The Asbestos Strike

Map of the Asbestos Region

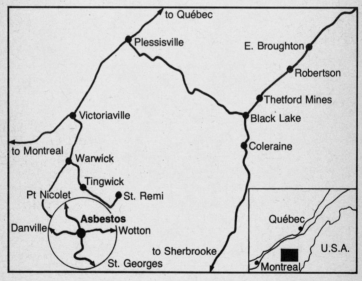

The Asbestos Strike

Joint authorship

Edited by
Pierre Elliott Trudeau

Translated by
James Boake

James Lewis & Samuel
Toronto, 1974

ISBN 0-8862-055-I paper
      0-8862-056-X cloth

Published with the assistance of the Social Science Research Council,
using funds provided by the Canada Council.

Design by Lynn Campbell

James Lewis & Samuel, Publishers
35 Britain Street
Toronto M5A 1R7
Canada

Printed and bound in Canada

Table of Contents

List of Joint Authors

Gilles Beausoleil, economist; graduate student at the Massachusetts Institute of Technology.

Réginald Boisvert, journalist and television writer.

Gérard Dion, priest; assistant chairman, Department of Industrial Relations, Laval University; member of the Sacerdotal Commission of Social Studies; editor of the review *Relations Industrielles* (Industrial Relations).

Fernand Dumont, sociologist; professor at the Faculty of Social Sciences, Laval University.

Jean Gérin-Lajoie, union representative for the United Steel Workers of America (C.C.L.).

Charles A. Lussier, lawyer; member of the firm of Perrault, Décary and Lussier.

Gérard Pelletier, editor of the weekly *Le Travail* (Labour); director of public relations for the C.C.C.L.[1]; co-editor of the review *Cité libre*.

Maurice Sauvé, technical advisor (on leave of absence) for the National Metal Trades Federation (C.C.C.L.); assistant secretary of the (federal) Royal Commission on Canada's Economic Prospects.

Pierre Elliott Trudeau, lawyer; economist; co-editor of the review *Cité libre*.

Editor's note: Almost all the joint authors of *The Asbestos Strike* now have different jobs, but we felt it would be useful to give here the positions they held when the first edition of this book appeared in 1956.

---

[1]Canadian and Catholic Confederation of Labour. As of 1960, it is known as the Confederation of National Trade Unions (C.N.T.U.).

This edition of *The Asbestos Strike* contains the complete text of the original 1956 edition of *La Grève de l'amiante,* and includes the original preface, foreword, and appendices. The translator has added a brief Reader's Guide which appears as Appendix V (page 377ff.) and occasional translator's footnotes.

Foreword

Recherches sociales (Social Research) is the name of a group, still little known, of colleagues in teaching and research. Since 1950, this group has been in charge of funds, the donor of which has left us free to use them as we see fit, for the general purposes of social education. Our chief aim has been to give financial support to a few daring and imaginative Canadians who are involved in worthwhile intellectual or social pursuits, but who are not in a position to receive one of the too few Canadian government grants available. In particular, we have tried to promote or encourage attempts to make the two great cultural groups of Canada better known to each other. We have made it possible for a Quebec organizer of cooperatives to pay an extended visit to the western provinces; we have enabled two union leaders, one English-speaking, one French-speaking, to take intensive labour education courses in the United States; we have financed the publication of first volumes by three young poets.

To date, however, Recherches sociales has devoted most of its time and money to this series of studies on the asbestos strike of 1949, which we are now publishing.

The original idea of this book arose five years ago, out of a concern shared by our group and by a few trade unionists who had participated in or observed the asbestos strike of 1949. We were all convinced that this event marked a turning point in the social history of Quebec. We did not yet have, of course, the necessary historical distance to encompass it in all its magnitude nor to make a fully accurate assessment of it. A great number of important facts, however, were still fresh in our minds and were in danger of being soon forgotten. Significant observations and interpretations, worthy of record, were about to disappear, and we felt we should inform the general public of the cruel or reassuring lessons we had learned.

A group of co-authors was thus eventually formed. Though very busy with their own affairs, they generously consented to describe, comment on, or analyze one of the essential aspects of the "great upheaval" of 1949. The group devised a work plan based on an outline by Gérard Pelletier, who remained throughout a tireless and valuable advisor. At the beginning, Jean Gérin-Lajoie was the coordinator of the project and kept things moving. Later on, Pierre E. Trudeau assumed this role, and afterwards took on the thankless task of revising the manuscripts, putting them together, adding the finishing touches, and arranging for the publication of the book in its final form. Eugene Forsey, Director of Research for the Canadian Congress of Labour, kindly read over most of the chapters and made valuable suggestions. J.C. Falardeau, Chairman of the Department of Sociology at Laval University, has continually shown a great interest in the project; he has generously offered his advice and agreed to write the preface.

In the preparation of this book, Recherches sociales has only served to bring people together and assist them in their work. We are pleased with our efforts, for we know that we have done something significant. It is up to the reading public to judge our work and to evaluate the opinions and judgments expressed in this volume. They are, naturally, those of their authors alone.

F.R. SCOTT, Director

Recherches sociales

Preface

One can easily predict that this book will be discussed for a long time to come.

On February 13, 1949, the asbestos industry workers went on strike at Asbestos, Quebec. The strike lasted to the end of June. It acquired an aura of quasi-revolution and became famous as "the strike at Asbestos." 5,000 miners took part in a strike which lasted 120 working days at Asbestos and 114 working days at Thetford Mines. Because of its length, the spectacular events it engendered, and its immediate repercussions on the trade union movement and on our society as a whole, this strike had a great emotional impact on public opinion. It awakened many people to the problems of our society.

A group of men of intelligence and goodwill, the authors of this book felt that it would be instructive from several points of view to set down the chronicle of this event. "Only when things are in a state of transformation, nay, complete dissolution," writes Karl Mannheim, "are men most able to perceive the interdependence of social facts." The asbestos strike was such a moment. A close examination of what preceded and followed it is most likely to show us, in the raw as it were, the real relations between the essential structures of our society and the play of forces which unites or separates them.

Some people will complain, I know, that this book has appeared too early, or too late. Some will ask why we waited so long to publish it—seven years after the strike. Let him who has already produced a book of joint authorship cast the first stone. This book has been in preparation for four years, and each of the joint authors is involved in one or more time-consuming activities. All those who shared in the writing of this book did so without pay, in addition to practising their professions. The coordination of their efforts required a little patience and perseverance, and much time and optimism. Through this in-

voluntary delay, certain overly romantic recollections of the strike
have given way to a more objective view of events. "That's just the
point," others will say, "isn't it too early to write adequately on this
subject? Are we not still too close to it to pass judgment? Would it not
have been better to wait twenty or thirty years?" Perhaps. As was
stated in the foreword, however, it seemed important to preserve a
record of many events which were still vivid in the memory of those
who participated in or observed them. In addition, the project was an
excellent way to make an original contribution to our meagre literature
of social documentation.

This book is essentially an effort at objectification. Its principal
value lies in taking an important point in the history of contemporary
Quebec and analyzing it from every point of view. The authors have
inevitably been led to discover the "meaning" of this event in the
larger perspective of our social development. Such presumption is
always dangerous, and the interpretations they offer remain open to
discussion. One must remember that this book aims at being realistic,
and does not represent the collective opinion of any group. Each of the
authors has reported the facts that he was familiar with, in accordance
with his personal point of view. No author is responsible for the
opinions of another. They are drawn together solely by a common
concern to discover the truth about an event which, in various ways,
has equally preoccupied and fascinated them all.

Several of the authors of this book subscribe to the idea that the
asbestos strike has revealed the recent divisions in our society with
greater clarity, that it has shattered social structures. What, then, has
been shattered, and why? To enable us to answer these questions, the
book needed an introductory essay like the one by Trudeau. After
reading it several times, I have come to regard it as a document of rare
candour. In this picture, as in a painting by Goya, we may find the
portrayal too bitter, the shadows too deliberately emphasized, and the
figures arrayed in distressing poses. Even so, it is hard not to admit, in
all honesty, that the spectacle so nimbly sketched is cruelly true to life.

The analysis of this strike is presented within the framework of an
overall interpretation of our social development over the last fifty
years, which historians of the future will have to accept or modify. We
are still poorly informed about our immediate past, and it is difficult to
assess the motives of those who have gone before us. Nevertheless,
some features of our social structure are revealed in quite a clear light.

Three main institutional orders have shaped and dominated French
Canadian society: the ecclesiastical order, the political order, and the
complex of commercial, industrial, and financial enterprises which
make up the economic order. The economic order has been guided

unconsciously by the ideology of capitalism, while the political order has subsisted without an ideology of its own. In a purely formal and rhetorical way, and for election purposes, it has adopted certain themes of nationalist thought. For the sake of security and comfort, it has nominally subscribed to the official thought of the Church. For all practical purposes it has fully endorsed capitalist ideology, of which it is the apostle and the guardian. Such was our Holy Alliance, the immemorial "understanding" between the governments of Quebec and the bosses of "our" big industries. The social thought of the Church in Quebec implicitly and explicitly sided with the existing economic and political orders. We see, then, what a triple rampart stood in the way of the first real attempts to promote the interests of the working class, what forces challenged every demand for social change, and what the stakes could ultimately become in a strike like the one at Asbestos.

Among the joint authors of this book, those who have asked themselves about the "meaning" of the strike have all thought along these lines, though they have expressed themselves in different ways. Trudeau writes: "In 1949 there was an asbestos strike because the national importance of the working class was out of all proportion to its low prestige." "We must consider the dispute in the light of this clash of forces," says Beausoleil; " . . . The strike at Asbestos was a power struggle." It also, he adds, "sought recognition of the trade union movement within the French Canadian community. . . ." Such a statement is correct as long as one does not apply it exclusively to the strike at Asbestos. One can say as much of the strike in the textile industry in 1937, and of all the major strikes that have been milestones in the progress of the trade union movement. French Canadian trade unions have had to become more and more concerned with economic demands. To obtain justice, or even to make themselves heard, the trade unions had to become recognized. To become recognized, they had to demonstrate their effective power. Reduced to the simplest terms, this is the significance not only of the strike at Asbestos, but of the entire recent history of the trade union movement, of which Asbestos is the most dramatic episode.

To take up a metaphor already in use, this strike was one of the *rites of passage* by which the French Canadian trade union movement has gradually reached adulthood. The steps involved in this rite were in no way unique. They are basic to the history of trade unionism in all the modern industrialized countries. The peculiar thing about them in French Canada is that they represent a break with the traditional formula by which labour conflicts were formerly settled, as by an institution vested with divine right. Up to that time in Quebec, every labour dispute of any importance involving the Catholic trade unions was originally defined and ultimately settled (officially or unofficially) by the trinity of management, government, and Church, or by some combination of these three: management and government, management and Church, or government and Church. At the time of the asbestos strike, this trade union movement decided to speak for itself, to define the purpose of the strike in its own terms, and to set its own conditions for a satisfactory solution. The Holy Alliance was not dissolved, far from it, but a new actor cast aside the classic scenario, improvised an original monologue, and came on stage with the traditional "three greats."

Serious ruptures developed in the relations among the latter. The government fell out of favour with the Church. For reasons suggested in the chapter by Abbé Dion, the social thought of the Church had recently moved in a new direction. The ideas of the Sacerdotal Commission of Social Studies were largely responsible for this change. When the strike occurred at Asbestos, the Church gave the trade unions a support hitherto unknown, by a resolute defence of the suffering workers against the economic guillotine of the companies. The strike was finally settled by the very patient intervention of the Archbishop of Quebec. This was, it is true, a return to the old formula, but with an important difference. This time, the unions were no longer treated as inferiors, and the terms of the settlement were based on their assumptions and on their definition of the situation.

There was nothing inevitable about a strike in Quebec in the spring of 1949; it was even less certain that it would occur in the asbestos industry. It is perhaps too easy to assert, as Trudeau does, that at the time, "our social framework was ready to come apart." All one can say is that, sooner or later, an event or series of events, set in motion by organized labour, were destined to meet our three great institutional orders head-on. In 1948, there was no indication that this event would occur the following winter, rather than in 1955 or 1960.

All the authors of this book have taken great pains, as I well know, to gather and to report as many facts as possible, with the most scrupulous honesty. What final judgment, though, may we make on the assessment of the strike at Asbestos which emerges from their writings as a whole? Has too much importance not been assigned to the strike? Have they yielded to the subtle temptation, in such cases as this, to endow a past event with a significance reflecting personal hopes and preferences? Again, only the historians of the future will be able to answer these questions.

To what degree has the clash of organized labour and the Establishment had a lasting effect? In society as a whole, how profound have been the changes in attitude brought about by the heady emotions of the four-month strike period?

Pelletier describes at length how, in the course of the strike, many newspapers experienced a "state of grace" (some almost in spite of themselves) regarding the "social question" and the problems of the working class. He concludes laconically: "I would not want to say that all the windows opened in 1949 have now been closed again. I believe, though, that very few of them are still open." What of the attitude of the population as a whole? Gérard Filion, whom Pelletier quotes, wrote in *Le Devoir* of June 6, 1949: "The asbestos strike was a great misfortune, but it was far from useless: the social climate of Quebec is no longer what it was six months ago. Today, we are beginning to acquire a social conscience." Trudeau adds, in his epilogue: "For many people, the drama at Asbestos was a violent announcement that a new era had begun."

Nobody has yet made a detailed study of the different ways in which the various strata of our society reacted to the asbestos strike. People were generally sympathetic. Students and university teachers soon took the side of the strikers. The statements and letters of bishops were mainly responsible for the interest which people began to take in the miners, but one should not forget the comments reflecting scepticism, mistrust, or antipathy to be heard on the way out of churches in bourgeois or middle-class parishes ... Collective interest in trade unionism was dissipated before the strike was over. Pelletier's words may serve to depict the aftereffects of this strike on popular thought. Four years later, following a strike of weavers at Louiseville, he wrote: "Our collective Christian conscience had digested the event and felt no nausea" (*Cité libre,* May 1953, p. 2). At the very time of this strike at Louiseville, Pelletier could speak from personal experience of the "crisis of confidence" which still affects our Christian trade unionism. In that article, he said: "The Church's attitude towards social issues is clearly revealed by the stand taken by our spiritual leaders. However, these ideas are still far in advance of the opinions which prevail among the rural masses and among the middle and bourgeois classes ..." (*Ibid.,* p. 4). This is plainly the situation in many countries, but we should still deplore the fact that those of us who are not workers seem not only to stay mentally remote from the working class, but to retreat ever farther from it.

It is more difficult to analyze the consciousness of the working class. First of all, in what sense may we say that there exists a collective consciousness among unionized French Canadian workers? The strike at Asbestos, more than any other event, helped to strengthen feelings of solidarity among the various sections of the C.C.C.L., and among them and the workers affiliated with other labour organizations. Have these feelings of solidarity lasted? If they have, how strong are they? Do the economic or social attitudes of the working-class groups have enough coherence to be described? Large segments of the working-class population appear to have acquired a more definite sense of their social responsibilities, and seem to want to move in new directions. Are these new directions, and this sense of responsibility, not mainly inspired by the leaders who have the confidence of the working class?

These leaders are the prime movers in a changing social universe. During the strike at Asbestos, labour leaders at all levels were much admired for the shrewdness and tenacity with which they carried on the struggle. They had to behave like generals: *they had no choice*. They had long known what the strike at Asbestos forced them to prove, that the French Canadian trade union movement, now come of age, can no longer define its position in abstract terms. In the first place, it must be wholly a working-class movement. Insofar as it is, it must formulate its problems in concrete terms, in economic terms, and in terms of a dynamic approach to things. This sense of realism and dynamism is a recent phenomenon in the "official" thought of the labour movement, and it is only beginning to affect the collective consciousness of the working class. The progress made at the time of the asbestos strike will have no future unless the working class becomes imbued with these ideas and convinced of their validity, so that it is able to plan a course of action and persevere in it.

These remarks are a very inadequate treatment of the main kinds of problems raised by this book. The reader must analyze and reflect upon them for himself. He will find that the following studies do not pretend to be definitive, and that they are partial, inasmuch as they approach the asbestos strike from the point of view of what it meant to the workers. Who could make a serious objection to that? In our time, whoever wishes to write on such subjects has little choice. Our society is being restructured, and nobody knows what tendencies will arise in it. If we try to discern them, to make a serious inquiry into our future, we must look at the forces of change on the level where they are now appearing most clearly: the level of the working class. Bruno Lafleur, in his introduction to the recent republication of *L'Appel de la race* (The Call of the Race), is perhaps psychologically right in saying that the "youth" of 1955 scarcely differs "in its profound aspirations" from that of 1925 or 1930. I feel, though, that he is seriously mistaken in claiming that the one differs from the other only in vocabulary, that, simply, "the word *social* has replaced the word *national*." There is more to it than that: the difference is intellectual. I am not opposing one generation to another, but only insisting on the fact that those who are now concerned with social problems favour a realistic approach. Because they are trying to understand our society as a whole, and its relationship to the rest of the world, their outlook must also be ecumenical. Theirs is not an entirely secure position. As Pierre Trudeau reminds us at the end of his remarks: "The future will either *thrust itself* upon us [my italics], imposing its own standards, or we will win ourselves a place in it, with the values that we cherish."

JEAN C. FALARDEAU

Faculty of Social Sciences
Laval University
Quebec

Chapter I

The Province of Quebec at the Time of the Strike

by Pierre Elliott Trudeau

I/Introduction

Events, like quotations, can be fully understood only in their context. This study, concerning the complex of events called "the asbestos strike," will not be completely intelligible to the reader unless he is familiar with the state of Quebec society at the beginning of 1949.

I shall therefore describe its main features by depicting the material facts, then the state of mind, and finally the institutions which, at the time, provided a framework for these facts and ideas.

The combination of circumstances existing in 1949 had a dynamic effect on our society. To grasp this important fact, we must go back a bit in time. A new state of affairs acquires its significance through the way in which it modifies the old; social thought reveals its logic and meaning through the history of its development. Similarly, a study of the development of our social institutions shows their profound effect on the patterns of our lives.

History knows no abrupt turns; the forces at work in the present have arisen in the past.

II/The facts

I surely do not have to belabour the point that in the half century preceding the asbestos strike, the material basis of Canadian society in general, and of Quebec society in particular, was radically altered.

The great upheaval usually known as the Industrial Revolution began to have a serious effect on our country around the turn of the century. Since then, radical changes in the techniques of production have occurred with such persistent rapidity that every Canadian reader can bear witness to this development from his personal experience. Still, I would like to present some figures here, not to please the lovers of statistics, but to show the extent of the changes. (Those who accept the greatness of the transformations as an established fact may skip the statistics which follow.)

1/Demographic changes

Between 1901 and 1949, the year of the asbestos strike, the population of Canada increased by 250%, from 5,371,000 to 13,447,000. During this period, the number of people in the work force went up even more rapidly, almost tripling. This increase occurred more in the cities than in the country. The population of Canada was 37% urban in 1901, 45% urban in 1911, 54% urban in 1941, and 57% urban in 1951.

The rate of change in Quebec becomes even more significant when we compare it with the rate in other provinces of Canada. Between 1901 and 1949, the population of Quebec increased by 136%, a rate exceeded only by the four western provinces. These provinces were our "frontier zone," and naturally underwent a prodigious development in those years. Still, the most heavily populated of them (British Columbia) contained only 8% of the total population of Canada in 1949, while Quebec contained 29%, or only 2% less than in 1901. (We can appreciate the stability represented by this last percentage if we consider that 41% of Canadians lived in Ontario in 1901, and that this figure had fallen to 33% in 1949.)

In 1901, 40% of the population of Quebec lived in cities. This percentage reached 48% in 1911, 56% in 1921, and 63% in 1931. After the Depression of the Thirties, in 1941, Quebec was still 63% urbanized, the most urbanized province in the country. From 1941 to 1951, the urban population of Quebec increased by 29% (a percentage exceeded only by Alberta and British Columbia). As a result, 1951 saw 67% of Quebec's population living in urban areas. In metropolitan Montreal alone, the population increased by 39% from 1921 to 1931, and by a further 22% from 1941 to 1951, so that by the latter year Montreal contained 34% of the inhabitants of the province.

Asbestos, which will figure largely in the rest of this book, had a population of about 600 at the turn of the century. This figure rose to 2,189 in 1921, and 4,396 in 1931. Incorporated as a city in 1937, Asbestos had 5,711 inhabitants in 1941, and 8,190 in 1951. In Thetford Mines, the population increased from 3,256 in 1901 to 10,701 in 1931, to 12,716 in 1941, and to 15,095 in 1951.

2/Economic transformations

Such demographic changes naturally corresponded to a profound transformation in the Canadian economy.

At the beginning of the twentieth century, the economy of Canada was still primarily rural, and 40% of the labour force was engaged in agriculture. Other occupations included fishing, trapping, logging, and gold mining. As a result, 44% of the work force was involved in primary industry, and only 17% in so-called secondary, or manufacturing, industry.

In 1949, however, the primary industries mentioned above employed only 26% of the work force, while the manufacturing industry alone employed more than one worker in four (27%), and was now the most important sector of the industrial economy. At this time, 30% of the *Net National Income* came from the manufacturing industry, 13% from agriculture, and 5.5% from the rest of the primary industrial sector. As for goods, 55% of the *net national production of commodities* came from the manufacturing industry, 20% from agriculture, 4% from logging, 6% from mining, and 1% from fishing and trapping. (The rest came from hydroelectric power, 3%, and from the construction industry, 11%. The total for the primary industries was thus 34%, and for the secondary industries, 66%.)[1]

This half century of intensive industrialization and urban concentration was necessarily accompanied by great improvements in the field of transportation. The railway network doubled in size between 1901 and 1919, after which motor vehicles took the lead, registrations increasing more than sixfold from 1919 to 1949.

Coal production tripled from 1901 to 1920, but increased little thereafter, coal having been replaced by other sources of energy: during the half century, Canadian hydroelectric capacity multiplied 67 times, and oil production rose from less than a million barrels to over 22 million barrels. In the same period, steel production multiplied 123 times.

Between 1900 and 1950, average weekly wages[2] in the Canadian manufacturing industry went from about $7.50 to $44.00, while the work week decreased from 60 to 43 hours. In the same period, the cost of living did not even triple.[3] In other words, the standard of living of the Canadian worker improved considerably in the half century. This rise in standard of living corresponds to an increase in the worker's productive capacity: as a result of industrialization, the annual productivity of the Canadian worker in all sectors increased by an average 2% per year over the fifty-year period, in spite of a considerable reduction in the number of hours worked per year.[4]

3/The economy of the central provinces

This transformation of the Canadian economy, stimulated by the industrial revolution, corresponded chiefly to the profound changes that occurred in the two central provinces of Quebec and Ontario. At the turn of the century, these two provinces produced four fifths of the total net value of Canadian manufactured goods;[5] in 1949, this fraction was still the same.

But it must be noted that Quebec played only a secondary role. Its production of manufactured goods remained, from 1917 at least, in a ratio of 3 to 5 to that of Ontario. This proportion, much lower than the ratio of the respective populations of the two provinces (3.8/5 in 1901, 4.4/5 in 1949), is a first indication that industrialization performed differently in these provinces.

A second indication is the income of the workers. In 1926, as in 1949, Quebec and Ontario together contained about 61% of the population of Canada. Their workers received 66% of the salaries, wages, and other income paid to all Canadian workers in 1926, and 68% in 1949; but the ratio of the Quebec workers' share to that of the Ontario workers was 3.1/5 in 1926 and 3.15/5 in 1949. [6]

There were various reasons for these differences. Apart from the great importance of ideological and institutional factors, which we will explain later on in this chapter, economic geography also played a very significant role. Southern Ontario was close to the sources of iron and coal, and linked to them by an excellent system of communication; it also had easy access to the western markets. Quebec had a lesser share of these advantages. [7] Furthermore, the Canadian market as a whole was protected by customs tariffs, and entrepreneurs were bound to seek profits from this situation by tapping the abundant labour pool in Quebec.

As a result, Ontario benefitted immediately from the phase of industrialization based on iron, coal, and steam, and was able to found its economy on highly mechanized industries producing machinery and durable consumer goods. Quebec, on the other hand, experienced more difficulty, and took longer to go from a commercial economy to an industrial one. Because its development was based on a docile and numerous work force rather than on capital intensive enterprises, the chief products of its manufacturing industry were non-durable consumer goods, protected as far as possible by customs tariffs. In the 1929 Dominion Bureau of Statistics reports, for example, the (gross) value of manufactured goods was greater in Quebec than in Ontario only in the following industries: some foods and beverages, tobacco, some leather goods, several clothing and related items (furs, silk, cotton thread, etc.). To this list we may add, in different categories, some asbestos and forest products, railway rolling stock . . . and musical instruments. Twenty years later, in 1949, the list remained basically the same, except for a greater diversification in certain categories (textiles, articles made of hair, etc.). We should, however, mention some additions which reveal a new orientation in Quebec's economy: aircraft and aircraft parts, ship construction, electrical appliances and supplies, petroleum products, plastics... and the publication of periodicals.

This false start affected the process of industrialization in Quebec for a long time, and largely explains why this province always had higher levels of unemployment and lower wage scales than Ontario. This inferiority of Quebec in relation to Ontario naturally extended to almost every sector of their economies. From 1901 to 1948, for example, the hourly wage of a printer increased from $0.24 to $1.52 in Montreal, but from $0.26 to $1.78 in Toronto; of a streetcar conductor, from $0.16 to $1.00 in Montreal, and from $0.18 to $1.10 in Toronto; of a plumber, from $0.18½ to $1.45 in Montreal, and from $0.27½ to $1.60 in Toronto; a bricklayer, from $0.30 to $1.60 in Montreal, and from $0.37½ to $1.75 in Toronto.[8]

More general comparisons may be found for the prewar period in Appendix V of the Report of the Royal Commission on Price Spreads (appointed 1934) and in Appendix E of the Report of the Royal Commission on the Textile Industry (appointed 1936). These documents show that Quebec wage earners made less money than their Ontario counterparts in the same industries, and sometimes within the same company. This inferiority became less marked during the war, thanks in part to the National War Labour Board (a federal body!), which pursued a policy of wage stabilization and wage parity. But these improvements were only temporary. In the few years preceding the 1949 asbestos strike, the normal functioning of our economy had again widened the wage spread between Quebec and Ontario workers. In 1939, the total of salaries and wages paid by the manufacturing industry in Quebec was 59% of the total paid in Ontario. This percentage rose to 69% in 1944, but had fallen back to 60% by 1950. (See the National Accounts. For the postwar period, see Gilles Beausoleil, Salaires du Québec et de l'Ontario [Wages in Quebec and Ontario], published by the C.C.C.L.-C.C.L., 1954; Aurèle Gagnon, Contributions à l'étude des sciences de l'homme [Contributions to the Study of the Social Sciences], Montreal, no. 1, p. 145; and Labor Facts, Montreal, May 1955.)

Quebec was, however, abundantly endowed with the materials for the second industrial revolution: hydroelectric power and a number of metals which had become industrial raw materials in addition to steel. These advantages favoured a prodigious development of Quebec's industrial production in the last decade of the half century.

In the Quebec manufacturing industry alone, for example, the number of employees increased by 77% from 1939 to 1950, and the value of goods produced (in constant dollars) went up 93%. For Ontario, these percentages were 78 and 89, and for Canada as a whole (exclusive of Newfoundland), 79 and 92. From the point of view of incomes, however, partly because of lower rates of wage increase, Quebec was at a slight disadvantage. During the eleven-year period referred to above, real per capita income rose by 48% in Quebec, by 49% in Ontario, and by 54% in Canada as a whole.[9]

In the same eleven-year period, the hourly productivity of the Quebec worker increased 2% per year on the average; for Ontario, this percentage was the same, and for Canada as a whole it was 2.1%. (It is worth noting that between 1900 and 1950, the average annual increase in *hourly* productivity was 3% for Quebec and 3¼% for Canada as a whole.)

These statistics have been presented to bring out the vast extent of the changes produced by industrialization in Quebec. We may sum up the situation as follows. At the turn of the century, the dollar value of agricultural production accounted for 65% of the total net commodities produced in Quebec; in 1950, this percentage had fallen to 10.5. The equivalent percentage for the logging industry dropped from 25 to 4.2, and for fisheries, from 2 to 0.1. On the other hand, the percentage for the mining industry increased from 2 to 5.1, and for the manufacturing industry, from 4 to 65.3.[10]

Finally, if we consider the number of men working in each sector of the economy in relation to the total number of male workers in the province, we find that from 1901 to 1951, the percentage of men working in the agricultural sector fell from 45 to 17, in trapping and fishing, from 1 to ½. In the same period, the percentage of men working in the mining industry increased from ⅓ to 1; in logging, from 1 to 3; and in the manufacturing sector, from 16[11] to 21.

III/The ideas
It may seem somewhat arbitrary to undertake to analyze the social thought of French Canadians separately in this section, and then to examine the public institutions of French Canada further on (in Part IV of this chapter). Generally speaking, the leading ideas in a society tend to become embodied in its institutions and so identified with them that one cannot describe the thinking of its leaders without also revealing the propensities of the institutions which provide a context for their actions.

In Quebec, however, during the first half of the twentieth century, our social thinking was so idealistic, so a priori, so divorced from reality, in sum so futile, that it was hardly ever able to find expression in living and dynamic institutions. By isolating some aspects of this thought, we may show the reader just how little—at the time of the asbestos strike—people were prepared to accept, interpret, and influence realities in this highly industrialized province, as I have sketched it above.

In my analysis, I attach little importance to the few circles where liberal and realistic thought existed on the fringes of our monolithic ideology, as I call it. I am, of course, fully aware that such circles did exist. The profound repercussions of the asbestos strike on very different parts of our society later revealed the foresight and courage of those who had refused to accept our official thinking as an affirmation of eternal truths. This chapter, though, is not primarily devoted to handing out medals, but to describing a society which had arrived at a critical point in its development. Why does the upheaval we are studying have such a scope and importance? In my opinion, it is not because a few precursors were able to understand and influence reality, but because circumstances forced an entire people to choose one lifestyle (as I have shown above), while all its intellectual and moral training urged it to cling to another (as I will explain below).

1/The main focus

Up to the very end of the period studied in this book, nationalism was the main focus of almost all French Canadian social thought. This indisputable fact needs no explanation here. A people which had been defeated, occupied, decapitated, pushed out of commerce, driven from the cities, reduced little by little to a minority, and diminished in influence in a country which it had nonetheless discovered, explored, and colonized, could adopt few attitudes that would enable it to preserve its identity. This people devised a system of security,[12] which became overdeveloped; as a result, they sometimes overvalued all those things that set them apart from others, and showed hostility to all change (even progress) coming from without.

That is why our nationalism, to oppose a surrounding world that was English-speaking, Protestant, democratic, materialistic, commercial, and later industrial, created a system of defence which put a premium on all the contrary forces: the French language, Catholicism, authoritarianism, idealism, rural life, and later the return to the land.

From this set of values, focussed by nationalism, the social theorists created an astrology which claimed to regulate the destinies of French Canada with all the precision of the celestial system. In this way, they reasoned, our providential mission would be accomplished.

These thinkers were building, in the twentieth century, a super-structure which combined, in a logical and homogeneous manner, all the social ideas that had proved useful to the French Canadians at a period in their past history. Meanwhile, the French Canadian people themselves were busy meeting the challenges to their existence offered by everyday reality. Individuals, after all, must first worry about making a decent living for themselves and their families, even if they have to upset a few mental constructs in the process. The result of this in practice was that nationalistic ideas were continually threatened with extinction, and nationalism survived as best it could. In the last century, for example, the exodus to American industrial centres dissolved a little pastoral dream. Authoritarianism was considerably shaken when Laurier was brought to power by a people to whom Monsignor Laflèche had preached, during the election campaign of 1896, that "no Catholic could, without committing a serious sin, vote for a party leader" like Laurier.[13]

In the following pages, I do not intend to analyze what is sometimes (wrongly) called our "de facto nationalism." This is only the concrete result of the virtue of patriotic piety exercised, after a fashion, by an ethnic group, and one which men of action sometimes pretend to have served after the event. I shall, instead, be concerned with our "theoretical nationalism," as formulated and dispensed by those among us who were professional writers and teachers, and who were generally accepted as our leaders and intellectual masters.

In the present context, I can only mention a few people; they are, however, recognized as typical. Since I do not have the space to do justice to their thought as a whole, I feel I should say that these men are, almost without exception, worthy of respect. They have lacked neither honesty in their intentions nor courage in their undertakings; neither firmness of purpose, nor always imagination in their solution of problems. Surrounded by a materialistic civilization and confronted by politicians who were often shameless, the nationalist school was just about alone in constructing a *system of thought*. As I shall be chiefly concerned with social and economic questions, I shall rarely have a chance to mention the valid aspects of this thinking, but it would be wrong to conclude that I minimize the value of the services it was able to render. Was it, perhaps, necessary first to "save the race," so that others might later find what was worth saving in the man? The gestation of a culture is a matter of generations, and today's generation would perhaps have thought like those of yesteryear, if born twenty years earlier. Perhaps . . . but I do not want to judge anyone, and remote historical facts do not interest me very much. For the same reason, I will not shrink from emphasizing those aspects of nationalist thought which are a burden on the present, and harmful to free and honest action. In all fairness, however, I cannot undertake a criticism of this thought without offering its adherents this statement in their favour: there have been many varieties of "nationalists," but most of them were known by their spirit of loyalty, their faith in the intellect (if not always in man!), and a certain respect for culture. Had such men not concerned themselves with public affairs, our people would have had that much less experience of disinterested government.

Alas, the nationalists have been harmed by their very idealism. They loved not wisely but too well, and in their desire to obtain only the best for the French Canadians, they formulated a system of social thought which could not be realized and which, for all practical purposes, left the people without any effective intellectual guidelines. It is this social thought which I now wish to examine.

2/Nationalism as an intellectual discipline

In a sermon of 1902, which has become "the breviary of the French Canadian patriot," Mgr. Paquet declared: "It is our privilege to be entrusted with this social ministry, reserved for elite peoples . . . Our mission is not so much to manipulate capital, as to handle ideas; not so much to light the fires of factories, as to maintain the luminous hearth of religion and of thought, making it to radiate afar. While our rivals are laying claim to the hegemony of industry and finance, we shall strive above all for the honour of doctrine and the palms of apostleship."

The policies and principles of this school of idealism could not be more succinctly and forcefully stated. Our intellectuals had to subscribe to them, and one after the other they all aspired to "the honour of doctrine." It reduced them to complete intellectual sterility in the end, for the only doctrine they were permitted to expound had to be derived from the most unproductive traditionalism.

One hundred years apart, two mentors of "the doctrine" established a rigorous framework for all research. In the conclusion to his *Histoire du Canada*, F.X. Garneau wrote: "May the French Canadians remain faithful to themselves; may they be wise and persevering; and may they not let themselves be seduced in any way by the glitter of social and political innovations! They are not strong enough to give themselves free rein in this field. It is up to the great peoples of the world to put new theories to the test." In 1945, this counsel of excessive caution had become, in the writings of Mr. Esdras Minville, an imperious *Gleischaltung*[14]: "It is not enough for us to desire equally the welfare of the nation; we must wish *unanimously* for the means to achieve it. . . ."[15] As we shall see, a *unanimous* system of thought, as our nationalists understood it, could only be timid and reactionary.

Anyone whose thinking went beyond the limits of official nationalism or who tried to reshape it by changing a basic trait was thus automatically suspect: on all sides, he and his ideas were scrutinized. If he renounced nationalism, he was discredited and ignored; if he embraced it, his ideas were emasculated, then assimilated.

This happened to Edouard Montpetit and a few other young professors. Before World War I, they came back from Europe with the idea, rare at the time, that our people should enter the fields of industry and finance. This idea had been advocated in the nineteenth century by Etienne Parent, Edmond de Nevers, and Errol Bouchette, but had not yet found favour, although the yearly exodus of 20,000 people to the United States was due to the lack of industry in Quebec. Greeted with hostility and suspicion, the young professors were accused of atheism, on the excellent grounds that they taught economic liberalism.

Finally, they succumbed to attrition. By consenting to "think nationally"[16] in their scientific work, they arrested its development and gave official social thought the chance to overtake and engulf their own. Within a few decades, they were blithely teaching an obsolete science in our schools. In addition, a growing number of our thinkers had already begun to grapple with economic issues, in nationalistic terms of course.

In 1921 Joseph Versailles, a Montreal financier, addressed a convention of the Association catholique de la jeunesse canadienne-française (Catholic Association of French Canadian Youth [A.C.J.C.]) as follows: "Let us stop serving our enemies. With the help of material power and moral force, our race will win a place of honour . . . To succeed, we must get our most promising youngsters to take up careers in business and finance." In the same year *l' Action française*, then edited by Abbé Groulx, began a lengthy investigation of economic issues. In 1927, it carried a study of the French Canadians' economic status by Olivar Asselin. He concluded that, though French Canadians made up two sevenths of the Canadian population, they possessed only one seventh of the national wealth. "Given our numbers," he wrote, "we aren't half as rich as we should be."[17]

During the Depression, economic nationalism was discussed more than ever. In 1934, according to *Le Devoir* of October 30, Abbé Groulx asked: "There are 2,500,000 French Canadians in Quebec. Is it inevitable, then, that all big business, all high finance, all the public utility companies, all our hydro power, all our forests, all our mines should belong to a minority of 300,000 individuals?" (Groulx, of course, is speaking of an *ethnic* minority. We should not regard this passage as a restatement of the principle: "Property is theft.") In the same year Athanase David, Secretary of the Province of Quebec, writing in *En marge de la politique* (Speaking of Politics), dared to say:[18] "Has the day not come when the graduates of our classical colleges must no longer look upon commerce, industry, and finance as occupations unworthy of their culture and their education . . . ? I believe that we must have money. With money, we can do the great things which we are meant to achieve on this continent." In 1936, Victor Barbeau assessed our situation in *Mesure de notre taille* (Sizing us up). He showed (p. 24) that "apart from the land, in all her desolate and ravaged immensity, apart from a few islets where we hold on by the force of inertia, we have nothing, you see, nothing. We do not even enjoy the use of the innumerable riches bestowed on us by God."[19]

In a province which was 63% urbanized and already heavily industrialized, in a city which, in 1933, had a 30% unemployment rate and 280,000 people "on direct welfare," people saw the inadequacies of aspiring to "the honour of doctrine and the palms of apostleship" while despising industrialization. They began to think that the engineer, the merchant, and the businessman played as vital a social role as the priest, the doctor, and the lawyer. Because nationalism coloured our approach to these problems, however, we religiously avoided any solution that might challenge our basic assumptions.

Our assumptions about agriculture will illustrate our overall approach. Having suggested an *Achat chez nous* (Buy Quebec Products) program to solve our economic difficulties, Edouard Montpetit went on to say: "This will solve our problems in secondary industry, which will be largely supported by agriculture, the basic industry which furnishes the raw materials."[20] Two months later, Olivar Asselin published some striking work, in which he attacked the sellout of our natural resources and the exodus to the United States, but arrived at this strange conclusion: "To keep the natural increase of the population in the country, it will not therefore be necessary to have new industries, if there is some way of keeping the farmers' sons attached to the soil." He preached colonization in Abitibi and wanted to postpone the employment of "our race" in big industry.[21] Then, in 1928, in *l'Action française,* Asselin, drawing on the conclusions of his inquiry of 1927, which we discussed above, was principally concerned with rural affairs. He did recommend a revolutionary policy, the eventual return to the State of natural resources exploited by private interests, but the greater part of his reforms dealt with agricultural methods and products, handicrafts, the country schools, and fisheries.[22] Victor Barbeau declared that agriculture would have saved us from the humiliations of the Depression, and jeered at us for having "rushed to the fires that industry was lighting all over our hills."[23] Athanase David was careful not "to ignore the fact that Quebec is above all a field, that it is and will remain an agricultural province."[24] Henri Laureys, though Dean of the Ecole des hautes études commerciales (School For Higher Commercial Studies), hardly went any further: "To achieve its fullest development, Quebec agriculture must, by a certain industrial extension, strive for the expansion which is denied it by the facts of geography."[25] In 1945 Father Arès, S.J., took stock of our overall situation in *Notre question nationale* (Our National Question).[26] He wrote that the industrial revolution "was bound to be disastrous for our people . . . [because] we did not have money, we did not have any industrial and commercial tradition, we did not have any great technical schools. Above all, we did not have a clearly defined social and national doctrine." Arès, a theorist of nationalism, was ready to supply a social doctrine along the following lines: "This belittling of rural life is a great misfortune, because of the prime importance of the countryside in the lives of nations in general, and of our nation in particular. What Minville says is true: 'The countryside has always been a reservoir for the physical and moral forces of a nation. In our bustling, unsettled times, this is truer than ever. . . .'. . . From the social and moral standpoint the big city, especially in times of high unemployment, devours bodies and souls, disrupts family life, and arouses hatred and resentment. Social unrest and revolutionary ideas flourish in this environment."[27]

The theorists told city workers that they were naturally inferior, and proclaimed that Quebec must pursue its vocation for agriculture, in spite of the fact that less than five percent of its surface area was said to be arable.[28] Nevertheless, they had to suggest some cure for the "ills" introduced by industrialization.

Unfortunately, few were qualified for the task. Clergymen, journalists, lawyers, and accountants vainly tried to become sociologists and economists, but they could not free themselves from a social environment that was traditionalist, anti-modern, and imbued with authoritarianism and fuzzy thinking.

When, accordingly, they had diagnosed our intellectual, social, and economic plight with some vigour; had censured our people's lack of spirit and exhorted them to show initiative and perseverance; had preached the familial, rural, and national virtues; had spoken at length of reforming the educational system; had gone over time and again the ideas they clung to; then their social thinking stopped strangely short: they had not yet said anything about our absorption into the real world of the industrial revolution.

Now the same preoccupation with security that had made them incapable of resolving the problems of the new era by themselves also prevented them from studying the solutions other people were proposing.

Our official thinkers, with amazing constancy, ignored all the social science of their own day. To judge by their writings, we may say without exaggeration that until very recently they knew nothing of universal legal thought, from Duguit to Pound; nothing of sociology, from Durkheim to Gurvitch; nothing of economics, from Walras to Keynes; nothing of political science, from Bosanquet to Laski; nothing of psychology, from Freud to Piaget; nothing of pedagogy, from Dewey to Ferrière.

They filled in these gaps in their social thought with a set of ideas which they called the social doctrine of the Church.

3/"Our" social doctrine of the Church

We must distinguish clearly between Catholic social ethics as expounded by certain popes who have been particularly attentive to the upheavals of modern society and the social doctrine of the Church as it has been understood and applied in French Canada.

The first group of ideas does not concern me here; the second is exactly my subject. It is nothing more, in fact, than a continuation of our traditionalist assumptions, with a veneer of papal authority. Our official thinkers were scarcely willing to recognize the advent of industrialization and the conversion of the masses into a proletariat. They were totally unprepared to understand these phenomena and had great difficulty in seeing the profound significance of the social encyclicals, which were written to put an end to what Pius XI called the scandal of the Church. Consequently, in drawing on the social thought of the popes, our theorists adopted only formulas which might dignify our collective prejudices with a borrowed prestige.

This exploitation of papal authority for the sake of nationalism was favoured by a misunderstanding stemming from the popes' condemnation of capitalism. The popes reproached this system because it kept a certain proletariat in abject poverty and prevented most people from developing their truly human qualities; our clerical and nationalist doctrine seemed opposed to this system principally because it kept the French Canadians in a state of economic colonialism and prevented them from developing their truly nationalist qualities. Abbé Groulx, quoted by Father Arès with approval, said: "Here, not only classes are oppressed, but a nation. . . ."[29] Still, Abbé Groulx was more realistic than many others, for he also said: "I am certainly not claiming that if our captains of industry or finance were drawn from our own people, we would be socially better off . . . Social evil would remain social evil, but the passions which dangerously aggravate it would be entirely absent."[30]

An indigenous capitalism would probably have spared us every misfortune likely to be accompanied by "passions"! Our captains of industry would have protected us from the worldwide economic de-

pression and, had they failed in that task, they would not have aroused
any resentment among the unemployed, so long as they were of the
same blood! We see, then, that for our social thinkers, industrialization did not present any serious problem that was not already known at
the time of that *Maria Chapdelaine* they so loved to quote; their
complaint remained the same: "Strangers have surrounded us whom it
is our pleasure to call foreigners; they have taken into their hands most
of the rule, they have gathered to themselves much of the wealth. . . ."
They could not, then, imagine that to become part of a world transformed by the industrial revolution, they would have to make a few
modifications in their traditional ideas and methods. "For this is it that
we must abide in that Province where our fathers dwelt, living as they
have lived . . . nought shall suffer change. . . ."[31]

In other countries, the social doctrine of the Church did much to
prepare the way for the democratization of peoples, the emancipation
of workers, and the progress of society. In French Canada, it was
invoked in support of authoritarianism and xenophobia. What is more
serious still, our doctrine made it impossible for us to solve our problems. On the negative side, it rejected any solution which might succeed among our "enemies": the English, Protestants, materialists,
etc. On the positive side, it was content to set up conceptual systems
bearing no objective relation to reality; the application of these systems was frequently impossible.

4/Negative effects of the doctrine
In the field of economics, we rejected those corrective measures for
capitalism devised by the liberal economists of Sweden and England
and recommended for our use by the federal civil servants in Ottawa.
For example, one of the most tragic episodes of the Thirties was our
complete confusion in the face of unemployment, combined with our
unshakable opposition to any constitutional amendment that would
make it possible for Ottawa to attack the problem seriously. Our
economists even managed to see that the unemployed in Quebec obtained less relief from federal sources than those out of work in the
other provinces. As Esdras Minville remarked, the province of
Quebec "received less because it asked for less . . . Quebec had a kind
of instinctive fear of excessive expenses . . . The other provinces,
which do not have the same *traditional attitude towards expenditures,*
seem on the contrary to have wanted to profit as much as possible from
federal handouts: public works, etc."[32]

Our efforts in the social field were extremely feeble as well. Like
the popes, for example, we had long demanded family allowances, but
our influence on the capitalist organization of our society was slight.

In addition, we were obstinately devoted to the idea that the State was a bogeyman eager to devour the family. We were thus unable to introduce this reform either through private enterprise or social legislation, and family allowances—desired by the Church and constitutionally within the jurisdiction of the provinces—were ultimately offered to French Canadian families by the federal, "Protestant" government. Significantly, François Albert Angers, the most competent and estimable of our nationalistic economists, tried to preach the rejection of these allowances by personal example, on the grounds that they were a threat to paternal authority.

We should also mention the case of old age pensions. The federal act dates from 1927; the provinces decided, one by one, to permit their elderly inhabitants to profit by the scheme. The last province to act was Quebec: it waited until 1936. This should come as no surprise; as late as 1939, the most famous sociologist in French Canada taught the traditional doctrine in these terms: "Social welfare in the Province of Quebec is organized by *private initiatives*. The Catholics are generally agreed that this must continue to be so. Let the State intervene to supplement or to round out the program, not to oust it or dominate it... The urgency with which different measures are required varies from people to people and from age to age."[33]

Finally, in the area of politics, we condemned ourselves to an equally discouraging impotence, because our political ideas were imbued with authoritarianism and we continued to regard the State as an entity independent of its citizens. This native obstinacy in believing that even the provincial government (though elected by a French Canadian majority) could not be placed at our service and under our control is found even in a theorist who, to his credit, made a patient effort to rehabilitate democracy among listeners who scarcely believed in it. Maximilien Caron analyzes the grandeur and servitude of the State in these terms: "The masses are thus able to extort one concession after another [from the political parties]. These concessions ultimately weaken authority, gravely compromise the finances of the State, and bring about the ruin of the government... The State, *almost always impotent,* is a witness to these fratricidal struggles [between rich and poor]."[34] In a discussion of corporatism, the same author speaks of the legislative function of the State: "The regulation of society by corporations is a thousand times better than the cartel and state control of the economy. Corporative control is adopted in broad daylight, with the consent of the majority of those concerned, under the surveillance of government and of consumer protection groups."[35] How, then, does this jurist believe that a democratic government ought to pass laws?

This attitude, combined with the pope's condemnation of atheistic socialism, gave us an excuse to reject the new Canadian social-democratic party, the Cooperative Commonwealth Federation (C.C.F.), though it was concerned neither with atheism nor philosophy, but offered us concrete political means for putting an end to the economic colonialism which our nationalism found so offensive.

In expounding the social doctrine of the Church, Cardinal Villeneuve rather neatly summed up our political thought. His judgments include the following: "The C.C.F. doctrine was condemned in a pastoral letter by Mgr. Gauthier, Archbishop of Montreal. The C.C.F. differs from communism mainly in that it does not seek to obtain its ends by violent means . . . [As for Social Credit], the Church is neutral with regard to the Social Credit Party . . . As for fascism, [Mussolini] has made a great contribution to saving the peace of Europe by his presence at Munich. The Italian mode of government involves certain dangers, it is true, but one should not forget that the democratic form of government involves certain dangers as well."[36]

Obviously, expressions of doctrine of this kind—in a society where a bishop's opinion was equivalent to an order—were not likely to foster, in the people, that spirit of inquiry and liberty of judgment which are basic to democratic practice. Our thinkers seemed, at heart, to be deeply suspicious of the people, who had, in a way, betrayed their providential mission by abandoning the land—where they were starving—to go and work in the cities. Furthermore, in our interpretation of the social doctrine of the Church, political society was viewed much more in terms of elites and leaders than in terms of the political education of the masses.

This was, in fact, the era when the *Editions de l'A.C.J.C.* (Publications of the Catholic Association of French Canadian Youth) published their book, *On demande des chefs* (We Want Leaders).

Elsewhere Abbé Groulx wrote in connection with the subject of "language and survival": "We have, however, a magnificent army of masters at our disposal. They are waiting only for a doctrine, a method, an impulsion. Who will be the mover, the supreme distributor of impetus, of will-power? Who will be the national leader, the de Valera, the Mussolini, whose policies are debatable but who, in ten years, have in psychological terms created a new Ireland and a new Italy, as a Dollfuss and a Salazar are in the process of making a new Austria and a new Portugal? Alas, we had better admit frankly: we do not have this national leader. Will we ever have him? . . . With anguished heart we shall demand this man of Providence, the man that every people needs. Meanwhile . . . etc."[37]

The editors of *L'action nationale* put it as follows: "French Canada demands a leader... Our survival urgently requires a leader, a real leader, with our traditions in his bones, strong in our faith, clear-headed, determined, high-spirited. May Providence bring him forth."[38]

Albert Lévesque, an editor of nationalist publications, also wrote: "For some years, in fact, young people have been demanding leaders; they are even sorry that they have lacked some. They complain that there are no directives, and they beg their elders to provide them."[39] In 1945, Esdras Minville wrote two volumes on *The French Canadian Citizen (Le citoyen canadien-français)* in which he called upon the elite to play a role of great importance.[40] He had already distinguished, as one of the "peculiar qualities" of our popular mentality, "an acceptance, spontaneous so to speak, of authority and hierarchy in the family, in society, and in the State. *The French Canadians like to be governed.* ..."[41]

Before we turn to an analysis of the positive content of our social doctrine, we ought to point out one final characteristic of it: an idealism bordering on schizophrenia. An escape by the high road offered the only exit from the blind alley where our social thought had ended up.[42] Our ethnic group really had no influence on the private sector of the economy; we could always seek consolation in aspiring to the "palms of apostleship," but this course of action did not offer us an effective means of demanding improvements in a social order which assigned us the role of servants. Furthermore, we abhorred state intervention on principle, and we also rejected any political action likely to result in economic reforms, for the irrefutable reason that liberal economic reforms were proposed by the "English," socialist reforms by "materialists."

Still, we proudly aspired to ideal solutions, despite the great poverty of our social sciences. Our attitude was: "A Catholic is too rich to borrow from communists or socialists." Our social policies had hardly been successful, and yet we said: "Let's keep it [political power] for ourselves, entirely for ourselves. Let's tear it away from the domination of financial powers, from the tentacles of Ottawa." Our trade union movement may have been pretty feeble, but still we said: "Let's not abandon our workers to agitators from outside our borders."[43]

Esdras Minville, in commenting on an investigation into "25 years of national life," summed up our economic position as follows: "The evident inability of the capitalist system to solve the painful problems arising from its own functioning, and the inhuman character of the so-called reforms advocated by the adherents of communism and totalitarianism of all kinds, have convinced [the French Canadians] of an elementary truth, that they can expect to obtain a solution to their problems from no one other than themselves. For the past few years, instead of looking to the outside world for directives, an orientation, a system of thought, or a doctrine, they have set out to find these things within themselves, in their own social philosophy and in the examination of their actual situation.''[44]

The young people were no less filled with national pride than their elders. André Laurendeau, in his *Alerte aux Canadiens français* (Warning to French Canadians),[45] blamed Mr. Godbout for his acceptance of an amendment to the constitution enabling the federal government to deal (finally) with the problem of unemployment. He thus explained why it was necessary to prevent Ottawa from invading the field of social legislation. "In this event, a Protestant majority will screen the reforms which have been or are to be undertaken to make our social life conform more closely to Catholic morality. The dreams of corporatism will be shattered. Our hopes of readapting social legislation to the needs of the family will disappear for a long time (because Anglo-Saxon thought is more firmly individualistic than ours), and so will our hopes of altering that legislation to meet the needs of the human and geographical context (since Ottawa will legislate for the country as a whole and not for this or that part of it) . . . We cannot compromise on social legislation for any reason; *we need to control all of it.*" (Laurendeau's italics and parentheses.)

This attitude is rather surprising, considering the retrograde attitudes which had always been typical of Quebec social policies. The search for self-government is truly an admirable step, provided that one fully intends to govern oneself. We must now look at what positive recommendations we made, as substitutes for those harmful reforms offered us by the outside world.

5/The positive message

I do not, of course, intend to consider each of the panaceas put forward by the social theorists of French Canada in the last fifty years. Some, like handicrafts, were too obviously futile to detain us. Others, like our opinions on immigration, amounted to a rejection and became associated with the negative effects of the doctrine. Still others, like certain statements on state control or nationalization, were too sporadic, timid, and especially too contradictory to amount to a really "positive message." Essentially, then, our nationalist "social doctrine of the Church" proposed the renewal of economic and social life by five means: the return to the land, small business, the cooperative movement, the Catholic trade union movement, and corporatism.

a) The return to the land

Any proposed remedy for the upheavals caused by industrialization almost always featured colonization and the return to the land. As I have already shown above, agriculturalism[46] was an integral part of our nationalism, and anyone who wished to deal with our economic problems first had to sacrifice to the rural gods. Here, then, I will simply offer some other typical examples.

In a series of articles on the Depression, written in September 1931, Henri Bourassa recommended a return to the land as the principal remedy for the situation.[47] In May 1933, *L'action nationale* informed us that the Ecole sociale populaire (People's School of Social Studies) had just worked out a program of social renewal; this led Father Alexandre Dugré, S.J., to remark: "We must be loggers or die; we must be farmers or be unemployed ... We must remain a race of farmers, or we will stop increasing, we will disappear."

We have already quoted the 1939 study, *La législation ouvrière et le régime social dans la province de Québec* (Labour Legislation and Social Services in the Province of Quebec). Its author, Esdras Minville, was farsighted enough to recognize the tendencies to industrialization in Quebec at quite an early date, but he still spoke of reform in the following terms: "From the sociological point of view, unemployment insurance and certain other measures of social legislation seem to us *more or less advisable* in the Province of Quebec. In an appendix to our brief on trade unionism, we have explained the seriousness of the *rural problem* in the Province of Quebec at some length. Most of the economists and sociologists who have studied the situation share our opinion: the present economic instability is rooted in the desertion of the countryside and the extreme congestion of the cities, particularly Montreal. Any measure tending to *improve the lot of the industrial worker even more,* or to give the illusion, at least, that the life of the urban worker is becoming more and more secure and easy, would almost fatally accelerate the *movement away from the countryside,* unless equal advantages were guaranteed to the rural population. ... "[48]

b) Small business

Edouard Montpetit declared: "My study of our needs has long convinced me that, in the field of production, we must stick to medium and small industry for now."[49] Maximilien Caron touched on almost all our reforms in a paragraph: "Let us develop small and medium industry, applying the principles of the cooperative movement to assure success. By our efforts, our fellow citizens will become thoroughly convinced that a healthy prosperity must be based on

sound corporatism. . . ."[50] An American sociologist quotes the following extract from the sermon of a small town priest on St. John the
Baptist Day: "The patriotic way for the true French Canadian to live is
to save and become a small proprietor. English methods are not ours.
The French became great by small savings and small business. Don't
borrow the commercial ways of others."[51] Henri Laureys, at the end
of the talk cited earlier, expressed the hope that "the French Canadians will make a determined effort to enter the field of medium and
small industry."[52]

Minville also reports that many people say: "Let's take over small
industry." He goes on to demolish this aspect of our doctrinal mytho-
logy: "The economists have never been able to give a satisfactory
definition of small industry. We might also ask how small firms could
meet the competition of big industry, and above all whether a community could ever attain enough independence, by small industry
alone, in an economy planned and managed to suit big business, and
dominated by it."[53] Needless to say, these timely questions remained
unanswered. Strangest of all, even their author seems to have forgotten them. In 1945, he suggested that a reform of the industrial system
be an integration of part-time manufacturing into the rural economy:
agriculture, logging, fishing . . .[54]

c) The cooperative movement

Our theorists certainly deserve credit for realizing that cooperatives
might have become—had we approached them differently—a means
of emancipation for a people without capital, whose only leverage on
the economic world was the force of numbers. In this field, Alphonse
Desjardins and his pupils were admirable pioneers.

Although the cooperative movement was somewhat successful in
the countryside and among the fishermen, it failed miserably in the
cities, for a good reason. This institution presupposes a firm belief in
democratic responsibility and in collective property. Our fear of
socialism led us to stifle these ideas systematically, especially in the
cities. In addition, people used the worst possible methods, it seems,
in their attempts to win acceptance for the cooperative idea. Some
apostles of the movement appear to have directed most of their efforts
towards the St. John the Baptist societies and towards other organizations of small property owners and merchants. The idea of committing
economic suicide for the sake of a hypothetical nationalism did not
particularly appeal to this group. Others did spread their ideas among
the workers, but their efforts came too late in our industrial development. The cooperative movement was no longer capable, in itself
(i.e., without the aid of political action), of winning a place in a world

where capitalist institutions had complete control of the economy. The last straw was the Jesuits' strong campaign to make the cooperatives denominational. Such a policy did nothing to further the adoption of cooperatives in urban areas, with their variety of language and religion. The provincial leader of the Dominicans at the time came to the defence of Father Lévesque, who had been attacked by the Jesuits for recommending that the cooperatives be non-denominational: "I fear, though I have no positive proof, that some people want to turn the issue of religious affiliation into a narrow question of nationalism."[55]

d) The Catholic trade union movement
One cannot exaggerate the role played by Catholic French Canadian trade unionism in the development of a working-class consciousness in Quebec. Largely through this movement, the Quebec worker has managed to formulate—in his own language and with his own concepts—problems and solutions in his particular industrial world. One would, however, almost be tempted to say that this result was a chance by-product . . .

Catholic trade unionism, in fact, was not in the main an offspring of liberal thinking, an attempt to alleviate the real hardships afflicting our Catholic proletariat in Quebec. Like much of our social doctrine, our ideas on trade unionism emerged from a nationalist reaction against reforms which arrived from the outside world, after we, in our indifference, had neglected to apply them in time. Our denominational trade unionism was conceived by artificial insemination; its birth is not the most glorious episode in its history. The xenophobic, authoritarian, and unrealistic character of the movement is reflected in the words of the tireless zealot of the Ecole sociale populaire, who rationalized our long blindness as follows: "Necessity [of uniting after the Conquest] made the French Canadians one big family without distinctions of caste or class rivalry. Little by little, with the increase of the race, social differences were established among its members, but barely perceptible ones. There were no great gaps between the rich and the wage earners, such as one finds elsewhere; above all, no animosity divided them . . . Because of these circumstances, the Church in Quebec was slow to establish trade unions . . . Faced with new economic facts, such as the increasing cost of living and the development of foreign-owned joint stock industries, the Church *believed that the time had come* to organize the workers. The difficulties that it then encountered almost all originated [sic] with American organization. The employers had already suffered at the hands of the international trade unions, and their lack of social consciousness made them generally hostile to the movement. There were many workers who belonged to unions or who, though not members, had been won over to the ideas of neutrality spread among the masses by the unionists: they were not well disposed towards this undertaking . . . But the difficult times are over. Thanks to the very clear directives of the bishops, based on the teachings of Rome, the energetic efforts of the chaplains, and the pious attitude of several managers and *a good number of workers,* Catholic organization of the workers is now doing well. . . ." Father Archambault concludes that "the elite acts upon the masses," and that to serve "the race and the Church," the doctrine should be preached everywhere in society: in the Church, in Parliament, in the press, among industrialists and financiers, *and even* (!) "in the factories where one finds a restless proletariat, which is too often embittered and menacing."[56]

During the same Semaine sociale (Symposium on Social Issues), Mgr. Lapointe, one of the founders of our Catholic trade union movement, blandly remarked: "At the right time, when it was possible, the clergy did for the workers what they had done for all the citizens of other classes. Here again we must, I feel, admit that they have broken new ground with wisdom and foresight."[57]

What, then, inspired Cardinal Taschereau to condemn the Knights of Labour (Chevaliers du travail), an act which, according to Alfred Charpentier (before he "converted" and became the first president of the Catholic trade unions), was due to "lack of reflection, haste, and incompetence"?[58] Wonderful, indeed, is the "farsightedness" which—in Chicoutimi and Jonquière in 1913, for example—led "the Catholic authorities" to make "a most aggressive appeal" against the international unions, calling upon "the workers to cast them out with all their works, if they wished to keep their Catholic faith."[59]

With the passage of years, the aggressive character lessened, of course, but the gist of the appeal was unaltered. In 1937, for example, during a strike in the Montreal garment industry, the religious authorities strongly supported the Catholic unions against the I.L.G.W.U. (International Ladies' Garment Workers' Union) by approving a collective agreement which violated the minimum wage law.[60]

In 1938, Father Arès wrote in the *Petit catéchisme d'éducation syndicale* (The Little Catechism of Trade Union Education): "In the Province of Quebec, is the Catholic worker permitted to prefer the non-denominational union to the Catholic union? No, unless in leaving the non-denominational union for the Catholic union, he would suffer severely; for example, if he were to lose *the only job available* to him" (p. 28, my italics). In 1939, the sociologist Esdras Minville had this to say about international (American) trade unionism: "The unreligious character of the group makes it almost inevitable that the members will have to choose between two loyalties: to their religion or to their trade association.'' A bit farther on he added: ''International trade unionism, given its doctrinal inspiration, is no more a guarantee of order than the revolutionary individualism from which it springs, or the communism towards which, by a natural tendency as it were, its ideas carry it.'' Mr. Minville candidly adds that his comments ''are, in short, just a summing up of the great campaign waged last November [1937], in the French Canadian Catholic press and on the radio, in favour of national, Catholic trade unions.'' Turning, at last, to matters of fact, he admits that the ''trade-unionism'' which he so nonchalantly libels ''has not really gone so far or so fast as its principles allow it. Still, it is left-wing. Its demands have followed a pattern which shows its tendencies clearly enough, particularly where hours of work are concerned. Before 1872, it fought for the nine-hour day ... [and today] it is calling for the six-hour day and the thirty-hour week.'' There can be no doubt: this is the pattern of the purest bolshevism! The whole piece ends with a speech in favour of ''the employer who has the same right to live as the worker.''[61]

Is there a fairer indictment of this phalanx of social thinkers than the words of a ''neutral'' trade unionist, reported by Mgr. Lapointe? ''Abbé ... for many years we have suffered, toiled, laboured for starvation wages ... When we complained of our poverty, and were greeted with rifle shots as rebels and revolutionaries, what were you doing? You counselled patience, pointing to heaven, and you read us some fine little sermons on respect for the social order ... Abbé, you offered us no solution. Then, organized labour from the States opened its arms to us, and we rushed into them. Today you say that's no good. Why didn't you say so before?''[62]

Our sociologists ignored the destitution of the working class until they were led, by nationalism, to denounce the international unions. They now favoured a paternalistic labour movement, controlled by clergymen and employers. They advocated religious affiliation for the unions, because ''without this system, *no authority will be able to enforce the principles of Christianity* in these organizations, where men of every opinion will come together. ....''[63] Forgetful of the deep scars they had left on the labour movement, and of the serious disturbances they had created in Christian consciences, our social thinkers again withdrew into the cozy myth of our providential mission. Bourassa concluded a series of editorials on the trade union movement with an appeal to working-class nationalism, isolationism, and social conservatism.[64] It is not surprising that the next year found him denouncing ''the plague of industrialization and its inevitable consequence, the depopulation of the countryside."[65] Alfred Charpentier sent *Le Devoir* "a public profession of faith in the nationalism of the working class." He later wrote: "God, it seems, intended that our race should flourish in this part of the country, in spite of past persecutions, to become the purifying salt of the entire Canadian nation . . . Providence calls upon our Catholic workers to do their part as well, namely, to lead a defence of this country's working class against the dangers which threaten it."[66]

e) Corporatism

Corporatism is without a doubt the most important reform to delight our social thinkers. The greatest variety of men, in the most different circumstances, and for the most opposed ends, proclaimed the gospel of corporatism. Their voices were as one, and they preached their futile homilies with unflagging enthusiasm. Nothing more starkly revealed the monolithic nature of our ideology.

From year to year, in connection with everything and nothing, lecturers at the Semaines sociales (Symposiums on Social Issues) found ways to apologize for corporatism. They included Mgr. Paquet and the future Mgr. Desranleau (1921), Jean Bruchési (1936), and Maximilien Caron (three times from 1938 to 1942). Caron relied upon such disparate authorities as Cardinal Villeneuve ("Corporatism all the way!") and the prime minister of the province ("Anything that brings us closer to corporatism is a step forward."). At the Semaine sociale of 1942, Gérard Picard was still speaking of trade unionism as a means of achieving a corporative organization of society.

The contributors to *L'action nationale* also went through a phase of hard-line corporatism. In November 1937, Roger Duhamel expressed the opinion that nationalism would emerge victorious from a national and Catholic trade union movement, which could reach full maturity within a corporative framework. The next year, a long inquiry into corporatism began. In the course of it, the greatest variety of learned doctors found themselves in agreement with one another: Abbé J.B. Desrosiers (in a Semaine sociale held at Jean-de-Brébeuf College, November 1937, he also recommended that family allowances be obtained through corporatism); François Hertel (who advocated a corporatist version of personalism; he still adhered to this doctrine in 1945, in his *Nous ferons l'avenir*[We Will Make the Future]); F.A. Angers (who held that the unions must develop towards corporatism). We should also add the names of other zealots who participated in this inquiry: Hermas Bastien, Gérard Filion, Esdras Minville. Father Lévesque was also part of the group: he recommended joint action by the adherents of the cooperative movement and the supporters of corporatism.[67]

Father Arès devised a corporatist catechism, and in his trade union catechism, he emphasized (Question 45) that the trade union movement is a first step towards corporatism. Victor Barbeau made a remarkable inquiry into our economic hardships; he concluded it with a statement in favour of an economic and political order based on corporations.[68] In the same year, the Jeunesses patriotes (Young Patriots) published a book on separatism, *Le séparatisme,* by Dostaler O'Leary. O'Leary called for "the establishment of a corporative regime in the Free French Canadian State."[69] The Bloc universitaire (University Coalition), at its Duchesnay convention of 1939, passed a resolution that "each of our Schools of Social Sciences should make a special effort to interest all students . . . in corporatism."

We could add to the list indefinitely, but the nature of our philosophic idealism is clear enough. Several decades of social thought are summed up almost in a word: corporatism. Since the word had crossed the lips of the Pope, and since the English were hardly enthusiastic about corporatism, we were glad to regard it as a universal panacea. Everybody was happy to recommend this miraculous remedy, which had the advantage of *not requiring any critical reflection.* Nobody felt that he had to search for an approach to social issues in tune with the course of history. Anyone who endorsed the fashionable prejudice was granted the title of Catholic and national sociologist.

I do not intend to deal here with the question of whether or not corporatism has some contribution to make to a political theory based on the idea of progress. Objective political economy and sociology have certainly not yet shown how a legal superstructure, which makes no essential changes in capitalist institutions, could reconcile the opposed interests of capital and labour, except in limited areas and for limited periods of time. Social and economic tendencies to monopoly, inherent in these reconciliations, would very likely create conflicts of interest (cartel against cartel, cartel against the consumers, etc.). These conflicts could be resolved only by oligarchy, eliminated only by dictatorship. It would therefore be most dangerous to attempt corporate organization, except among people whose democratic development was so far advanced that one could be utterly certain that special interests (the concern of the corporations) would be subordinate to the general interest (the concern of the State).

Now, most of our thinkers saw corporatism in a completely different light: they regarded it as a means to tame the *democratic* thrust of the trade union movement. They tolerated unions only because they believed that they would soon be contained by corporations. Our brand of corporatism was actually devised for an "elite," who saw it as a means to discipline popular movements and to maintain its authority over the masses organized in this fashion. The people were not at all taken in by this. When we finally made an objective inquiry into the results of nearly half a century of theoretical corporatism, we realized that defeat was total: "There is not one organization whose administrative structure corresponds exactly to the ideal type described by the militants."[70]

The Book of Ecclesiastes still offers the finest comment on our social ideas in general in the half century before the asbestos strike: *mataiotès mataiotètôn, ta panta mataiotès*.

IV/The institutions

Our people had suddenly, and as it were inadvertently, been thrust into the industrial era; our doctrinaire thinkers were totally opposed to this situation. Our institutions tried to bridge the gap between reality and theory.

Such a posture is not conducive to energetic action. It explains the lethargy, during the first half of the twentieth century, in those of our institutions which were primarily based on thought, but of necessity had to keep in touch with reality. Our Church and our universities are examples. Other institutions refused to straddle this gap: they took a stand, so to speak, either on the side of pure theory or on the side of concrete reality. The first group became petrified in grand abstractions, like most of our nationalist organizations. The second group renounced all ideology, like our major political parties: opportunistic, they recognized no master but the passions.

Within the scope of this section, I obviously cannot examine all the major institutions that conditioned the thinking of French Canadians and established a framework for their actions. (Our thinkers have so far done little more than outline this critical task—a typical example of the lack of realism in our culture.)[71] I shall mention only a few institutions as examples. Even so, the treatment will be superficial, because my sole aim is to draw attention to the inescapable truth that emerges from the deep contradiction between Part II (the facts) and Part III (the ideas) of this chapter: when we were faced with the powerful upheaval of the asbestos strike, the "social habits" of French Canadian society (I mean our habitual, or institutional, ways of thinking) left us in the lurch.

We will consider, then, some examples of institutions which became bogged down in theory; which strayed into a complete pragmatism; or which, immobilized by these opposing tendencies to theory and practice, found themselves somewhere between the two.[72] (Of course, this division is only a rough approximation to the general orientation of our institutions. Many of them, no doubt, had their valid aspects; insofar as these aspects prevail, the institutions offer some promise for the future.)

1/A national organization: the St. John the Baptist Society

The St. John the Baptist Society of Montreal is a prime example of an institution where an obliging attitude to "the doctrine" made it impossible to understand reality. "The oldest national society of Franco-Canadians," it was founded in 1834. In the course of its history, the Society had its days of glory and its successful undertakings. One of its more important ventures was the Prêt d'honneur (Loan on Trust). Good intentions, however, are no substitute for realism in pursuing a course of political action. This is clearly shown by the brief that this society presented, in 1938, to the Royal Commission on Dominion-Provincial Relations, under the title *Les faits sociaux dans la province de Québec* (Social Facts in the Province of Quebec).[73]

After a long discussion of the Canadian constitution, which it regards as a pact, the brief expounds the moral principles that govern the social organization of the Province of Quebec. Among other platitudes, it states that "Catholic social doctrine distinguishes the individual from the person." It then examines the consequences of this social morality on the practical level: 1—Reform of principles ("an equitable conception of the law of property, an improvement in the condition of the proletarians and wage-earning classes," etc.). 2—Reform of institutions ("A renewal of the true role of the State, which is to coordinate, not to absorb; planned economy; trade associations"). 3—Reform of morals. The brief goes on to say that "the family constitutes the keystone of our social organization," and laments the fact that "it seems that the politicians have borrowed abroad their examples and models of legislation."[74]

A fine attitude, indeed. The confrontation with industrialization is seen in these terms: "Accordingly as the lot of the worker was improved, the rural class was incited to desert the soil . . . One must seek a formula of organization . . . This formula does not consist in social legislation which in turn rests on wages. It can thus only aggravate the evil by making the disadvantage of rural life more disproportionate in relation to urban life . . . The protection and stabilization of the family imply a wide policy of agricultural expansion to the full extent that the soil and the climate permit, completed by a prudent and daring industrial policy, but recognizing to the fullest possible degree small and average-sized industry."[75]

The brief notes in passing that the rural population is "the guardian of the moral inheritance." Peculiar ideas of political economy are presented (it is necessary to "provide outlets for excess production *and* excess population"), and the creation of a proletariat and of unemployment is examined. The brief then turns to "the necessary restoration." Having stated that the population of Quebec is 63.1% urbanized, it coldly declares that "the French Canadian family is bound up in the soil by tradition. The agricultural problem is the first to call for solution."[76] Farther on, it continues: " . . . the labor legislation remains a dangerous palliative by accentuating the too pronounced tendency of expecting everything from the State, and, on the other hand, of creating a privileged situation for the workers in the cities. In the present instance, it is a step in the direction of state socialism. In the second instance, the city-country industry-agriculture contrast will accentuate the movement of urban centralization. Legislation that aims at improving the lot of the worker—good in itself——cannot fail to attract the rural to the city. Now, our population is traditionally rural and legislation that may appear good in other environments may cause in our province very grave social disturbances."[77] The brief concludes with an apology for decentralization " . . . in order to allow the Province of Quebec to orientate the social policy in the direction of its specific needs and in keeping with its traditions."[78]

Such a document raises the question: are such "decentralizers" leading us along the path of true progress? . . .

2/The Ecole sociale populaire (People's School of Social Studies), et hoc genus omne

The Ecole sociale populaire was the prime institution involved in teaching the social doctrine of the Church in French Canada (it later became known as the Institut social populaire [People's Institute of Social Studies]). From its establishment in 1911 by Father Hudon to our own day, this Jesuit institution has shown an admirably zealous concern for social issues. Unfortunately, these enthusiasts seemed to regard sociology, economics, and political science as deductive tools, by means of which—starting from "great principles" rather than from facts—a docile people might be led in the right direction. This institution must therefore assume a large share of the blame for the fact that, in contempt of reality, social thought in French Canada took a narrow nationalist path, blinkered by clericalism, agriculturalism, and a paternalistic attitude towards labour.

The Ecole sociale populaire voiced its opinions through the monthly publication of pamphlets and through tracts. According to the titles, attention was focussed on the following issues: agriculture, colonization, corporatism, and especially labour and trade union problems. The content of the teaching has been discussed above in connection with agriculturalism, denominational trade unions, etc. The Jesuits set the tone for the discussion of all these issues. Perhaps the most "advanced" doctrine published by them is found in pamphlet no. 232-233 of the Ecole sociale populaire.[79] Minville begins by making the most absolute and categorical denunciation of capitalism imaginable, but he crowns it with these words: "Capitalism can do better than merely accumulate riches: it has a social role to play. If, one day, it comes to understand this role, prosperity and peace will reign in the world." The Dominican Father Georges Lévesque makes a denunciation of the C.C.F. which offers a contrast to this benevolent and tolerant attitude. Lévesque first rejects Cardinal Bourne's endorsement of English socialism with this ridiculous argument: "English socialism, by abandoning several fundamental and anti-Christian principles of the socialist school, is not a true socialism."[80] He then proceeds to condemn C.C.F. doctrine on three points, but all he really does is to criticize its presumed and hypothetical intentions. Although the C.C.F. has condemned communism, it is still a fact that "Mr. Woodsworth has gone to the trouble of visiting Russia personally, to study the result of the Soviet experience"! The C.C.F. expressly condemns violence, "but we are inclined to believe that they would, with deep regret, admit it as an exceptional means. . . ." They proclaim "the primacy of man in the economy" and "the priority of the common good over the interests of a few individuals," principles which "are far from being materialistic" and "are entirely Christian in appearance," but are *still materialistic* because "they only recommend reforms on the material plane: reforms of things, not persons"! After these two expositions of doctrine, Father Louis Chagnon, S.J., has no trouble proving that there is nothing more perfect than the 13 clauses in the "program of social renewal" advocated by the Ecole sociale populaire. These 13 clauses contain very welcome suggestions for the regulation of financial institutions, the state control of "certain forms of wealth," and social legislation. Then, necessarily, they advocate cooperatives, colonization, agriculture, and corporatism.

From 1936 to 1940, the Ecole published *L'ordre nouveau* (The New Order), a review which was considered to be "the official publication of the Semaines sociales of Canada." According to the index, agriculture was treated 4 times; cooperatives 16 times; corporatism 64 times; trade unionism 20 times; employers' organizations 7 times; labour 3 times; employers 10 times. (I admit at once, and once and for all, that this sort of evidence can be imprecise, especially as the indexes are often poorly compiled.)

At the beginning of the war, *L'ordre nouveau* was replaced by the
monthly review *Relations* (Relations). According to the table of contents, which covers the period 1941-1950, agriculture was treated 33
times, colonization 54 times, cooperatives 18 times, corporatism 8
times, industry 5 times, the worker 16 times, work and wages 10
times, women at work 20 times (mostly deplored), trade unionism 16
times, strikes 6 times (4 times to oppose them), Catholic trade unions
5 times, Anglo-American trade unionism once (to say that membership in the C.C.F. was a threat of totalitarianism), the Catholic Union
of Farmers 7 times.

It was chiefly through the Semaines sociales, however, that the
Ecole sociale populaire was able to spread our social doctrine of the
Church. From 1920, these symposiums were held annually (with 4
exceptions) in different centres of French Canada. Prominent and
respected clergymen and laymen gathered to reiterate a traditional and
unquestioned doctrine. An analytical and critical (?) study of this
teaching was made by Sister Marie Agnes of Rome Gaudreau and
published in 1946 as *The Social Thought of French Canada as
Reflected in the Semaine sociale.*[81]

This well-disposed observer summed up the Semaines sociales'
attitude towards the economic order as follows: "The Semaine sociale
rejects that exaggerated capitalism which is responsible for so many
economic disorders. It advocates rural life for the French Canadian
population aware of its various benefits, thereby offering practical,
economic, social and political remedies for bettering conditions on the
land."[82]

Sister Marie Agnes devotes only one page each to the Semaines
sociales' condemnations of such perverse doctrines as individualism,
liberalism, and racism, but more than 13 pages to their condemnation
of socialism and communism.[83]

On our sociologists, Sister Marie Agnes remarks: "The conception
of sociology used in French Canada is the ordinary Catholic one, not
the conception of American materialists . . . If an attempt were made
to formulate a definition of sociology in the light of the teachings of
the Semaine sociale, it seems that this definition would apply only to a
Catholic sociology. To the French Canadian elite of the Semaine
sociale, sociology is a practical discipline, based on sound philosophy
and theology, which studies the doctrine of the social encyclicals and
examines the data on social problems in the light of the social teachings of the Church. For instance, the study of criminology would not
be included in French Canadian sociology, for crime, in the opinion of
several followers of the Semaine sociale, does not reach large enough
proportions to constitute a major social problem."[84] She adds:

"Rather than inquire into how many industries the French Canadians control, the Semaine sociale is more concerned with the number of Catholics who have remained faithful to their religious practices ... A politician or a professional who incurs the displeasure of the Church must bear with ostracism of one kind or another."[85]

Finally, on trade associations, she remarks: "The Semaine sociale would make these Catholic syndicates form the basis for the establishment of corporative organizations as advocated by the social Popes, and insists on the immediate establishment of such a corporative system...."[86]

For further information, I refer the reader to the numerous quotations drawn from various Semaines sociales and already reported in the third part of this chapter.

3/From the Ligue des droits du français (League for the Rights of the French Language) to **L'action nationale** (National Action)

The Ecole sociale populaire concentrated on our social doctrine of the Church. A parallel Jesuit institution, which invited more participation by laymen, was set up to develop and spread a nationalist doctrine. The Ligue des droits du français was founded in 1913 by Father Joseph Papin Archambault. It first published an Almanac; then, in 1917, it launched a review, l'Action française. Abbé Groulx became its first editor. This review brought together an enthusiastic team who favoured a more doctrinaire and ethnocentric nationalism than Bourassa. In particular, a "sacred union," which was the result of the conscription crisis followed by the economic crisis of 1920, led several contributors to speculate about the creation of "our French State." We should also mention that in 1921, the review conducted a remarkable inquiry (already cited) into the economic problems of French Canadians, with the collaboration of men like Montpetit, Asselin, Georges Pelletier, Antonio Perrault, Léon Lorrain, Beaudry Leman, Henri Laureys and Omer Héroux. Abbé Groulx concluded the inquiry by showing the urgent necessity of economic nationalism. In the following year, l'Action française published some other very interesting studies, by Asselin and Pelletier especially, on economic nationalism. In going over all these writings, one cannot help thinking that nationalism blinds people to the *real forces* which direct the economy of a country. The common good would doubtless have been better served if our researchers had studied the unequal distribution of our provincial wealth less from the ethnic point of view and more from the point of view of social classes and the inequities inherent in economic liberalism. To do so, however, they would have had to attack the economic dictatorship with more vigour and to devote to real reforms of structure (teaching, nationalization, planned economy, etc.) some of the energy that was lavished on organizing the *Achat chez nous* (Buy Quebec Products) program and on making up "white lists" (fair lists) of Catholic and French Canadian employers.

In January 1928, one year after Rome had condemned Maurras's *l'Action française*, the Montreal review took the name of *l'Action canadienne-française*. Then, in March 1929, in the euphoria of prosperity and an atmosphere of good federal-provincial and international relations, the review ceased to appear.

The Depression revived the sacred union. Towards the end of 1932, *L'action nationale* was founded to take up the cause of nationalism again. The nationalist Old Guard recruited people from the younger generation (which was just starting the Jeune-Canada [Young Canada] movement). In the ensuing years there was further talk of economic dictatorship, and worthwhile political and social reforms were advocated. It was apparent, though, that the sacred union was again regrouping on the ethnic rather than on the economic or social level. Capitalism and trusts were attacked *because* they were foreign, and the reforms offered by the outside world were naturally rejected as well. Father G.H. Lévesque, though recognizing "the excellence of certain principles" supported by the new C.C.F. Party, again concluded that "it is our duty to ask all Catholics, and all citizens who desire the real welfare of the country, to oppose this socialist movement and to struggle vigorously against it."[87]

F.A. Angers's great sincerity obliged him to recognize the advantages of socialism, but his conscience forced him to condemn it. Ten years later, in the pages of the same review, he wrote: "In some respects, the Blum government was harmful to France, due to the errors of French socialism, which are common to other forms of socialism as well. It did, however, make a fine effort, doubtless shortsighted but in the right direction, to restore human dignity to the worker. The unions took advantage of the socialist government in power, calling for paid holidays, leisure time activities, and travel within the workers' means ... By their methods of action and their demands on behalf of labour, the socialists have upset many applecarts, but they have made some remarkable achievements."[88]

In sum, the "structural reforms" advocated by *L'action nationale* again featured an *Achat chez nous* program and bilingual currency. On the theoretical level, they were supplemented by the magnificent mental constructs discussed earlier: return to the land, corporatism, etc. Between 1933 and 1946, the review's tables of contents show that there were 13 articles written on rural and agricultural issues, 14 on cooperatives, and 15 on corporatism, while only 4 articles dealt with social security and 6 with labour and union issues (one of these, however, was a courageous article on the strikers at Arvida in 1941).

When André Laurendeau became editor of *L'action nationale* late in 1937, the review lost its racist overtones and purged itself of extreme right-wing doctrines. Some currents in Quebec political thought favoured autonomy; *L'action nationale* tried to give them a more socialist orientation, but the war and the events preceding it soon revived the anti-imperialist and anti-conscription controversies. Social issues were more or less shelved until 1947, when the review made an inquiry into labour humanism. It lasted eight months, and led Laurendeau to conclude, in June 1948: "Almost all our correspondents have been harsh judges of French Canadian nationalism. They have accused it, in particular, of paying too little attention to social issues, of retaining very bourgeois attitudes. This is, I feel, a fair criticism on the whole . . . [but] French Canadian nationalists should not be used as a scapegoat. Of all the people in our society, they have held the most open-minded and liberal opinions, along with a bourgeois outlook . . . Social concern and national concern now seem to be antagonists . . . We must see if we can make the synthesis in time."[89]

This is not the place to examine the possibility of such a synthesis. We wonder, though, if Mr. Laurendeau, in trying to do the opposite, has not denied the possibility. In the article cited above, he wrote: "Neither the bourgeois nor the intellectual stop being themselves because they are nationalists; a nationalist who does not react to the labour problem as I do is still a nationalist." One might well agree with this. The nationalist in question, though, is less "socially concerned," and the "synthesis" is all washed up . . .

Nevertheless, on the eve of the asbestos strike one nationalist institution, at least, was certainly prepared to reconsider its doctrinal positions in the light of economic and social realities. One month before the strike, the editors of *L'action nationale* signed an article on asbestosis entitled "The East Broughton Morgue."[90] As we shall see later on in this book (especially in the chapters by Beausoleil and Pelletier), some usually traditionalist institutions adopted very progressive social attitudes at the time of the asbestos strike.

But let's not get ahead of ourselves . . .

4/Educational institutions in general
The development of our educational institutions has been strongly influenced by our industrial revolution; our institutions' influence on that revolution is less certain. Let us examine the problem on its various levels.

a) Primary and secondary education

The physical development of our institutions has been affected by industrialization. In one of the chapters in *Essais sur le Québec contemporain,* Léon Lortie has shown that the development of the business world, as well as the nearby presence of English schools, led us to establish better elementary schools; that during the second quarter of this century, the number of engineering students at the Ecole polytechnique (Polytechnic School) in Montreal quadrupled . . .[91] In the same book, Arthur Tremblay remarks: "On the level of basic professional training, apart from the apprenticeship centres which have just recently been created and which are still few in number, we have been content to assure a better geographical distribution of two types of school already in existence: the technical school and the agricultural school. On the other hand, almost all our middle-level technical schools were set up scarcely 25 to 30 years ago; until about 1920, our university faculties offered training only in the liberal professions: theology, medicine, and law."[92]

Consequently, "industrialization has profoundly modified the structure" of our educational institutions. It seems, however, that we agreed to these changes only with the deepest reluctance: our traditionalism prevented us from redesigning our social structures to the point where we might have become the masters of the industrialization process, rather than its passive slaves. Lortie writes of our present-day school system: "It corresponds to the mentality that prevailed when it was created, shortly after the troubles of 1837 . . . It displays a certain distrust of the State, because it fears its interference, and it upholds a strong particularism."[93] Lortie adds that secondary education "offered a deep-rooted resistance to the effects of industrialization,"[94] and that its masters "especially saw, in the rising tide of industrialization, the spectre of materialism and of Americanization." Tremblay tells us that he has "diagnosed a kind of resistance to the industrial movement on the part of graduates in Arts. At the university, the industrial and commercial faculties owe their numerical importance less to them than to graduates in other fields."[95]

We should also refer briefly to the incredible struggle of the apostles of compulsory education against an entire intelligentsia, which stubbornly refused to see this reform as anything but a radical and atheistic measure. Mgr. Paquet in 1909 and 1916, Mgr. Philippe Perrier in 1912, and Father Hermas Lalande in 1919 opposed compulsory education on theological grounds.[96] In 1920, Abbé Groulx equally condemned compulsory education and the divorce law, which he regarded as the work of Protestant parliaments.[97] At the Semaine sociale of 1923, held at Montreal, the future Cardinal Villeneuve stated: "People are demanding the compulsory school, the public school, the national school, the state school, as if this were not tantamount to violating the family, and thereby enfeebling society."[98] As a result, the Roman Catholic Committee of the Council of Education ignored "premature school leaving" until 1942. During the deliberations of this committee, Mgr. Charbonneau declared himself in favour of compulsory education. As for Cardinal Villeneuve, "he recognizes that up to the beginning of the century, most of our professors of social philosophy challenged the State's right to impose compulsory schooling ... It was not clearly apparent, in the past, that school instruction was a matter of public concern ... His Eminence also admits that he formerly questioned the right of the government authorities to make schooling compulsory. Today, Catholic doctrine is clear and firm on this point, formerly the subject of debate, and there is no longer any reason to have the least doubts about the government's rights in this area." Nevertheless, when the Committee produced a statement in favour of adopting compulsory schooling, the following dissenting voices were recorded: Monsignors Comtois, Langlois, Douville, and Belleau, as well as Sir Mathias Tellier and Judge H.A. Fortier.[99]

In 1943, a bill was prepared to put the Committee's recommendation into effect. The Secretary of the Province, Hector Perrier, won over most of the bishops by explaining that his law was modelled on the Vatican's law. Still, some were intractable, and so were organizations like the J.O.C. (Jeunesse ouvrière catholique, Catholic Labour Youth) and the St. John the Baptist Society of Montreal. In the Legislative Assembly, the National Union MPPs, led by Duplessis, were solidly opposed to the law, but the government majority of Godbout won out. On May 26, 1943, school attendance became compulsory for children aged 6 to 14. The National Union came into power a year later, however, and has since made hardly any efforts to enforce this law.

b) Post-secondary and university education
Two documents span the period studied in this chapter; a comparison of them shows that our university instruction had little of the dynamism required to keep abreast of change in a century of rapid developments. In 1905, André Siegfried had this to say about French Canada: "The university is far from being, as it is in some countries, a place where new ideas are in ferment, where future developments are in preparation; rather, it is an effective instrument of conservation ... Left to itself, French Canadian higher education tends to remain what it is: its leading principles do not push it in the

direction of development. The energies of exceptional leaders would be needed to change it profoundly and organically."[100] A half century later, these reforms were apparently still not in view, to judge by the University of Montreal's brief to the Tremblay Commission. The University stated: "Research is not really an essential university activity." Further on, one encounters these unspeakable sophistries of constitutional law and political "science": "The provinces are by definition guardians of property and civil rights, and will therefore prove more conservative than the federal government under our present constitution, taking the word conservative here as meaning opposed to socialism, communism, and new social experiments. This rule, applied to the universities, once more proves valid: *the role of the university is to preserve and to transmit knowledge much more than to increase it.*"[101]

No doubt, some professors at Laval and Montreal shuddered at these strange ideas. In our two French Canadian universities, there are teachers whose competence and courage excite only admiration. Thanks to these people, some branches of our university knowledge have undergone a rapid development, such as our official attitudes gave us no right to expect. The teaching of the exact and social sciences at Laval and of psychology at Montreal are examples. Still, the above quotations are a painfully accurate reflection of the views of university administrations. Their systematic and persistent narrow-mindedness has produced generally poor results.

Access to higher education was limited by its high cost in relation to our means; niggardly scholarships were tainted by subservience to the political order.[102] As a result, our society was hardly able to renew itself intellectually through the constant circulation of its social types in accordance with talents and vocations. In 1951, for example, of the 1,130,194 people who earned wages or salaries in Quebec, 10.4% were professional or business men, but the students who came from these social strata accounted for 47.8% of the enrolment at the University of Montreal. On the other hand, skilled and unskilled workers made up 43.1% of the wage or salary earning group mentioned above, but their sons represented only 13.9% of the university students enrolled.[103] These statistics are obviously not perfect, but even if we allow for the fact that the percentage of businessmen and professional men would be higher if we added those who were not salaried employees, these figures suggest that financial and social status are of prime importance in determining access to university studies. The great majority of children born into poor families, then, must be satisfied with a few years of primary school, where their readers and their arithmetic problems extoll the bourgeois virtues and illustrate the glories of the free enterprise system.

Traditional university faculties still attract the highest enrolment,[104] but let's look first at the other faculties.

The figures below reveal the success of the technical and industrial faculties. In 1951, 79.6% of all workers in the Province of Quebec were French Canadian (75.5% in 1931); in the same year, 49% of Quebec's architects were French Canadian (48% in 1931). French Canadians made up 54% of all civil engineers (46% in 1931), and 51% of all chemists and metallurgists (47% in 1931). Of all chemical, mining, electrical, and mechanical engineers, no more than 25% were ever French Canadian.[105] In short, the French Canadians have always been the hewers of wood and the drawers of water in the industrial revolution. Over a period of 20 years, our educational institutions have not caused our percentage of technicians to increase more rapidly than our percentage of workers.

In the first half of the twentieth century, did any of the other faculties train an elite capable of redesigning our social structures in the light of contemporary realities?

In the teaching of history, our institutions have done their best to prevent people, often very serious and capable people, from raising their discipline to the level of a social science. Our first historian, F.X. Garneau, wrote his *Histoire du Canada* in a spirit of nationalist recrimination; one hundred years later, the men who held the chair of history in our two French-language universities could still fascinate the cultivated public with a discussion of whether our history should promote nationalism or a spirit of tolerance and understanding.[106] Within this interval of a century, our universities were without a professor of history for fifty years, and when the authorities finally appointed one (Abbé Groulx), they wanted to make him sign an agreement that he would attack neither the Canadian Confederation nor the English Canadians.[107]

Our French Canadian faculties of law need not detain us. Busy lawyers came there to teach students how to find their way among the different law codes of the Province of Quebec. Any notions of the sociology of law were scrupulously avoided; the major currents in the philosophy of law were ignored by our law faculties; the infrequent courses in constitutional law were completely worthless, and the very names of Jean Bodin and Jeremy Bentham were unknown. With such a background, it is no wonder that the Quebec Bar had yet to recognize the industrial revolution as the first half of the twentieth century drew to a close. In 1949, for example, Quebec still had no family courts, no legal clinics, and no legal aid system to deal with the problems of a disinherited proletariat.[108] From 1941 to 1949, less than half a dozen lawyers discussed the problems of Quebec labour legislation in the pages of the *Revue du Barreau* (Quebec Bar Review).

The Ecole des hautes études commerciales (School for Higher Commercial Studies), founded in Montreal in 1907, was also a professional school rather than a university faculty properly speaking. It was simply an intermediate level school of commerce (like the much more recent one in Quebec City), and could not be expected to generate profound and dynamic thinking. The Montreal institution has, however, done some useful preliminary work through its industrious compilation of facts and statistics. The Ecole also made notable contributions in the field of commerce and business, but its institutional orientation and its choice of deans and professors fostered an essentially conservative atmosphere. Its teaching remained in a state of perpetual obsolescence, though French, Canadian history, and physical geography were readily offered! The scant social and political theory taught was merely nationalism and its corollaries: the social doctrine of the Church, small business, the virtues of country life, etc. This was the state of things in the Ecole at the time of the asbestos strike.

We can obtain a general idea of the Ecole's leading preoccupations by analyzing the topics covered in its quarterly review, *l'Actualité économique* (Current Economics). (I shall first give the data for the period 1925 to 1946, and then add in parentheses the corresponding figure for the period 1946-1950; this will enable the reader to recognize a certain shift of interest during the latter years of the quarter century in which the review appeared.) For the years 1925 to 1946, titles dealing with agriculture occupied about 154 lines of the general subject index (plus 33 lines for the period 1946 to 1950); with colonization, 24 lines (plus 10); with cooperatives, 83 lines (plus 25); with corporatism, 18 lines (plus 4); with Canadian trade unionism, 2 lines (plus 12); with land and soil, 36 lines (plus 6); with industry, 132 lines (plus 50); with insurance and social security, 12 lines (plus 11); with industrial relations, 13 lines (plus 10). There were, finally, 10 lines of titles dealing with Social Credit, but none on the C.C.F., nor on the big strikes at Arvida, Sorel, and Asbestos. The Coopérative Fédérée de Québec (*Société coopérative fédérée des agriculteurs de la province de Québec,* Quebec Federation of Farmers' Cooperatives) is mentioned 4 times, the Catholic Union of Farmers 7 times, and the Catholic trade union once (in connection with corporatism).

5/The teaching of the social sciences

A word must be said, finally, about the schools of social science properly speaking.

a) In Montreal

In 1920, the very year that the University of Montreal received its charter, Mgr. Gauthier invited Edouard Montpetit to establish a "School of social, economic, and political sciences." From the beginning, "the School has incorporated other subjects": courses in hygiene for nurses, the School of Tourism, business administration... As for real sociology, "the School, because of insufficient funds, has retained approximately the same program for twenty years." In 1941, however, "a year was added to the program"; in 1942, "the University gave the School the status of a Faculty"; and in 1943, an Institute of Sociology was founded.[109]

This was a misrepresentation. In its brief lifetime, the so-called Institute hardly did any more sociology than the compilers of telephone directories. The "Faculty" did not offer any instruction at the university level. Right up to the time of the asbestos strike, only night courses were offered, and (except for the course on "Politics and Diplomacy") no more than a grade 12 high school certificate was required for enrolment. The professors had no tenure at the Faculty, and for the most part they had never published anything to indicate their competence in the social sciences. The very titles of the courses reveal a lack of the kind of organization needed to provide a university education. The offerings were made in a desultory fashion, through the devotion of worthy people or the random contributions of visiting firemen. Keynes may have been ignored among the recent economists, but his absence was duly counterbalanced by courses on health services, the protection of infants, colonization, the French minorities, Anglo-Saxon psychology, small industry, and diplomatic technique...

Such an institution, in sum, did nothing to prepare people for the social upheaval in Quebec. At the most, it helped to prolong the hostility to change cultivated by the nationalist school system and by the professors of our social doctrine of the Church. Furthermore, the teaching staff in all these institutions was almost always the same, and interchangeable.

Brother Marie-Victorin may have had these social sciences in mind when he deplored the fact that we had contributed nothing to the scientific capital of humanity and begged us to stop "being too preoccupied with a science which is specifically subordinated to a racial point of view."[110]

To complete our survey, we should mention the work of Father Bouvier. In 1945, this Jesuit created the Department of Industrial Relations in the Faculty of Social Sciences. This department was, however, peripheral to the main organization of the Faculty: a few competent men were added to the mediocre teaching staff, and the instruction was organized so that it might, in time, offer a respectable university training. The same was true of the Department of Social Work. Instruction in this field, which had been organized within a different framework, was already flourishing under the guidance of the Dominican Father Guillemette. He was appointed chairman of the Department of Social Work, which became part of the Faculty of Social Sciences in 1948.

This arrangement had a number of drawbacks. Internal intrigues and power struggles pitted the Faculty against the two departments, and each department against the other, dissipating their energies. Secondly, the avowed purpose of these departments was to train technicians—social workers, heads of personnel, etc.—rather than economists and sociologists who could revise our traditional doctrines in the light of new realities. Furthermore, the Department of Industrial Relations was partly financed by the Association professionnelle des industriels (Professional Association of Industrial Managers),[111] a kind of management union of which Father Bouvier had been the leading light. In these circumstances, one could hardly expect the teaching in the Department to approach the sociology of our industrial upheavals in a spirit of strictly scientific objectivity.

b) In Quebec City

Developments were different at the University of Laval. A School of Social Sciences, attached to the Institute of Philosophy, was founded in 1932. It was "an ordinary evening school offering popular courses to the general public."[112] In September 1938, however, the School began to give day courses leading to bachelor's and master's degrees, and Father Georges-Henri Lévesque was appointed Dean. At the time, this Dominican was one of the rare examples among us of a man who, in his mature years, permits reflection and scientific research to overthrow the idols of his youth. Father Lévesque, now a liberal, organized the teaching on a rational basis, fostered the intellectual development of his professors by giving them the opportunity to study abroad, accepted the fact that science eliminates prejudice, and recognized that the teaching of Catholic social morality cannot dispense with intellectual integrity. In 1943, the School became a Faculty, and in 1948 the course was extended from three to four years. When the asbestos strike broke out, there was thus at least one centre in Quebec where a team of fifteen full-time professors were trying to formulate and teach a system of social thought that would be scientifically valid for the present day. Young people, former students of the School, were already beginning to feel their way towards an effective and committed social activism, as revealed, for example, by their work in the field of adult education.

The political and religious opposition to the Faculty shows how much our society is shocked by iconoclasm. In the face of it, the Dean and his staff displayed an admirable firmness and calm. Unfortunately, the Faculty had been remiss in creating a department of political science to go with the School of Social Work and the Departments of Sociology, Economics, and Industrial Relations. This led, inevitably, to regression: it was precisely in its political theory and practice that the Faculty lacked realism and perhaps enduring grandeur. It did not love our homeland less, as the chauvinists have claimed; rather, it did not pay enough attention to the problem of the *political* destiny of our people. In this field, the Laval school produced only vague and abstract notions and concentrated on attacking monolithic nationalism.

6/The Church and our industrial revolution

The Church is such an important institution in French Canada that it is impossible, in a few pages, to sum up the role that it has played in the development of our thought and the guidance of our actions in the social field. Still, a few facts repeated here will enable the reader to understand that our Church had assumed the impossible task of bringing a stagnant system of thought into alignment with a changing reality. This effort so exhausted our Catholics that they were scarcely able to function as the galvanizing force in social change.

a) Physical presence

Our church institutions were in fact firmly rooted in social realities. The "French Canadian" Church consists of a people that is 97% Catholic and a clergy that is drawn from every rank of society. In Quebec, there is roughly one priest, religious brother, or nun for every forty Catholics, and this figure does not include the many French Canadian clergy working overseas as missionaries.

In our history, the Church has always been a distinctly national institution, inseparable from the basic structure of our society. Of course, the Church ceased to be "established" at the time of the English Conquest; i.e., Catholicism was henceforth not the official religion of the State, but its influence was all the greater. With the disappearance of the French civil authority, the church hierarchy became the unofficial spokesman of the French Canadians. After a painful beginning, this function of the Church was recognized by the British, and later the English Canadian, authorities. The hierarchy knew how to make judicious arrangements with the secular power. The latter, by abandoning its hopes of religious and ethnic assimilation, gained a loyalty which proved invaluable at the time of the American invasions of 1775 and 1812, the rebellions of 1837 and 1838, and the disputes over social participation in the twentieth century.[114]

The French Canadian people, on the other hand, readily accepted the church hierarchy as their legitimate interpreter. Apart from the fact that their faith enjoined obedience, they owed their very survival largely to the clergy; they knew it, and were frequently reminded of it. Moreover, the foreigners dominated us in political, economic, and social life, and frequently scoffed at us as well. There is nothing remarkable about our respect for the clergy. They were the only power structure to which we had free access. People adopt such "self-government" as they can...

True enough, the British institutions slowly taught us to build up an independent political authority which, in certain circumstances, might offend the church authorities. It is no accident that our clergymen were always more or less hostile to democracy, nor that leaders like Papineau, Mercier, Laurier, and even Bourassa were the objects of clerical wrath. Nevertheless, first Mercier, then Laurier were victorious at the polls, in spite of ultramontanist bishops, the condemnation of the Liberal Party by the French Canadian Institute, the Guibord affair, the excommunications, the placing of books on the Index, and the denunciations to Rome. Their triumphs showed conclusively that our people would follow laymen as willingly as bishops, depending on who seemed to offer the best guidance for achieving national well-being. The bishops had the wisdom to understand this. Apart from a few, who made the same mistake about the C.C.F. that they had formerly made about the Liberal Party, the bishops now remained aloof from party politics for the most part, at least where doctrine was concerned.

The priests, on the contrary, became even more ardent about social and educational questions and jealously defended their territories. On the level of primary education, they fought against the establishment of a department of education, then vigorously opposed compulsory schooling. In secondary education, they retained an undisputed monopoly, with the unforeseen result that higher education was all but inaccessible to the mass of people who were not well-to-do. They possessed powers of supervision and control which are only now becoming less absolute because of financial difficulties.

In the field of social education especially, the clergy have adopted a realistic attitude. They finally stopped their outcries against a victorious liberalism and heeded the gentle voice of Leo XIII, who called upon his Church not to lose its footing in the midst of rapid technological change. Twelve years after the encyclical *Rerum Novarum*, there begins that long series of works in which tireless clergymen have tried to spread the social doctrine of the popes among us. As I have shown above, the social aspect of this teaching was set aside in favour of the national aspect; I shall return to this theme later on.

Abbé Lionel Groulx, Abbé Emile Chartier, and Father Hermas Lalande organized Catholic groups for social action in different communities in the Montreal area. In 1903, these social action groups were united as the Association catholique de la jeunesse canadienne-française (Catholic Association of French Canadian Youth, A.C.J.C.). In 1905, Abbé Lortie and J.E. Prince founded the Société d'économie sociale et politique (Society of Social and Political Economy) in Quebec City. This society eventually published the daily newspaper *L'action sociale* (Social Action, now called *L'action catholique*). Founded in 1907 by Abbé Paul Eugène Roy, this paper was not edited by Léon Bloy, as had first been hoped, but by Jules Dorion and Omer Héroux. Bourassa founded *Le Devoir* in 1910; a group of priests and Ottawa civil servants established *Le Droit* in 1913. The groundwork for a daily Catholic press was thus completed. Later on, *L'action catholique* came under the control of the Archbishop of Quebec City, *Le Droit* became the property of the Oblate Fathers of Ottawa, and *Le Devoir* became a subsidiary of the Archdiocese of Montreal.

Meanwhile, the Jesuit Father Hudon founded the Ecole sociale populaire with the help of Arthur Saint-Pierre. Through tracts and monthly publications, the Ecole tirelessly disseminated the Jesuit interpretation of the social doctrine of the popes. We have already discussed these activities in Section 2 above, as well as *l'Ordre nouveau, Relations,* and the Semaines sociales, which were all created by the Society of Jesus.

We have also seen that Father J. Papin Archambault, S.J., had been instrumental in founding the Ligue des droits du français in 1913. It eventually gave birth to *l'Almanach* (The Almanac), then to *l'Action française* (1917), edited by Abbé Groulx.

Let us recall, finally, that Mgr. Gauthier, the administrator of the Montreal diocese, was associated with the establishment of the School of Social, Economic, and Political Sciences at the University of Montreal; and that in Quebec, the school of the same name was founded by a Dominican priest, Father G.H. Lévesque. Priests were everywhere in the fields of social work and education. To complete our account of their activities, we should also mention their work as chaplains, "moderators," or directors of many charitable organizations (adoption societies, societies for the protection of young girls, colonization societies, Boy Scouts, etc.); of professional groups (teachers' associations, farmers' unions, etc.); of different Catholic social action groups (J.A.C., J.E.C., J.O.C., etc.);[115] and of trade unions. Their participation in all these ventures (often as founders, as in the case of the Catholic trade unions) reflects a more or less conscious effort of the Church to adapt its structures and its influence to new social conditions. In the rural parish of former times, the priest could be in fairly direct contact with fifty different families. This was no longer possible in working-class parishes containing ten or fifteen thousand people.

The Church, through two thousand years of experience, had learned how to adapt its administration to new situations. It skilfully applied this knowledge in Quebec: our church institutions made a remarkable effort to adapt themselves physically to the changing realities of the industrial era.

Was it just a conditioned reflex? Heart and mind were certainly not in it, but longed for the golden age, when an obscure rural people was accustomed to hide behind the skirts of its clergy.

b) Intellectual absence

The clergy strove to assure the *physical* presence of the Church in the midst of our social tribulations; this very zeal shows its tragic alienation from reality on the intellectual and moral planes. Our Catholic social thought, a mere attribute of our nationalism, mirrored its lack of realism. They were both equally installed in "the truth"; they both shared the same retrograde "orthodoxy," the same poverty of invention, the same passive acceptance of arguments from authority, and the same fear of adventure. Their artificial mental constructs necessarily embodied clericalism and reaction, sometimes in the religious, sometimes in the political domain. The alliance of Catholicism and nationalism was also manifest in each of the institutions discussed above. The A.C.J.C., its flag resplendent with carillon and Sacred Heart, combined separatism with Catholic social action; *Le Devoir, Le Droit,* and *L'action catholique* formed a national and religious triad; the same people were active in *l'Action française* and the *Semaines sociales,* etc.

Consequently, the analysis of our official thought in the third part of this chapter will suffice here as well. In the overall group of quotations presented in that analysis, clergymen and laymen appeared with equal frequency, and their idealistic speculations were of equal weight. I shall, then, simply note here a few stages in the development of the official social thought of the Church as teacher, i.e., of the bishops.

In 1873, during the massive exodus to the industrial regions of the United States, the Fathers of the Fifth Quebec Provincial Council wrote that for many people "The great attraction of the foreign land is the hope of being able to make money and live more comfortably, with less hardship . . . Ever since an unbridled luxury invaded our countryside, this emigration has assumed alarming proportions . . . Luxury appears all too often in the countryside, in the urgency with which foolish parents demand that their daughters learn music, drawing, embroidery, and other things which will be of absolutely no use to them. Unfortunately, these accomplishments set our dear children at odds with their social class . . . You need not be surprised if we later take measures to overcome this great evil, by protecting our country convents against importunate and dangerous demands . . . One thing is certain in our eyes, and that is that the emigration would no longer be necessary and would cease if parents used the money which they now squander on luxury and intemperance to prepare homes for their children on new lands."[116] In 1880, in a pastoral letter, Cardinal Taschereau called upon Christian parents to devote their children "to colonization, or rather to our native land, to religion, even to God." This cardinal did not, however, have the same high opinion of the vocation of trade unionist: on February 2, 1885, with the support of a Holy Office decree, he condemned membership in the workmen's brotherhoods of the day, the Knights of Labour, as a serious sin, which he identified with the prohibited secret societies. Cardinal Gibbons and the American archbishops did not see the matter in the same light. In 1887, following their protests to Rome, Cardinal Taschereau reluctantly authorized his priests to absolve the Knights of Labour.[117]

In 1891, the bishops of Quebec City circulated the encyclical *Rerum Novarum,* but in the archdiocese of Montreal, though the most industrialized region in the province, there was no official echo of it for twelve years. The episcopal documents dealt several times with agriculture, colonization, and Freemasonry. On one occasion, they mentioned Sunday labour, to allow it in butteries and cheese factories, but the labour question was not tackled until April 1903. At that time, Mgr. Bruchési expressed a great concern for the welfare of the working classes. He demanded fair wages for them, supported the right of free association (while disapproving of the international unions), and advised the workers to choose their parish priests and their archbishop as arbitrators in industrial disputes. It would have been unwise to expect much from such arbitration, for Mgr. Bruchési also wrote, concerning inequalities in the human condition: "It would be chimerical to try to banish this inequality from the earth or to revolt against it . . . Men will not change by one iota from what God has decreed and

Christ has upheld. To the end of time, then, God's creatures will be divided into two great classes, the class of the rich and the class of the poor.'' Later, he adds: ''You cannot reasonably demand that the wages of the laborer be continually increased, while his working hours are reduced at the same time. O son who art subject to the commands of the Gospel, accept with generous heart the fate that Providence has prepared for you. Think of Heaven; then thou shalt receive thy eternal reward.'' Mgr. Bruchési offered the same kind of advice on the consequences of strikes: ''To remedy these evils and prevent them, we again advise the workers to submit patiently to their condition, their eyes turned towards Heaven, their future home, and towards the Saviour, their brother and their model.''[118]

In 1909, the Plenary Council of Canadian Bishops condemned the principle of non-denominationalism in the ''economic societies,'' but in the diocese of Montreal, the labour question seems to have faded into the background once more. We hear that the bishop participated in the Labour Day festivities and took an interest in the problems of fruit trees and agricultural cooperatives (1913), but little else. Then, on March 19, 1920, Mgr. Gauthier issued a circular letter suggesting that money be taken from parish incomes to pay for full-time labour organizers. In 1922, the bishops of Quebec jointly issued a letter in which they asked that Sunday be respected in industry, the railways, etc. Another joint letter, published in 1928, supported the Catholic Union of Farmers.

Then came the Great Depression. Mgr. Gauthier, Coadjutor to the Archbishop of Montreal, overcame his reticence about social issues; on January 4, 1932, he signed a circular letter dealing with the economic crisis, in which he drew attention to the encyclical *Quadragesimo Anno* and attacked the social abuses produced by capitalism.[119] On the other hand, he took issue with the economists who advocated that wages should be maintained at their present level to avoid a further drop in consumption. The archbishop's point of view is interesting, no doubt, but one wonders what was to be gained by using the authority of the archbishop's office to uphold a thesis originally propounded by an economist of the Chase National Bank. This thesis was not only disadvantageous to the wage earners; it has since proved to be false.

In June of the same year, the bishops and archbishops of the church districts of Quebec City, Montreal, and Ottawa published a ''joint pastoral letter and directive'' concerning ''the present economic difficulties.'' The letter condemned the misdeeds of capitalism and communism, and went on to offer a remedy to the situation, proposing that the armies of unemployed should ''practice thrift and save their money." The traditional solution was not omitted: "The most profoundly human solution to the present problems is a return to the land, and the concern of each household to produce what it requires for itself."[120]

In 1933, the bishops and archbishops issued another collective warning against the dangerous propagandas of communism and socialism. During a period of ten years, Mgr. Gauthier continually recommended these warnings as sermon topics to the priests in his diocese, who repeated them incessantly. On February 11, 1934, the Coadjutor to the Archbishop of Montreal issued a "Pastoral letter to the congregations of the diocese on the social doctrine of the Church and the C.C.F.," in the tradition of political meddling which had once tried to destroy the Liberal Party, but had mostly proved harmful to the Church. Mgr. Gauthier again began by declaring his preference for the land, "the basic requisite of our stability," over industry. He then went on to warn the Catholics of Montreal "against the socialist propaganda which threatens them," and which, among other things, called for freedom of speech and assembly for all! He explicitly attacked the C.C.F. for being materialistic, for undermining the principle of private property, and for advocating the class struggle. He then offered another argument which has, it is true, nothing to do with morality, but which clearly reveals the old connection between nationalism and clericalism: the C.C.F. believed in a strong central government.[121] Finally, he quoted the profound remark of Cardinal Villeneuve: "The twentieth century ought to be more devoted to social solidarity, and less individualistic."[122]

On April 14, 1937, Mgr. Gauthier distributed Pius XI's encyclical on communism to his priests. On November 30, 1937, the return to the land was once more advocated in the "Joint pastoral letter on the rural problem in the light of the social doctrine of the Church." The people who lived in the country were once more advised that "the exodus to the cities . . . is a great menace to their Christian spirit and to their morals."[123]

On the other hand, at the 1938 Semaine sociale, held in Sherbrooke, Cardinal Villeneuve criticized the laws of Duplessis (the first Bills 19 and 20) which made closed shop clauses illegal.[124] Mgr. Gauthier, however, on March 15 of the same year, issued a circular letter which to all intents and purposes was an endorsement of the Padlock Law. He added: "Are people not even trying to create the impression that the true danger we must guard against is not communism, but fascism?" The circular letter appears to hold that there is a great difference between Nazism and fascism, and warns French Canadian fascists of the dangers of Nazi influence: "The program of the Christian

National Socialists contains a number of involved doctrines, and a Catholic would do well to examine them closely before he adds his name to the membership roll.''[125]

Then the war broke out against Nazism *and* fascism, Mgr. Charbonneau became archbishop of Montreal, and the French Canadian Fascist leaders were imprisoned by the R.C.M.P. Russia had not yet become our ally. On May 15, 1941, in a joint pastoral letter to celebrate the anniversary of *Rerum Novarum* and *Quadragesimo Anno,* the Cardinal, archbishops, and bishops of Quebec repeated their condemnation of economic liberalism, socialism, and communism, but added this admirable and astonishing sentence: ''Had one the time to go over all the laws passed by our federal and provincial assemblies in the last fifty years, one would be (one has to admit) impressed above all by the influence wielded by high finance and by the concern to protect the interests of private property . . . Capitalism in our country exploits the worker, and our legislation does not protect him enough.''[126] In spite of this, the letter ends with a reversion to our pet solutions: return to the land, corporatism, non-international trade unionism, cooperatives.

This joint pastoral letter is perhaps a turning point in the development of the Quebec Church's official thought. In 1944, Abbé Gérard Dion and a group of priests devoted some Journées sacerdotales d'études sociales (Sacerdotal Social Study Days) to the problems of our industrial environment. The bishops encouraged this initiative, which finally gave birth to the Sacerdotal Commission on Social Studies towards the end of the war. Shortly before the asbestos strike, this commission took up a courageous and far-sighted stand against a projected Labour Code (Bill 5); their attitude did much to nip this reactionary legislation of the provincial government in the bud. The Commission was also responsible for the publication of the joint pastoral letter on the labour problem.[127]

This pastoral letter on the labour problem was not published until February 1950, one year after the asbestos strike. Accordingly, I do not intend to speak of it here, except to note that although some clergymen tried to update their social thought, many others resolutely swam against the current; the Jesuits in particular remained firmly attached to obsolete ideas. Towards the end of 1942, Mgr. Charbonneau had appointed a committee to reconsider the problem of the C.C.F., *in relation to Catholic doctrine.* Due to the intrigues of the priests of the Ecole sociale populaire, however, the committee was allowed to study the problem only *in relation to national survival.* It concluded that the C.C.F. was incompatible with the doctrine of nationalism! This theological sabotage was intended to prepare the way for the Bloc populaire (Popular Coalition), but it could not prevent the Plenary Council of Canadian Archbishops and Bishops, meeting on October 13, 1943, from declaring that Catholic believers were "free to support any political party in Canada that upholds the basic Christian traditions." Unofficially, this statement was supposed to annul the warnings once made by Mgr. Gauthier against the C.C.F. As Omer Héroux put it in *Le Devoir* of October 20: "The bishops have implicitly endorsed the idea that the faithful may act freely with regard to the C.C.F." The Ecole sociale populaire rejected this interpretation, making much of the fact that the bishops had not exonerated the C.C.F. by name. The Jesuits again revealed their peculiar ideas on society at the beginning of 1946, when they managed to enlist a part of the hierarchy for an attack on the Laval Faculty of Social Sciences, the dean of which had dared to support the idea that cooperatives should be non-denominational.[128]

It would thus be dangerous to conclude that the church hierarchy in Quebec had joined the avant-garde of the movement for social change in the years which preceded the asbestos strike. For every bishop like Mgr. Charbonneau who looked for real social advances, in housing for example (letter of January 1948), there were several who remained attached to the "traditional" doctrine. In March 1943, for example, the Quebec Bishops' Assembly called for intensive agricultural production, and in October 1946, the archbishops and bishops of Quebec circulated a joint pastoral letter on colonization, apparently because they were afraid of an increase in unemployment after the war. "When should this colonization movement begin? We are convinced that time is short. Our people have been suffering for so long . . . let us not delay the remedy for their ills any longer." The bishops of the province, then, were still adherents of the "golden age" tradition. Fearing "the fascination of the city," they urged the "descendants of the pioneer apostles . . . to carry on their mission, to increase the mystic body of Christ by establishing new parishes and by baptizing the Canadian earth. . . ."[129]

The opposition to the international unions remained as virulent as ever. At the Granby convention of the Canadian and Catholic Confederation of Labour (C.C.C.L.), held in 1943, Mgr. Douville still regarded the international unions as communist and anti-nationalist; according to Mgr. Parent of Rimouski, communism slithers in their shadow like a serpent.[130]

7/The State, or the ways of expediency
Having dealt with the Church, we must now consider the State and its related institutions.

a) The political parties

Let us begin with the political parties. They are the antechambers of power where, as a rule, the theorists and practical politicians in a democracy meet to find compromise solutions to given social problems. In Quebec, in the half century before the asbestos strike, the major political parties had hardly needed economic or social theories. When political nationalism waxed virulent enough, it alone decided the outcome of elections; when it was dormant, a well-oiled political machinery assured success.[131]

When Laurier was made leader of the Liberal Party in 1887, the French Canadians were convinced that their national aspirations would be treated with more respect by the Liberals than by the Conservatives. It was, in general, true that the Liberals showed more toleration of French Canadian rights than their opponents, and they also claimed to be more respectful of provincial rights. The Conservatives, on the other hand, directly opposed our national passions, especially during the two world wars.

From 1891 to the present, Quebec has thus elected a Liberal majority to the House of Commons. (The reduction of this majority in 1911 was due to the influence of Bourassa, who effected a slight change of direction in our nationalism.) Still, the Liberals had control of Quebec's Legislative Assembly from 1896 to 1936. Their later defeats were inflicted on them by a party which had nominally detached itself from the Conservatives and which was able to present itself as the champion of a Quebec nationalism beleaguered by foreign "trusts" (in 1936) and by the central government (in 1944, 1948, and 1952).

Throughout this period, there was so little reason involved in our political discussions, at election time or in Parliament, that our politicians did not have to bother with the education of the Quebec voter. Elections were decided, now by the emotions of nationalism, now by the blandishments of "white whisky." In our political arenas, the passions dominated the scene, and the most unspeakable of them affected the governing process.

The following paradox resulted: the theorists of nationalism, who so ardently strove for "the honour of doctrine and the palms of apostleship," were mainly responsible for the fact that our political life, by concentrating its energies on nationalism, has never evolved beyond the level of emotional response, and finds itself incapable of dealing with ideas. In our politics, the apostolate wins fewer victories than party loyalties and political machines. "You don't win elections with prayers" was Israël Tarte's habitual comment on politics in the Province of Quebec.

Another indication of the unrealistic outlook of our social thought is the fact that it has never found an outlet in the field of practical politics. On the other hand, our elected parties have never had any coherent system of thought, and in the exercise of power have been unable to make any use of the inapplicable "social doctrines" of theoretical nationalism.

The great crash of 1929, followed by a long period of economic hardship, certainly forced some of our people to shake off their political torpor and helped to revive economic nationalism. For the moment, Quebec abandoned its usual practice of electing hardly anyone but Liberals to the federal parliament. In 1930, of the 65 Members of Parliament to which it was entitled, the province elected 25 Conservatives. The change was particularly noticeable on the provincial level. The "traditional doctrine" was not renovated; it merely added the "abuses" of capitalism to its list of false doctrines. Some new people, however, began to make an inference from these abuses: the State ought to intervene to prevent them. The French Canadian youth organizations were mostly preoccupied with "saving the race," but still found time to attack the electricity trust; Dr. Philippe Hamel demanded that it be nationalized. Paul Gouin and a handful of progressive Liberals founded the Parti d'action libérale nationale (National Liberal Action Party); its platform included social legislation and nationalization. In 1935, this party was able to undermine the Taschereau forces, but in 1936 it joined the Conservative elements led by Maurice Duplessis, who became leader of a new political entity, the National Union Party. His precise mandate was to nationalize the Montreal Light, Heat and Power Co. Once in power, however, the conservative leader did nothing of the sort, and the program of social reforms disappeared, for the most part, in a flood of nationalistic and conservative verbiage.[132]

People were very disappointed at this, but because the French Canadians never use their head when it comes to politics, the same people made the same mistakes a few years later. The Bloc populaire was, in fact, a curious mixture of conservative money and progressive hopes, all under the banner of nationalism. Paul Gouin, René Chaloult, Philippe Hamel, and Jean Martineau advocated the nationalization of public utility companies and other radical measures, while the national leader, Maxime Raymond, and the eventual party organizer, Edouard Lacroix, both adopted a position of extreme right-wing conservatism. As a result, the "provincial platform of the Bloc" was a very strange mixture. The "economic dictatorship" of the trusts was denounced along with "socialism . . . the trust of the State"; "the reestablishment of private enterprise" was advocated as well as "nationalization"; the platform advocated that "big industry be left in the hands of private enterprise," but regulated by "commissions free of political ties." Colonization, cooperatives, "absolute freedom of choice of union, [?]" and all the rest were supposed to bring about "the corporative society." In other words, the whole platform had a Jesuitical flavour.[133]

The Bloc populaire collapsed in confusion; yet another attempt to introduce some elements of ideology into our political discussions had failed. There remained the Communist Party, the C.C.F., and Social Credit. The first two parties were, as always, forbidden by the theologians of nationalism and the politicians of clericalism. The third, however, had enough economic truth in its doctrines to appeal to the uninitiated, and many doctrinaire people were brought together under its banner. The theories of Major Douglas were first discussed in Quebec at the time of the Depression, and their popularity was not surprising, considering that the other economic theories, liberalism and socialism, were condemned out of hand. Social Credit filled an ideological vacuum for those who had many good intentions and little economics. Some clergymen became ardent propagandists for Social Credit, particularly Abbé J.B. Desrosiers and the Dominicans G.H. Lévesque and Thomas Lamarche. Even bishops were impressed. Social Credit was well on its way to becoming an important political and religious movement when Cardinal Villeneuve intervened and stripped the Social Credit rallies of their sacramental character. Since that time, the movement has grown unobtrusively by thoroughly exploiting nationalist sentiments. From time to time it draws upon anti-Semitism and anti-unionism as well (which does not stop it from having an influence on many trade union members; for all too long, they had not been allowed any other form of political self-expression). We are continually alarmed at the way this doctrine is compelled to feed upon the most reactionary passions. Its converts display a zeal and a political consciousness which are absolutely remarkable; it is a pity that they often display a fanaticism and an admiration for the monolithic which are rather unsuited to democracy.

Duplessis, in power since 1944, manipulated nationalism so successfully that social issues simply did not come to the fore. As a result, in the elections of July 28, 1948, the French Canadians still felt obliged to "save the race" from the "Ottawa centralizers" by electing 82 conservatives who claimed to be nationalists but were merely the representatives of high finance and (secondarily) of the professional, middle, and agricultural classes. The "opposition" to this National Union consisted of 8 Liberals and 2 Independents, none of whom had a well-defined attitude towards social problems (except for René Chaloult). Of these 92 members of the Legislative Assembly, eleven were classified as farmers and three as workers.[134] Such, then, was the character of government at the time of the greatest labour crisis our province had ever known.

b) *Social legislation*

As I have explained above, our political parties were able to get themselves elected without espousing our official social doctrines. Accordingly, the State did not have to pay much attention to these doctrines in the concrete exercise of power. It and the political parties had only to pay lip service to this social thought; they were then free to follow the dictates of a perfect expediency. The State in Quebec thus made a better adjustment to the social realities of a rapidly industrializing province than the theorists. Often, of course, there was a time lag in this process of adaptation: when the legislators found themselves intellectually incapable of grappling with a problem, their own interests and those of their financial supporters led them to adopt highly conservative solutions to the social and economic problems arising from industrialization. As a result, the State frequently did nothing to eliminate injustices in the legal system until they became a matter of public scandal. The provincial government also passed many questionable laws, which reflected haste or compulsion and were obsolete from the day they were enacted. In spite of everything, though, our legal system was not as far removed from reality as our ideological labours might suggest. In spite of our "providential mission" and our unhealthy dislike of other people's laws, the Quebec legislator eventually became something of a plagiarizer of statutes that had been more skillfully and swiftly enacted elsewhere. Henri Mazeaud rightly said that social and economic pressure causes different systems of law to develop in the same direction.[135] A glance at some aspects of our social legislation will make this clear.

Private charities had traditionally provided almost the complete spectrum of social welfare in the Province of Quebec, but the upheavals caused by the industrial revolution made this system plainly inadequate. After the First World War, the provincial government consequently offered to give financial assistance to private institutions and municipalities providing social services. Our leaders, adherents of clericalism and nationalism, were strongly opposed to such a policy, which they regarded as socialist. Needs were so great, however, that the bishops finally had to advise the charitable institutions to make use of the public assistance made available through the enactment of our first Public Charities Act in 1921.[136]

This was the beginning of our social legislation. In 1924, we passed an Adoption Act which was such a servile imitation of the Ontario act

that it eventually had to be changed. In 1936, Quebec was the last of
the provinces to agree to participate in the federal old age pension
scheme, established in 1927. Our province was also one of the last to
pass (in 1938) a needy mothers' assistance act. At this time, Quebec
spent only three quarters as much per capita on social welfare as the
other provinces of Canada on the average.[137]

c) Labour legislation

Our labour legislation, properly speaking, reveals the same tendency
to imitate the work of others.[138] Faced with similar social upheavals,
the Quebec government usually reacted in the same way as the other
provinces. We do not mean that legislation was everywhere uniform;
in Quebec in particular, legislation differed from that of the other
provinces in its framing, in the administrative and judicial procedures
it established, and in the scales set for hours of labour, wages, etc.
Moreover, some of the laws of the other provinces had no equivalent
in Quebec. For example, British Columbia had laws protecting the
working woman who became pregnant dating from 1921. Other provinces had enacted that men and women should receive the same pay
for the same work. Several provinces made union payroll deductions
compulsory, where previously they had been voluntary and could be
cancelled. Such laws did not exist in Quebec. On the other hand, some
of our labour laws are unique in Canada, for example, our law on
communist propaganda (the Padlock Law). In most cases, however,
both the spirit and the letter of labour laws were the same from province to province, even in Quebec, which had a social doctrine with
great claims to originality.

Quebec occasionally led the other provinces in social legislation,
for example, in our Workmen's Compensation Act (1909), inspired by
French law. The next year, Quebec enacted the first Canadian Employment Bureaus Act, modelled on an English labour exchange law
of 1909. In 1924, Quebec's Professional Syndicates Act, based on
French statutes of 1884 and 1920, was the first in Canada to recognize
unions and trade associations as legal entities. In 1934, our province
was the first to follow the lead of several European and Commonwealth countries in legislating the Collective Labour Agreements Extension Act. In 1939, Quebec enacted a Public Charities Act, the first
in our province to deprive a group of wage earners absolutely of the
right to strike. It seems, then, that our particularist spirit had some
effect on our eclecticism. The law passed in 1934, for example, was
particularly pleasing to us because it hinted at corporatism. On other
occasions, our social doctrine betrayed its influence in matters of
detail, revealing an extraordinary meanness of spirit. In 1938, for

example, the Quebec Unemployment Insurance Commission decided to refuse assistance to unmarried mothers and to persons living common law; in 1939, the law on needy mothers was similarly altered. In the great majority of cases, however, the Quebec legislator differed from those of the other provinces only in his slowness and stinginess.

In 1872, the federal government passed a law permitting the existence of labour unions. The Quebec courts did not allow the enforcement of this law until 1898, when they were compelled to do so by a decision of the federal Supreme Court.

In 1884, Ontario established a minimum age for employment on the basis of an English law, and Quebec copied the Ontario enactment the following year. In 1888 Nova Scotia, in 1894 Ontario and British Columbia, and in 1900 the federal government passed laws on the voluntary conciliation of industrial disputes. Quebec followed suit in 1901. In 1900, Ottawa decided to pay a fair wage to people employed on federal public works; the analogous Quebec law was passed only in 1915. In 1900, Ontario encouraged the development of a paper industry by a law forbidding the export of wood pulp; Quebec only followed suit in 1910. In 1906, the federal government passed a Lord's Day Act; the equivalent Quebec law dates from the following year. The federal Industrial Disputes Investigation Act (the Lemieux Law), enacted in 1907, forbade strikes in a certain number of industries affecting the public interest, until a public inquiry had been made. The law was valid for all of Canada until the Privy Council ruled against it in 1925. From 1926 to 1932, all the provinces except Prince Edward Island extended the federal law to their own jurisdiction; Quebec was the last to accept it, in 1932. Ottawa's Department of Labour was created in 1909, those of British Columbia and Ontario in 1917 and 1919 respectively. Quebec only acquired its own Department of Labour in 1931. Manitoba and British Columbia passed minimum wage laws for women in 1918, as did Quebec in 1919. In 1919, the federal government allocated funds to encourage the provinces to develop technical training and apprenticeship programs. From 1928 on, the provinces enacted apprenticeship laws; Quebec was the last to do so, in 1945. British Columbia began to limit hours of work in 1923; Quebec was the second province to do so, but only ten years later. In 1937 and 1938, four provinces made conciliation compulsory in the settlement of industrial disputes; the equivalent Quebec law dates from 1944. Ontario made paid vacations compulsory in 1944; Quebec was the fourth province to pass a similar law, in 1946.

The above paragraphs, though very incomplete, are enough to show that the pace and direction of the State's development in Quebec were very different from those envisaged by our theory-loving institutions.

The State, after all, cannot govern without considering the real relations of forces in the country. As we indicated in the second part of this chapter, the forces of industrialization dominated the Quebec scene in the fifty-year period before the asbestos strike. The ideological forces have done little but divert or slow down these developments.

It would thus be logical, before drawing our conclusions from the study in this chapter, to examine the two main institutions in which the forces of industry have found their most eloquent expression, namely capitalism and trade unionism. Once more, alas, the limits imposed on this chapter do not permit me to study the matter in depth. I shall limit myself to a few notes and statistics, to give the reader some idea of the particular forms assumed by these institutions in Quebec. The two following chapters excuse me from doing more, as they contain special studies of capitalism and trade unionism. Here, we are looking at these institutions from a particular point of view, but we can still recognize the characteristics of capital and labour as they revealed themselves everywhere in the province.

8/The contradiction between capital and nationalism
a) Concentrations of joint-stock capital

As elsewhere, capitalism in Quebec has developed through concentration: wherever technology permitted, small firms have been replaced by larger ones. For Canada as a whole, from 1870 to 1930, the average capitalization of manufacturing concerns increased from $1,900 to $217,000,[139] while the number of firms dropped from 75,964 (in 1890) to 22,532 (in 1920), and 22,618 (in 1930). From 1900 to 1933, there were 374 mergers of companies competing in the same field (not including the public utility companies and the private or semi-private companies); 1,145 formerly distinct companies were thus swallowed up.[140]

In the Province of Quebec alone, of the 23,000 manufacturing firms existing in 1890, there were only 7,530 left in 1920, and 6,948 in 1929.[141] It is true that the number has since increased, to 8,373 in 1939, and 11,670 in 1950, but here again the concentration of capital has had its effects. While the number of firms increased by 39% between 1939 and 1950, the number of people employed went up by 77%, and the value of goods produced (in constant dollars) by 93%.[142] The average capitalization per firm increased from $94,600 (in 1917) to $179,300 (in 1929), $141,200 (in 1939), and $201,600 (in 1942).

These developments had a very serious effect on the French Canadians, because of their attachment to small business and because they belonged to a culture that was restricted to a relatively small geographical area. Gradually, businesses owned by families or syndicates gave way to joint-stock companies, which were less national in that the great suppliers of capital did not belong to our ethnic group.[143] The administrative structures of these new giant corporations have given rise to the phenomenon which sociologist E.C. Hughes calls "the circulation of technicians"; this phenomenon forces our people to choose between stagnation and being uprooted from their communities. Hughes adds: "Quebec is fated to experience its colossal industrial expansion at a time when capitalism has reached full maturity. It is no longer the bold and adventurous work of small groups of entrepreneurs, but a mass assault by impersonal institutions, from which there is no escape."[144]

Clearly, then, the capitalist institutions in our province have developed in full contradiction to most of our nationalist assumptions (small business, cultural isolation, etc.). Now, our social thinkers excused themselves for their slowness in accepting trade unionism, and justified the meagreness of their reforms, by claiming that we were "one big family . . . without . . . class rivalries," and that social welfare in the Province of Quebec . . . [should be organized by] private initiatives." These statements compel us to note that capitalism was no more free of abuses in the Province of Quebec than elsewhere. The trade union movement was just as badly needed to correct these faults here as elsewhere, regardless of the statements of our official theorists.

b) The opposition between labour and capital

In 1889, the Royal Commission on the Relation of Labour and Capital in Canada found that women in Quebec were working more than twelve hours per day in manufacturing; children ten years of age were working from a quarter to seven in the morning to a quarter to six in the evening, with an hour and ten minutes off for lunch, and received one dollar and a quarter per week. The commissioners remarked: "Nothing could be more striking than the contrast furnished between organized districts and others where as yet the principles of a trade organization are little known . . . The claim that workingmen do not receive full value for their labor, that they are too frequently unable to make ends meet, and that capital often takes advantage of their necessities to regulate the price of labor, appears to be well founded, when judged by the evidence given before the Commission. This state of affairs is, however, more apparent in the places that are not organized. . . ."[145]

In 1934, another royal commission (on price spreads) supplied information on working conditions in Canada. The following examples show what was found in the Province of Quebec.[146] A man with ten years' experience in the garment industry in Montreal worked 70 hours per week for ten cents an hour.[147] In the country, there were people working 54 hours a week for five and a half cents an hour. In the shoe industry, boys aged 14 to 20 earned from 2½ cents to 6 cents an hour. Male workers tended to be used in the place of females, as the latter were protected by a legal minimum wage. This protection was, however, often no more than theoretical, for girls were discovered working 75 hours a week for the sum of $1.50. When the employer was found out, he was obliged to pay a fine of $10.00.

The same commission made inquiries into a large number of industries and found that conditions were deplorable even where production and profits had increased in spite of the Depression. This was the case, for example, in the silk industries. At Montmagny, the average hourly wage for men was ten cents an hour. At Louiseville, there was an American company which had continually increased its profits since 1929; it paid its female workers $9.73 for a working week of 55 hours. In the chain stores, the work week was often more than 60 hours, and in several cases was 80 to 84 hours. The commissioners also mentioned the case of a company which declared a dividend on its shares of 80%, but paid 90% of its employees less than $10 per week. In another case, a company reduced the wages of its Canadian employees by 10% and made a net profit of $1,800,000 for its New York owners.

Among its other conclusions, the commission recognized the need for a trade union movement and for better labour legislation. In particular, it recommended that those Quebec and Ontario laws be changed which, in some circumstances, permitted employers to keep women at work for 72 hours per week.[148]

A few years later, things were not exactly rosy in the industrial world. A series of serious strikes led to a royal commission on the textile industry. The commissioners deplored the fact that "this industry, in Canada, has always refused to negotiate with the labour unions," and quoted the testimony of Quebec employers who were categorically opposed to the negotiation of collective agreements. In this case as well, the commissioners concluded that capitalism would finally have to recognize the trade union movement.[149]

9/The trade union movement, and the search for realistic ideas
a) The social climate
Labour organizations in Quebec have had a rather complex history. The social climate of the province was no more hostile to them than

elsewhere in the early days; indeed, the first labour union in Canada, a printers' union, was founded in Quebec City in 1827.[150] Later, unions were established in Quebec in the shoe industry, in shipbuilding, and among stevedores and other workers.

The Order of the Knights of Labour, founded in Philadelphia in 1869, spread rapidly to Canada. Although the Order was condemned in Quebec (but later exonerated), the Knights had a great influence on the Quebec labour movement. Their organization claimed to be more than a simple device for making economic demands: it aimed at reforming the structures of society, undertaking political action, and laying the groundwork for a pan-Canadian trade unionism. This speculative side of the Knights helps to explain their popularity among French Canadians, and the taste for ideology which was long cultivated by Quebec unionists. Newspapers, intellectuals, and even priests were eventually won over to this brand of trade unionism. After the Knights were expelled from the Trades and Labour Congress in 1902, they remained active in Quebec up to 1910, long after the Order's demise in the United States.

The turn of the century marked a new stage in the history of trade unionism in Quebec. At the time of the strike and lockout in the shoe industry in Quebec City in 1900, Mgr. Bégin was called in as an arbitrator. Because of his decision, the unions heeded the encyclical *Rerum Novarum* by accepting chaplains, though the non-Catholic members were not given inferior status. Mgr. Bégin's intervention created a precedent which was often followed. In 1906, for example, Mgr. Bruchési, the Archbishop of Montreal, acted as arbitrator in a leather workers' strike in that city. Later on, Cardinal Villeneuve and Mgr. Gauthier of Montreal intervened in the textile industry disputes of 1937. The later chapters in this book reveal that this tradition was still very much alive at the time of the asbestos strike.

From the beginning, the union leaders had mixed feelings about these interventions by the bishops. Their own influence was thereby diminished, and they were also afraid that the trade unions would grow accustomed to paternalistic solutions, imposed from the outside. This is one of the reasons why the non-denominational unions made such an effort to obtain legislation allowing capital and labour to solve their problems on the sole basis of law.

Some Catholics, on the other hand, felt that Mgr. Bégin had not gone far enough by offering trade unionism a Christian doctrine, and in a way baptizing it: they thought that the Church should take it over. In this spirit, Abbé E. Lapointe promoted the idea of the Fédération ouvrière de Chicoutimi (Chicoutimi Labour Federation). The Federation had its first meeting in 1907, and was the first denominational union properly speaking. In 1921 this federation, which drew most of its membership from pulp and paper workers, was incorporated under the name Fédération mutuelle du Nord (Mututal Federation of the North),[151] a strictly national and Catholic organization to which Protestants were not admitted even as honorary members. One branch of the trade union movement thus embraced the nationalism of our official social thinkers, along with all its assumptions. These tendencies (in a somewhat less severe form) later found expression in the establishment and growth of the Canadian and Catholic Confederations of Labour. In 1918, Father Joseph Papin Archambault and Alfred Charpentier called a meeting at the Villa St. Martin. "Each delegate was requested to ask the bishop of his diocese to appoint a priest to take charge of the Catholic labour movement. On June 2 of the same year, the foundations were laid for a national and Catholic trade unionism featuring constitutions approved by a diocesan authority; the presence, in labour organizations, of a chaplain; full membership restricted to Catholics, with admission of non-Catholics as associate members; the organization of study circles, etc."[152] This kind of activity intensified over a period of several years. Finally, the C.C.C.L. (Canadian and Catholic Confederation of Labour) was founded at Hull in 1921. Led by militants imbued with the mystique of trade unionism like G. Picard and Jean Marchand, the C.C.C.L. eventually adopted policies in which ideas foreign to trade unionism proper became less and less important. By the time of the asbestos strike, the Catholic unions had shed most of the attitudes and tactics of clerical nationalism. At the Granby convention of 1943, the C.C.C.L. deprived the chaplain of the right to veto any resolution "which, *in his opinion,* would call in question Catholic morality, the teachings of the Church, or its directives." Non-Catholics were already being admitted to the C.C.C.L. as associate members, but they were not permitted to hold office. This vestige of religious discrimination finally disappeared as well, so that one authority could say that the C.C.C.L. had "lost its denominational character, becoming purely and simply a socioeconomic organization which is Catholic in inspiration."[153]

The point of all this is: there were bitter struggles among Catholics divided into denominational and non-denominational unions, denunciations by jingoists, condemnations by the clergy, anti-clerical and anti-nationalist counterblasts. In spite of them, the Quebec labour movement forged ahead with implacable determination, impelled by internal forces and a logic which ignored whatever was not dictated by its own nature. Our peculiar ideologies certainly had the capacity to slow the progress of the movement, dam up its forces, and disparage its logic, especially in the early stages. Ultimately, though, it seems

that the fortunes of the trade union movement, in Quebec as elsewhere, were largely determined by the degree of industrialization, the
attitude of capitalism, and the political climate.

b) Union membership
It is unfortunate that the statistics on trade unions in the Province of
Quebec are inaccurate and sometimes contradictory, especially for the
first decades of the twentieth century, because many labour organiza-
tions failed to make the report requested by government statisticians.
Still, it is possible to make some rough estimates.

The trade union movement grew rapidly in Canada in the first two
decades of this century. In particular, from 1911 to 1919, the number
of trade union members almost tripled, from 133,132 to 378,000. The
economic slump after the First World War caused a sudden drop in
membership. There was a gradual recovery up to 1930, when there
were 322,000 union members. There was another fall in membership
with the coming of the Depression, and membership fluctuated until
1936, when things began to improve again. In 1937, there were
383,000 union members, a figure which for the first time surpassed the
high point attained in 1919. A temporary drop in 1938-1939 was
followed by a great increase during and after the war. Between 1939
and 1945, the number of Canadian trade unionists doubled from
359,000 to 711,000; between 1939 and 1949, it tripled, reaching
1,006,000 in the year of the asbestos strike.

In Quebec, the fortunes of the trade union movement followed more
or less the same course, although the amplitude of the fluctuations was
sometimes different. The number of trade union members quadrupled
from 1911 to 1919. It reached a peak at the end of the war, fell, then
steadily recovered (except for 1926) until 1930. There was another fall
in membership during the Depression, but a recovery (with a dip in
1935) from 1934 on. Quebec union membership revealed the same
downward turn in 1939, and a rapid increase since (except for
1944-45), though somewhat less rapid than in the rest of the country.
In 1939, 1945, and 1949, the stated membership of the Quebec labour
unions was 105,000, 171,000, and 236,000 respectively.

Between the two world wars, trade unionism in Quebec developed
more rapidly than in the rest of Canada on the average, so that in 1939
the province had almost one third of all trade union members in
Canada. During the war, however, Quebec lost its relative advantage,
so that in 1949 our province had 29% of all Canadian wage earners
employed in non-agricultural industries, but only 26% of all Canadian
trade union members.

In the year of the asbestos strike, Quebec wage earners were 24%

unionized, slightly more so than in Ontario (23%); in the rest of Canada, the figure was 29%. In British Columbia, 37% of the labour force was unionized, which contributed greatly to the higher figure for Canada exclusive of Quebec and Ontario.

Comparisons of the numbers of union locals are interesting as well. From 1900 to 1930, the Quebec locals were barely 33% as numerous as in Ontario, but in 1936 the percentage had climbed to 52%; in 1943, to 56%; and in 1949, to 59%. In 1951, the wage earners of metropolitan Montreal were 23% unionized, and those of Toronto were 22% unionized.

The labour movement in our province seems, then, to have developed independently of our official social thought. The effect of this thought on the movement, if any, was probably to slow its growth. A favorite with clergymen, nationalists, and even employers on occasion, the C.C.C.L. grew more slowly than the other labour movements. In three years, the Catholic unions lost almost half of the 45,000 members they had had in 1921, and continued to stagnate until 1934. From 1934 to 1949, the C.C.C.L. gradually increased its membership (except for a few fluctuations, especially at the beginning of the war), but much more slowly than the other labour movements both in Quebec and in the rest of Canada. In 1934, the Catholic labour unions had 30,346 members; in 1939, 49,401; in 1945, 61,723; and in the year of the asbestos strike, 83,272 members, or 35% of all Quebec trade unionists.

c) *The ideas*

In conclusion, we should stress one point: though official thought in our province did not support the development of trade unionism, the movement was not wholly subject to the dictates of expediency. To win a place in our society, and upset its legal framework, the labour movement had to do more than just fight. It had to develop a doctrine that suited its nature; reeducate a population that was suspicious and often hostile; win over the electorate; and force the hand of the legislators. Its adversaries could count on the natural social conservatism of the French Canadians, the power of money, and the organs of public opinion to influence the legislators in their favour; the trade union movement could only appeal to reason and the sense of justice (supported by the power of numbers). As elsewhere, this militant union thinking was essentially the child of necessity, and had little opportunity to lose touch with the social realities of our industrial world. The "list of demands" of any labour union one cares to name has done more to influence the destinies of our changing society than all the libraries filled by our official social thinkers.

All the labour unions participated in this work of social education. Most of the legislative reforms discussed above were obtained through the influence of Canada-wide or international unions: recognition of the right of association, amendments to the Criminal Code regarding labour "understandings" and picketing, minimum wage laws, hours of labour laws, regulations assuring at least one day off a week, shop inspection, safety standards in working conditions, and various reforms in social security, such as workmen's compensation, old age pensions, etc.[154]

The C.C.C.L. had a more complex value system than the other labour movements, but it too was responsible for several legislative reforms, especially on the provincial level. The C.C.C.L.'s borrowings from our official social doctrine often remained a dead letter, such as its infatuation with corporatism and the return to the land[155] and its opposition to compulsory schooling and to immigration.[156] On the other hand, the C.C.C.L. could arrive at autonomous and fruitful policies where the interests of the workers were more directly affected. In 1938, it advocated a federal system of unemployment insurance in opposition to our entire official thought. In 1924, it obtained the enactment of the Professional Associations Act, which it had demanded the year before. The C.C.C.L. supported the extension of collective agreements in 1930; the measure became law four years later. In 1940, it obtained the establishment of a Superior Labour Council, which it had requested since 1923.

In some cases, the denominational and non-denominational organizations worked together to exert a greater influence on legislators and on public opinion. Around 1923, for example, the C.C.C.L. joined a labour coalition which had been created a few years earlier to improve the Workmen's Compensation Act. The coalition lasted for a number of years. On March 2, 1938, the Quebec Provincial Federation of Labour (T.L.C.) and the C.C.C.L. formed a temporary coalition in an effort to block the passage of Bills 19 and 20 which, in particular, made certain forms of union security illegal. Nine years later, on March 28, 1947, the same two organizations joined the unions of the Canadian Congress of Labour in a new coalition to prevent the Duplessis government from enacting its first "provincial Labour Code."[157] This coalition, known as the Conférence conjointe du travail syndiqué de la Province de Québec (Joint Conference of Organized Labour of the Province of Quebec), remained active; on the eve of the asbestos strike, it was fighting against the passage of Bill 5, an extraordinarily inept and reactionary provincial labour code.[158] The following chapters (especially Boisvert's) show that the Joint Conference played a fairly important part in the events of the asbestos strike itself.

V/Conclusions

Let us not belabour the obvious.

Having worked our way through the clumps of data in this chapter, are we not forcibly struck by one fact: in the first half of the twentieth century, Quebec enjoyed material progress, though we fought it body and soul?

Twenty years ago, Victor Barbeau passed this judgment on our intelligentsia: "There is an opinion called enlightened (God knows how often by a pale and flickering lamp), which through lack of awareness or cowardice first tries, as a rule, to deny what it lacked the intelligence to predict, what interferes with its habits, or simply what compels it to make an effort of thought. Enlightened opinion is the child of wayward circumstance, the fruit of mismatched, varied, and ill-digested learning. It pulls up short before anything new, unexpected, or seemingly exceptional. How it hates to be jostled, surprised, or turned aside from the path of mediocrity where all is familiar, down to the last blade of grass... Many of the professional cretins exercise their congenital defect on the mob, to earn their living. Apart from them, no one still doubts that we are in a state of advanced decadence. We are experiencing the end of a world."[159]

Father Ernest Gagnon, S.J., in discussing "the psychological development of French Canada," had this to say in 1951: "We have a secret love of morbid submissiveness... We like a standardized system of thought, ideas off the peg. From one end of the country to the other, even among our intellectuals, it's the same: break through the shell of empty phrases and you find the ideal that everyone should think and say the same thing, expressing themselves as far as possible in the same way. This passivity ignores the problems. It does not confront obstacles: it goes around them or tries to shunt them aside. We're eclectic, we have nothing we can call our own: not our ideas, our decisions, our enthusiasms, not even our faith... In some ways we make fine seconds, dull and obsequious fellows that we are... This inner obsequiousness is hostility turned inward against the self, the hostility of the weak. Nourished by fear, this hostility sometimes lends us the air of eternal protesters. To accomplish, to create, to *do* something in spite of difficulties: that is a noble attitude. We prefer to complain about others, especially if they are far away or anonymous."[160]

Morbid submissiveness, passivity that ignores the problems, eclecticism, the denial of whatever interferes with one's habits... This is what we ought to have written about, and especially proved, as an introduction to the special studies in this book. The asbestos strike assumed the proportions of a social upheaval, and its causes and effects are worthy of analysis, only because it occurred in a society which was inept at preventing it, impotent in controlling it, and unaware of its deep significance.

We could no longer find relevance in our ideologies, which featured a ready-made suspicion of industrialization, withdrawal into the self, and peasant nostalgia. Bullied by the forces of modern capitalism and beset by foreign influences, we were displaced persons in a modern Capernaum where the family, the neighbourhood, and the parish—our traditional safeguards against the collapse of the personality—no longer offered the same help. In industrial society as developed by capitalism, we needed other remedies for ignorance, insecurity, slums, unemployment, disease, accidents, and old age than the parish school, good neighbours, individual charity, and private enterprise. Our social thought had contrived very inadequate solutions to these problems: accordingly, it had taken root, at most, only in the paper programs of artificial, otiose, and debilitating organizations. Our vital institutions were compelled, by their very nature, to cling pragmatically to reality; they had either to renounce all ideology or sacrifice their dynamism.

How have we managed to survive such torments? Precisely by thumbing our noses at every ideology. Paradoxically, our ethnic group, though entrusted with a providential mission and the honour of doctrine, owes much of its survival to its "materialism." Peoples are not doctrinaire, thank God. Their life is lived on the level of immediate experience. The imperious necessity of earning their living, of meeting their present needs, obliges them to rediscover practical possibilities by the constant application of the empirical method. A people, it is true, may revolt, storm the barricades, endure a siege (psychological as well as military); in a word, it may rise momentarily to the heights of heroism, but heroism, by definition, is not the permanent condition of most individuals. Sure instincts guide peoples to diminish the contradictions between their systems of thought and their plans of action, and to eliminate, on a pragmatic basis, those values which demand heroic opposition and a continual lack of adjustment to normal everyday life.

In the social field, this explains why the nationalism of our social thought, and its assumptions about society, were never accepted by our people in the half century preceding the asbestos strike. There was little return to the land and not much development of cooperatives. Small business became increasingly anemic, corporatism remained in limbo, and Catholic trade unionism did not eliminate other kinds. As we saw at the beginning of this chapter, the province went through a period of intensive industrialization, which bore a near-perfect resemblance to the industrialization of less messianic countries than our own.

I have already shown that the number and the standard of living of industrial workers rose considerably in the half century. Here, I shall simply add a few more facts concerning the second quarter century. Between 1926 and 1949, the hourly wage index of workers doubled, while the cost of living went up only by one third. In the same period, Canada's Net National Income (in variable dollars) increased 315%, the income of workers (the "labour" factor in production) 329%, and income from investment (the "capital" factor in production) 356%. The workers' share in this national income was naturally the largest: in 1926 they received 56% of the national income, in 1949, 59%.

The Net National Income, however, includes the incomes of companies, societies, etc. Let us, then, compare the income of wage-earning and salaried workers with the total of *personal incomes*. In 1926, the workers received 58% of personal income in Canada. In 1949, this percentage was 61%. In Quebec, these percentages went from 62 to 66, and in Ontario, from 61 to 66.

I am not saying that these percentages correspond to the respective "economic values" of workers and other recipients of income, given their number and their industriousness. Under the present economic regime, the remuneration of the worker is probably less than the surplus value of his productivity retained by his employers, and his contribution to society. This point need not be discussed here. Even if we suppose that the above distribution of incomes is fair, it is clear that in Quebec in 1949, the wage-earning and salaried workers accounted for close to two thirds of our economic production. Now the present chapter has shown that *for all practical purposes* they counted for almost nothing in our social thought, our Church, our institutions devoted to teaching and propaganda, our national societies, our political parties, our deliberative assemblies, or the legislative and executive branches of government.

In 1949, the memorable asbestos strike occurred because the industrial workers of Quebec were suffocating in a society burdened with inadequate ideologies and oppressive institutions; because the national importance of the working class was out of all proportion to its low prestige; because its economic gains as a class were accompanied by a loss of social status (the peasants became proletarians only through sacrificing their social standing as parishioners, voters, patriots, etc.); because our moral and political philosophy of labour did not take enough notice of the fact that we had become an industrialized people.

There had been, of course, other major strikes in French Canada before the asbestos strike, and there were to be others after it. The

asbestos strike, however, was significant because it occurred at a time
when we were witnessing the passing of a world, precisely at a moment when our social framework—the worm-eaten remnants of a
bygone age—were ready to come apart.

It is the date, rather than the place or the particular industry, that is
decisive. The strike might well have happened elsewhere, for at this
time the Quebec proletariat had been led, by the logic of its own
development, to win a place for itself in the community corresponding
to its numbers and its social utility.

As it happened, it was the asbestos that caught fire! This book is
dedicated to the history of that conflagration.

Bibliography for Chapter I

BEAULIEU, Marie-Louis. "Législation du travail: la Loi de la convention collective," *La Revue du Barreau de la province de Québec (The Review of the Quebec Bar)*, Vol. 14, 1954, pp. 385-396; "Législation du travail: la Loi des relations ouvrières et la Loi des différends entre les services publics et leurs salariés," *Ibid.*, Vol. 14, 1954, pp. 425-432.

Canadian Labour Force Estimates, 1931-1950. Ottawa: Bureau of Statistics, Labour and Prices Division, 1951.

FIRESTONE, O. J. *Private and Public Investment in Canada, 1926-1927*. Ottawa: Department of Trade and Commerce, 1951.

GOUIN, L.M. *Des syndicats ouvriers au point de vue légal*. Montreal: Beauchemin, 1921.

GRAUER, A. E. *Labour Legislation*. A study prepared for the Royal Commission on Dominion-Provincial Relations. Ottawa: The King's Printer, 1939.

GUILBAULT, Jacques. "Les lois québecoises de conciliation et d'arbitrage," a series of four articles, *La Revue du Barreau de la province de Québec*, Vol. 11, 1951, pp. 221-245; 277-297; 329-353; 384-403.

Health, Welfare and Labour (a reference book prepared for the Dominion-Provincial Conference on Reconstruction). Ottawa: The King's Printer, 1945.

Highlights of Industrial Development in the Province of Quebec. Ottawa: Department of Trade and Commerce, 1951.

The Labour Force, November 1945-January 1955. Ottawa: Bureau of Statistics, Special Surveys Division, 1955.

Ninth Census of Canada, 1951. Ottawa: Bureau of Statistics, 1953-1955.

Progress and Impact of Canadian Industrial Development, by Provinces, 1939-1952. Ottawa: Department of Trade and Commerce, 1952.

SPECTOR, J. J. *Essays on Labour Law in the Province of Quebec.* Montreal: 1952.

Notes to Chapter I

[1]*Canada Year Book, 1954* (Ottawa: Bureau of Statistics), p. 360. The revised figures of the *Survey of Production, 1948-1952* (Ottawa: Bureau of Statistics, 1954), Table 2, are 53% for manufactured goods and 14% for construction.

[2]The figures are for the wages of employees paid by the hour.

[3]The index approximately doubled from 1914 to 1950. See *Labour Gazette* (Ottawa: Department of Labour), September 1950, p. 1364. From 1900 to 1914, the increase cannot have been very great.

[4]For estimates of productivity, see O.J. Firestone, "Comments" to Chapter 1 of *Essais sur le Québec contemporain (Essays on Contemporary Quebec)*, ed. J.C. Falardeau (Quebec City: Les presses universitaires Laval, 1953), pp. 38-44; and the *Labour Gazette* (Ottawa: Department of Labour), September 1950, p. 5.

[5]*Report of the Royal Commission on Dominion-Provincial Relations* (Ottawa: The King's Printer, 1940), Vol. 1, Table 16.

[6]*National Accounts, Income and Expenditure, 1926-1950* (Ottawa: Bureau of Statistics), Table 28; and *National Accounts, Income and Expenditure, 1949-1952* (Ottawa: Bureau of Statistics), Table 28.

[7]An excellent account of these matters is offered by Albert Faucher and Maurice Lamontagne, "History and Industrial Development," Chapter 1 of *Essais sur le Québec contemporain (Essays on Contemporary Quebec)*, ed. J.C. Falardeau (Quebec City: Les presses universitaires Laval, 1953), pp. 23-37.

[8]See the *Labour Gazette* (Ottawa: Department of Labour) Vol. 50, September 1950, p. 1363. Several other statistics were also obtained from this source.

[9]Later on in this chapter I make so many remarks about the sterility of the spirit of recrimination that the reader will hardly be tempted to suspect me of economic nationalism. I compare the economy of Quebec with that of the other provinces only to show the reader our actual situation in a true light. Wage parity for the Quebec worker could be achieved only by immediately consenting to integrate Quebec into the national or even the continental economy, something our "traditional leaders" have always refused to do. In an age of joint stock companies and mass production, one cannot ask both for an industrial structure of one's own and for wage scales comparable to those in the industrial world as a whole.

[10]In this paragraph, the percentages for the beginning of the century are supplied by Lamontagne and Faucher, *op. cit.* (note 7), p. 28. Those for 1950 are taken from the *Canada Year Book, 1954* (Ottawa: Bureau of Statistics), p. 364. Their comparison yields only an approximate idea, because the early figures likely contain some duplications.

[11]This is an approximate figure. In the census of 1901, manufacturing and construction were lumped together, giving a percentage of 23. The *Quebec Yearbook, 1950* (Quebec: Bureau of Statistics), p. 52, informs us that in 1911 and 1921 construction accounted for 6% or 7%. It is unlikely that construction was any more important in 1901.

[12]Marcel Rioux, "Remarques sur l'éducation secondaire et la culture canadienne-française," *Cité libre,* no. 8 (November 1953), p. 35.

[13]Robert Rumilly, *Histoire de la province de Québec* (Montreal: Editions Valiquette), Vol. 8, p. 63.

[14]The techniques of making thought "mesh in unison" were, as we know, perfected under an authoritarian regime not so long ago. (*Translator's note:* Correctly, *Gleichschaltung,* "coordination, streamlining," the term used in Nazi Germany to denote the imposition of political conformity.)

[15]Esdras Minville, *Le citoyen canadien-français* (The French-Canadian Citizen) (Montreal: Editions Fides, 1946), Vol. 1, p. 101. Abbé Groulx had also reproached us for "not protesting with enough perseverance, nor with enough *unanimity.*" (Lionel Groulx, "Langue et survivance," *L'action nationale,* Vol. 4, September 1934, p. 46.)

[16]An expression of Edouard Montpetit ("une science joyeusement acquise et pensée nationalement," 1938) quoted by Maurice Tremblay, "Orientations de la pensée sociale," Chapter 9 of J.C. Falardeau, ed., *Essais sur le Québec contemporain (Essays on Contemporary Quebec)* (Quebec City: Les presses universitaires Laval, 1953), p. 207.

[17]Olivar Asselin, "Les Canadiens français et le développement économique du Canada," *l'Action française,* Vol. 17, May-June 1927, p. 319.

[18]Louis Athanase David, *En marge de la politique* (Montreal: Editions Albert Lévesque, 1935), p. 120.

[19]Victor Barbeau, *Mesure de notre taille* (Montreal: *Le Devoir,* 1936), p. 24.

[20]Edouard Montpetit, "L'indépendance économique des Canadiens français," *l'Action française,* Vol. 5, January 1921, p. 19.

[21]Olivar Asselin, "Les lacunes de notre organisation économique," *l'Action française,* Vol. 5, March 1921, p. 133.

[22]Olivar Asselin, "L'industrie dans l'économie du Canada français," *l'Action canadienne-française,* Vol. 20, September 1928, pp. 151-175.

[23]Victor Barbeau, *Mesure de notre taille* (Montreal: *Le Devoir,* 1936) p. 17.

[24]Louis Athanase David, *En marge de la politique* (Montreal: Editions Albert Lèvesque, 1935), p. 151.

[25]Henri Laureys, in a talk reported in *Le Canada,* May 30, 1934.

[26]Richard Arès, S.J., *Notre question nationale* (Montreal: Editions Action nationale, 1944) Vol. I, pp. 145-152.

[27]These are extraordinary views, as is shown by a comparison with the liberal views of a specialist, W. B. Munro, art. "City," *Encyclopaedia of the Social Sciences* (New York: Macmillan, 1950), Vol. 3, pp. 474-482, who says in part: "In all ages and areas, from ancient Egypt to modern America, the highest development of mentality, initiative

and achievement has been in urban communities. So long as men remained in the pastoral or agricultural stages, there was little stimulus to the differentiation of economic functions; the entire energies of men were absorbed in the task of raising the food supply. But with the city came the division of labor and possibilities for economic surplus, hence wealth, leisure, education, intellectual advance and the development of the arts and sciences . . . The city, in any event, is bound to be a controlling factor in the national life . . . Its population supplies most of the national leadership . . . He who makes the city makes the nation, and indeed it is the cities of the future that will determine the character of the world."

[28]Gérard Filion, "L'agriculture," Chapter 5 of *Notre milieu: aperçu général sur la province de Québec* (Our Environment: A General Survey of the Province of Quebec) (Montreal: Editions Fides, 1942), p. 135. The *Canada Year Book, 1954* (Ottawa: Bureau of Statistics, 1954), p. 20, puts Quebec's arable land at 12% of its surface, and states that 40% of this arable land is already occupied.

[29]Richard Arès, S.J., *Notre question nationale* (Montreal: Editions Action nationale, 1944), Vol. 1, p. 105.

[30]Lionel Groulx, *Faites-nous des hommes* (Give Us Men) (Montreal: Editions de la Jeunesse indépendante catholique, 1938), p. 17.

[31]Louis Hémon, *Maria Chapdelaine: a tale of the Lake St. John country,* trans. W.H. Blake (New York: The Modern Library, 1934), pp. 282-283.

[32]Esdras Minville, *Labour Legislation and Social Services in the Province of Quebec.* A study prepared for the Royal Commission on Dominion-Provincial Relations. Appendix 5 of the *Report of the Royal Commission on Dominion-Provincial Relations* (Ottawa: The King's Printer, 1940), p. 85. My italics.

[33]*Ibid.*, p. 97. My italics.

[34]Maximilien Caron, *L'organisation corporative au service de la démocratie* (Montreal: Ecole sociale populaire, 1942), p. 18.

[35]*Ibid.*, p. 24.

[36]These remarks of Cardinal Villeneuve were excerpted from *L'action catholique* and distributed by the Jesuit fathers to their pupils in the form of leaflets dated December 1, 1938. Through the efforts of their college J.E.C. *(Jeunesse étudiante catholique,* Catholic Student Youth), these students also had the good fortune to receive the text of a speech by Cardinal Villeneuve, dated October 31, 1937, in which he said: "I approve of the resistance which has been shown to the communist rallies. [These were rallies concerning the war in Spain, at which Malraux had attempted to speak] . . . I call upon you, should the occasion arise, to do the same. If someone should object that this is against the law, I would reply that the law of nature is above human law . . . On the pretext of respecting a sick democracy, people raised the scarecrow of an illusory fascism . . ." The Cardinal's address to the *Cercle universitaire de Montréal* (University Club of Montreal) on January 25, 1938, on the subject "Liberty and Liberties," is in the same vein. Here, the Cardinal sets forth his political credo, in which "tolerance" takes on a rather totalitarian character.

[37]Lionel Groulx, "Langue et survivance," *L'action nationale,* Vol. 4, September 1934, pp. 61-62.

[38]*L'action nationale,* Vol. 5, January 1935, p. 4.

[39]Albert Lévesque, in a letter to Louis Athanase David, published as part of a preface to Louis Athanase David, *En marge de la politique* (Montreal: Editions Albert Lévesque, 1935), p. 8.

[40]Esdras Minville, *Le citoyen canadien-français* (Montreal: Editions Fides, 1946).

[41]Esdras Minville, *L'avenir de notre bourgeoisie* (The Future of our Bourgeoisie) (Montreal: Editions Valiquette, 1939), p. 34. My italics.

[42]On the unrealistic attitudes in our culture, see the penetrating articles by Pierre Vadboncoeur: his contribution to "Pour une dynamique de notre culture," *Cité libre,* no. 5, June-July 1952, pp. 11-30; "Henri Bourassa," *Cité libre,* no. 6, December 1952, pp. 71-72; "Critique de notre psychologie de l'action," *Cité libre,* no. 8, November 1953, pp. 11-28. Also of interest on this subject are Guy Cormier's article in *Cité libre* no. 1, and Maurice Blain's contribution to "Pour une dynamique de notre culture," *Cité libre,* no. 5, June-July 1952, pp. 11-30.

[43]These three sentences are taken from Lionel Groulx, *Pourquoi nous sommes divisés* (Montreal: Editions Action nationale, November 1943).

[44]Esdras Minville, "L'économique: progrès ou régression?" *L'action nationale,* Vol. 21, January 1943, p. 26.

[45]André Laurendeau, "Alerte aux Canadiens français!" *L'action nationale* Vol. 16, November 1940, pp. 177-203. This article was later published separately as a pamphlet: *Alerte aux Canadiens français!* (Montreal: Editions Action nationale, 1941).

[46]The word has been popularized by Michel Brunet, who rightly calls it one of the "Three Illusions of French Canadian Thought" (lecture reported in *Le Devoir,* June 2, 1954). The two other illusions he refers to are anti-imperialism and French Canadianism. I shall not deal with either of these, nor with other popular topics such as bilingualism, the schools in the West, etc. For the purposes of this chapter, I regard them as aspects of our political nationalism, not of our socioeconomic thought as such. For the same reason, I do not say much about the champions of political nationalism, like Bourassa, Lavergne, etc.

[47]See also R. Parenteau, "Les idées économiques et sociales de Bourassa," *L'action nationale,* Vol. 43, January 1954, pp. 166-179. Parenteau portrays Bourassa as "hostile to the establishment of industry," guiding the people towards colonization.

[48]Esdras Minville, *Labour Legislation and Social Services in the Province of Quebec,* a study prepared for the Royal Commission on Dominion-Provincial Relations. Appendix 5 of the *Report of the Royal Commission on Dominion-Provincial Relations* (Ottawa: The King's Printer, 1940) pp. 96-97. My italics.

[49]Montpetit is quoted by J.H. Marcotte, *Osons!* (Let's Dare!), 3rd ed. (Montreal: Thérien frères, 1936), p. 28. The quotation from Henri Laureys (note 25) was also obtained from this source.

[50]Maximilien Caron, *La Corporation professionnelle* (Montreal: Ecole sociale populaire, 1939), p. 17.

[51]Everett C. Hughes, *French Canada in Transition* (Chicago: University of Chicago Press, 1943), p. 151.

[52]See above, note 25.

[53]Esdras Minville, "L'économique: progrès ou régression?" *L'action nationale,* Vol. 21, January 1943, p. 23.

[54]See Mason Wade, *The French Canadians, 1760-1945* (London: Macmillan, 1955), p. 1098.

[55]P.M. Gaudrault, O.P., *Neutralité, non-confessionnalité et l'Ecole sociale populaire* (Ottawa: Les Editions du Lévrier, 1946), p. 56.

[56]J. Papin Archambault, S.J., "L'Eglise et le syndicalisme," *Semaine sociale du Canada: deuxième session, Québec 1921* (Montreal: Editions Action paroissale, 1922), pp. 15-17. My italics.

[57]Eugène Lapointe, "Les syndicats catholiques au Canada," *Semaine sociale du Canada: deuxième session, Quebec 1921* (Montreal: Editions Action paroissale, 1922), p. 388.

[58]Alfred Charpentier, *Ma conversion au syndicalisme catholique* (My Conversion to Catholic Trade Unionism) (Montreal: Editions Fides, 1946), p. 77.

[59]*Ibid.*, p. 47. On this period, I would also like to quote the following paragraph taken from an unpublished work by Fernand Dumont:

The chaplain general of the Catholic trade unions, Abbé Maxime Fortin, wrote in the Quebec City publication *L'action catholique* for April 3, 1916 (under the pen name of Albert du Lac): "These labour organizations [the international unions] are the fruit of the social revolution which, at the beginning of the last century, followed the French Revolution as a daughter follows in the footsteps of her mother. Political in appearance, they were really born of the hatred of God, of the Church, of religion, of order, and of all authority, especially that of employers. . . ." This is a rather strange summary of the labour struggles of the nineteenth century: the Revolution was responsible for everything, the poverty of the workers for nothing. In short, Villermé was a dreamer. Our author, engrossed with his principles, continues: "Today the Church has undertaken the awful task of rehabilitating the working class, even in our own society. Your assistance in this must be enlightened and obedient; you promise that it will be liberal. If it is, it will truly serve a cause which is not only yours, but ours: the cause of God himself." Having made his rapid sketch of the labour movement, the author assigns the workers no other function than obedience. The chaplains, who know working class life only from the outside, will do the rest, with the help of good employers, of course.

[60]See the article by Eugene Forsey, "Clerical Fascism in Quebec," *Canadian Forum*, Vol. 17, no. 197, June 1937, pp. 90-92.

[61]Esdras Minville, *Labour Legislation and Social Services in the Province of Quebec*, a study prepared for the Royal Commission on Dominion-Provincial Relations. Appendix 5 of the *Report of the Royal Commission on Dominion-Provincial Relations* (Ottawa: The King's Printer, 1940) pp. 19-21.

[62]Eugène Lapointe, "Les syndicats catholiques au Canada," *Semaine sociale du Canada: deuxième session, Quebec 1921* (Montreal: Editions Action paroissale, 1922), pp. 387-388.

[63]J. Papin Archambault, S.J., "L'Eglise et le syndicalisme," *Semaine sociale du Canada: deuxième session, Quebec 1921* (Montreal: Editions Action paroissale, 1922), p. 15. My italics.

[64]*Le Devoir*, May 7, 1919.

[65]Henri Bourassa, in a speech to a labour rally at Lafontaine Park, Montreal, June 24 (St. Jean Baptiste Day), 1920. As reported in *Semaine sociale du Canada* (Montreal: 1920), p. 171.

[66]Alfred Charpentier, *Ma conversion au syndicalisme catholique* (Montreal: Editions Fides, 1946), pp. 54 and 134.

[67]*Translator's note:* See Roger Duhamel, "La victoire par le syndicat national," *L'action nationale*, Vol. 10, November 1937, pp. 173-180; J.B. Desrosiers, P.S.S., "Principes et déscription de l'organisation corporative," *L'action nationale*, Vol. 11, February 1938, pp. 143-155; François Hertel, "Position du personnalisme," *L'action*

nationale, Vol. 11, February 1938, pp. 95-116, and "D'une civilisation person-naliste," *L'action nationale,* Vol. 11, March 1938, pp. 205-228; F.A. Angers, "Le miroir aux alouettes," *L'action nationale,* Vol. 12, September 1938, pp. 65-74, "Où nous mènent les syndicats?" *L'action nationale,* Vol. 12, October 1938, pp. 153-161, "Esprit patronal et problèmes ouvriers," *L'action nationale,* Vol. 12, December 1938, pp. 342-353, and "Le type économique et social des Canadiens," *L'action nationale,* Vol. 11, April 1938, pp. 338-340. See also Hermas Bastien, "Corporatisme et liberté," *L'action nationale,* Vol. 11, April 1939, pp. 305-313, and "Le bilinguisme au Canada," *L'action nationale,* Vol. 11, January 1938, pp. 5-10; Gérard Filion, "La coopération agricole," *L'action nationale,* Vol. 12, November 1938, pp. 201-208; Esdras Minville, "Le corporatisme et le national," *L'action nationale,* Vol. 12, October 1938, pp. 131-140; G.H. Lévesque, O.P., "La nouvelle chaire de coopération à l'Université Laval," *L'action nationale,* Vol. 12, November 1938, pp. 217-221.

[68]Victor Barbeau, *Pour nous grandir* (To Make Us Great) (Montreal: *Le Devoir,* 1937), p. 232.

[69]Dostaler O'Leary, *Séparatisme: doctrine constructive* (Montreal: Editions des Jeun-esses patriotes, 1937), p. 215.

[70]Pierre Harvey, "Les corporations professionnelles dans la province de Québec," *L'actualité économique* (Revue trimestrielle publiée par l'Ecole des Hautes Etudes Commerciales) , Vol. 30, April-June 1954, p. 62. See also the letter of F.A. Angers, secretary of *L'action corporative,* in *Le Devoir,* November 22, 1954, where a bill "in preparation for 17 years" is discussed.

[71]We must make exception for the remarkable *Essais sur le Québec contemporain (Essays on Contemporary Quebec)* (Quebec City: Les presses universitaires Laval, 1953), which we have already mentioned above (notes 4 and 7), and for a very valuable study by Maurice Tremblay, *La pensée sociale du Canada français* (French Canadian Social Thought), written at Laval University in 1950, but still unpublished. I would also add the very useful and voluminous researches of Mason Wade, published under the title *The French Canadians 1760-1945* (London: Macmillan, 1955).

[72]Our discussion will deal mostly with institutions in the legal sense (public organiza-tions more or less complex in structure) rather than in the sociological sense (socially well established norms of conduct).

[73]Société St. Jean Baptiste de Montréal, "Social Facts in the Province of Quebec," part of a brief to the Royal Commission on Dominion-Provincial Relations (appointed 1937) entitled *Canada, an Anglo-French Country.*

[74]*Ibid.,* p. c.

[75]*Ibid.,* pp. e-f.

[76]*Ibid.,* pp. f-h.

[77]*Ibid.,* pp. i-j.

[78]*Ibid.,* p. j.

[79]*Pour la restauration sociale* (For a Renewal of Society) (Montreal: Ecole sociale populaire, 1933).

[80]*Ibid.,* p. 21.

[81]Sister Marie Agnes of Rome Gaudreau, *The Social Thought of French Canada as Reflected in the Semaine sociale* (Washington, D.C.: The Catholic University of America Press, 1946).

[82]*Ibid.,* p. 183.

[83]*Ibid,* pp. 203 f.

[84]*Ibid.,* p. 239. The consequences of such prudishness may be gauged in an article by R.B., "Nos frères bagnards" (Our brothers, the convicts), *Cité libre,* no. 14, December 1955, pp. 35-37, and in a further article to which it refers: D.S., "Bordeaux," *Canadian Forum,* Vol. 35, no. 415, pp. 99-102.

[85]Gaudreau, *op. cit.* (note 81), p. 243.

[86]*Ibid.,* p. 248.

[87]G.H. Lévesque, "Socialisme canadien," *L'action nationale,* Vol. 2, October 1933, p. 116. In the same vein, see also Léopold Richer, *Nos chefs à Ottawa* (Montreal: Editions Albert Lévesque, 1935). The author paints a fine picture of the C.C.F. leader, and praises his sincerity, intelligence, hard work, and sympathy for the French Canadians, but adds this warning, which speaks volumes on the open-mindedness of our local Catholicism: "In seeking support from the Church, Mr. Woodsworth is meeting an adversary" (p. 40).

[88]F.A. Angers, "Avons-nous compris nos ouvriers?" *L'action nationale,* Vol. 22, October 1943, p. 103.

[89]André Laurendeau, "Conclusions très provisoires," *L'action nationale,* Vol. 31, June 1948, p. 424.

[90]"La morgue d'East Broughton," *L'action nationale,* Vol. 33, January 1949, pp. 3-4.

[91]Léon Lortie, "Le système scolaire," Chapter 8 of *Essais sur le Québec contemporain (Essays on Contemporary Quebec),* ed. J.C. Falardeau (Quebec City: Les presses universitaires Laval, 1953), pp. 169-186.

[92]Arthur Tremblay, in his "Commentaires" to Lortie's chapter in *Essais sur le Québec contemporain,* p. 188.

[93]Lortie, *loc. cit.,* note 91, p. 169.

[94]*Ibid.,* p. 175.

[95]*Ibid.,* p. 176.

[96]See Dollard Morin, *La griffe maçonnique sur les écoles du Québec* (The Schools of Quebec in the Clutches of Freemasonry) (Montreal: Editions de l'Union, 1943), p. 12.

[97]Lionel Groulx, *Méditation patriotique,* Bibliothèque de l'Action française, no. 1 (Montreal: Editions Action française, 1920), p. 11.

[98]Rodrigue Villeneuve, O.M.I., "La famille, cellule sociale," *Semaine sociale du Canada. IVe session, Montréal, 1923* (Montreal: Bibliothèque de l'Action française, 1924), p. 53.

[99]See *Procès-verbaux du Comité catholique du Conseil de l'instruction publique* (Minutes of the Roman Catholic Committee of the Council of Education), sitting of December 17, 1942.

[100]André Siegfried, *Le Canada, les deux races* (Paris: Armand Colin, 1905), pp. 123-124. This passage from Siegfried is quoted by Maurice Tremblay, *La pensée sociale du Canada français* (unpublished; see above, note 71).

[101]*Mémoire de l'Université de Montréal à la Commission royale d'enquête sur les problèmes constitutionnels* (Brief of the University of Montreal to the Quebec [Province] Royal Commission of Inquiry on Constitutional Problems [The Tremblay Commission: appointed 1954, Report 1956]), pp. 36 and 73.

[102]We should note, for the edification of future generations, the unspeakably base act of a Prime Minister of Quebec who, in the middle of the Legislative Assembly, accused an

opposition member of ingratitude because the latter had not espoused his political ideas although, thanks to the Prime Minister, he had received a small amount of financial aid when he was a student. The incident is reported in *Le Devoir,* February 15, 1955.

[103]These figures are taken from the results of an inquiry made by J.Y. Morin and published in *Le quartier latin* (The University of Montreal student newspaper), March 19, 1953.

[104]See Arthur Tremblay, in his "Commentaires" to Léon Lortie's chapter on the Quebec school system in *Essais sur le Québec contemporain (Essays on Contemporary Quebec),* ed. J.C. Falardeau (Quebec City: Les presses universitaires Laval, 1953), p. 189.

[105]These national census figures were compiled by Léo Roback and published in *Le Devoir,* February 2, 1955.

[106]See the radio talks by Abbé Maheux, broadcast between September 1942 and January 1943, which were subsequently published by the C.B.C. as Arthur Maheux, *Pourquoi sommes-nous divisés?* (Montreal: Beauchemin, 1943). See also Lionel Groulx, *Pourquoi nous sommes divisés* (Montreal: Editions Action nationale, November 1943).

[107]See Mason Wade, *The French Canadians, 1760-1945* (London: Macmillan, 1955), pp. 873 and 894.

[108]In the last fifty years, almost every French Canadian who has dealt with our social problems began by stating that the family is the basic social building block and by urging us to protect it from "Protestant and individualist" legislators. As we have seen, family allowances and old age pensions finally came from Ottawa, the latter under socialist pressure. Other provinces, "Protestant and individualist," have established family courts with jurisdiction over the family considered as a unit, but in Quebec, different courts must jointly pass judgment on the separate members of the same family, thus tending to destroy the "basic social building block." Mrs. W. Holmes, a lawyer in Montreal, has given a number of lectures on Quebec courts and the family; see, for example, the *Montreal Gazette,* December 1, 1953.

[109]See *Annuaire de la faculté des sciences sociales, économiques et politiques* (Yearbook of the Faculty of Social, Economic and Political Sciences) (Montreal: University of Montreal) for the year 1946-1947.

[110]Brother Marie-Victorin, "Vingt-cinq ans de vie scientifique au Canada français," *L'action nationale,* Vol. 21, January 1943, pp. 45 and 47.

[111]*Translator's note:* This organization is now known as the *Centre des dirigeants d'entreprise,* or *C.D.E.* (The Industrial Managers' Centre).

[112]*Annuaire de la faculté des sciences sociales, économiques et politiques* (Yearbook of the Faculty of Social, Economic and Political Sciences) (Quebec City: Laval University) for 1947-1948 and 1948-1949, pp. 20 f.

[113]This ratio is based on the approximate figures of J.C. Falardeau, as given in the Parisian journal *Esprit,* August-September 1953, p. 224. The whole issue, which is devoted to French Canada, is worth reading.

[114]This loyalty was evident even at the time of the Fenian raids. On May 28, 1870, Mgr. Truteau, the administrator of the diocese of Montreal, urged his priests to "use all your influence on your parishioners to get them to join those who have already taken up arms to repel these brigands." See *Mandements, lettres pastorales, circulaires et autres documents publiés dans le diocèse de Montréal* (Instructions, Pastoral Letters, Circular Letters and Other Documents Published in the Diocese of Montreal), Vol. 6 (Montreal: J.A. Plinguet, 1887), p. 94.

[115]*Translator's note:* These abbreviations stand for Jeunesse agricole catholique (Catholic Farm Youth), Jeunesse étudiante catholique (Catholic Student Youth), and Jeunesse ouvrière catholique (Catholic Labour Youth) respectively.

[116]*Mandements, lettres pastorales, circulaires et autres documents publiés dans le diocèse de Montréal,* Vol. 6 (Montreal: J.A. Plinguet, 1887), pp. 398-400.

[117]*Ibid.,* Vol. 10 (Montreal: J.A. Plinguet, 1887), p. 334.

[118]*Ibid.,* Vol. 13 (Montreal: 1903), pp. 525 f.

[119]*Ibid.,* Vol. 18, Mgr. G. Gauthier, "Circulaire de Mgr. l'Archevêque-coadjuteur au clergé du diocèse sur la crise économique," no. 49 (Montreal: Arbour & Dupont Ltee, 1940), pp. 196-214.

[120]*Ibid.,* Vol. 18, "Lettre pastorale et mandement des Archevêques et Evêques des Provinces Ecclesiastiques de Québec, de Montréal et d'Ottawa, à l'occasion du malaise économique des temps présents," no. 52 A (Montreal: Arbour & Dupont Ltée, 1940), pp. 229-240. The quotations are taken from p. 234.

[121]*Ibid.,* Vol. 18, "Lettre pastorale de Mgr. l'Archevêque-coadjuteur aux fidèles du diocèse," no. 60, pp. 324-358.

[122]*Ibid.,* Vol. 18, Gauthier, *loc. cit.,* pp. 355-356.

[123]*Ibid.,* Vol. 18, "Lettre pastorale collective de Son Eminence le Cardinal Archevêque de Québec et de Leurs Excellences les Archevêques et Evêques de la Province civile de Québec. Sur le problème rural au regard de la doctrine sociale de l'Eglise," no. 79, pp. 542-584. The passage cited is taken from p. 545.

[124]Rodrigue Villeneuve, O.M.I., "Allocution" on the theme "L'oeuvre social de l'Eglise," *Semaine sociale du Canada, 16e session, Sherbrooke, 1938* (Montreal: Ecole sociale populaire, 1938), pp. 382-389.

[125]"Circulaire de Mgr. l'Archevêque-coadjuteur au clergé du diocèse," no. 82, *Mandements, lettres pastorales, circulaires et autres documents publiés dans le diocèse de Montréal,* Vol. 18 (Montreal: Arbour & Dupont, 1940), pp. 593-605. The two passages cited are from pp. 596 and 598. Mgr. Gauthier is referring to the Parti national social chrétien (Christian National Socialist Party), a French Canadian fascist party led by Adrien Arcand.

[126]*Ibid.,* Vol. 19, pp. 56 f.

[127]On the role played by the Sacerdotal Commission of Social Studies during the strike itself, see Chapter VI below.

[128]This attitude of the French Canadian Jesuits is strikingly different from that of their French colleague Father Daniélou, who said at the Semaine des intellectuels catholiques de France (Symposium of French Catholic Intellectuals) at Paris, November 13, 1955: "A philosophy should not concern itself with being Christian, but with being true. A civilization should not be concerned with being Christian, but with being just and free." Their attitude is even more at odds with the assertion of the Bishop of Chartres: "The new Christianity will no longer be sacred and clerical, but profane and lay. This means that religious institutions will not strive to develop a Christian faith and religious values directly, but rather humane and true values." (Quoted by François Mauriac, *L'Express,* Paris, December 8, 1955.)

[129]*Mandements, lettres pastorales, circulaires et autres documents publiés dans le diocèse de Montréal,* Vol. 20, pp. 256 and 259.

[130]See Mason Wade, *The French Canadians, 1760-1945* (London: Macmillan, 1955), pp. 979 and 1019.

131See P.E. Trudeau, "Réflexions sur la politique au Canada français," *Cité libre,* no. 6, December 1952, pp. 53-70.

132Onésime Gagnon, the Provincial Treasurer in the Duplessis government, later referred to the proposed nationalization of the Montreal Light, Heat and Power Co. as a "dictatorial" and "Bolshevik" measure. See Mason Wade, *The French Canadians, 1760-1945* (London: Macmillan, 1955), p. 1074.

133Bloc populaire, *Document no. 10* (Montreal: Imprimerie populaire, October 1943).

134The classification is by Dominique Beaudoin, *Le Devoir,* July 11, 1952.

135Mazeaud made this remark in a lecture given at the University of Montreal in November 1953.

136This paragraph and the following are based on the work of Esdras Minville, *Labour Legislation and Social Services in the Province of Quebec,* a study prepared for the Royal Commission on Dominion-Provincial Relations. Appendix 5 of the *Report of the Royal Commission on Dominion-Provincial Relations* (Ottawa: The King's Printer, 1940). This work has already been quoted above: see notes 32, 33, 48, and 61.

137Leonard C. Marsh, *Report on Social Security for Canada;* prepared for the Advisory Committee on Reconstruction (Ottawa: The King's Printer, 1943). Appendix 6, "Rental Variations and the Minimum Standard," p. 140, under the heading "Public Welfare Expenditures (per capita)."

138A very useful table of comparison of the labour legislation in the different provinces of Canada is given in the *Labour Gazette* (Ottawa: Department of Labour), Vol. 50, September 1950, pp. 1437-1441.

139See the *Report of the Royal Commission on Dominion-Provincial Relations* (Ottawa: The King's Printer, 1940), Book I, "Canada: 1867-1939."

140See the *Report of the Royal Commission on Price Spreads* (Ottawa: The King's Printer, 1937), p. 28.

141See Wilfrid Bovey, *Canadien, a Study of the French Canadians* (London: Dent, 1933), p. 223. See also Georges Pelletier, "Notre industrie," *l'Action française,* Vol. 5, June 1921, p. 322.

142These percentages are based on the figures in the *Canada Year Book, 1954* (Ottawa: Bureau of Statistics, 1954), p. 621. See also the *Canada Year Book, 1943-1944,* p. 363.

143This is not the place to make a critical study of the different estimates which have been made of the French Canadian share in the national wealth. They all agree that it is far inferior to our numerical importance. (For example, see the work of Olivar Asselin quoted above [notes 17, 21, and 22], and the books by Victor Barbeau, *Mesure de notre taille* [quoted above, note 19] and *Pour nous grandir* [mentioned above, note 68]. Mason Wade, *The French Canadians, 1760-1945* [London: Macmillan, 1955], p. 864, quotes from the works of well-known economists which show that, in 1934, one third of all industrial capital invested in Quebec was American.) This situation occurs, please note, in a country which is only partially owned by its inhabitants. On this last point, we offer only one piece of evidence, but an important one. The (then) Governor of the Bank of Canada, Graham Towers, made the following remark in a speech to the Canadian Club of Toronto on November 9, 1950: "Apart from the war debts of certain countries, it is true to say that Canada has a *larger foreign debt than any other country in the world.*"

144Everett C. Hughes, "Regards sur le Québec," Chapter 10 of *Essais sur le Québec contemporain (Essays on Contemporary Quebec),* ed. J.C. Falardeau (Quebec City: Les presses universitaires Laval, 1953), pp. 217-230. The passage cited is on p. 229.

[145]*Report of the Royal Commission on the Relation of Labour and Capital in Canada* (Ottawa: The Queen's Printer, 1889), pp. 111-112.

[146]See the *Report of the Royal Commission on Price Spreads* (Ottawa: The King's Printer, 1937).

[147]This was also the normal working week at Asbestos at one time. This fact is innocently revealed by a little brochure hymning the glory of the Canadian Johns-Manville Co., written by one Francis Hand, and entitled *Asbestos . . . "Magic Mineral."* It contains the statement: "The work week is now 40 hours compared with 48 in 1948 and 70 in 1929."

[148]See the *Report of the Royal Commission on Price Spreads* (Ottawa: The King's Printer, 1937). Of particular interest are pp. 105-142, and also some of the testimonies taken. (Some of these testimonies are quoted in Michel Brunet, Guy Frégault and Marcel Trudel, *Histoire du Canada par les textes* [Montreal: Editions Fides, 1952].) Appendix 5 of the *Report* clearly shows that the wages of unionized workers are always higher, and often much higher than those of non-unionized workers; and that Quebec wages are almost always lower than Ontario wages, even for the employees of the same company.

[149]See the *Report of the Royal Commission on the Textile Industry* (Ottawa: The King's Printer, 1938), especially pp. 146 and 191.

[150]Robert H. Coats, *History of the Labour Movement in Canada* (Dominion Training School, Communist Party of Canada, 1937). Coats's work is quoted by H.A. Logan, *The History of Trade Union Organization in Canada* (Toronto: Macmillan, 1948). The following paragraphs are partly based on Logan, who also quotes G. Tremblay, *Programme-souvenir du premier congrès, C.T.C.C.* (Souvenir Program of the First Convention, C.C.C.L.).

[151]See *Le Travail* (an official publication of the C.C.C.L.), September 1943.

[152]See J.P. Desprès, *Le mouvement ouvrier canadien.* Publiè sous les auspices du Département des relations industrielles de la Faculté des sciences sociales de Laval (Montreal: Editions Fides, 1947), p. 57.

[153]*Ad usum sacerdotum* (a bulletin published under the editorial supervision of Abbé Gérard Dion), March-May 1955, p. 122.

[154]See Esdras Minville, *Labour Legislation and Social Services in the Province of Quebec.* A study prepared for the Royal Commission on Dominion-Provincial Relations. Appendix 5 of the *Report of the Royal Commission on Dominion-Provincial Relations* (Ottawa: The King's Printer, 1940), p. 13.

[155]For example, at its annual convention in 1932, the C.C.C.L. adopted a resolution on rural settlement because "according to men of sense, a return to the land offers the most practical solution to the problem of unemployment." The first resolution of the convention held in 1934 is even more surprising: it denies the possibility of full employment without a return to the land.

[156]For example, the C.C.C.L. opposed immigration at its first convention because, among other things, "many of these immigrants come here filled with socialist and revolutionary ideas." In 1937, the C.C.C.L. tried to keep out American labour organizers, whose "most important activity is making trouble for Canadian industry. . . ."

[157]L.L. Hardy has an unpublished work on this subject, as well as an article on it in *Le Travail,* February 19, 1954.

[158]*Labour Research* (a bulletin published by the Research Department, Canadian Congress of Labour, Ottawa), January 1949, has a cruel and very intelligent analysis of this proposed legislation.

[159]Victor Barbeau, *Pour nous grandir* (Montreal: *Le Devoir,* 1937) pp. 195-198.

[160]Gagnon made these remarks in a lecture at the Radio College, which was reported in *Le Devoir,* February 27, 1951.

Chapter II

Financial History of the Asbestos Industry

by Jean Gérin-Lajoie

I/Introduction

In 1948, asbestos mines were a relatively unimportant part of the Canadian mining industry as a whole, and they contributed .003 of the Gross National Product. From the economic point of view, their importance lay chiefly in the 40 million American dollars they brought into the country each year, and in the jobs they provided for approximately 5,000 workers. In Mégantic, Wolfe, and Richmond townships, however, these mines were the only significant industry, and their prosperity was thus of vital importance to this part of the Eastern Townships, hence to the Province of Quebec as a whole.

The strike of 1949, which brought this sector of our economy to the attention of the general public, was the climactic event in a long history marked by many changes of fortune. These changes were brought about both by general factors like war and depressions and by factors peculiar to the industry.

The strike revolved around two issues. It broke out over a wage dispute (the union asked for 15 cents, the employers offered 10), but it was really provoked as well by a conflict over the acceptance of trade unionism and the prerogatives of management.

We do not intend to study the causes of the strike here, but to give an outline history of the industry and to describe the economic conditions of the employers and employees. We[1] shall then situate this industry in the context of the postwar economy in order to obtain a better understanding of its present structure.

Here, then, is a rough sketch of its chief characteristics:

The product: Asbestos exists in the form of long or short fibres; in Canada, the short fibre asbestos is the most common, and is worth little in comparison with the long fibre variety, which comes mostly from Africa.

The market: Almost all our asbestos is exported to the United States, where it is used mainly in the automobile and construction industries. It is also used in the manufacture of a few other industrial products. Thanks to their geographic proximity, the Canadian producers have cornered the short fibre asbestos market in the United States; this also has the disadvantage of making them almost completely dependent on this market.

The industry: In 1948, there were seven companies producing asbestos, four of which were owned by American manufacturers. These firms are heavily capitalized and mechanized, and they no longer have to face the financial difficulties and the savage competition which troubled them for so long. One of the characteristics of the industry, in fact, has been a great instability which has constantly menaced not only the producing companies but also the workers whose jobs and wages were affected.

The main stages in the development of this industry are as follows:

1878: The production of asbestos begins in Canada. From 1891 on, heavy capital investment is needed because of the market structure and the nature of production. The importance of capital has continually increased since then, due to fluctuations in sales, price wars, and the need for intensive mechanization to produce shorter and shorter asbestos fibres on a commercially viable basis.

1914: At about this time, American manufacturers make a serious effort to buy up the Canadian primary producing industry in order to control production.

During and after the First World War, asbestos prices rise dramatically. These developments stimulated the establishment of African mines, which within twenty years are to dominate the world market for long fibre asbestos, the most lucrative kind.

1921: A severe depression engenders new price wars, so savage that many Canadian mines that are either only marginally prosperous or burdened with excessive debts go out of production.

1925: Many producers who until that time had managed to retain their independence are forced to merge.

1929-33: The industry reels under the effects of the Great Depression. A very gradual recovery is won only at the price of a closer and closer integration of our production with the American market.

1951: After ten years of continual prosperity, Canadian production is almost totally absorbed by the United States.

We shall now attempt, in spite of a dearth of published figures on the subject, to show how these successive repercussions and changes affected employment and wages. We shall then be in a position to analyze the relationship between these wages and the industry's situation in the year 1948.

We have often rounded off the figures obtained from statistical compilations in order to make the text and the numerical comparisons readily understandable. We ask the reader's indulgence for a work of popularization.

II/From a small to a large industry (1878-1896)
1/Asbestos: a family of products

There are many kinds of asbestos, all of which are more or less totally resistant to fire, heat, and friction. This property accounts, in the main, for the economic value of the mineral. The chemical and physical properties of the mineral vary from one deposit to another, and several kinds of asbestos may occur together in the same deposit. To understand the problems of the industry, we must retain the fact that asbestos is not so much a product as a family of products, in which each category attracts a different market and has its own particular uses.

Commercial production of asbestos began around 1850 in Italy, which had a monopoly in the field until 1880. Italian asbestos is a long fibre type occurring in irregular deposits, and it is rather hard to mine.

In 1876, asbestos deposits were accidentally discovered in the Thetford hills during the construction of the Quebec Central Railway. At first the fibres of this asbestos seemed too short to be useful, but it proved to be so easy to spin and weave that its economic value soon surpassed that of the Italian asbestos. In 1878, three open pit mines were opened close to the new railway. The first year's production amounted to fifty tons.

2/The first market slump

As soon as industrialists became aware of the quality of this new asbestos, its price jumped to a high level. Up to 1890, new pits mushroomed. (See Table I.)

Table I

Asbestos production, 1878-1892

Year	Tons produced	Average value	Workers employed	Number of producers
1878	50	$ 65.00	—	3
1885	2,240	$ 58.00	350	7
1890	9,860	$128.00	—	16
1892	6,082	$ 64.00	—	19

Source: F. Cirkel, *Chrysotile-Asbestos,* Department of Mines, Ottawa, 1910.

Prices, however, could not long remain at this high level. The rise in prices was due largely to the fact that customers were stockpiling asbestos in order to protect themselves against a further price increase. Based on speculation, the market naturally collapsed. The crisis had an especially drastic effect on the value of the two highest grades of asbestos. The situation was further aggravated by the defensive action taken by some American customers, who merged in the hope of having some control over the prices that speculation and competition forced them to pay.

3/Capitalization

This market crisis obliged the producers themselves to accumulate stocks of asbestos for the first time. Those who did not have the capital to carry these inventories were forced out of the industry. Of 19 producers in 1892, only 9 were left two years later. By 1899, the number had shrunk to 6. From the very beginning, market instability eliminated the weakest competitors from the industry.

Changes in production methods had the same effect. Up to 1885, these methods were fairly primitive, but thereafter, particularly after the crisis of 1891, the producers had to find ways to increase their return and reduce their costs by perfecting their mining methods and making greater use of machinery.

The capital needs of the asbestos industry have steadily increased up to our own day; they have directly affected the structure of the industry.[2]

III/The threat of instability (1896-1914)

The first market crisis in the asbestos industry created a precedent which repeated itself during the twenty-year period prior to the First World War. The heavy capitalization required for production limited the number of competitors. The few survivors continued to fight it out among themselves. As a result, prices, wages, employment, and even financial structures were chronically unstable. After many years of suffering the chaotic effects of this competition, the producers and their customers wanted to curb it. Manufacturers who used asbestos bought mines, and the independent producers tried to consolidate their position. This latter effort was a failure, however, and a majority of the firms were left with a heavy burden of debt.

Prior to 1896, asbestos was for the most part spun and woven, and the commercial value of very short fibres was thus negligible. When the industry suddenly found a way of using these short fibres, they immediately became an important factor in the market. Up to that time the short fibres had accounted for 5% of total sales; now this percentage quickly rose to 35%. In 1948, long fibres represented only 1% of the total value of asbestos produced. The early situation had completely reversed itself.

1/Varieties of Canadian asbestos

The different kinds of asbestos must be carefully distinguished. Canadian asbestos occurs in the form of veins running through rock, 1/8 to 2½ inches in width. Once removed from the rock, these veins may be separated into fine silky fibres. Crude asbestos—the higher quality long fibres—are obtained where the mineral can be removed from the rock by hand. This type of asbestos is mainly found in the district of Thetford Mines (Asbestos Corporation, Johnson's, Bell), and occurs with less regularity around Coleraine and Black Lake (Asbestos Corporation, Johnson's). None is found at East Broughton (Quebec Asbestos). The narrower veins are sent to the mill, where the separation is done mechanically. A third type of asbestos is obtained by crushing the rock that surrounds the veins of pure mineral. The value of the asbestos produced by these methods decreases with the length of its fibres. In 1913, for example, a ton of crude fibres was worth 175 dollars, while a ton of short fibres had fallen in value to 22 dollars. In 1951, the difference in prices was even greater, as shown in Table II.

Table II

Price scale for asbestos in 1951

Category	Price per ton f.o.b. mine	Canada
1. - Crude no. 1	$1,100	$1,500
2. - Crude no. 2 and other	485	900
3. - Spinning stocks	275	450
4. - Shingle stocks	135	151
5. - Paper stocks	95	119
6. - Waste, plaster or stucco	70	70
7. - "Shorts"* and waste	32	63

*"Shorts" are microscopic bits of asbestos.
Source: *Asbestos*, April 1951.

The growing demand for short fibre asbestos was accompanied by a general expansion of the industry which lasted up to the First World War. The combined effects of these two developments were:

—a strong increase in production and mechanization;
—the opening up of the Broughton region for the production of short fibres;

—heavy competition threatening the stability of the mining companies;
—changes in the financial structure which affected the industry up to 1939;
—unstable working conditions.

This period deserves study because, in spite of considerable growth, the industry has often been in trouble, sometimes in a state of chaos. To remedy the situation, it has made structural reforms which still exist today.

We can illustrate this precariousness by an example. Between 1911 and 1913 there was a depression, and from 1912 on, all the East Broughton mines were out of production. (They were not reopened until 1917, and the only East Broughton mill still operating around 1949 belonged to Quebec Asbestos, one of the smallest firms in the industry.)

2/Production

In this period, sales of Canadian asbestos increased roughly by a factor of ten, reaching $4 million in 1913, a considerable sum at the time. (See Graph I.)

Graph I

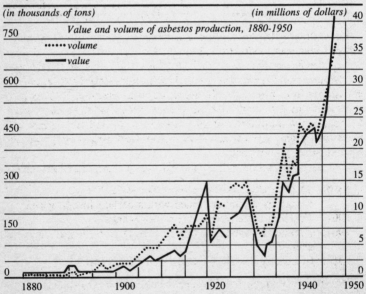

(in thousands of tons)   (in millions of dollars) 40

Value and volume of asbestos production, 1880-1950
•••••• volume
——— value

Source: *Asbestos in Canada: Surveys and Forecasts,* Toronto, 1950.

One might think that such a pace of development would bring about a general prosperity in the industry. A close examination of the statistics, however, shows that this is not the case, as this increase in production coincided with the phenomenon we have just discussed above, namely the increase in importance of short fibres. While sales were increasing, the price of asbestos was going down. Thus the producers made less profit per ton. To understand the importance of this last development, let us consider Graph II (derived from Graph I).

Graph II

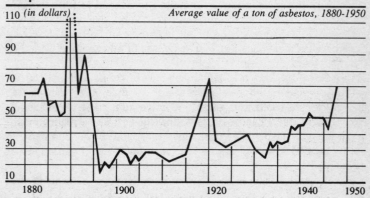

Average value of a ton of asbestos, 1880-1950

These graphs help us to understand the brutality of the new conditions to which the industry had to adapt itself.

The producers not only made less per ton; they also saw their production costs increased by mechanization. We have explained above that long fibres may be removed from the rock by hand, but short fibres have to be milled. Bigger mills thus had to be constructed to separate the short fibre asbestos from the rock, and at the same time the whole mining process had to be modernized to increase productivity and offset higher costs.

Four dates will serve to illustrate this change in production methods:

1898: The extraction of the asbestos is done entirely by hand, as is shown by a contract made with a certain Joseph Parent.

1902: The Bell mine puts a steam shovel into use.

1904: American Asbestos (Black Lake) introduces electrical energy.

1917: Electricity has almost entirely replaced steam.

The capital required for this mechanization was considerable, and many small producers were unable to raise it. Moreover, it was possible to improve the return on investment only in those mines which had sufficiently rich mineral deposits. The others had to be given up. Thus, even before 1914, one needed plenty of capital and a good property to make money producing short fibre asbestos and "shorts." This explains why the number of active producers has never greatly exceeded ten, except in abnormal circumstances.

3/East Broughton

The district of Broughton has no long fibres, but with the growth of demand for short fibre asbestos, it acquired a new economic importance. The first mine in East Broughton was opened in 1901. Around 1910 there were five active mines in the area, but their prosperity was precarious. They were less profitable than those of Thetford and Black Lake because they made less money per ton of mineral, and were thus the first to be affected by a slump.

Of course, the import of American capital was not due only to this particular crisis in the industry, since at the time all of Canada was becoming industrialized through a massive influx of foreign capital. Nevertheless, there can be no doubt that the desire of American manufacturers to reduce mining company profits, and above all to stabilize their source of raw materials, had an important effect on this import of capital.

The American manufacturers were responding to the same stimuli that were urging Quebec's independent producers to unify their forces. Faced with the disastrous effects of free competition, everyone realized that the industry had to be reorganized if it were going to remain viable.

The most serious effort of the period to unite the independent producers was made in 1909. Two mines at Thetford and three at Black Lake came under the control of the Amalgamated Asbestos Corporation, which at the time had a capital of $25 million. At the same time, four other mines in Black Lake formed the Black Lake Consolidated Asbestos Company, capitalized at $5 million.

Both these attempts at consolidation failed, because prices started to rise again the year after, bringing new producers into the field. The number of mines climbed from 14 to 18. When the market collapsed, the cutthroat competition described above was taken up with even greater ferocity, in spite of the efforts of the two large organizations. Furthermore, it soon became apparent that their financial obligations were much too heavy for a period of crisis, and alterations in the financial structure had to be made.

4/Instability

The price fluctuations of asbestos are a complex phenomenon. In general, all types of asbestos are vulnerable to a fall in price, but sometimes the price of one kind of asbestos goes down while that of another goes up. The producer is hard put to defend himself against fluctuations of this kind. It is very hard for him to control the production of this or that kind of asbestos, because each type makes up only a tiny proportion of all the rock that is extracted and milled.

This inflexibility in production has clearly contributed sometimes to the rise, and sometimes to the fall, of prices. In 1901, for example, the price of no. 1 crude asbestos (the most lucrative kind) increased from $107 per ton to $165 per ton on the American market, while in 1910, no. 2 crude fell in price from $152 to $100.

This kind of instability, even if of slight magnitude in any individual case, obviously did a lot of harm to the industry as a whole. Between 1896 and 1914, only three mines did not have to shut down at some time or another, for a shorter or longer period. Irregular production was a characteristic of the period. The situation became so serious that in 1912, the provincial minister of mines remarked that economic conditions in the industry were so unstable that some firms were abandoning electricity in favour of less costly steam.

Fortunately, this retrogression did not last long.

5/The effects of instability
Such an unhealthy situation was bound to provoke a reaction, which expressed itself on two levels: the import of American capital and the merger of independent producers.

6/Employment and wages
From the year 1900 on, we have annual figures on the number of workers employed in the asbestos mining industry and on the total wages paid to them. These two figures enable us to calculate the average annual wage. From 1900 to 1914, this wage climbed from $270 to $430, but within that period it fluctuated as much as 40% per year.

Table III

Number of workers and their annual wages (1900-1914)		
Year	Number of workers	Total wages (in $1000s)
1900	1,000	270
1914	3,000	1,300

Source: Quebec Department of Mines. Annual report on the mining industry.

Two different factors explain this fluctuation in wages: the changes in the nominal wage rate and those in the length of employment. As a rule, people were employed on a very irregular basis in this industry; consequently, the annual wage that we have quoted is only a poor approximation to what a worker would have earned if he had been employed all year round.

The figures on the number of people employed are not very good either. Not only did the duration of employment vary, but so did the number of workers employed. In 1902, for example, 200 more workers were employed in the industry as a whole than in the previous year (a 13% increase), but many of these people worked for only four months. In 1904 in Black Lake, the irregularity of production caused annual incomes to drop from $320 to $260. The next year, on the other hand, three mines in the area were shut down and three provided jobs on a regular basis; the average annual salary increased to $350.

In short, there might be very heavy employment at the beginning of the year, including a night shift of ten hours, but a few months later, workers might be laid off because some mines were forced to curtail their operations or shut down completely.

Clearly, then, this whole period saw truly extraordinary fluctuations in the number of workers employed, the length of their employment, wage rates, and average income, in spite of the fact that the industry had made definite progress even in such unstable circumstances. Frequently, the total number of workers employed in the industry increased by ten, twenty, or even fifty percent (1901), but it sometimes decreased just as sharply (by 40% between 1910 and 1912). (See Table IV.)

Table IV

Instability of employment

Year	Decrease in relation to the previous year
1903	27%
1905	7%
1911	22%
1912	25%

Source: Quebec Department of Mines. Annual report on the mining industry.

7/Nominal wages
Unfortunately, we have little information on wage rates, because the reports of the provincial Department of Mines have almost nothing to

say about this aspect of the industry. We know, however, that these rates were extremely flexible. In 1900, for example, a strong demand brought about the establishment of new mines. Night shifts had to be added, and wages increased 25% on the average. The years 1914-1915 are instructive in this respect. In the spring of 1914, as a result of increasing demand, wages rose to $1.25 per day, then to $1.40. Wages did not increase beyond this point because the war came along, dislocating the European market and causing Canadian production to slow down. Many workers were dismissed. After a few weeks, only heads of families still had jobs, at a maximum wage of $1.00 per day. Soon the war created a new market; the situation in the asbestos industry began to improve in the spring of 1915. A year later, wages reached the level of $2.50 per day.

This wage flexibility should not surprise us. Most of the workers came from a society that was still rural, and had not been able to create a lasting union. Asbestos prices varied greatly, and employers had little trouble in adjusting wages to suit. They could raise wages, secure in the knowledge that they would not meet with organized resistance when they came to lower them again. In all probability, the producers would not have engaged in such chaotic economic battles among themselves if they had had to reckon with a sufficiently strong labour organization.

8/The precedent becomes a general rule

At the beginning of our study we noted that a dangerous precedent had been created by the market crisis around 1891. In the period 1896-1914, this precedent became the general rule. The industry enjoyed a really spectacular expansion in this period, but its development followed a typical pattern: chronic instability of prices, wages, and employment, and an unfettered competition which created havoc in the industry, eliminating the small producers or forcing them into efforts at consolidation which were sometimes hazardous.

As we shall see, except around the two wars, chronic instability was the norm in the asbestos industry.

IV/Wartime prices and their effects (1914-1926)

The period 1914-1926 is interesting because some of its features will help us to understand what happened after the Second World War, in the period just before the strike of 1949.

The wartime demand for asbestos provided a stimulus for the industry that was first felt in 1915 and lasted until 1920. However, this rise in prices did not result in an immediate increase in production, because military recruitment and the scarcity of manpower created by the war effort made it impossible to expand rapidly.

The high prices made asbestos production extremely profitable, and eventually new producers managed to invade the field, in spite of the obstacles we have discussed above. By 1920, there were no fewer than 20 producers operating in Canada.

To simplify our analysis of the First World War's effects on the asbestos industry, we shall limit our study to three main aspects: foreign competition, the stabilization of the industry after the formation of the Asbestos Corporation, and the behaviour of wages. These three phenomena are closely related to the spectacular rise in prices resulting from the war.

1/Foreign competition

Before the First World War, Canada was the only important producer of asbestos. The price increases created by the war led to the establishment of large-scale mining operations in Southern Rhodesia. This new competition soon became serious. In 1920, for example, Canada was still producing 180,000 of the 213,000 tons marketed in that year, but Rhodesia was beginning to get control of the most lucrative area, the market for long fibre asbestos. In 1928, Rhodesia contributed only 10% of the world's asbestos production in quantity, but 20% in value, while Canada, producing 70% of the market's tonnage, accounted for only half its value.

Table V

Long fibres in Canadian and Rhodesian production (in thousands of tons)

Year	Canadian production	Rhodesian production
1920	18	21
1921	6	22
1922	9	16

2/New producers

The Canadian asbestos industry had lost control of the most profitable markets, which was bad enough. The crowning misfortune, however, was the excessive increase in the number of producers, with its unhappy aftermath. In 1921, there were 22 active asbestos mines in Canada. In 1923, after a short but severe slump, 17 remained. The following year, a price war eliminated four others. In the end, only 10 companies (controlling a total of 13 mines) were left. They were still too many: as we shall see, more were to fail before prices and production stabilized.

This crisis did have one advantage: it made people realize that the financial structure of the industry was at the root of the troubles. It had become clear that unless this structure was radically overhauled, the producers would be confronted with the same problems indefinitely. The strongest companies thus embarked on a new scheme. Instead of allowing their most feeble competitors to linger on, they bought them up. In this way, the Asbestos Corporation came into being in 1925, grouping 11 different companies and providing a central management for the mining of a very extensive asbestos deposit. This financial operation was conducted by the New York firm of Dillon, Read & Co.

3/Wages

In the aftermath of the economic battles, nobody was spared. In the course of the whole period that we have just discussed, the average wage and the number of workers employed both dropped by about 30%. From 1920 to 1921 alone, the total of wages decreased by 50%. Had work not been provided by the opening up of new pits and the maintenance of old ones, employment and wages would probably have fallen even lower.

We should point out, however, that these variations were less radical than the fluctuations in sales and profits. Between 1920 and 1921, wages fell by 50%, but sales dropped 67%. In the previous years 1914-1920, on the other hand, wages increased 270% while the margin of sales over production costs went up 510%.

This phenomenon is typical of industry as a whole. It is easier, in fact, for an employer to manipulate profits than wages. He can, of course, easily raise wages, but if he has to reduce them at a later time. he meets with great resistance. We thus have the paradox that the more workers organize, the more employers are reluctant to raise their wages.

In the very period we are studying, the growth of working-class consciousness was beginning to make wage manipulations more difficult. In particular, there were strikes in the asbestos industry in 1915, 1916, and 1920. The strike of 1920, for example, resulted from a demand for higher wages. This demand, it seems, could easily have been met, yet the employers refused it, and succeeded in breaking the strike.

In the development of the asbestos industry, a new social law thus emerged: a strong labour organization always had trouble obtaining a fair share of the industry's prosperity for the workers precisely because this prosperity was seldom of long duration. One naturally wonders how important this factor was in the strike of 1949; I myself cannot say exactly.

V/The modern asbestos industry and the Depression (1926-1939)

With the creation of the Asbestos Corporation in 1925, the modern phase of the industry begins. In this period, we will be dealing with the same problems as before, because they remain characteristic of the industry. These problems are: changes in demand, international competition, the capitalization of the industry, its structure, and its producers.

1/Changes in demand

Between the two wars, Canadian industry continued to be drawn to the markets for shorter fibre asbestos. Technological advance in the automobile and construction industries made the long fibres less important, and the short fibres themselves gradually gave way to a very short asbestos fibre, in powder form. Of course, these changes resulted in a decline in the value of asbestos per ton.

Furthermore, the construction and automobile industries were severely affected by the Depression of 1929-1933. When their markets collapsed, the effect on the asbestos industry, already weakened by technological change, was disastrous. The price of asbestos sunk as low as 25 dollars per ton, one of the lowest levels ever experienced by the industry.

2/International competition

The Canadian asbestos industry has never met with serious competition in its principal market. Canada supplies 90% of American asbestos imports (short fibre and powder). The Americans usually import 3% or 4% of their asbestos from the Soviet Union. This figure rose exceptionally to 10% in 1936, but returned to the normal level the following year.

In the long fibre asbestos market, however, Canada's position continued to deteriorate in the period 1926-1933, due to African competition. In fact, the asbestos industry in Southern Rhodesia and the Union of South Africa enjoys many advantages which are not shared by the Canadian industry.

In the first place, the industry is largely controlled by a single company, Turner & Newall, of London. Secondly, it pays very low wages to its black workers, a factor which loses its importance if the productivity of this labour is lower. Finally, the main reason for African dominance in the long fibre asbestos market is the quality of the mineral itself. The proportion of (long) spinning fibres is greater than in Canada (30% instead of 8%). Consequently, the average value per ton is higher and can easily absorb the costs of overseas transportation. As a result, the African mines are more profitable than those in

Canada. The Canadian product becomes very expensive if it has to be transported over a great distance. The results of these advantages can be seen from the following statistics: in 1929, Canada supplied 40% of the long fibres imported by the United States; in 1938-1939, this percentage had fallen to 20%, and during the Depression had sunk as low as 10%; at the present time, Canada's share of this market is minimal.

3/Capitalization

The Asbestos Corporation was formed with two ideas in mind: first, to unite the independent producers and prevent new competitors from breaking into the field, and secondly, to consolidate the financial structure of the industry. The first aim was fully realized, but the second had to be abandoned.

To keep new producers out of the industry, the Asbestos Corporation had to acquire vast territories. In 1927, it controlled 16 asbestos mines. Each of these mines had to be bought at a high price, because most of them had a lot of capital tied up in them and suffered from overinvestment.

To mitigate the effects of this overcapitalization, the value of all these properties was reduced by half (from thirty to fifteen million dollars, of which eight million was in debentures and the rest in preferred and common shares). Even this reduction was not sufficient, and of the 16 mines owned by the company, only 5 were still active in 1927, although that year was relatively prosperous.

The real problem lay in the fact that the capitalization had not been arranged to finance a given production, but to get control of all the mines. This is why the company did not pay any dividends on its common stock, even before 1929. After this date, it did not even pay dividends on preferred shares. In 1930, the company stopped paying the interest on its mortgages.

In 1932, a decision was made to reorganize the company. A capital of $3 million replaced the issued capital of $15 million. In 1935, the company made a net profit, and by 1939, all the old obligations had been redeemed, leaving a capital made up exclusively of common shares. From this time on, the Asbestos Corporation did not have any more financial trouble. No public information is available on the financial history of the rest of the industry.

The above information, though, gives us some idea of the excessive and disorderly investment of capital in the industry between 1900 and 1926. The fact that one company was forced to reduce the value of all its holdings from $30 million to $3 million speaks volumes on the poor investment policy and the financial camouflage typical of the period.

4/The internal structure of the industry

In spite of the simplifications that it had introduced in the internal structure of the industry, the formation of the Asbestos Corporation had not eliminated all the causes of the price wars. The very close ties between certain mines and their American customers sometimes created serious disorders. In general, when an American manufacturer gained possession of an asbestos mine, he aimed at controlling the production, which henceforth passed exclusively to him. Under normal conditions, this production was thus not offered for sale on the open market. Sometimes, however, the manufacturers found themselves suddenly burdened with a surplus, which they proceeded to dump, thereby wrecking the market and doing serious harm to those producers who had remained independent.

To alleviate this situation, the Asbestos Corporation signed an agreement with three American producers (Johns-Manville, Keasbey & Mattison, and Quebec Asbestos) in 1926 to buy back all of these surpluses, but the following year Keasbey & Mattison broke the agreement. The Asbestos Corporation took the matter to court, and in 1934 the Supreme Court of the United States handed down a decision that the agreement was in violation of the antitrust laws and was consequently devoid of legal value.

Nevertheless, the Great Depression induced collaboration among the various producers who managed to survive. In 1931, for example, a uniform classification of the different varieties of asbestos was adopted. A committee was also formed to set up uniform safety regulations. This atmosphere of relative cooperation, and the fact that only six producers remained in business, explain how the asbestos companies were able to enjoy financial stability between 1929 and 1939 despite great fluctuations in the markets.

5/The producers

The internal structure of the industry has not changed much since 1926. At that time, competition had reduced the number of producers to five. In 1949, there were seven (not including the United Asbestos Corp., which had just been incorporated with independent capital and which was later—and indirectly—to carry on mining operations under Black Lake). (See Table VI.)

Table VI

List of asbestos producers in Quebec in 1949

Name	Capital	Centres of production
Asbestos Corp. Ltd.	independent	Thetford Mines (Beaver mine)
		Black Lake (Vimy and Brit. Canadian mines)
		Coleraine
Johnson's Co. Ltd.	independent	Thetford Mines
		Coleraine
Bell Asbestos Mines Ltd.	British	Thetford Mines
Canadian Johns-Manville Co. Ltd.	American	Asbestos
Nicolet Asbestos Mines Ltd.	American	St. Rémi de Tingwick
Quebec Asbestos Corp. Ltd.	American	East Broughton
Flintkote Mines Ltd.	American	Thetford Mines

Two of these companies are independent (Asbestos Corporation and Johnson's) in the sense that they have no ties with the manufacturers who are their customers. Four are owned by Americans (Johns-Manville, Nicolet Asbestos, Quebec Asbestos, and Flintkote). One is owned by the British firm of Turner & Newall through an intermediary in the United States (Bell).

It looks as though this structure will remain more or less the same in the future. The capitalization of these companies appears to be solid, and they seem to have achieved some success in bridling the savage competition which was the scourge of the industry for so many years.

Furthermore, short fibre asbestos predominates in Canada, and considerable mechanization is required to extract it. This asbestos is, however, of relatively low value compared to high-grade asbestos. These circumstances make it difficult for new producers to enter the field, as enormous sums of capital are required.

The rigid portioning out of the market offers a final obstacle to the would-be producer. This does not mean that the various companies have divided it up equally, but simply that sales patterns have become fixed and permanent. The prosperity of the Canadian industry depends almost exclusively on a small number of American customers. This situation offers all the advantages of a de facto monopoly of the short fibre asbestos market in the United States, but has the drawbacks inherent in a rigid structure of exchange. Certain companies, though, the Asbestos Corporation in particular, still have to confront a mild competition from other countries, even in the United States markets.

VI/Prosperity and increasing wages (1939-1948)

Between 1938 and 1948, the industry experienced a remarkable growth. The wartime demand for asbestos began in 1939 despite the revaluation of the Canadian dollar, which in other circumstances would have resulted in a slowdown in the industry. The demand for asbestos quickly became insatiable.

Let us examine some of the features of that prosperity, which has continued down to the present day.

1/Asbestos powder

Asbestos powder was in future to account for 65% of the total Canadian production. During our period, then, it gradually replaced not only long fibres, but short fibres as well. The latter accounted for 50% of our production before the war. Today, they make up a mere 35%.

We have already seen that this tendency towards the extraction of shorter and shorter fibres brought about a decrease in the relative value of the asbestos produced.

During the war the average price per ton declined. The full significance of this phenomenon becomes apparent if we recall that at this time the Canadian government had to impose price controls to halt the inflation that was rampant everywhere in the country.

Inflation eventually had its effects even on this apparently recalcitrant industry. Between 1946 and 1949, the average price of asbestos went from 45 to 69 dollars.

The increase in production accounts for the new prosperity of the industry in spite of the unorthodox behaviour of asbestos prices. During the war (1939-1945), production jumped from 364,000 to 467,000 tons. In the postwar period it accelerated even more, reaching 717,000 tons in 1948.[3]

In keeping with the traditions of the industry, this enormous production was absorbed by the American market, and the dependence of the asbestos mines on the U.S. economy became even greater. Since 1940, we have been selling about 85% of all our production to our neighbours to the south. Our near-monopoly in the United States offers us a security which largely compensates for the fact that asbestos powder is less profitable than long fibre asbestos.

2/The position of the Asbestos Corporation

Whatever the future may hold, it is a fact that the Canadian asbestos industry has enjoyed continual prosperity for over a decade, and yet it has been argued that the Asbestos Corporation was in a rather weak position despite this prosperity, and therefore could not grant large wage increases. This weakness was allegedly due to a number of causes.

Firstly, it was pointed out that the Asbestos Corporation had no official ties, even through its directors, to any *manufacturer of asbestos products*. As an independent producer, it was obliged to offer its asbestos on the general market, and could not count on the special market of a parent company. Moreover, the Asbestos Corporation exported a part of its production to Europe, where the competition was much more severe than in the United States, and where the additional transportation costs made this European market even harder to penetrate.

Without detailed information, it is difficult to assess this argument properly. We may, however, note that the Asbestos Corporation has one advantage: it produces an asbestos of better quality, which assures it of solid profits. In 1948, for example, its asbestos sold for 70 dollars a ton, while the average price for the industry as a whole was only 50 dollars. This no doubt explains the financial soundness of this company in 1948.

At that time, it had the King, Vimy, Beaver, and British Canadian mines in production. It had plenty of financial reserves, and its liquidity ratio was close to 4/1, which is more than adequate. The amount paid out annually in dividends had gone up slightly since 1946, and the profits—increasing almost as rapidly as sales—continued to exceed 11% of sales, which is a more than comfortable ratio for an industry of this type.

3/The workers' share

Were the workers able to obtain a fair share of this prosperity of the asbestos industry?

It is difficult to reply to this question. We know very little about most of the companies involved. The Asbestos Corporation, in fact, is the only firm that publishes adequate statistics, and it can hardly be considered as typical.

We shall, then, have to be satisfied with the statistics on the industry as a whole, published annually by the Dominion Bureau of Statistics. We do not intend to discuss the relative merit of the economic claims advanced by the union and the companies in the asbestos conflict. To explain the origins of this dispute, a more detailed study than ours would be required. As the parties involved admit, there was more than money involved.

A comparison will help us to understand how big a slice the workers took out of the asbestos pie, namely the ratio between wages and salaries on the one hand and *net* sales on the other (i.e., total sales minus the cost of containers, fuel, electricity, and various other materials). (See Table VII.)

Table VII

Wages and sales (in thousands of dollars)

Year	Sales (net) $000	Wages and salaries $000	%
1935	4,998	1,904	38
1936	7,561	2,643	35
1937	10,433	4,233	41
1938	9,705	4,024	41
1939	12,399	4,347	35
1945	19,857	6,680	34
1946	20,270	7,772	38
1947	26,192	9,165	35
1948	34,422	12,137	35

Source: Ottawa. Bureau of Statistics. Annual report on the asbestos products industry.

These percentages are revealing if one compares the fluctuations from one series of years to another. For example, the ratio of wages and salaries to sales, from 1945 to 1948, was a little more than 35% on the average; from 1935 to 1939, however, this ratio reached 38%. The workers' share in the income from asbestos sales was thus greater before the Second World War than after.

Other comparisons further our knowledge. The figures quoted in Table VIII show the major changes that occurred in the industry from 1945 to 1948; they offer additional evidence of the strange behaviour of the wage index.

Table VIII

Changes in the industry from 1946 to 1948

Changes in % from one year to the next for	*1946-45*	*1947-46*	*1948-47*	*Average*
Wages only	16	17	33	22
Number of workers	7	7	1	5
Sales (net)	2	29	31	21
"Profits"*	− 5	53	33	27
Expenditure for equipment	114	− 17	52	50
"Profits" less the expenditure for equipment	− 42	134	26	39

*The real profits are not published. The word is loosely used here to designate the surplus of net sales over the main costs of production and over taxes. It therefore includes, in addition to profits strictly speaking, depreciation and certain other general expenses (interest, insurance, etc.). Our calculations are based on the assumption that these general costs vary more or less uniformly with profits strictly speaking.

Source: Ottawa. Bureau of Statistics. Annual report on the asbestos products industry.

The chief characteristic of this four-year period is heavy capital outlay. This gives no grounds for complaint in principle, because this is the way in which an industry becomes modernized, increases its production, and becomes more competitive. Still, if the above approximations are fair, these investments seem to have been made even more to the detriment of wages than of profits. The "profits" less the expenditure for equipment increased 39% on the average each year, while wages went up 22%. The invested capital, though, becomes the property of the stockholders, not of the wage earners. If, in future, it should become mandatory for shareholders and wage earners to divide the profits (in the strict sense of the term) on the basis of the contribution made by each group to the invested capital, there is no doubt that the workers would obtain a goodly portion of these profits.

4/Conclusion

One might well ask why, in the period from 1939 to 1948, wages did not increase in proportion to the growing prosperity of the industry. There appear to be a number of reasons:

—In the first place, wages are adjusted only once a year, while prices vary from month to month and sometimes from week to week.

The workers had only one chance per year to demand a wage increase, and on that occasion other forces of resistance came into play.

—Secondly, a regular increase in profits can become a tradition in a given industry at a given time; in such a case, a powerful resistance develops to breaking with that tradition.

—Finally, companies hesitate to increase wages when they know that the unions will do everything in their power to make these increases permanent. We have already seen in the history of this industry that the companies were more inclined to raise wages when they could be sure of having little difficulty in lowering them again later on, if need be. In other words, the presence of a strong labour organization makes the employees more resistant to a decrease in wages, but at the same time hardens the resistance of management to higher pay.

The industry had once suffered from chronic instability, and this fact no doubt contributed to making management more than usually reluctant to raise wages. In spite of obvious improvements in the internal structure of the industry, it did not believe, in 1949, that it could count on a prosperity without end. The employers recalled, for example, that in 1920 they had preferred to endure a strike rather than increase wages, and that in the very next year, a slump resulted in a 30% drop in wages.

In any case, it is hard to evaluate the importance of these various economic and psychological factors in the employers' decision to resist the demands that were made prior to the strike in 1949. Moreover, such a task would carry us beyond the limits imposed on this chapter.

Bibliography for Chapter II

Periodicals:
Asbestos. A monthly review published in Philadelphia, Pa.
Canada Year Book. Ottawa: Bureau of Statistics. Published annually.
Ottawa. Bureau of Statistics. Annual report on the asbestos products industry (title varies).
Quebec. Department of Mines. Annual report on the mining industry (title varies).

Books:
Asbestos in Canada: Surveys and Forecasts. Toronto: 1950.
CIRKEL, Fritz. *Chrysotile-Asbestos, its Occurence, Exploitation, Milling, and Uses*. 2nd ed. Ottawa: Bureau of Mines, 1910.
GILLIES, E.W. *The Asbestos Industry Since 1929*. McGill University thesis. Montreal: McGill, 1941.
JONES, R.H. *Asbestos and Asbestic*. London: 1897.

Notes to Chapter II

[1]More than a royal "we" in this case! It expresses my debt to Fernand Dansereau; without the help of this friend, the chapter would still be a clumsy and shapeless draft.

[2]This phenomenon also explains the absence of local (or French Canadian) capital in the development of our asbestos resources. For many years the accumulation of private capital was thwarted by historical vicissitudes and by the social structures and lifestyles of French Canada. The greater the capital required, the less chance there was for French Canadians to become industrial entrepreneurs.

[3]In 1954, Quebec was to export about 915,000 tons, with a value of $79 million.

Chapter III

History of the Trade Union Movement in the Asbestos Industry

by Fernand Dumont

I/Introduction

Our purpose in this study is to trace the history of the asbestos labour unions prior to the conflict in 1949. While it is true that the creativity of the moment plays an important part in every event, we must recognize that every social situation is also, to a great degree, a crystallization of the past. We wish to cast some light upon the workings of those historical forces which slowly prepared the scene for the asbestos strike.

It is not easy to decide upon the arrangement of an historical account, especially when the author wants the scheme of presentation itself to serve as an attempt at explanation, and still follow the actual rhythm of events. These difficulties were aggravated in the present case by the fact that we had to describe, in one account, the evolution of three unions which, as we shall see, have often developed along different lines, but which had to grapple with so many common problems that they deserve to be considered as aspects of one historical reality. We simply wish to point out here that we have tried to take into account, at the same time, both the developments within these unions and the factors that were determining the general course of Quebec's history.

We shall primarily be concerned with the unions at Thetford, Asbestos, and East Broughton, but we shall from time to time refer briefly to the effects of their activities on the small locals in the area (Robertson and Black Lake).[1]

II/Trade unionism in the asbestos mines: 1915-1926
1/The origins: Thetford

Trade unionism did not take root in Thetford until 1915, but by that time the town had already had a brief and rather strange encounter with it. In 1909, the Fédération canadienne des travailleurs de Thetford Mines (Canadian Labour Federation of Thetford Mines) was established there. This organization was defined by the terms of its constitution as follows: "The aim of this association is to establish a cooperative store, to carry on therein a general retail business, and to do so for the benefit of the members of the Federation (par. 2); to maintain harmony and understanding between the employer and the worker (par. 3); to combat by legitimate means all difficulties that might degenerate into a strike (par. 4); to support the temperance crusade that has been started in the city of Thetford Mines (par. 5); to promote and safeguard the interests and rights of the Federation without infringing upon those of the employers and the church authorities (par. 6); to keep abreast of municipal and educational affairs, and, in these fields, to look after the interests of the Federation and of the workers in general (par. 7)." The society also proposed "to come to the aid of indigent members." A man could not join this organization if he belonged to an international union, but the first Thetford union does not seem to have been directly connected with the Catholic trade union movement, which was beginning to develop in the province at that time. Towards the end of 1909, a cooperative store was opened in Thetford under the auspices of the labour union, but by 1911 it had been sold back into private hands. The new association was dissolving. Clearly, this was only an incident, which does not seem to have had a very strong influence on the consciousness of the Thetford working class. The history of trade unionism in this city properly begins in 1915.

On the fifteenth of October of that year, Jacob Asbestos Mines granted a wage increase to some Russian workers then in its employ. For them alone, the company raised the daily wage from one dollar and a half to one dollar and sixty-five cents. The very next day, the French Canadian workers were informed of this by the Russians themselves. The Canadians then demanded a raise for themselves as well, but not principally for this reason. At the beginning of the First World War, the wages of the miners had been cut because of the uncertainty of the markets. In 1915, the situation had changed; the deliveries of asbestos were as great as before the war, and asbestos prices had returned to the same level, as everyone knew. The workers explained all this to a reporter from Le Soleil (October 19, 1915): "The workers have been employed at reduced wages since the beginning of the war, and they have suffered real hardship. They are almost all in debt. Until last Saturday, they calmly accepted their fate. They said to themselves that they would have to put up with the hard times; they realized that the war in Europe had affected their industry. . . ." The partial increase—unfair to the other employees—which the mining company awarded to the Russian workers was thus no more than the incident that triggered the strike on October 18, 1915.

As soon as they had gone out on strike, the miners of Jacob Asbestos went around in succession to the Beaver, Martin-Bennett, Bell, Johnson, and King mines. One hour later, all the miners in Thetford had left their work. A committee was immediately formed, of which the mayor and an alderman were members. "There is little hope that the measures they have taken will meet with success," as *La Presse* put it on October 19, "because the owners of the Jacob mines have declared that they do not intend to yield to the demands of their employees." Furthermore, the manager of the Jacob Asbestos Mines was regarded by the miners as the man behind the policy of wage reduction in all the mines, even in those where he had no authority.

The following is the text of the demands made through the committee to the mine managers: "1. We want the mining companies to pay us the same wages we received in the past, i.e., we want to be paid the 14 percent of wages that was withdrawn from us at the end of last summer. 2. We want the King and Johnson companies to give us complete freedom to spend our wages in the stores of our choice, and no longer force us to buy in their own stores. 3. We want all the mining companies to pay their workers on a regular basis every fifteen days. 4. When a worker is not able to finish his hour of work, we want him to be paid for the fraction of the hour he has worked if that fraction is greater than half an hour[2]." The strikers also demanded that "all the workers be rehired in the positions they held before the strike, and that the representatives of the strikers suffer no harm for the part that they have taken in this strike."

In a meeting held on October 19, the miners received the order to prevent the departure of the asbestos shipments that the companies were preparing to make. The two real leaders of the strike seem to have revealed themselves at that session. They were two foreign workers, J.R. Coupren and Nicholas Kachook, employees of the Jacob Asbestos Co., who addressed the gathering on that occasion. They had most likely been sent to Thetford by the Western Union of Miners (American Federation of Labour) to establish a union there. At least, the role they later played in the foundation of the international union would lead one to suspect so.

On October 20, the mine managers jointly replied to the workers' delegation. They stated in part: "We find that it is impossible for some of the companies to obtain a confirmation of their decisions by their head offices in so short a space of time. However, to avoid further delay in this matter, we jointly consent to your demand for an increase of fourteen percent, on condition that work in all mines begin again tomorrow."

The strike was not over. A few hours later, the Jacob Asbestos Co. refused to grant the promised fourteen percent to those workers who were making one dollar and seventy-five cents before the strike. At Robertson (a small mining centre near Thetford), the workers greeted the managers' refusal with blows. On October 22, however, the victory of labour was complete.

It appears that at the time of the strike, Coupren and Kachook suggested the idea of a labour union; it was actually founded a few days after the strike by a special representative from Montreal, who was sent by the Trades and Labour Congress. The Union catholique ouvrière des mineurs (Catholic Miners' Labour Union) was founded about the same time.[3] A struggle at once began between the two infant unions.

Narcisse Arcand, who seems to have been the chief promoter of the international union in Thetford, held a meeting on November 17 at which he expressed harsh criticism of the priests who had arrived to take charge of the Catholic union. Some of the methods used by the leaders of the Catholic organization had nothing to recommend them, either. On December 13, the chaplain of the Catholic union wrote to Abbé Fortin: " . . . In the above-mentioned mine [the King mine] and the Bell mine we have a fortress of the international union. I assure you that these people [the members of the international union] are not going to be won over easily. I doubt that we will be able to succeed by direct methods. If only the management of these mines would help us out; if we act discreetly, I have hopes that we will win out against them. . . ."[4]

In early December 1915, the rumour of a new strike began to circulate: the international union was going to start another dispute with management on January 18, to obtain a wage of two and a half dollars per day for day laborers. The chaplain of the Catholic union thereupon decided to take advantage of this opportunity to destroy the rival organization. In a letter of December 15 to Abbé Fortin, he wrote: " . . . A committee is going to visit the mine managers, to explain the situation to them and to suggest that they help us, seeing that we are ready to help them. The international union wants to obtain the recognition of management and then take charge of the situation. As you see, it is trying to achieve this by immediate recourse to violence. I intend to suggest that we get rid of the most influential members of the international union when work starts again after the holidays. If people listen to me, here is how we will go about it: the employers will lay these men off until the following day on the pretext that they do not need them; the next day they will lay them off again, and so on, but without telling them that the purpose of all this is to get rid of them. In this way, we will not arouse the anger of the mob. . . . '' The chaplain soon devised a yet more subtle tactic. In his letter of the sixteenth, he says to the employers that he had also ''decided to send a petition via the council, demanding an increase in wages of 25 cents per day to counteract the scheme of the international union, which is going to ask for a raise of 75 cents per day or a wage of $2.50 for common day laborers. In this petition we will also ask those employers who have not already done so to come out openly in favour of us . . . I will pay a visit to the employers in the next few days to discuss these very matters. . . .''

That was not all. The chaplain did not hesitate to supply strike-breakers to the employers in the small strike which occurred spontaneously at the Jacob mine on February 7, 1916. On his initiative, the Catholic union changed itself into a union of scabs. On February 17, the chaplain wrote to Abbé Maxime Fortin: '' . . . A strike of Russians at the Jacob mine. The manager phones to ask me for 25 to 30 men. I promise him to get right on it tomorrow. I telephoned to Robertson tonight. I hope to have several men from there for tomorrow. I will round up the others here, wherever I can find them. . . .''

The employers did not pass up the opportunity that was so benevolently offered them. Father Houle, a Thetford parish priest, could write in a letter of February 16, 1916: '' . . . This morning two strikers managed to get hired on at another mine—they were not recognized—they are going to be fired at noon. At the Jacob mine —the Russian stronghold—they decided to get rid of them quietly. Forty have been dismissed in the last fifteen days, which is not bad! . . .''

On March 20, the managers put up notices in all the mines announcing a wage increase of 25 cents, effective April 1. A few days before, the wages had been raised similarly at Black Lake and at Robertson.

Though the leaders of the international union did not initiate the strike they had threatened to call in January, they did not abandon the idea. On June 13, 1916, the executive sent a proposed wage scale to the mine managers and demanded that the international union be recognized by the employers. The chaplain of the Catholic union wrote, on June 14: '' . . . Whatever the defections from our ranks, I am sure our members will accept our guidance and remain calm despite the agitation of their fellow workers. At this moment, three thirty, the employers are holding a meeting, and I am waiting to hear the results. I shall go to see them with President Rousseau and we will arrange things for the best. It's going to be interesting. . . .'' On the evening of the fifteenth, at a meeting held by the international union, the speakers accused the clergy of trying to divide the workers.

The Catholic union soon brought its tactics out into the open. At a meeting on June 18, it passed a resolution which sanctioned this very division of the forces of labour. The text of the resolution had been prepared by the union chaplain and had earlier been accepted by the executive council at its meeting of June 14. We quote this document here in full, because it offers a synthesis of the ideology which inspired the foundation of the Catholic union in Thetford:

"Whereas rumours have been circulating for several days to the effect that work will soon be stopped in the mines in the hope of obtaining another wage increase;

"whereas certain information sent to the newspapers is likely to give the public the impression that the Catholic Labour Union of Thetford Mines is ready to join forces with the international union in an effort to make trouble for the employers and to extort another wage increase from them;

"whereas we have grounds for believing that the actions undertaken by the international union will have unfavourable consequences for the working class of Thetford Mines and for the employers and other classes of citizens in our town;

"whereas the members of the Catholic Labour Union of Thetford Mines deplore and disapprove of the actions and undertakings of the sowers of discord who spread confusion among the workers;

"whereas the Catholic Labour Union has always been concerned with the improvement of wages and working conditions, the members of this council declare that they are satisfied with the present condition of the workers and express their gratitude to the employers for what they have already done for the workers.

"It is resolved that the Council use all its influence to support the employers in these difficulties; that it ask the employers to protect the members of the Catholic Labour Union in return; and that the employers offer these workers an adequate recompense for their efforts on behalf of management. Adopted unanimously."

The strike had not yet been declared at this time. The Catholic union tried to arrange a meeting with the employers, who only agreed to it on July 27. On the first of August, representatives of the Catholic union met Mr. Larue, a Quebec City lawyer acting for the employers, and requested a raise of fifty cents per day for all workers. The next day, the employers offered twenty-five cents for the men who worked by the day. The mine managers also promised, within ten days, to make a special agreement with each man who was working by the month or on contract.

On August 3, 1916, the international union started a strike in all the mines, except at the Martin-Bennett mine, where most of the employees belonged to the Catholic union. Mr. Bennett himself soon had the mine shut down to avoid any complications. The international union asked the Department of Labour to set up an arbitration board, but it refused on the grounds that it would have to appoint a board for each of the five companies involved. The employers refused to take part in any negotiations, and the strike soon degenerated into a lockout. The Catholic union held a meeting at which it formulated a request that the mines be opened. The international union had demanded an inquiry into the working conditions in the asbestos industry; this request was turned down. The parish priest of Thetford, in a letter to the Minister of Labour, had asked that the inquiry not be made.[5]

At a meeting on August 17, the miners decided to accept the employers' offer of twenty-five cents, on condition that all the miners be rehired without discrimination. The employers refused to accept this condition. The reporter for *Le Soleil* (August 17) justified their actions in these terms: "When the strike was declared, they paid everyone off and shut down the mines because of the strike. At the present time, they consider that they have nobody in their hire, in short that they have no employees. They want to exercise their right to rehire whomever they please. By this they mean that they intend to rehire the great majority of the strikers, but they do not feel obliged to rehire the fomenters of the strike in their old positions. In the employers' opinion, these strike leaders have devoted the last several years to sowing discord in the mines, to stirring up the workers against their employers, to vilifying and abusing the latter, and to undermining every principle of authority in the mines. . . ."

The miners were forced to yield all along the line. On August 25, 1916, the two parties signed the following document, which ended the lockout and sealed the doom of the union:

"1. An increase of two cents and a half per hour is granted to the employees, with the exception of those who work on contract and those who are paid by the month;

"2. Whereas, for the latter group, working conditions differ from one mine to another, separate agreements will be concluded with them within ten days;

"3. The above wages will be paid as long as the present market conditions prevail, and as long as the employees' work continues to be satisfactory;

"4. This agreement is made with the employees individually, without regard to the unions to which they belong, and it shall be signed by two employees from each mine on behalf of all the employees of said mines;

"5. The employees who are rehired promise to do their best to make their work as productive and efficient as possible, to the satisfaction of their employers;

"6. The mines will reopen on Thursday, August 24 instant."

The document is signed by two representatives of the workers in each mine, by Maître (Lawyer) J. Lane on behalf of all the proprietors of the mines at Thetford, and by C.A. Blanchet, of Ottawa, representing the federal minister of labour.

From then on, the trade union movement went steadily downhill. The divisions among the workers became more pronounced; the two unions lingered on, always at odds with one another. In July 1919, the Catholic union was officially recognized at the Bennett mine, but this was hardly a real victory for the trade union movement. It seems that the union won this privileged position only because Mr. Bennett was a Catholic (as the other mine managers were not). In October 1920, there was a strike at the King and Beaver mines which lasted for five weeks, but it also ended in failure. By the end of 1920, the asbestos industry had already been affected by the wave of unemployment that followed the First World War. Two mines shut down in the course of the winter, and a third stopped production in November 1921.

In the ensuing years, the trade union idea faded from the consciousness of the miners. The rivalry of the unions was not the only cause of this; the impotence of labour organizations in the face of rising unemployment was undoubtedly an even more important factor. The number of dues-paying members of the Catholic union decreased in a few years from 1,500 to 100. In 1921, union meetings were attended by between sixty and one hundred members.

The Canadian and Catholic Confederation of Labour was founded at the Hull convention of 1921. The Thetford union joined the Confederation at once; though still in existence at this time, it no longer had a real role to play. The many conflicts which arose in the following years, as a response to the Depression, were spontaneous mass movements in which the union, as such, had no part at all. We shall consequently describe only the highlights of the period.

At the end of November 1921, the Asbestos Corporation[6] announced to its workers that it was going to shut down its operations on the first of December. A few days before the appointed date, a group of miners accompanied by fifty unemployed men went to the Beaver mine and invited the workers there to walk off the job. In the afternoon, a hundred miners went to see the general manager of the Asbestos Corporation and ordered him to keep the Beaver mine open day and night for six days a week or get out of town forthwith. They even tried to make him sign a pledge at the City Hall, where they wound up dragging him. Since he was unable to do anything without "orders from Montreal," he was given a respite. The next day, the same group paid a visit to the other managers and handed them a similar ultimatum. A few days later, the employers agreed to open the mines for four days per week.

In April 1923, the workers at the King and Beaver mines resorted to force in an even more spectacular way. The manager of these mines, C.H. McNutt, had always been harsh in the treatment of his workers. When he fired two miners of long standing with the company, he provoked a strong response. On April 23, the workers seized the manager, took him to the railway station, and advised him never to return to Thetford. While awaiting the arrival of the new manager, they went out on strike. On the 25th, however, Mr. McNutt returned with a bodyguard of forty private detectives. McNutt and his men were subjected to a regular siege of the company offices, to which they had fled. They left for Montreal again that very evening, escorted by an unsympathetic crowd. The strike continued until April 30. Following some difficult negotiations, the company agreed to replace McNutt as manager.

During this whole period, the Catholic union restricted itself to finding work for some of its members. Unemployment was gradually increasing. In Novemebr 1926, the union stopped holding meetings and collecting dues, and the accumulated funds were divided up among the regular members. The first Catholic union of Thetford miners was dead and gone.

2/Asbestos: off to a bad start

The Catholic union at Asbestos appears to have come into being under the aegis of the Thetford organization. In any case, the founders' meeting of October 12, 1919, was addressed by two representatives from Thetford. The minutes of this first meeting report as follows: ". . . The workers at the asbestos mine in the town of Asbestos were seeking ways to improve their lot and to put an end to the many things that had given rise to complaints. Several people had been unjustly treated, and the situation was such that some workers, both tenants and property owners, had been forced to leave the parish because they were unable to find work. They made all kinds of efforts, and finally obtained the services of Abbé Maxime Fortin, the priest appointed in the Archdiocese of Quebec . . . Abbé Maxime Fortin, greeted by applause from the assembly, rose to speak of the good works performed by Catholic labour unions in the Province of Quebec over the past few

years. He added that the miners at Asbestos would have everything to
gain from the establishment of a local Catholic labour union. Turning
to the subject of international labour unions, he clearly explained their
purpose, namely the ruination of the employers, which in turn makes
paupers of the worker and his family. . . .'' That very day, three
hundred people joined the new union.

The union asked for a wage increase almost at once. A motion put
to the meeting on February 1, 1920, demanded that ''wages be
equalized and then raised by 20%.'' At a subsequent special meeting,
the members passed a motion which emphasized the fact that wages
had not been increased for a long time, while the cost of living had
gone up considerably. Towards the end of February, the Johns-
Manville Company, which had operations at Asbestos, granted its
employees a small raise in pay. In practice, not everyone received the
increase, and the many complaints about this led the union to submit a
new request. At a meeting of May 23, 1920, the miners adopted a
resolution that ''the wages should be raised by five cents per hour or
50 cents per day, over and above the increase which is to take effect on
May 24, 1920; and that the said mining company, to remedy the
present financial distress of the workers and to maintain the good
relations which ought to exist between employers and employees, take
this demand into serious consideration, and reply to it in the near
future in the way that we expect.'' The Company put off making an
answer to this, and finally the whole subject was dropped. The union,
which seems to have been created under the stimulus of propaganda
from outside, had already begun to sink into a torpor. The minutes of
its meetings suggest listless gatherings where all the resolutions, without exception, were devoid of interest and without real importance for
an authentic labour movement. Everything about them smacks of
artificiality. Meetings were also held less and less frequently. In 1925,
as much as seven months went by between one meeting and another.
At the meeting of November 1, 1925, and again on March 7, 1926, the
union formulated a request for help from the chaplain of the diocese,
which appears to have been ignored. At the meeting of October 3,
1926, a temporary committee of four members was struck to manage
the affairs of the union, which was by now in the doldrums. The
organization continued to exist, but as a mere shadow. The defects of
this first union at Asbestos seem to have been congenital.

III/The Depression and the labour situation. Renaissance of the unions (1929-1936)

Consumed by internal strife, founded not upon the resources of the
community but upon an imported ideology, trade unionism had

aborted in the asbestos region. One should not, however, minimize the effects of the Crash of 1929 on developments in the trade union movement. It was a time, unquestionably, of terrible trial. The unions were unable to alleviate conditions by any radical means. There was, of course, no longer any question of asking for higher wages, and so one of the major aims of the labour struggle was lost to view for years.

1/Thetford: from the Cercle ouvrier (Workers' Study Group) to the union

In 1929, there were nearly twelve hundred unemployed miners at Thetford. Abbé Pierre Gravel, who at that time was the assistant parish priest at St. Alphonse de Thetford, has told us how everyone there was violently opposed to any form of labour union. The miners were convinced that they had been duped by both the Catholic and the international unions. The parish priests themselves, according to Abbé Gravel, wanted no more to do with trade unionism.

In 1931, Abbé Gravel founded two study groups (cercles d'étude). He would have preferred to revive the old union, but the workers and the parish priest were firmly opposed to this. He regarded these groups, in any case, as stepping stones to the creation of a new union. In this he was perfectly correct. A brief analysis of their ideology is thus of some importance if we wish to understand the nature of the union which came into existence a few years later.

Abbé Gravel first founded the Pius XI Study Group. It was open to workers, foremen, merchants, and the employees of small businesses alike. Probably it was intended as a device for breaking down the barriers between the classes. There is a résumé, in the minutes of the meetings, of a speech given by the chaplain, which clearly illustrates the nature of the association: "Abbé Gravel explained the purpose of this social study group, which is to examine all the issues of the day, the problems and projects affecting the public welfare, in the light of the common interests of our people; to consider these matters from the particular point of view of the various groups among us; to arrive at a practical conclusion; and then to work at disseminating this scheme among our people; and in some circumstances, to act as intermediaries or promoters for parties to a dispute. ..." Further on, the résumé continues: "The chaplain then read the material which he had prepared for this meeting, a presentation of the reasons justifying the formation of this study group, which aims at the education of the people and the rectification of certain ideas. The group will work especially to stem the tide of communism which threatens our country, and to show us how imminent this danger is." The agenda of these meetings was almost always the same. The chaplain would begin by reading a few pages from an encyclical or from a book on the social role of the Church.[7] One of the members would then give a résumé of current events, and lastly a "keynote address" would be presented, usually by one of the local professional people. The very titles of these short papers have a certain zest: "Social Consciousness," "Family Allowances," "Feminism," "Carbonated Water Factories," "The Trappists," "Common Decency," etc. The study group also concerned itself with problems closer to home. For example, it made many attempts to establish new industries in Thetford, since its members saw this as the great way of counteracting the effects of the Depression. Another scheme was to send settlers to Abitibi; at that time this was regarded almost everywhere in the province as the great cure for unemployment. Finally, the study group was constantly getting mixed up in municipal affairs. Above all, the struggle against communism was the great preoccupation, under the influence of the chaplain no doubt.

The Workers' Study Group, founded a few months later, was organized along similar lines. In principle, it was open only to workers, but professional people frequently came to meetings to give the "keynote address." Some of the topics treated by the workers or by their guests were: "Trusts," "Albert de Mun," "Teeth," "Safety in the Home," "The Collective Agreement" . . . At the end of each meeting, Abbé Gravel, who had already given his usual reading at the beginning, would deliver a speech on unemployment, communism, the eight-hour day, wages, the Workmen's Compensation Act, etc. In August 1932, J.P. Wiser, a superintendent of the Asbestos Corporation, came to a meeting of the study group and answered questions asked by the workers.

In August 1934, the provincial Minister of Labour, Mr. Arcand, was invited by the Workers' Study Group to give a lecture at Thetford. In his speech, Mr. Arcand suggested that the workers should form a union and ask the employers for a collective agreement. "The government will force them to accept" are his alleged words on this occasion. We shall see later on what became of these promises.

The two study groups undoubtedly played an important part in the renaissance of trade unionism at Thetford. As in 1915, inspiration came from on high. The minutes of the meetings reflect the ideas that were current in French Canada at the time. Still, the groups' efforts were often directly concerned with the community: the problems of Thetford, the effects of the Depression on the community, and municipal affairs were a regular part of the agenda, and the workers themselves often tried to formulate the issues.

Like the union of 1915, the Workers' Study Group was paternalistic. Apart from small concrete problems, everything was referred to the chaplain, who had assured himself of this role. Paragraph VI of the constitution of this study group reads as follows: "The chaplain-*director* is appointed by the proper religious authority; his function is to assure the maintenance of moral discipline by the members, and he is *exclusively* responsible for the religious, intellectual, and moral guidance of the Study Group...."[8] This paternalism was less pronounced than in the union of 1915, however, where there had been little concern with allowing the workers to think for themselves, or even with exposing them to ideas. The chaplain there did everyone's thinking for him and made decisions according to his lights. In the Workers' Study Group, some effort was made to provide the workers with intellectual nourishment; it had, at least, reached the level of indoctrination.

A Catholic union was officially founded at the meeting of April 28, 1935; it plainly represents an extension of the Workers' Study Group. The executive was maintained from one organization to the other by a simple motion. The agenda of the meetings remained largely the same: the "keynote address" occurs less frequently, and the chaplain comes more and more to dominate the speaker's platform... and the minutes. He continues, in fact, to provide the real leadership of the organization.

2/Renewal at Asbestos

The union at Asbestos had been vegetating since 1926. Meetings were held less and less frequently. The establishment of a study group was discussed at a meeting of October 12, 1930, but it seems that nothing came of it. The union saw its membership gradually melt away. On November 26, 1933, there were only twenty-nine paid-up members. The rot did not stop short of the ideas, either; there was, it seems, nobody around to play the intellectual mentor for the union. The minutes of 1933 report that the president "spoke from the heart about the need for a strong and active union here at Asbestos, if we want to be victorious in our defence of Labour against one of its worst enemies: communism. He went on to list some of the advantages of having the union in case of some grievance at work, etc...." Some members appear to have been alarmed at this decline of the union. At the meeting of January 28, 1934, there was "a discussion about the possibilities of reactivating the union. It was finally decided to take this matter into consideration, and it will be brought up at each subsequent meeting until a decision is taken...." Towards the end of 1935, the union did not even bother to have an election. By an ordinary motion, all the members of the executive were retained in their positions.

This puppet union no longer had the slightest influence on the miners. In reading over the minutes of its meetings, one cannot help thinking of some little club where a few village locals, punctilious devotees of the fine phrase, get together occasionally for a quiet evening of chat. At Asbestos, there was no movement similar to the study groups at Thetford, though Abbé Gravel frequently came to town and held workers' meetings at which he must have delivered speeches like those he usually gave at the end of each meeting of the Workers' Study Group in Thetford. He continued this practice until the parish priest of Asbestos, who was violently opposed to trade unionism, rather bluntly told him to stay home.

The coming revival of union activity was already in the wind in 1935. We have seen that at Thetford, this revival was the logical extension of the Workers' Study Group; there was a smooth transition from one organization to the other. At Asbestos, on the other hand, trade unionism came awake with a start. At the beginning of 1936, according to the minutes, there was a "great purge." The new chaplain, at the behest of the Sherbrooke Central Labour Council (of the Catholic unions), went about his task in a rather draconian manner: he appointed a new council without even asking for the resignations of the old one. At the meeting of January 26, 1936, the minutes inform us that "Chaplain Aubert... made a fine speech thanking the audience for appearing in such large numbers and for being so well behaved... [he] also read a fine speech by Chaplain Camirand of Sherbrooke on the Catholic trade union, which had been published in an annual. Chaplain Aubert also stated that there were some bad apples in our union and that a purge was needed at all costs, because these bad apples had spread a lot of rottenness about in the past, and unless some changes were made, they would do us more harm in the future. He mentioned that at the next meeting of the executive, a committee of inquiry would be struck...."[9]

Without any authorization, Abbé Aubert proceeded to get in touch with the authorities of the Company. The minutes of the meeting of February 10 have this account of that interview: " ... He spoke to us of a meeting he had had with the manager, Mr. Shoemaker, in which he had been well received and had made many promises. Mr. Shoemaker had said that he would have to wait and see if Abbé Aubert was sincere in his promises, but he invited him to come and visit him often. He said that he was willing to cooperate with the union, but he would not put up with meetings of workers on company property during working hours, assembling and discussing matters whenever they felt like it. Mr. Aubert said that the thing he really deplored was that hundreds of men were obliged to work on Sunday, when most of the union meetings were held on that day. He said that there was certainly ill will on the part of the Company, which was mainly concerned with the protection of its financial interests. He added that if we had any life in us, now was the time to get together and demand our rights, that 18 or 23 cents an hour wasn't enough for the head of a family. . . ."

3/A new union: East Broughton. The establishment of a Federation

In March 1936, a union was founded at East Broughton. This area had never had a labour organization. Before this time, the union members of the East Broughton mine belonged to the Thetford union as associate members. In 1936, there were enough of them to create a union of their own. The executive had scarcely been appointed when the manager, Mr. Spafford, fired all its members. In May, some members of the union had an interview with the manager in which they asked him not to dismiss a worker because he belonged to the union. In a letter to Lauréat Morency, Aimé Nadeau—one of the first union leaders at East Broughton—described this incident as follows: " . . . At the time set for the interview, the foremen, acting in concert with the manager, brought all work to a standstill with no further explanation, and the word spread that the union had had the mine shut down. You know how it is, it's the only industry that gives a whole population the chance at some kind of a living. Most people were quick to put the blame on the union. Three days later, the mine started up again, after a meeting with a mediator, without another word from the workers. Still, this lost time was always looked on as the union's fault. . . ." We shall later see that Mr. Spafford had other tricks up his sleeve.

At a meeting held on April 19, 1936, the Fédération nationale des syndicats de l'amiante (National Catholic Federation of Asbestos Employees of the Province of Quebec) was founded,[10] grouping the unions of Asbestos, Thetford, and East Broughton. The elected officers of this federation immediately took steps to obtain an interview with the Minister of Labour and with the three provincial Members of Parliament from the area. It was even proposed that a brief be prepared which would list the major grievances of the mine workers and would also contain a suggested scale of wages.

In the asbestos region as in the province as a whole, a new era was beginning for Catholic trade unionism.

IV/Developments from 1936 to 1942
1/At Thetford
Immediately after its revival, the Thetford union made efforts to ob-

tain a collective agreement. At the meeting of July 7, 1935, it passed a
proposed wage scale, which was to be discussed at a meeting of the
Minister of Labour and union and company representatives at the
provincial department. This meeting took place on September 11. In
spite of the promises made by Mr. Arcand, the companies refused to
make a decision in the matter and the government could do nothing.
Mr. Taschereau, who was Prime Minister of Quebec at the time, was
present at the meeting. He was clearly not well disposed towards the
workers.

At this moment, Abbé Gravel was recalled from Thetford. At the
meeting of December 22, 1935, "the entire assembly" recommended
"that a protest be lodged against the decision of His Eminence the
Cardinal." This happened at the very time when the new union, years
in the planning, was proving to be something of a failure from the
outset.

The next year, the union again approached the Department of
Labour. In September 1936, its leaders met with the provincial Members of Parliament for the area. Tancrède Labbé, MPP for Mégantic,
and Albert Goudreau, MPP for Richmond. According to the minutes
of the meeting, both of them "stated that they were prepared to support the demands of the asbestos union. . . ." In October, the leaders
of the new Federation met with the Minister of Labour (of the Duplessis government, which had just been elected), and discussed a wage
scale, as well as the main grievances of the workers throughout the
asbestos region. The brief in preparation was also mentioned. Written
by Abbé Campagna, the new chaplain, it was actually delivered to the
department in November. A reply was slow in coming. At the meeting
of December 6, "it was proposed that the secretary be authorized to
write to the Department of Labour, to ask it to speed up the process of
obtaining a collective agreement for the asbestos workers. . . ." The
brief was also sent to the federal government in Ottawa. The Prime
Minister, the Minister of Labour, and the Minister of Justice sent their
congratulations and promised their support. In January 1937, meetings
were held of the managers, the chaplain of the union, and the representatives of the provincial department. They did not produce any immediate results.

In spite of all this, here is what *La Presse* reported on March 27,
1937, under the title "The Conditions of the Asbestos Workers":
"The lot of the asbestos worker is continually improving in our province, thanks to steps taken by the Hon. William Tremblay, Minister
of Labour,[11] and to the goodwill of the companies who control this
vital Quebec industry. The Johns-Manville Co. has recently signed a
collective agreement with the Syndicat catholique des ouvriers en

amiante (National Catholic Union of Asbestos Employees). The Company has granted a wage increase of 25% to 30%. The basic hourly wage is now 33 and a half cents. The Minister of Labour has also been informed by Mr. J.G. Ross of the Asbestos Corporation, which controls five of the most important asbestos mines in the province, that this company has just recently put a new policy into effect. Its mines will now be operated by three shifts working eight hours each. The basic hourly wage paid by the Company has been increased by five and a half cents, for both surface and underground workers. The basic hourly rate is thus now uniform throughout the Asbestos Corporation. This new policy means not only that the current wages have been considerably increased, but also that many unemployed people will be able to find work, because the Company is increasing its number of shifts. In his letter to the Hon. Tremblay, Mr. Ross says: 'The Company greatly appreciates your cooperative attitude, and the employees appear to be very pleased with the present conditions and wages. . . .' ''

The asbestos unions quickly made indignant protests to the Department. Gérard Picard, at that time a Quebec City journalist and Secretary of the C.C.C.L., voiced the unions' point of view in *L'Action catholique* of March 30, 1937: '' . . . Thus, the trade unions in the asbestos industry have been utterly useless, and the Department of Labour, now a propaganda bureau for the Minister himself and the employers who oppose unionism, will henceforth be the buffer organization whose good works will bring about a renewal of society in our province. . . The Hon. Minister, member of a National Union cabinet devoted to social renewal, has deemed that the trade unions could in fact only spoil things by expressing their opinion in the matter . . . The official statement by the Department of Labour might have left it to others to decide how much credit the Minister of Labour and the employers deserve for the improvements in the condition of the asbestos workers. It might also have pointed out that the wage increase announced by the Asbestos Corporation applies to the Vimy Ridge mine at Coleraine and the British Columbia mine at Black Lake, but not to the mines at Thetford. The official statement could also have added that the eight-hour day will go into effect in the shops and not in the mines. . . .''

In June 1937, the leaders of the Thetford union were able to meet with the officers of the companies and to submit the wage scale that had been worked out by the union. The companies refused to deal with the labour organization. In July, the Minister of Labour asked for time to settle the matter with the managers. The companies soon granted a wage increase (less than that which had been demanded): two cents as of July, and two cents more as of October. The union members decided to accept the offer, and the agreement was signed. In this way the union became recognized by the companies. But its success was only temporary. At a meeting on September 19, the union members of Thetford complained "about the raise of two cents per hour, which some workers have not received, especially the cleaners at the Asbestos Corporation, who have been given an increase of only one cent." Towards the end of 1937, when negotiations were taking place to renew the contract, some companies tried to deal directly with the "works committees"; they were trying to get rid of the unions by this means, and thus they made a mockery of the recognition which they had granted the union the previous year.

In November, the miners of Thetford decided to seek a new contract for 1938, which would create a basic rate of 40 cents an hour for the first six months and 42 cents for the second. In January 1938, the company offered to pay a basic rate of 40 cents for the entire coming year. At a meeting on January 9, the union chaplain observed that "if the union refuses to sign the new contract as drawn up by the management, in other words 40 cents as the base rate for the year, we shall have to resort to the Fair Wage Board. From the information that we have received, it seems that the Board's decision would be much less favourable than the contract. . . ." The companies were still able to dictate their terms, and the union was obliged to accept.

The membership of the union was already shrinking appreciably. As early as January 1938, this problem was discussed at nearly all the meetings, sometimes at great length. The contract for 1939 was obtained only after long, hard negotiating. The workers requested, among other things, that the base rate be maintained, that wages be adjusted in all the mines, and that the companies give one week of paid vacation per year. On May 13, representatives of the union and of the Asbestos Corporation met at the Department of Labour. A slight wage increase was obtained from the company, which refused a further request for a bonus. At the end of 1939, it was the companies' turn, following a meeting, to propose a wage scale. At a meeting of the union on December 24, "the president of the union explained why the wage rates in this scale were much lower than the actual wages paid in almost every job category. He said that the wage scale was designed for all the mines, and had thus been based on the lowest rate in each case. The officers, however, were assured that no job category would suffer a pay cut in any mine." At the same meeting, the workers asked for an increase of five cents. The employers later offered a raise of three cents, and this proposal was finally accepted by the miners after lengthy discussions. The contract for 1941 had the same base rates as the previous year, with a provision for read-justments as of January 1, 1941. At the end of this year, the union executive drew up a new wage scale, but soon came to the conclusion that it would be impossible to incorporate it in the contract for the coming year.

The National War Labour Board was soon to enter the picture. War measures were enacted which gave the federal government jurisdiction over some aspects of industrial relations.

2/At Asbestos

We have seen that at a union meeting in Asbestos, the chaplain had advised the workers to ask for a wage increase. In March 1936, Abbé Aubert and two other officers of the union were authorized to ask Shoemaker, the manager, to raise wages and put an end to Sunday work. By the end of August, nothing had been done. In September, Abbé Aubert returned from an interview with Shoemaker to report the good news: a salary increase was in the offing. In November, wages were still the same as before, and the workers began to talk of striking. The next month, Shoemaker and the representatives of the union at Asbestos were present at the meeting held by the Minister of Labour which we discussed above, along with management and labour representatives from Thetford. At the union meeting of December 20, MPP Goudreau was asked about this particular meeting. He reported the comments made by the Minister after it: "He said that the managers seemed ready to cooperate with the government and the workers, except for our own Mr. Shoemaker, who refused to compromise himself in any way. Mr. Shoemaker would not recognize the Federation of Asbestos Employees in any way...." At this meeting, Mr. Shoemaker had also said "that he would be happy to see the works committee reorganized with some competent people in it, for as far as he was concerned the members of the old committee did not have the intelligence to be able to negotiate with him."

The Deputy Minister called upon the union to form a new "works committee." The miners, allowing themselves to be humiliated in this way, appointed new members. In January, another interview took place in Quebec City, and on this occasion the Deputy Minister is reported to have said: "This will be the last trip." It seems that the Johns-Manville manager promised nothing at this new meeting.

The miners were tired of waiting, and went on strike on January 22. Mr. Shoemaker was soon run out of town by the workers in circumstances not unlike those we have described in connection with Mr. McNutt. The union had nothing to do with the strike. At a meeting held on the night of January 23, "the president said that he was surprised that the strike had broken out so quickly. He added that the asbestos union, though it had not been informed of the strike, would still be willing to take charge of it if the strikers so desired.'' The strikers met the next evening and unanimously passed a motion authorizing the union to act as intermediary between the workers and the Company. At a meeting on the 28th, the officers of the union were given the power to sign an agreement which would be binding upon all the workers. The union thus succeeded in taking charge of the strike, which was no mean victory. At the meeting of February 14, 435 miners asked to be admitted as new members. Mr. Sherry, who succeeded Mr. Shoemaker as manager, proved to be more amenable, and a collective agreement was signed in March 1937. In December 1937, the contract for 1938 was also arrived at without any difficulty.

Bills 19 and 20, passed at the provincial session of 1938, had their repercussions at Asbestos. This particular incident is well worth telling. On the whole, the miners strongly disapproved of these bills, as did almost all the workers in the province.[12] At the union meeting of March 27, 1938, MPP Goudreau (who, it seems, often invited himself to these gatherings) made a defence of the government policy. The minutes of the meeting state: ''Mr. Goudreau declared that the ministers, before submitting bills for a first reading, consult with the religious authorities.'' Furthermore, ''The chaplain . . . called upon the workers to have confidence in their elected representatives, and not to believe the newspapers, which for the most part are full of lies.'' Another orator added that ''the present laws are based upon the encyclicals, and the criticism we are now hearing is completely unjustified.''

In December 1938, the contract was renewed for the following year.

In February 1940, a Canadian affiliate of the American Federation of Labour tried to set up a union at Asbestos. Its organizers called a meeting for the 18th. Some seven hundred workers attended, but at a prearranged signal from the president of the Catholic union, the majority of them quit the hall, leaving the speakers of the American Federation with an audience of twenty. International unionism did not put in a second appearance at Asbestos.

When the collective agreement came up for renewal in December, the union asked for an increase of three cents per hour. The Company refused, but offered to raise the rates for some job categories. The employers' terms were accepted and the contract was signed. In June of 1941, however, there were further discussions concerning the rise in the cost of living. At the meeting of June 1, ''whereas taxes and the prices of goods have gone up considerably in the last few months; and whereas, in addition to its usual orders, the Company has several war contracts, it was proposed that the union ask for a bonus equivalent to the increase in the cost of living; this bonus should be the same for everyone. . . .'' On the other hand, the Company demanded the following: no wage increases for 1942 and amendment of the contract to eliminate the bonuses corresponding to the 15% increase in the cost of living. At the union meeting of July 27, it was proposed "that the assembly authorize the union executive to make amendments to the collective agreement between the Johns-Manville Co. and the Union of Asbestos Employees which will bring into effect the system of cost of living bonuses. . . ." The contracts for 1942 and 1943 were signed, but the miners did not receive the wage increases they had asked for.

The National War Labour Board was soon to intervene at Asbestos as well.

3/The disappearance of the East Broughton union
We have already described the difficult beginnings of the union that was founded at East Broughton in 1936. The conciliator appointed by the provincial Department of Labour intervened, but to little avail. As early as June 17, Abbé Campagna wrote a letter to the Deputy Minister of Labour, in which he stated that the company was not upholding the agreement that had recently been made. He said in particular: ". . . The foremen, and even the head foreman who was given a stern warning by Mr. Gosselin [the conciliator], as well as the non-unionized workers, are continually engaged in harassing the union workers at the mine. The unionized workers represent approximately 80% of the workers. On Monday, June 15 of this week, a union worker and head of a family was dismissed for no reason, and was replaced by a boy who did not belong to the union. The foreman of the department told the man he fired that he had to do this to please somebody . . . The other union workers, especially the members of the executive, are frankly being told that they can expect the same treatment. . . ."[13]

In these somewhat trying circumstances, the officials of the Federation persuaded the members of the East Broughton union not to undertake any further negotiations with the mining company. At Thetford, a collective agreement was about to be signed, and the Federation was convinced that this contract could be extended to include the miners of East Broughton by governmental decree, in virtue of the Judicial Extension of Collective Agreements Act. This project did not materialize, and the unionists of East Broughton felt that they had been duped.

In December 1937, the union obtained an interview with the manager, who gave every appearance of goodwill. Negotiations were at once begun to arrive at a collective agreement, but the workers soon realized that the management had not changed its tactics. In January 1938, the company closed the mine, and at the beginning of February called a meeting of its employees. Let us listen to the words of a worker from the area:[14] "Dr. Cliche was chairman of this meeting, at which a vote was to be taken. The chairman began by saying that he had accepted this role at the request of Mr. Hill, who was representing the company in the absence of the manager. Mr. Hill then took the floor and said to the doctor: 'Excuse me, Doctor, you are quite wrong to say that; I do not represent the company, nor is it the company which is asking for a vote, but a group of unemployed workers.' The chairman then hastened to retract his remarks, but he still made it clear to the workers that if they voted in favour of the company, work at the mine would start again at once, but if they did not vote in favour of the company, that wouldn't be such a smart idea, things would stay just as they were. The vote was taken, and there were 13 against and 54 in favour of the company. Everyone voted, from Art. Jacques (head foreman) down to the servant of the private house, and the doctor offered to vote as well. The doctor gave the workers to understand that the manager was afraid there might be demands for wage increases in the spring, and that if he had definite guarantees that the workers would not bother him about this, work could begin again in the spring. . . ."

Apparently the manager was not pleased with the vote, because the mine remained closed. A few days later, the company made its employees sign individual contracts in which they stated that they were satisfied with the working conditions and agreed, for the coming twelve months, to accept the wage rates established by the company. The unionized workers were opposed to this contract. They were not very demanding, merely asking to sign the same paper but in the form of a collective agreement. The company, which was precisely attempting to undermine the union by these tactics, refused. The union asked for time to communicate with the general secretary of the C.C.C.L., and the secretary advised the union members to sign, claiming that the contract in question was not legally valid. The miners signed reluctantly, but many left the union. Some time later, the president of the Federation offered to get in touch personally with the company in an effort to reach a collective agreement. This project also failed. The union was completely routed. The officers themselves abandoned their duties. Only a few members continued to hold meetings, but they did not dare to do anything. In March 1939, the company tried to get the East Broughton miners to sign the same individual contracts that they had agreed to the previous year. This attempt failed — one doesn't quite know why.

A letter of Madame Aimé Nadeau to Abbé Campagna (Nov. 22, 1939) gives us a good idea of the situation at that time: ". . . You must know that a group of workers have been laid off at a time when others are working 15 to 18 hours per day . . . As for the few union members who have held out until now, we can see that they will have to give in soon. The assistant parish priest, Mr. B., has volunteered to take over the leadership of the union. The union members don't hear anything about what is going on; the priest did not even mention the last meeting at the beginning of October in his weekly announcements. You can see that its opponents are sure that there will be no more trade unionism here. . . ."

Trade unionism was dead in East Broughton. The industrial feudalism which oppressed this small town, with the complicity of a few prominent citizens and the silence of the clergy, still seemed to have an assured future in 1939.

V/World War Two and the postwar period: 1942-1949

For the trade union movement in the asbestos industry, the years immediately before the strike in 1949 were a time of intense and extremely varied activity. In this period, the East Broughton union revived, and struggles in common brought the unions at Thetford and Asbestos together within the framework of the Federation of the asbestos unions. The Federation became a determining factor in the situation in late 1946 and early 1947, especially when two full-time union representatives were hired: Rodolphe Hamel and Daniel Lessard. Another important factor in these developments was that over the previous fifteen years, the union members of the asbestos region could count on the close and enlightened support of their chaplains.

1/The rebirth of the East Broughton union

The workers of Thetford and Asbestos had received a cost of living allowance in October 1941, and their success in this seems to have encouraged the East Broughton miners to turn once more to thoughts of trade unionism. An opportunity arose from the fact that the East Broughton workers were having trouble figuring out the many decrees on wage controls and cost of living allowances which had been issued since the beginning of the war. At the request of several miners, the leaders of the Federation of Asbestos Employees came to East Broughton to explain these decrees to a large assembly gathered for that purpose. Trade unionism was discussed in passing, and some of those present called for another meeting on the following Sunday to debate the reactivation of the local union. At a meeting on December 21, one hundred workers joined the new union.[15]

As early as the meeting of December 28, the union members decided to write to the manager, Mr. Spafford, to advise him that the union had been started up again and to inform him that in the future, his workers would deal with him only through the intermediary of their union. Their interview with the manager on January 2, 1942, marked the beginning of a long series of negotiations. Six weeks later the union representatives explained their requests to Hugh O'Donnell, a lawyer acting for the company. They demanded that the company recognize the union, sign a collective agreement, and accept a scheme of cost of living allowances and wage adjustments, subject of course to the approval of the National War Labour Board. The company soon showed its hand: it refused to recognize the union and attempted to replace it with a "workers' committee." Reverting to a familiar tactic, it started a lockout. At a meeting on February 27, "Mr. O'Donnell said that it is not part of company policy to deal with a National Catholic Union. . . ." After this interview, there was a five-day lockout. On the fourth of April, Mr. O'Donnell "stated very clearly that the company was not opposed to the existence of an employees' union, but that it had no desire to deal with the present one, nor to sign a collective agreement with it. . . ." A conciliator from the federal Department of Labour intervened at this point to propose a contract "to be signed by a committee representing the workers." The unionists refused to give in. On June 19, the miners went out on a wildcat strike. The union managed to get them back to work three days later; the federal Deputy Minister of Labour had promised the union that negotiations would be started again, and three months later, on September 10, a preliminary agreement was finally reached. It was decided to sign a contract containing the following terms: that the officers and members of the union be immune from company reprisals; that the company pay the wage scale decreed by the National War Labour Board; that the workers and the employers meet at least once a month to discuss their mutual problems; that if the discussions did not yield results, the two parties would accept the decision of a federal arbitration board.

The workers enjoyed a triumph, but not a definitive victory: the contract had not yet been signed. In September, however, the National War Labour Board replied to the requests for higher wages made by the miners. This reply did not satisfy every group of employees, but it was accepted anyway. On November 22, Spafford called a meeting with the three contractors employed by Quebec Asbestos to work out the arrangements prescribed by the National War Labour Board, particularly those concerning cost of living allowances. One of the contractors, Cloutier by name, was unable to get the company management to pay the arrears in the cost of living allowances which were owing to his employees. He was informed that he could either sign the contract as drawn up by the company or refuse it and lose his business. Cloutier refused, but still went with his men to the mine the following day. At nine o'clock, they were told to stop work. Cloutier, however, had learned from the Selective Service Advisory Board that neither he nor his men could be dismissed without six days' notice. The company sent workers to replace Cloutier and his men, who decided to prevent them from doing their work. The company made no effort to settle the matter, and production ground to a halt because of this work stoppage in the so-called "bagging" section. On November 25, the company itself sent the last workers home. The union sent a telegram to the National War Labour Board, informing it of this incident. On November 27, Mr. Maclean, Director of the Industrial Relations Branch of the Department of Labour in Ottawa, referred to the "illegal strike" in his answer to it! The union naturally protested. The lockout lasted two months, in spite of several representations by the unions to the Department of Labour and in spite of the legislation making strikes and lockouts illegal in wartime. The settlement of the dispute, which was reached on January 16, 1943, at Sherbrooke, was in favour of the company: a "workers' committee" rather than the union was a party to the collective agreement signed that day.

On October 1, 1943, this committee and the company renewed the collective agreement signed on January 16, adding a wage scale. In 1944, the situation began to improve, and the union and the company henceforth negotiated with one another on a regular basis. The union was able to obtain small wage increases in 1945, 1946, and 1947; in 1947, the eight-hour day was also accepted. The real fate of trade unionism in the asbestos industry, however, depended on what happened in Thetford and Asbestos.

2/The asbestos unions and the National War Labour Board
From January 1942 on, there was a copious correspondence between the Thetford union and the National War Labour Board about the contract renewal and the new wage scale which was to be included in it. One after the other, the Bell Co., the Johnson Co., and the Asbestos Corporation offered wage increases. After discussion at the union meetings, the union and the companies made a joint proposal to the National War Labour Board. In December, after long negotiations, these improvements were allowed: a wage increase; time and a half after eight hours' work; regular rates of pay for beginners; permission

granted to the union to employ a business agent; settlement of the problem of foremen paid by the hour; a guaranteed minimum on piece work rates; a guaranteed wage for baggers and sewers; a special clause protecting workers incapacitated by accident, sickness, infirmity, or old age. The latter might in future be employed at a lesser wage than that stipulated for their job classification, with the consent of the union and the employer. These arrangements were accepted by the National War Labour Board, and the collective agreement was signed in February 1943.

More difficulties arose over the contract for 1944. On this occasion, the policies of the National War Labour Board proved to be unworkable (see below). The union itself was beset by serious internal problems. From 1939 to 1943, the asbestos unions had not been able to make substantial improvements in the working conditions of the miners. During this period, the length of the work week had indeed been shortened, from 60 to 54, then to 48 hours, but the workers were divided by problems in internal structure. The employees of the three companies operating mines at Thetford were all lumped together in a single union. The workers for the Johnson and Bell companies were unhappy with this arrangement, as the Asbestos Corporation employees far outnumbered them and were able to assure that their own interests came first in the negotiations. The story of the establishment of the Canadian Congress of Labour at Thetford, at the end of 1943, should be told in the light of this latent crisis situation within the Catholic union.

Paul Emile Marquette, the regional director of the Congress, was in charge of this organizing campaign. He had just scored a brilliant labour victory in winning over the employees of Montreal Tramways from a C.C.C.L. union and an international union. The campaign at Thetford also coincided with a C.C.L. organizing drive throughout the province.

Mr. Marquette accused the Catholic unions of being in league with the employers, and of not having made any serious attempt to improve the lot of the miners. He went even further; according to him, there was a more or less unspoken collusion among the chaplains, the parish priests, and the employers. Moreover, he had no trouble proving to the Thetford miners that their wages were much inferior to those paid in the rest of the Canadian mining industry. It was therefore quite easy for the Canadian Congress of Labour to gain control of the Bell and Johnson mines. We have emphasized that the workers in these mines felt themselves to be a minority in the sole Catholic union which still existed. These mines also employed the lowest proportion of French Canadians. When the time arrived to negotiate the contract for 1944 with the Johnson mine, the Congress already had a solid majority in terms of membership, but the Catholic union still had certification accorded by the National War Labour Board. As the C.C.L. had not met the statutory deadline for the intervention of a new union in negotiations, the Catholic union was able to complete the contract with the company for 1944. At the Bell mine, the Canadian Congress of Labour accepted the same conditions as those granted to the Catholic union in the other mines. Mr. Marquette claimed that he couldn't do any better because the C.C.C.L. still controlled the employees in the two biggest companies.

This whole dispute was without a doubt an important event in the life of Catholic unionism at Thetford, which seemed on the point of sinking back into torpor when it was happily revived by the C.C.L. campaign. When the C.C.C.L. appointed a special organizer for Thetford, a new era began for the Catholic union there, and even for the one at Asbestos, as we shall see.

Shortly after the arrival of the appointed organizer, Jean Marchand, three separate unions were formed at Thetford, thereby resolving the internal crisis which had greatly facilitated the entry on the scene of the C.C.L. About the same time the Catholic union at the Johnson mine put the question of certification to a vote. As the majority of union members there now belonged to the Canadian Congress of Labour, the certification soon was transferred to the C.C.L. Marquette thus had the opportunity to make good his promises.

An incident helped spoil his chances of success at the very outset. He had actually come up with a rather original stratagem, namely to invite all the Thetford miners to a meeting for a debate on trade unionism. This meeting, attended by the great majority of the workers, took place on October 15, 1944. Pat Conroy, the C.C.L. secretary-treasurer, and Marquette spoke on behalf of the C.C.L.; Marchand and Gérard Picard replied for the C.C.C.L. Conroy, who seemed unaware of the nature of the gathering, stressed the necessity for a united labour movement to combat the combined forces of the employers. The speakers for the C.C.C.L. naturally did not fail to agree with him. They had no trouble showing that it was precisely the Canadian Congress of Labour which had divided the workers, who were formerly all united in the Catholic union. Such a meeting could not help but produce the opposite effect on most miners from that intended by Marquette.

In December 1943, the members of the Catholic union at Thetford had voted that the following clause be added to the contract for 1944: "It is recognized that the wage rates as well as the working conditions which directly or indirectly affect the wage rates are subject to government regulations now in force. Consequently, the National Catholic Union of Asbestos Employees Inc. reserves the right to make application to the appropriate government authorities regarding the wages and working conditions which will become effective by the terms of this contract. The company agrees that it will not apply for a reduction in the present wage rates, nor for overall changes in working conditions. The company also agrees that, if the increases in the present wage rates are allowed by the appropriate government authorities... these increases will take effect as of January 1, 1944..." Negotiations were undertaken with the National War Labour Board concerning wage increases and adjustments. The Catholic union asked for a raise of 12½ cents, while the Canadian Congress of Labour demanded 15 cents. The Board handed down its decision on April 13, 1944.

This decision also affected the union at Asbestos. Before discussing it, we should say a word about the situation at Asbestos, which was far less complicated than that at Thetford. In November 1943, the union had decided to propose the following changes for the new contract: a general wage increase of ten cents per hour; a full cost of living bonus; time and a half after eight hours' work, and double time on Sunday; five cents an hour supplementary pay for night work, to be paid to employees working continually at night on the four o'clock to midnight and midnight to eight o'clock shifts, as well as to women working the midnight to morning shift; wage adjustments. In December, the Company's offer of a four-cent raise was rejected, and the union decided to appeal to the National War Labour Board. The executive of the union signed the contract for the following year, except for the clause concerning wages. The workers hoped that the Board would make a favourable reply.

The union members of Thetford and Asbestos were disappointed by the Board's reply. At this time, the federal government was pursuing a policy of wage controls, and Order in Council P.C. 9384, of December 9, 1943, stipulated that wages were not to be increased except in cases of "gross inequalities and injustices." In other words, the increase was only granted if the wages were too low in themselves, or if they were too low in relation to wages in similar industries located in economically comparable regions. The requests of the unions at Thetford and Asbestos offered the National War Labour Board its first opportunity to issue a decision on the basis of this new Order in Council.

The petitions from Thetford and from Asbestos were heard separately, but in April 1944, the Board issued a single decision in reply to the two unions. The Board noted that Order in Council P.C. 9384 was recent, and went on to emphasize that "the unions have not developed the case as it could have been developed under the terms of the Order in Council. That is a matter easily understood as this is a first attempt. We do not propose to deal with it in a technical fashion except insofar as that is necessary in doing justice to the employers." The Board insisted that there had been "no really scientific job evaluation" either at Thetford or at Asbestos, and the new order made it hard to find the wages insufficient. Further on, the Board added: "The unions endeavored to establish a case of inequality based on comparison with Eldorado Gold Mines, International Nickel, and Hudson Bay Mining and Smelting Company. No evidence was introduced to establish that there was any real similarity of operation. Put in the bald general way the case was presented, it is akin to comparing a grocery store with a hardware store. Some classifications in the Asbestos Mines have names similar to classifications in the Nickel Mines, but that in itself proves nothing. Certainly to establish an inequality one must find a comparison. An inequality arises when something is not equal to something else. But there must be a reasonable degree of similarity between the things sought to be compared. P.C. 9384 cannot be construed to level off wages in the mining industry generally throughout the whole country. That would be a far cry from the stabilization of wages. In our view no case of gross inequality was made out." After a few general remarks on labour and management, the Board finally allowed a four-cent increase to all the applicants from Thetford and Asbestos.[16] This concession corresponded exactly to the employers' offer, and introduced a striking contradiction into the judgment of the Board. By accepting the offer made by the Johns-Manville Co., the Board disregarded the rule of "gross inequalities and injustices" and thereby recognized the validity of the arguments advanced by the union representatives, who had had to draw comparisons with wages outside of the asbestos industry, because the only asbestos mines in the country were those of the Thetford and Asbestos regions.

The first phase of the negotiations between the asbestos unions and the National War Labour Board thus ended with this reply to union demands. Such an arbitrary decision could only be temporary. The second phase began in 1945, baring a crisis which had festered under the remedies of 1944.

The Catholic union and the Canadian Congress of Labour continued their struggle during 1945. The workers now showed less enthusiasm for the Congress, which had failed to live up to its promise to obtain higher wage increases than the Catholic union. At the end of the year, the Catholic union took the necessary steps to replace the C.C.L. as the representative of the Johnson Co. workers. Marquette had just made a noisy departure from the C.C.L. in order to found a new union of his own: the Association ouvrière canadienne (Canadian Labour Association). Only the miners of the Bell Co. remained faithful to him. In the face of delays and hesitations by the National War Labour Board, the Catholic union declared a strike at the Johnson mine. The Board finally authorized a vote on the question of representation, and the Catholic union won.

At the beginning of 1945, the unions of Thetford and Asbestos sent a new petition to the National War Labour Board requesting a general increase of ten percent. The petition was quickly rejected. In its reply, the National Board declared: "After having given the submissions in support of the applications the most careful consideration, we have come to the conclusion that we have been furnished with no new arguments or evidence to justify a further general increase beyond or above that awarded in the said decision of April 13, 1944."[17] The Catholic unions immediately protested to the Minister of Labour, Mr. Mitchell, who sent two industrial engineers to the asbestos region to study the problem of job evaluation. These engineers proposed that the conditions in other mines be examined in order to establish points of comparison for justifying wage increases, and recommended that this inquiry be undertaken by company, union, and government representatives. The companies first accepted this proposal, then rejected it at the last minute. One can imagine the deep disappointment of the miners, who had pinned their hopes on this inquiry. Henceforth, the unions changed their tactics in favour of direct action.

The union at Asbestos declared a short strike to support its demand for a ten percent wage increase. The Johns-Manville Co. finally gave in to this, and the union and the Company sent a joint petition to the National War Labour Board, asking that this agreement be allowed. In spite of its previous decision, the Board approved the request.[18] The unions of Thetford followed Asbestos' example of direct negotiations. The companies did not want to grant ten percent, but around seven or eight percent, to bring the base wage into line with that of Asbestos.[19] The unions went on strike from May 16 to 20, and thereby won their point.

3/The activities of the Federation
As has likely been noticed already, the Federation of Asbestos Unions did not play a determining role in labour disputes until 1947. It was far too concerned, from its inception in 1936, with union education and with the problem of asbestosis. It had sent many reports and petitions concerning asbestosis to the authorities, and we may sketch the history of this activity here. In 1937, the Federation requested a re-enactment

of the provincial law on silicosis, which had been rescinded in 1933. From 1940 to 1942, it tried to get asbestosis included among industrial diseases in the (provincial) Workmen's Compensation Act. It also tried to have a medical board of the Workmen's Compensation Board set up in the asbestos region. In 1943, the Board appointed an examining doctor at Thetford. In 1945, the Federation drew up an important brief in which it demanded that the provisions of the law be applied in a truly satisfactory way (medical examination of all the miners, compensation for workers attacked by asbestosis, etc.), and also asked that a detailed inquiry be made into the problems of asbestosis. Frequent representations were made to the departments concerned following the presentation of this brief. It was not until October 1946, however, that the president of the Federation could announce that he had had an interview with the provincial Minister of Labour, and that the latter had appointed a doctor and a lawyer to study the question. The Federation continued to concern itself with the asbestosis problem, but henceforth devoted most of its energies to other concerns.

The summer of 1947 marks the beginning of a new era for the Federation. At its convention on August 3, the Federation approved a uniform contract for all the mines, and the member unions authorized the Federation to negotiate this contract on their behalf.

A few weeks later, the Johns-Manville Co. made an offer to the union at Asbestos. The Company said that it was ready to "reopen" the contract which ran until January 1, 1948. The Company proposed a wage increase of 17 cents per hour in addition to the bonus of 10 cents which its employees were already receiving at that time. The union members accepted the company offer on October 12, but they handed over "all powers to negotiate and sign the agreement to the Federation." This decision slowed down the negotiations, because the Federation was still waiting to hear from the provincial Labour Relations Board about a request for certification made on the recommendation of the C.C.C.L. The Company was ready to negotiate and used its influence to get the Federation certified without delay. The certificate was issued after a very brief inquiry, and the Federation was now able to negotiate legally on behalf of the member unions. The contract was signed at Asbestos on November 7, 1947, for the period from February 1, 1948, to January 31, 1949.

The union members at Thetford at first reacted very unfavourably to the news of the separate negotiations at Asbestos. They were afraid that their employers would refuse to sign the same contract with them. It seemed, for a time, that this situation would undermine the Federation's new scheme to make working conditions uniform throughout the industry. However, once the agreement was signed at

Asbestos, the agents of the Federation received the authorization to offer the same contract to the mining companies in Thetford, and to ask that the Rand formula be granted as well. This last request was made because of the attitude of a group of employees of the Johnson mine who were C.C.L. sympathizers and refused to belong to the Catholic union. The Rand formula was rejected by the companies, and when they persisted in their refusals, the unions held an authorized meeting during working hours on January 5, 1948, a meeting which threatened to go on indefinitely . . . Consequently, after negotiating all night, the companies decided to accept the Rand formula, but only if they were asked to make this concession by an arbitration board. The board was appointed at once; the arbitrators were chosen from among the negotiating agents, and the provincial conciliator, Mr. Lépine, was made chairman. The board "imposed" the Rand formula . . . As at Asbestos, the contract was signed for a one-year period, starting January 1, 1948. It was not signed, however, until April 1, 1948.

4/Conclusions

We shall not relate the events that followed the signing of the contracts in November 1947 at Asbestos and in April 1948 at Thetford. They belong to the history of the conflict proper and are treated in another chapter of this book. By way of conclusion, we shall merely emphasize to what degree the strike of 1949 was bound up, inevitably as it were, with the events we have described.

In particular, people have been very shocked by the fact that, throughout the entire course of the strike in 1949, the workers did not avail themselves of the hallowed judicial remedies. They have failed to see that this situation is partly explained by the fact that the National War Labour Board had, in the preceding years, considered and passed judgment upon the workers' demands in a very superficial way. The union members' distaste for seeking redress from official sources is also explained (perhaps best explained) by certain facts that led them to believe that there was collusion between the companies and judicial or political institutions. At Asbestos in 1948, there was an arbitration (undertaken by virtue of the provincial law) concerning a grievance. The union lost. The chairman of the arbitration board had stayed, at the hotel, in the suite reserved for the president of the Johns-Manville Co. . . .

Furthermore: for many years the union members had, in their disputes with the employers and their agents, found themselves caught up in a strange network of influence woven by the goings and comings of politicians and managers. The workers were aware of this network both before and during the strike. At the Asbestos Corporation, the legal firm of Duquette and Ralston was empowered to represent the company; Mr. Ralston had been, as we know, the Minister of National Defence. At Johns-Manville, the legal counsel of the Company was Yvan Sabourin, president of the Quebec wing of the Conservative Party. In 1944, Judge McTague presided over the deliberations and decisions of the National War Labour Board regarding the unions of Thetford and Asbestos. He later became leader of the federal Conservative Party—for all of Canada. As for Hugh O'Donnell, whose actions on behalf of the company at East Broughton have been described, he was the son-in-law of Mr. St. Laurent, who was at that time Minister of Justice in the federal government.

The various coincidences were, no doubt, the work of chance, but we know from our interviews with a number of the actors in the drama of 1949 that these coincidences had a great influence on the political opinions of the unionists at Thetford, Asbestos, and East Broughton. We mention them here for that reason, not because we want to make fun of people. Those who are tempted to take offense would do well to recall that one does not explain the behaviour of societies in the same way that one strings pearls. Before attempting to explain any social event, one must first discover how the actors in that event explained it to themselves. We hope to be forgiven for this final digression, which illustrates the spirit in which we have conceived this entire study.

Notes to Chapter III

[1] In our research, we have used documents more extensively than interviews, but we should mention here that Jean Marchand, General Secretary of the Canadian and Catholic Confederation of Labour (C.C.C.L.), Rodolphe Hamel of Asbestos, and Daniel Lessard and Abbé Masson of Thetford have provided us with information of great interest.

Of written sources we have, firstly, used the documents in the archives of the C.C.C.L. and of the unions at Thetford, Asbestos, and East Broughton. The minutes of meetings have been particularly valuable as a source of information. Secondly, we were allowed to consult a great mass of correspondence. Finally, we have examined the newspapers as carefully as possible: the relevant issues of *Le Soleil* (Quebec), *L'Action catholique* (Quebec), and *La Presse* (Montreal). These are authentic historical sources, as almost all of the articles which we have read were written by local correspondents, and thus amount to true personal testimonies, to be subjected to scrutiny of course, but of great value.

I wish to express here my profound thanks to my friend Yves Martin. I was obliged, in rather peculiar circumstances, to leave him my chapter in the draft stage. In his scrupulous and amiable fashion, he persevered in the tedious job of revising and typing the manuscript. Let his·name be here associated with mine.

[2] Reference to.a fairly common policy in industry at that time: uncompleted hours of work were paid or not paid at the discretion of the foremen. My mother and father, who worked at that time in an altogether different industry, have told me exactly the same thing about their working conditions.

[3] It is difficult to determine the date exactly: Nov. 1, according to C. Adams in his monograph on Thetford; Nov. 7, according to Abbé Maxime Fortin in a letter to Alfred Charpentier (reproduced by the latter in his book *Ma conversion au syndicalisme catholique* [My Conversion to Catholic Trade Unionism], Montreal, Editions Fides, 1946, p. 218). It is just as hard to establish who the founder of the union was. According to Abbé Fortin's letter, he himself was the founder; C. Adams claims that Mgr. Paul Eugène Roy was responsible.

[4] Archives of the C.C.C.L.

[5] A letter from Abbé Maxime Fortin to Alfred Charpentier, quoted in *Ma conversion au syndicalisme catholique* (My Conversion to Catholic Trade Unionism), p. 79 " ... Acting through the parish priest of Thetford Mines, the Catholic union made a declaration to the Minister of Labour that it was satisfied with the existing conditions. It protested against the government paymaster who, without the knowledge of the Catholic

union, had collected the signatures of its members and had added them to those of the members of the international union, to ask for a commission of inquiry...."

[6]Not the company which bears that name today, which was not incorporated until 1925, and resulted from the merger of several companies.

[7]A careful study of the minutes shows that these passages were usually chosen for their apologetic value.

[8]Our italics.

[9]Here, as we can see, a real worker has become secretary. (Translator's note: The French text contains grammatical errors.)

[10]It later changed its name to Fédération nationale des employés de l'industrie minière incorporée (National Federation of Mining Industry Employees, Inc.).

[11]In the National Union government which had come to power the previous year.

[12]Bills 19 and 20 made amendments in the law of collective agreements and the Fair Wage Act which, in the name of the worker's right to freedom of work, invalidated all "closed shop" and "union preference" contracts. The C.C.C.L. made an energetic but futile protest against these measures, which its president referred to at the time as "the two fateful bills" (see minutes of the seventeenth annual convention of the Congress of the C.C.C.L., Thetford Mines, 1938, pp. 27-30).

[13]We have found, among the documents concerning this affair, a certain number of sworn statements in which workers described threats made to them by the foremen on the subject of the union. Here is an example: " ... Mr. X., head foreman, warned me in the presence of Mr. Y and Mr. Z that if we wanted to work at the mine we would have to give up the union, otherwise there would be no work for us at the mine, and that even if nobody said so in so many words it would be understood that the very fact of coming to work amounted to a renunciation of the union...."

[14]Letter of Aimé Nadeau to Abbé Campagna (Archives of the C.C.C.L.).

[15]The Quebec Asbestos Corporation, of East Broughton, at that time employed 120 workers.

[16]The decision of the National War Labour Board was published in the *Labour Gazette*, 1944, pp. 602-603.

[17]See the *Labour Gazette*, Vol. 45, 1945, p. 1638.

[18]We quote here a good part of the note of the National War Labour Board: " ... It has not been proved, and in fact the brief accompanying the present petition does not try to argue that the actual rates are low in comparison with those paid by employers operating other types of mines, but it argues nevertheless that the general increase which is now demanded is necessary to completely eliminate the situation of 'flagrant injustice.'

"In their written briefs and verbal presentations, the petitioners have claimed that their demand was 'reasonable in the circumstances,' owing to the fact that the Company was in the process of changing its extraction methods completely, which would ultimately do away with the present open-pit operation; that it was increasing the output of its crushing mill, modifying its methods, and introducing other improvements demanding a greater efficiency than the actual production units had, so that more and more effort was required of the workers; and that the wage increase they were seeking would eliminate any injustice 'presently' remaining.

"In support of its request, the Company asserts that it would be able to absorb the cost of the proposed increases without raising its prices correspondingly. Moreover, coming after the above-mentioned demands and prolonged negotiations, the signing of a two-year collective agreement equally satisfactory to both parties would create stable conditions for the workers and would thus improve efficiency . . ." *(The Labour Gazette,* Vol. 46, 1946, p. 605.)

[19]The wage of day laborers, at Asbestos, had been two cents an hour less than that of day laborers at Thetford.

Chapter IV

History of the Strike at Asbestos

by Gilles Beausoleil

I/Introduction

In the first six months of 1949, one of Quebec's most serious postwar labour conflicts occurred at Asbestos and at Thetford Mines, the two centres of the asbestos mining area in the Eastern Townships. Five thousand miners stopped work for over four months. Two thousand of these were employees of the Canadian Johns-Manville Co. at Asbestos; the rest worked for the Asbestos Corporation, the Flintkote Co., and the Johnson Co. at Thetford. In the two cities, the workers struck within a day of each other; the people at Asbestos were the last to go back to work, by a few days. At Thetford, work stopped completely—not one ton of mineral was taken from the struck mines. At Asbestos, the Canadian Johns-Manville Co. put some of its units back in production a few weeks after the strike had begun.

I intend to focus my account on the strike at Asbestos. This may seem arbitrary, but there are in fact many good reasons for doing so. The real drama was acted out in this city, and the historic asbestos strike is popularly known as "the strike at Asbestos." The two thousand union members at Asbestos were the ones who decided to call the strike that later proved so meaningful for the working class in Quebec; they were the strikers who witnessed the daily arrival of the scabs at the Johns-Manville Co. plant. Several weeks after the strike began, the Company recruited these strikebreakers through an intensive, and partially effective, campaign in which it promised them that they would have first chance at permanent jobs once the dispute was settled. The miners' hostility to this policy led to the active intervention of the Provincial Police. The police, assigned to Asbestos from the very first days of the strike, were a constant challenge to the unionists. They were also a symbol of the reprisals that menaced them because the provincial government, through the Prime Minister and the Minister of Labour, had repeatedly declared the strike illegal.

The prime importance of Asbestos became clearer on May 5 and 6, 1949, when the "picketing" of the city became so effective that the number of Provincial Policemen in the city was substantially increased, the Riot Act was read, and strikers were arrested en masse. This tragic occurrence was the decisive event of the strike. It revealed the determination of the miners who, even after these reprisals, refused to go back to work, and it made a great impression on public opinion: soon everybody felt that some solution should be found to this terrible conflict. By resorting to force, the strikers remained masters of the situation at a moment when many different influences were weakening their control.

The strikers in the other centres were, however, more than complacent spectators of the struggle at Asbestos. The asbestos strike was brought to a successful conclusion only because all the strikers made common cause. The least failure on the part of the Thetford strikers would have upset the balance of forces, and might even have induced the workers to give up. The Thetford miners came to the aid of the unionists at Asbestos on several occasions, and took an active part in the battles of May 5 and 6.

The strike was equally intensive in both cities, but at Thetford things were quiet, almost monotonous, while at Asbestos the course of events was marked by incidents, violence, and what nearly amounted to a pitched battle. The historian of this conflict has a prime obligation: to recount the most noteworthy events. To analyze the precise role of each actor in this drama would require a very detailed study, and one which would carry us beyond the limits imposed on this chapter.

II/The strike from day to day

The 1948 negotiations in the asbestos industry began on December 10 with a meeting between representatives of the˙Asbestos Corporation and the Johnson Co. and officials of the National Federation of Mining Industry Employees, affiliated with the Canadian and Catholic Confederation of Labour. The same group of negotiators reconvened on December 11, 20, and 21 and on January 7, 1949.

At Asbestos, representatives of the Canadian Johns-Manville Co. met with officials of the Federation on December 24, 1948. Further meetings were held on January 4, 5, and 10, 1949. Direct negotiations were broken off on January 14, after an exchange of letters between the Company and the Federation. On February 1 Léopold Rogers, a conciliator from the provincial Department of Labour, arrived in Asbestos. He held several meetings with the two parties to the dispute. Finally, on February 10, the representatives of both management and labour agreed to resort to arbitration.

1/Act I: February 13 to 20

On Sunday evening, February 13, the union members at Asbestos met to decide whether or not to accept the recourse to arbitration. The union officials explained that the negotiations had reached a dead end: the representatives of Johns-Manville had offered a mere 5% wage increase and had refused to consider the complete set of union demands. The many union members who filled the St. Aimé Hall regarded the union and management positions as settled, and so they did not bother to debate them.

The discussion turned instead to the question of tactics to be used to force the Company to change its stand. Jean Marchand explained that the workers had a choice between arbitration as prescribed by law and immediate recourse to an illegal strike. The general secretary said that as far as he was concerned, labour arbitration in Quebec was seriously compromised. The unionists of Asbestos had only once resorted to arbitration. On that occasion, the chairman of the arbitration committee had upheld the management position without taking the arguments of the union into account.

As the evening progressed, it became evident that the gathering was in favour of a strike. Marchand had not finished speaking before there were cries of "we want a strike" and "we're not going back tonight." When the secretary of the C.C.C.L. stopped speaking, the hall resounded with a unanimous call for a strike. Marchand asked for forty-eight hours, to meet with the Minister of Labour; the workers would not grant him twenty-four. Midnight was approaching, and a few groups of unionists left the hall to go and tell the night shift that the strike had been declared. In the hall, several people were insisting that the maintenance crews be kept on the job to prevent damage to the company buildings and equipment. This suggestion was accepted. The secretary of the union, Raymond Pellerin, was ordered to give passes to these workers, who were the only ones who were to enter the company grounds. An English-speaking electrician tried to go to work without a pass, but he was prevented from doing so.

During the night, groups of picketers occupied all the entrances to company property, whether factory, railway, mine, or mill. It was cold outside, and they went into the guard posts and even into the factory. The executives of the Company did not show up at their offices the next day, except for the head foreman. He was escorted home by the strikers, who advised his wife to take good care of him.

That morning the Johns-Manville Co. sent a communiqué to the provincial government announcing that an illegal strike had been de-

clared at Asbestos, and that no settlement would be considered until
the strikers returned to work. A little later, company representatives
Foster, Soutar, and McGaw had a short meeting with the union
spokesmen, who included Hamel, Larivée, and Pellerin. They decided
that the watchmen would remain on duty at all company properties, and
that a list of these men would be given to the city police chief.
Johns-Manville representatives wanted all maintenance personnel, including foremen, to be allowed to continue their work. The union
argued that the subordinate personnel alone would provide adequate
maintenance. This was the union position before the arrival of the
Provincial Police.

The manager of the factory, Morrison by name, came to visit it
around noon. He was making his rounds in the company of two
picketers when a group of strikers put an end to his inspection and
forced him to return home.

The town council held an extraordinary meeting that morning. Albert Bell, the chief of police, reported that everything was in perfect
order. The town hall was put at the disposition of the strikers free of
charge, and part of the office of the chief of police was turned over to
the representative of the C.C.C.L., Maître J.P. Geoffroy. The city
police chief was given the authorization to swear in "special dep-
uties" among the strikers, who would be responsible for maintaining
order on the picket lines and at meetings. He was also given the
authority to hire extra constables, to be paid by the municipality.

It was like a big holiday in the city. Groups of happy people strolled
about the town. They were full of optimistic talk, and laughingly
remarked that the miners, by stopping work, had hit upon the most
effective way of eliminating the asbestos dust. In the evening there
was dancing and singing everywhere. Throughout this whole first day
of the strike, people were constantly coming and going in the town
hall, the basement of St. Aimé Church, the restaurants, and the other
public places of Asbestos.

At that time people had two questions on their mind: would the
strike spread to the rest of the industry, and what would the provincial
government do about it in that case? The asbestos unionists at Thetford
Mines met on the evening of February 14 and unanimously declared
themselves in favour of a strike. At midnight, the Asbestos Corporation, Flintkote Mines, and the Johnson Co. shut down their operations. The industry was now almost completely paralyzed. The only
mines still in operation were at Thetford (Bell Asbestos), East Broughton (Quebec Asbestos Corporation), and St. Rémi de Tingwick
(Nicolet Asbestos Mines).

The only workers who did not belong to unions of the C.C.C.L.

were the Bell employees, who belonged to the Canadian Labour Association, headed by Paul Emile Marquette. They were not directly involved in the strike, but they still quit work temporarily during the second week of the work stoppage to avoid trouble with the unionists of the Federation (see below). The Bell mine, like the mines of East Broughton and St. Rémi de Tingwick, was not of great importance in the Quebec asbestos industry as a whole.

At the East Broughton mine, the union was weakened by the constant threats of the Quebec Asbestos Corporation to stop production. A strike did not occur at this mine because of its marginal character and the consequent weakness of the union there. It was the only mine that continued to operate without any work stoppage throughout the whole period of the strike.

At St. Rémi de Tingwick, there was a kind of sit-down strike on February 11, two days before the strike was declared at Asbestos. On the morning of the 13th, however, the workers at the Nicolet Asbestos Mine returned to work before an agreement had been signed. Discussions continued between the union leaders and the negotiators for the company, but came to a deadlock. The miners quit work again on March 2. When they returned on June 6, they had won a very good agreement, especially where reprisals against the strikers were concerned. The C.C.C.L. had been quick to accept this settlement, in the hope that it might serve as a basis for the resolution of other conflicts that were still in progress.

Now that we have seen the extent of the strike in the asbestos industry as a whole, let us return to the town of Asbestos.

On Tuesday, February 15, the provincial government expressed an official opinion on the strike in a telegram sent by the Minister of Labour, the Hon. A. Barrette, to Jean Marchand. The telegram read as follows: "1. We can only condemn a general strike made in formal violation of Article 4, Paragraph 1 of the Labour Relations Act. 2. We are prepared to form an arbitration board, but this board will not be appointed until the workers have shown their respect for legality by returning to work. 3. If the present situation continues, we will be obliged to notify the Labour Relations Board of the illegality of the strike, and to ask it to consider the withdrawal of certification. We therefore suggest that you ask the workers to show respect for the law, in their own interest and in the interest of their cause, by ending the strike and by leaving it to an arbitration board to do justice to the two parties to the dispute."

On the afternoon of February 16, the Minister offered further comment on the strike in the course of a long debate in the Legislative Assembly. The Hon. Barrette mentioned the joint efforts of the government and the asbestos companies to mitigate the effects of industrial disease: the mine managements had modernized equipment and improved the methods of extraction and treatment, while the Department of Labour specialists had succeeded in limiting these diseases to a great degree, and had seen to it that the sick received adequate treatment. Mr. Barrette added that instead of recognizing these facts, the labour leaders were aggravating the danger of a class struggle by resorting to illegal means. The only reply to the Minister's speech came from an independent member, René Chaloult, who maintained that the companies had not done what they ought to have done and that working conditions in the asbestos industry were still bad.

Locally, the strike continued without incident. In the afternoon of the same day, the chief of police went to the Johns-Manville foremen's club, which was located in the Iroquois Club. He asked the people in charge to close the club in order to avoid any possible incidents. In the course of the day, the workers on maintenance duty stopped phoning the superintendents for orders. According to the Company, they did this on the orders of the union. The union claimed, however, that it had not given any order to this effect, and that the telephone calls were probably not necessary, as everything was functioning properly.

On the evening of the next day, February 17, the two thousand strikers at Asbestos had a mass meeting. The most important union leaders were present. Rodolphe Hamel, President of the National Federation of Mining Industry Employees, corrected a misapprehension about a letter which the Minister of Labour had quoted, alleging that in it Mr. Hamel had thanked him for his help in the fight against asbestos dust. The letter had been sent two years before and the problem of asbestos dust had been ignored since that time. Jean Marchand explained that the increase of $0.27 per hour (also used by the Minister in building his case against the strikers) had not been obtained by arbitration in 1947. This increase had been obtained through direct negotiations and included a cost of living bonus which had already been paid. As for the threat of decertification by the Labour Relations Board, Marchand noted that one did not have to have an illegal strike to lose the certificate of recognition, as the Board had withdrawn certificates in connection with perfectly legal strikes. He added that decertification would be discriminatory, because the certificate of recognition was no more than an attestation of the existence of a union, and the existence of a legal person cannot be denied as a result of civil infractions. The strikers again declared their support for the union leaders, and were pleased to hear that the Flintkote Co. of Thetford had just offered a blank contract which guaranteed all the increases obtained by the strike in the other mines, provided that the Flintkote employees return to work immediately. This offer was refused so that the work stoppage might make its full impact.

During this time, the officers of the Canadian Johns-Manville Co. were debating whether or not to ask for the protection of the Provincial Police. They were worried by the fact that the miners were taking little interest in maintenance, in the repair of machinery, and in keeping up the reserve supplies of coal and oil. The union officials said that these matters would be taken care of. They did not seem very urgent because everyone thought that the strike would last only a few days.

The strike still made the managers of the Company very nervous. They regarded it as a device whereby the workers might overturn the regime of industrial private property, and they could already imagine the Company forced to share rights and even property with the workers if the strike resulted in a labour victory. Was it such a foolish anxiety? In trade union circles there were social reformers, inspired by the social doctrine of the Church, who spread such ideas, and who were convinced that their schemes would be realized in the near future. Trade unionism had been militant in the last few years; the miners seemed to be deeply discontent, and their demands had taken an ideological and radical turn. In the minds of the Johns-Manville management, all this could only lead to excesses; they reasoned that the union leaders were bound to lose control of the situation in a very short time because the democratic structure of the trade unions so easily lent itself to anarchy. The company executives should have realized, however, that radical reforms would require a complete transformation of the legal and economic organization of the province; they ought to have considered the volubility of the French Canadians, their abstract and sometimes utopian ideals, and the fact that the union leaders had to supply the rank and file with the kind of notions that would inspire them to defend their interests. Things had happened so rapidly, and the declaration of the strike had been so dramatic, that a lucid and objective analysis of events had given way to fear edged with panic.

The Company's last doubts about police protection were dispelled by an incident that occurred the next day, February 18. The pay owing for the working days preceding the strike had been distributed. About twelve thirty in the afternoon, several hundred workers appeared and headed for the company offices, led by a group of drummers. They burst into the offices and invited the employees there to quit work. Half a dozen people left the premises, and the picketing within the building continued all afternoon.

When they heard that the offices had been occupied, Mr. Foster and Mr. Sabourin, the company solicitor, departed in haste for Sherbrooke to obtain an injunction against the union. Around four o'clock in the afternoon, an injunction was issued ordering the strikers to stop the picketing and put an end to illegal activities. The same day, the Company also initiated a $500,000 suit for damages jointly against the union at Asbestos, the National Federation of Mining Industry Employees, and the Canadian and Catholic Confederation of Labour.

Saturday morning, February 19, rumours began to circulate that a contingent of Provincial Police were going to arrive in Asbestos that very day. Albert Goudreau, who was both mayor and National Union MPP for the area, did not deny the report. The city police chief felt that there might be trouble if the Provincial Police came to Asbestos. Meanwhile he hired four new constables, thereby increasing his force to eleven, and deputized fifteen strikers to maintain order.

Shortly before noon, a hundred Provincial Policemen under the orders of Inspector General Norbert Labbé entered the city and went directly to the company grounds. They found nobody at the gates, for as soon as the arrival of the police was confirmed, the union had recalled all its members to a plenary meeting to avoid any scuffles with the police. In the afternoon, the parish priest, Father Camirand, held a meeting of the leaders of the Ligue ouvrière catholique (Catholic Labour League) to decide what should be done to avoid unfortunate incidents.

When the union meeting was over, the union executive and the municipal council conferred with Inspector General Labbé. He assured the aldermen and the unionists that the police had come for the sole purpose of protecting the properties of the Company and that they had no intention of interfering with the progress of the strike. The policemen would remain on company grounds.

After the arrival of the police, the maintenance personnel and the watchmen quit work on the orders of the union. The union leaders were afraid that there might be altercations between the police and this group of miners, or that these workers might be held responsible for acts they had not committed.

When Mr. Sears, head of security at Johns-Manville, heard about this, he got in touch with the union officials and asked them to at least leave the watchmen on the job. They told him that the union had decided otherwise, but that he was free to come to the meeting that evening to give the Company's point of view and perhaps persuade the union members to change their minds. Mr. Sears thus presented himself at the meeting and tried to show that the union had nothing to lose by allowing the watchmen to keep on working. The workers heard him out, but did not grant his request, mainly because of the presence of the Provincial Police. The foremen and even management personnel thus had to replace the workers to assure the maintenance of company property. They quickly brought in a carload of coal and immediately had oil delivered, as the reserves were, it seems, low at the time. They also cleaned the furnaces and emptied out the accumulated ashes.

The closing of the small Bell mine at Thetford marked the end of the first week of the general strike in the asbestos industry. All during the week, the workers at this mine, who were members of the Canadian Labour Association, had not wanted to go on strike. On Saturday, the strikers at Thetford wanted to force them to quit work. The chief of police intervened, and in a meeting with the workers at the Bell mine requested that they leave their work to avoid any altercation between them and the strikers. This work stoppage lasted nine days.

2/The conflict defined: February 21 to 25

On Monday, February 21, the city council of Asbestos protested against the presence of the Provincial Police in the following resolution:

"Whereas on February 14, 1949, a strike was declared at Asbestos in the asbestos industry;

"Whereas during the week of the 14th to 19th, all has been peaceful at Asbestos;

"Whereas on the 19th, at the request of the Canadian Johns-Manville Co., a detachment of about 150 members of the Provincial Police were sent to Asbestos, allegedly to protect the properties and the salaried employees [still at work] of the Company;

"Whereas on their arrival, many of these policemen were under the influence of alcohol;

"Whereas a certain number of these policemen have even been guilty of indecent acts on the streets of the city and have caused a disturbance in public places;

"Whereas in certain cases the members of the Provincial Police have used violence against the employees in charge of maintenance [of the factories] during the strike, and against the constables of the Canadian Johns-Manville Co.;

"Whereas these acts [of violence] have been committed without warning and with the evident intent of creating trouble;

"It is resolved unanimously by the members present to lodge a protest against these men with Mr. Hilaire Beauregard, Chief of the Provincial Police, and to send a copy of this resolution to various radio stations and newspapers for publication."

The mayor of the city, Albert Goudreau, who was not present at the meeting, had this to say about the declaration of the City Council: ''In returning from Montreal, I learned from the newspapers that the City Council of Asbestos, of which I am mayor, has decided to censure the conduct of the Provincial Policemen sent to our city on the occasion of the Asbestos strike. I was surprised to find my name mentioned in this resolution, as I had not taken part in the meeting. I can state that I am partially in favour of this resolution, but I do not believe that violence was committed. It is, however, undeniable that there have been abuses.''

Late in the afternoon, it was confirmed that the Labour Relations Board had decertified the unions in the asbestos industry as well as the National Federation of Mining Industry Employees. A rapid settlement of the conflict was becoming less and less likely.

During the night of February 22, A. Larivée, president of the union at Asbestos, was invited to join a delegation from the Asbestos City Council which was planning to meet with the Minister of Labour the following day. The reply of the Minister of Labour was received the next afternoon: he agreed to see a joint delegation of representatives of the unions and of the City Council. A little later on the same afternoon, the executive of the union received a second telegram couched in the following terms: ''Please ignore my first telegram of February 22. Will receive only representatives of the National Federation of Mining Industry Employees at 3 p.m. in my offices in Quebec. It must be understood that only officials of the National Federation of Mining Industry Employees or of the unions will be present at this interview. Antonio Barrette, Minister of Labour.'' The City Council was thus set aside.

The following afternoon, the union delegation arrived at the offices of the Minister of Labour. The Hon. Barrette first admitted R. Hamel, with whom he discussed the illegality of the strike for a few minutes. He then called in A. Larivée and announced to the two delegates that the Prime Minister would see the delegation of unionists in the late afternoon. When Hamel and Larivée came out of the Minister's office, J. Marchand expressed his surprise at the length of time they had spent there, as it had been firmly decided that the delegation would not split up.

There was further discussion of the asbestos strike in the Legislative Assembly, as reported by *Le Devoir* on February 24: ''It is interesting to note that between Mr. Barrette's refusal to receive the people he had invited and the meeting with the Prime Minister, there occurred the debate in the Assembly on Bill 60 and the vehement declarations of Mr. Duplessis concerning 'the leaders of the Catholic unions, who are saboteurs rather than labour leaders.' '' The debate on Bill 60 (containing the provisions for a system of arbitration to apply to disputes between municipal or educational corporations and their employees) turned into a discussion of industrial relations in the province, with special reference to the attitude of the labour leaders. Mr. Duplessis declared in part that "it is not the workers who are not satisfied, but certain labour leaders who place their own interest ahead of the workers' interests and who are out to make trouble. . . ." When Mr. Barrette was asked about the position of the chaplain in the Catholic unions, he replied: ". . .The chaplains are like us. They are putting up with the situation in the hope that we will put our house in order, and believe me, we shall." Jos. Matte, MPP for Quebec-East, rose to endorse the Premier's opinion that the labour leaders were acting solely from motives of personal interest.

About six thirty in the evening, the Prime Minister's secretary asked for the list of delegates. It contained the following names: Albert Goudreau, Rodolphe Hamel, Geo. Dionne, Daniel Lessard, Armand Larivée, Oscar Champagne, Raymond Pellerin, Emilien Maheu, Adélard Cliche, and Jean Marchand. Duplessis said that he was prepared to receive all the members of the delegation except Jean Marchand, the representative of the C.C.C.L. The delegates insisted that they all be received together. The Prime Minister informed them that he was not budging from his first offer, and the delegates thereupon refused to enter the Prime Minister's office. MPP Goudreau tried to split up the delegation and even started to drag A. Larivée into the antechamber, but the latter got free and joined the other delegates, who were on their way out.

On February 24, the Canadian Johns-Manville Co. issued a long statement containing fifteen points. Mr. Foster stated on the Company's behalf that negotiations could not be resumed until the miners returned to work, and also said that the Comapny was extremely pleased with the Provincial Police, who were providing adequate protection for company property and also maintaining law and order, a task which was beyond the competence of the municipal police. The statement ended with a reference to "the deep regret felt by the employers in reading of the accusations that have been made against the government and against the Provincial Police, because of the intervention of the latter."

The following day, the Minister of Labour offered to intercede in the conflict in order to obtain a settlement more quickly. The important part of his statement reads as follows: "I also told them that I was prepared to do this to assure them a prompt and just settlement of their strike, on two conditions: 1. Immediate return to work. 2. Resumption

of direct negotiations, without the presence of a government conciliator between the representatives of management and of labour.
Should these negotiations fail, I offered my services as a a mediator
who would bypass arbitration. I asked the leaders of the strike if these
offers constituted a satisfactory guarantee, and they said yes. I reminded them that this was not my role, that nowhere else did labour
ministers act as conciliators. I added that I had already done this in
major disputes which sometimes involved an entire industry, and that
these disputes had been settled to the satisfaction of both parties after I
had met with the management and labour representatives. I added that
were I to act as mediator, I would accept as labour representatives only
either union members or the directors of the Federation of Asbestos
Workers.''

The strikers refused the offer of the Hon. Barrette, because as far as
they were concerned a return to work without written guarantees was
tantamount to losing the strike. Moreover, the exclusion of the
C.C.C.L. from the discussions would have proved unworkable, since
the strikers' power to negotiate depended heavily on the support of this
labour body. Finally (and above all), the Minister's proposal was an
unacceptable attack on the basic principle that the union have free
choice of its representatives.

3/Battle lines form: February 28 to March 14

It was now evident from a number of things that neither side could
hope for a rapid victory. The negotiations had broken down, and the
parties to them had grown more rigid in their attitudes. Management
was in league with the government, certification had been withdrawn,
and the Provincial Police had been called in. The workers also realized
that the strike was beginning to slip out of their control, and could no
longer be settled without intervention on a high level. In the face of all
this, the two adversaries decided to dig in for a long struggle.

Encouraged by government support, the Canadian Johns-Manville
Co. took the offensive on two fronts. Where public opinion was concerned, the watchword of the Company was the illegality of the strike.
Through a fine orchestration of newspaper ads, news reports, and
press statements, the Company sought to make the outside world
hostile to the strikers. On the local level, the Company sent letters to
individual strikers, exploited the sympathy of professional and business people, and sought the collaboration of non-strikers and scabs in
a systematic effort to separate the strikers from their union leaders.

The union set up a number of committees: the Strike Committee,
the Recreation Committee, the Relief Committee, and the Stores
Committee. The Strike Committee was the most important, although it

did not have any specific duties. It was supposed to plan the strategy of the strike, coordinate activities, and launch new projects. The Strike Committee did not include any officials of the local union or of the Federation, but representatives of the C.C.C.L. and ordinary strikers. The Recreation Committee was in charge of organizing and supervising all demonstrations, parades, and receptions. The Relief and Stores Committees were to help the families of the strikers and see to their needs. The Relief Committee distributed vouchers which the strikers could use to go shopping in the stores in town. The Stores Committee was responsible for distributing the foodstuffs which were sent to the miners in the course of the strike. It became active around March 25, when the first truckloads of provisions arrived in Asbestos. This assistance was handed out on the basis of a striker's civil status and number of dependents. A bachelor received the equivalent of three dollars per week. The head of a family got the equivalent of four dollars for him and his wife, plus one dollar for each child. In addition, the union provided free bread and milk.

The solidarity among the unions increased in proportion as the Company and the politicians made ever greater efforts to separate the miners from their union leaders. People laughed at the slanders that were circulated about the strike leaders. The parish priest Father Camirand never tired of telling the workers that they should stick together and not lose confidence in their leaders.

On February 28, the three hundred fifty employees of Bell Asbestos at Thetford went back to work with no opposition from the strikers. This return to work was brought about by the intercession of the City Council, which discussed the problem with the committee of strikers.

On March 1, the Canadian Johns-Manville Co. sent out its first circular letter to its two thousand employees. It called upon them to return to work "in order that the dispute may be settled and a labour contract negotiated," and explained that the letter was part of "a company policy of keeping its employees informed of developments in the relations between the Company and them." The letter also mentioned that, when the supervisors had entered the mine following the arrival of the police, they found incontrovertible proof that the strikers were planning to discontinue the maintenance of equipment that very evening.

On March 2, the workers at St. Rémi de Tingwick went back on strike. A hundred in number, they had quit work at the beginning of the conflict but had later returned to the mine.

The next day the injunction issued by the Sherbrooke Higher Court in favour of the Canadian Johns-Manville Co. against the strikers in the first week of the strike was extended to the following April 5.

On Sunday, March 6, two union meetings were held at Asbestos. The afternoon session was organized for the wives of the strikers, and the problems discussed there were purely union matters like wages and paid holidays, or family and social issues. The evening gathering was reserved for strikers. The chief speaker, Jean Marchand, delivered an attack on the Canadian Johns-Manville Co. In his opinion, the machinations of the Company had no other aim than the destruction of organized labour. What else could explain the stubborn refusal of the Johns-Manville Co. to offer the unions the least security?

On March 9, Minister of Labour Barrette renewed his offer to mediate on the express condition that the workers return to their jobs, as is shown by his telegram to T. Labbé and A. Goudreau, mayors of Thetford and Asbestos respectively: "If the workers obey the law, return to work, and conform to legality, I will be pleased to recommend that your unions be recertified and I will also be prepared to act as mediator to obtain from this unhappy situation a just and advantageous settlement."

The Johns-Manville Co. continued to put pressure on its employees, and carried on with its attempts to influence public opinion. In a new letter sent on the same day (March 9) to its employees, the Company maintained that the workers wanted to return to work, thanked the governmental authorities for taking an interest in the problem, and declared that it was always ready to negotiate with the workers' representatives. The last paragraph of the letter included a referendum on the return to work. As soon as the union heard of this, it demanded that its members turn their copies in to the union if they wanted to show that they were worthy of being unionists. The next day a large advertisement appeared in the newspapers under the title: "This Strike is Illegal, Useless, and Expensive." The Company again insisted on the fact that the strike was illegal and tried to show that in addition to causing enormous wage losses, it was not benefitting either the workers or the Company in any way.

It was about this time that the Provincial Police began to patrol the highways systematically. A striker who had forgotten his driver's licence was taken to Sherbrooke and told that he would not get out of it with less than a thirty-dollar fine unless he agreed to return to work at the Company in the near future.

On March 12, the strikers received a sum of money that had been subscribed by the members of the Social Research Group, an organization of students at the University of Montreal. The subscription was accompanied by a letter stating that the donors were convinced that the strike was justified and were supporting the workers' cause.

A serious incident occurred on March 14. A section of the Johns-

Manville railway line was dynamited during the night. The dynamiting was done near Danville, on the company line that served to carry freight from Asbestos to the C.N.R. main line at Danville. The case was turned over to the R.C.M.P., but their investigation established nothing: no report was issued, nobody was brought to trial. On the same day, the City Council of Asbestos again approached Minister Barrette, but found his attitude unchanged: the unions would be recertified and the mediation undertaken only if the workers returned to their jobs.

4/Stalemate: March 16 to April 18
As the strike dragged on, the Company increased its publicity efforts and sent letter after letter to each of its employees. Above all, it started to hire all the workers that it could find. This recourse to scabs was to have a great influence on the course of the strike. It increased the tensions and frictions between strikers and non-strikers, and led to many altercations and skirmishes. According to company records, there were 122 employees at work in March and 252 in April. The figure for April included 65 new employees. Though the men who were working for the Company were few, they symbolized the menace of defeat. The strikers soon tried to stop them from going to work in the morning. The Provincial Policemen protected the strikebreakers and intimidated the strikers, thereby becoming more and more hateful in the miners' eyes.

The merchants and professional men of Asbestos, who were not yet very sympathetic to the workers, tried to win them over to dubious schemes of settlement or attempted to create divisions among the unionists. The political agents tried to divide them as well, and also made efforts to destroy the reputation of labour leaders and undermine the strike.

In the face of this opposition, the whole labour movement lent its support to the asbestos strikers. The C.C.C.L. emptied its treasury and asked its members for supplementary dues. Cheques and truckloads of foodstuffs began to arrive in the region of the strike from unions affiliated with the Trades and Labour Congress or with the Canadian Congress of Labour.

In the following weeks, the C.C.C.L. led the struggle to influence public opinion. The public at large was becoming more and more interested in the asbestos conflict, and the C.C.C.L. tried to get more cooperation from the newspapers, especially the labour papers and those published under the influence of the clergy. It also organized more demonstrations of the kind that were likely to attract the attention of the major news media, and undertook a systematic publicity campaign within the labour organizations themselves.

On the local scene, the pressures on the strikers increased rather than decreased their solidarity. Few strikers decided to go back to work. According to company figures, this number increased to more than sixty-five workers per month. The collective hostility was directed towards the strikebreakers from the nearby villages who were seduced by the attractive offers of Johns-Manville. Another phenomenon arose about this time—spontaneous groupings of men who attacked the strikebreakers, intimidated their families, and damaged their property. Idleness, insecurity, and an unspoken fear of losing the strike multiplied these incidents. They were not part of the union strategy, but arose inevitably from the course of events.

On March 16, a Johns-Manville delivery truck was parked at the corner of Panneton and Bourbeau streets. The driver was not well liked among the unionists, and his truck was almost turned over by a group of strikers gathered near the city hall. Seeing what was going on, the police chief and the union officials hurried over to stop the strikers. In falling back on its four wheels, the truck hit a striker, Edmond Delorme, who suffered a double fracture of the leg. On the same day, as an engineer employed by the Company was passing through a group of strikers near the city hall, he decided to make a few derogatory remarks to them. He was somewhat brutally escorted home.

On the same day, the City Council asked the union leaders to prohibit large gatherings of men on the streets of the city. This request was granted and the streets became less congested. The chief of the city police, Albert Bell, was given authorization to hire six new constables to maintain order in the city. The Provincial Police began to patrol the streets more zealously than ever, in an attempt to prevent the strikers from intimidating those who were on their way to work.

At a meeting that evening in the St. Aimé Hall, Gérard Picard, president of the C.C.C.L., announced a piece of good news for the strikers. The three great central labour bodies in the country had formed a coalition to provide help to the strikers and to study the best means of putting an end to the strike.

In the following days, the Company waged its publicity campaign with great vigour. On March 17, it sent a new letter to its employees, accusing the strike leaders of intimidating the workers by asking them to give the union the letter that had been previously sent out by the Company. The Company added that its employees were perfectly at liberty to decide for themselves whether or not they wanted to return to work. The next day, the Company placed a large advertisement in the Sherbrooke newspaper La Tribune, denying that it had any intention of breaking the union. It claimed that it had always trusted the union representatives and had committed itself to dealing with them even if the collective agreement was not renewed. The Company added that the secretary general of the C.C.C.L. had asked for arbitration and that the workers would have obtained a new collective agreement if the correct procedures had been followed. In an advertisement published in *La Tribune* the next day, March 19, the Company reproduced the letter it had sent to its employees two days before.

The inhabitants of Asbestos who attended mass on Sunday, March 20, heard quite different sermons, depending on the church they attended. Father Deslandes, of the St. Isaac-Jogues parish, declared that the strike was a great calamity which he had, moreover, predicted. Since he had not been consulted, he had not been able to warn the workers of the ills that attended them. Father Camirand, of the St. Aimé parish, read from the encyclical *Divini Redemptoris* and from a short speech given by Mgr. Desranleau at the Labour Day ceremonies in 1938. These documents embraced the following themes: the workers have a right to a fair wage and to self-respect; they need not await their salvation from other social groups.

On March 21, two Provincial Policemen went to the house of a striker by the name of Richer with a warrant for his arrest. Richer was accused of intimidating a non-striker. As he happened to be next door at his neighbour's, the policemen went there. It was subsequently claimed that Richer resisted arrest, and that in defending him his wife struck a policeman with a telephone. The two policemen left the house, but a few minutes later the street was invaded by eight Provincial Police cars. In a few minutes, the house was occupied. All those present were taken to the Iroquois Club, where two of them, Paul Lemay and Gérard Beauchemin, were released. The latter was taken to the doctor, because he had a deep wound on the head. Beauchemin was not a striker and had in fact just returned from the sanatorium. He was allegedly struck on the head with a truncheon before he had made a move. The other persons arrested remained in police custody.

When the leaders of the union heard of this incident, they asked the strikers to remain calm, and dispatched the following telegram to the Prime Minister of the province: "In view of the very serious situation created by the actions of the Provincial Police, the National Union of Asbestos Employees of Asbestos, Inc., has decided to bring the following facts to your attention: For the last three days, officers of the Provincial Police have detained strikers at the club of the Canadian Johns-Manville Co. for the purposes of interrogation for periods of up to seven hours at a time. These detainees have been intimidated and grossly insulted by the policemen in charge. A few hours ago, Provincial Policemen bullied a pregnant woman right on the street in full view of the population. This conduct on the part of the police can only be interpreted as an attempt to provoke the strikers out of the calm which they have displayed so far.''

During the night, two other strikers were dragged from their beds between two and five o'clock in the morning. Another was arrested in the course of the day. The arrest warrants were stereotyped and repeated the same accusations of malicious intimidation and threatening. That evening, there was a union meeting at which the arrested strikers mounted the platform in the place of the officers of the union. It was pointed out to the gathering that strong discipline was needed if the strikers were to avoid difficulties with the police.

On March 23, an altercation occurred at the entrance to the Mar-Lodge Club in Danville between a strikebreaker and five strikers, including J.N. Hamel, the son of the president of the National Federation of Mining Industry Employees. This strikebreaker had previously beaten up a striker; he was now beaten up in return. The following Wednesday, March 30, Hamel gave himself up to the police for this assault. The four other strikers were still being sought for their part in the affair. On March 31, the same strikebreaker appeared in the court of the Sessions of the Peace, accused of aggravated assault against the striker A. Demers.

In the last week of the month especially, aid arrived in money and in kind. The Alliance des professeurs catholiques de Montréal (Montreal Catholic Teachers' Association) and the Shawinigan Central Labour Council (C.C.C.L.) sent substantial cheques to the union at Asbestos. Truckloads of foodstuffs were sent from Sherbrooke, Montreal, St. Hyacinth, and Granby.

The asbestos dispute was discussed again in the Legislative Assembly. On this occasion, the Hon. Barrette attacked the Rand formula in these terms: "If I were still a worker belonging to a union, I would be opposed to the Rand formula. If I were an officer of a union or trade association, I would be equally opposed to the Rand formula for the following reasons: It is, I believe, extremely important to safeguard the worker's right to belong to the association of his choice . . . If the Rand formula were generally applied to all industries and commercial firms, it would effectively put a power of taxation in the hands of union officials.'' Duplessis emphasized the necessity of obeying the laws: "It is evident that contempt for laws leads to anarchy and disorder. It is also clear and certain that contempt for civil laws, enacted by the civil authority, engenders contempt for all other laws. Clearly the Attorney General, who is responsible for seeing that the laws are observed, cannot become an accomplice to the non-observance of laws, particularly of fundamental laws. If the laws are violated with impunity, it will be a disaster for the workers, the economy, and the nation.'' The Hon. Duplessis concluded his remarks with the observation that it was not the majority of workers but a small minority who did not respect the laws.

On Sunday, April 3, the union leaders thwarted a diversionary tactic attempted by a group of citizens of Asbestos. From noon to two o'clock in the afternoon, an automobile equipped with a loudspeaker drove through the streets of the city to announce a meeting of the workers of the Johns-Manville Co. at two o'clock. The meeting was sponsored by the mayor of the city, Albert Goudreau, and a group of businessmen. Right away the union leaders called a meeting at the St. Aimé Hall for one thirty. A great number of strikers attended. The president of the union, A. Larivée, and the secretary, R. Pellerin, went to the other meeting to debate the situation with its organizers. The whole question of the strike was again gone over in detail and the union representatives explained the union position. The meeting was a failure.

On April 4, the strike was debated at length in the Ottawa House of Commons for the first time. The socialist (C.C.F.) members emphasized that the asbestos strikers were only defending their rights and that the attitude of the Quebec government was therefore unacceptable. ''The only aim of the workers who have gone on strike,'' said Clarie Gillis, MP for Cape Breton South, ''was to get recognition for their elementary rights. In almost all the provinces, the law gives these rights to workers who are members of legally constituted unions and who have established bodies to negotiate on their behalf. The strikers are asking, first of all, for a wage increase in proportion to the rise in the cost of living, and secondly, for security in the exercise of their rights as union members.'' Ross Thatcher (C.C.F.), MP for Moose Jaw, declared: ''The asbestos cartel has not merely won the sympathy of the Duplessis government, but its active support as well, to the detriment of the taxpayers, the miners in the asbestos unions, and all the other workers in the Province of Quebec.'' Jos. Lafontaine, Liberal MP for Mégantic-Frontenac, said that he hoped for a quick resolution of the conflict, a resolution which could be obtained if the MPPs of the region had the nerve to force the hand of the Prime Minister of Quebec. The Hon. Humphrey Mitchell, Minister of Labour in the St. Laurent cabinet, stressed that this labour dispute fell within the jurisdiction of the Province of Quebec, and said that the settlement of it depended upon the cooperation of all the organizations involved in the conflict: ''I hope, then, that the dispute will be resolved to the satisfaction of the employees' organization, thanks to a sensible attitude on the part of the other party to the conflict. The member who drew the attention of the House to this question has performed a service for the entire population. Constant vigilance is the price of freedom. We know this, but we need to be constantly reminded of it. I repeat that there can be no substitutes for honesty and justice. Without them, one can pass all the laws in the world to little avail. It is easy to enact a law which makes strikes illegal, but what can one do when 20,000 to 30,000 men decide to stop work? We must use our common sense in this matter.''

The Social Credit MPs did not take part in this debate. The leaders of this party neither supported nor criticized the asbestos strike. The party organizations did not take any steps to help the strikers, such as sending food or money. This is somewhat surprising, as many rumours, originating no doubt with the managerial class, held that the strike was due to the subversive and revolutionary activity of the Social Credit. Certainly the newspaper *Vers Demain* expressed sympathy for the miners on several occasions. On the local scene, a number of union leaders were one-time followers of Social Credit, and the members of this party took an active part in the strike, but within the framework of organizations set up by the strikers. Their actions did not reflect any official political stance.

On the same day that the debate took place in the House of Commons, the Canadian Johns-Manville Co. made its first direct attack on the leaders of the asbestos unions, in an advertisement published in *L'Action catholique* under the title: ''Too Bad Our Employees Have Been Duped.'' The Company claimed that the strike had been planned, initiated, and led by a tiny group of pigheaded individuals. It added that it was ready to negotiate with its employees once they returned to work. That day the strikers received, in place of the Company's weekly letter, an issue of the Montreal paper *Le Moraliste,* which shamelessly attacked the union leaders as bad citizens, agitators, and revolutionaries while flattering the strikers as peace-loving citizens.

On April 6, the strikebreakers received a wage increase of ten cents per hour, and the Company announced that all workers who were willing to return to their jobs would get the same raise.

Two days later Antoine Rivard, Attorney General of Quebec, took up the subject of illegality in a speech he delivered at a luncheon meeting of the Jeunesse de l'Union Nationale (Young National Unionists) of Montreal. He spoke of a ''dismal example of this travesty of the basic principles of peace and order in the community . . . Again according to this law [the Labour Relations Act of 1944], a strike declared before recourse to arbitration is an illegal strike. It calls law and authority into question and becomes a source of disorder which is inadmissible to any legislator worthy of the name."

At a meeting of the Plenary Council of the C.C.C.L. on April 9, the officials of this organization voted to give $25,000 to the asbestos workers and decided to set up a strike fund of $100,000 in the near future. At this time, the industrial world was beginning to feel the effects of an asbestos shortage. The processing plants in the United States were supposedly ready to shut down for want of raw material.

A parade of several thousand people greeted the arrival of University of Montreal students at Asbestos on April 11. This group of students, representing all the faculties, were travelling in cars festooned with banners reading "Long Live the Asbestos Strikers." Two students addressed the meeting held in the St. Aimé Hall. The last speaker was Father Jacques Cousineau, S.J., who hoped that the students who were listening to him would become "a generation who value social justice more highly than legality." At this time, it was learned that the students of Laval University were organizing a similar subscription.

On April 16, representatives of the asbestos companies met with spokesmen of the C.C.C.L. The delegates of management stated that they were not opposed to the recertification of the unions, but the negotiations broke down anyway, as was announced the next day. On April 18, the Hon. Barrette sounded the death knell of union hopes in a radio speech: "The asbestos workers can return to their jobs whenever they like, because they quit work voluntarily. In the present circumstances, no settlement is possible because the strike is illegal. Disputes are not going to be resolved by the sabotage of legitimate authority. Moreover, a labour contract negotiated in these conditions would not provide the workers with adequate guarantees." Members of the union, who had gathered in the St. Aimé Hall, listened to this speech. While Gérard Picard was replying to the statements of the Minister, a telegram was sent to the Honourable Barrette in which he was described as the Minister of Capital, not the Minister of Labour.

5/Prelude to violence: April 19 to May 4

All attempts at negotiations had failed and the chances of a settlement were more remote than ever. The provincial government maintained its rigid attitude, and the Provincial Police protected the scabs that the Company succeeded in hiring. Unable to get enough strikers to return to work, agents of the Company went around to all the villages and farms in the surrounding area to hire strikebreakers. In the light of this activity, the strikers became persuaded that their most urgent task was to stem this invasion of non-strikers, and to persuade those already working that their attitude was bound to have deplorable consequences. The government, the Provincial Police, and the Company were no longer the chief preoccupations of the strikers. The strategy of the union leaders was to prevent the strikebreakers from going to work, while the resentment of the strikers focussed on the workers who had become the enemies of their cause.

On April 19, the Johns-Manville Co. put Mill no. 4 back in operation, and a company spokesman said that two to three hundred workers were on the job. The next day, the Company threatened to evict those strikers who rented houses owned by it. It made an official announcement that the strikers would have to leave their homes "soon," so that the new employees could take up residence in them, and representatives of the Company visited the strikers concerned to explain the situation clearly to them. The Company did not, however, deny that it had always refused to accept the rental payments which the strikers offered for these dwellings.

A general meeting of the union decided to establish massive picketing around the strikers' houses if the Company tried to put its eviction order into effect. Father Camirand advised his flock not to let themselves be evicted but to notify their priest. He said that the company agents would not take one stick of furniture out of the houses "except over my dead body."

The Hon. Barrette intervened in the housing affair on April 21, sending the following telegram to Mr. Foster, the manager of the Johns-Manville Co.: "The newspapers reported today that your Company has notified several of its employees, who are presently on strike, that they must evacuate the houses belonging to the Company which they now occupy. If this report is correct, I am sorry that you have taken this decision. As Minister of Labour, I would ask you to reconsider this decision and to cancel the eviction notices. I am also authorized to say that the government deems that these notices should be cancelled. We feel that in the present circumstances, it would be only fair and proper to annul these notices." In his reply to the Minister, Mr. Foster noted that the eviction was not to be carried out immediately, as the occupants of the houses had been notified that "sooner or later, we must find accommodation for the people who are in fact working for us."

Early in the morning of April 22, as the scabs were going to work, a long procession of strikers marched through the streets of Asbestos in an attempt to shame them. Gérard Pelletier, a reporter for the newspaper *Le Devoir*, and two friends, G. Charpentier and P.E. Trudeau, who were watching the demonstration, were arrested by the Provincial Police and given half an hour to get out of town. When they refused to leave, they were taken to the Iroquois Club where they were interrogated by a high-ranking officer by the name of Gagné. When he realized that he was dealing with a press reporter and with citizens who were not about to be browbeaten, his arrogance gave way to politeness.

On the same day, the president of the Johns-Manville Co., L.H. Brown, stated that in his opinion the strike was really an assault on fundamental principles, including that of private property, and had little to do with wages and working conditions. In commenting on this statement, Mr. Foster, the local head of the Company, stressed that the union leaders were trying to get partial control over the administration of the firm, while the Company remained faithful to the principles of collective bargaining.

On April 24, several people attended a public meeting in favour of the asbestos strikers at the Palais Montcalm in Quebec City. R. Hamel sketched the history of the asbestos unions, emphasized their efforts to improve working conditions, and set forth the aims of the present strike. J. Marchand traced the course of the negotiations. He placed the dispute in its context and showed it to be an important social problem. G. Picard offered a critical review of collective bargaining, showing that this procedure resulted much more frequently in settlements than in strikes. He said in part that "it is useless to try to apply the legislation of an era of individualism to the collective problems of today," and that for this reason the present generation should carry on the struggle in the economic and social spheres.

On April 26, the City Council of Asbestos decided to impose a curfew from 1 a.m. to 5 a.m., and to lock the doors of the city hall auditorium at half past midnight. Any person found on the streets without just cause during the curfew hours was to be immediately arrested. It is believed that this measure, taken to curb the growing vandalism in the area, was suggested by the Inspector General of the Provincial Police, Mr. Labbé.

On April 28, the newspaper *Le Devoir* published a letter from the Rector of Laval University, Mgr. Vandry, in which he criticized an article in the paper that had stated that a trip to Thetford planned by a group of Laval students had been formally prohibited by him due to political pressure. The Rector declared that he had freely made the decision because he was worried about the possible repercussions that this trip might have for the students. The reporter involved, Gérard Pelletier, made a few corrections in his article in a note to the editors, but did not retract the substance of his remarks. In the closing words of his note, he expressed his astonishment at the Rector's decision. A week later, Guy Rocher and Henri Schmidt, the organizers of the

Laval subscription, sent a precise description of these events to the newspapers. Their account tallied with that of Mr. Pelletier.

On April 29, the media reported a very serious new development: the negotiations in progress for several days between lawyers Théodore Lespérance and Yvan Sabourin had definitely been broken off. These two lawyers had been appointed as the union and management arbitrators respectively, to form an arbitration board to settle the dispute. This was the most important concession made by the C.C.C.L. as well as the formula in which it had placed the greatest hopes. This solution actually met the demands of government and management without compromising any of the parties to the conflict, and postponed the settlement until after the strikers had returned to work.

A first difficulty had arisen from the fact that the two arbitrators were unable to agree on the choice of a chairman of the committee, but this problem began to seem less and less important to the union arbitrator, who realized that the terms under which the strikers were to go back to work were not so well defined as the Minister had claimed in a statement about the formation of the arbitration committee. The Johns-Manville Co. appeared to have a very peculiar definition of the non-discrimination policy promised by the Hon. Barrette. Lespérance took it upon himself to break off the negotiations because the Johns-Manville Co. insisted on giving the scabs the first chance at jobs and was only prepared to promise work to the strikers according to the undetermined needs of production. For the workers, these terms—by destroying the rights of seniority—amounted to a regression to the conditions of several years ago, and a loss of the guarantees which had been duly acquired through years of struggle on the part of the union. As far as they were concerned, the Company was not making an offer of settlement but of capitulation. Given the intensive recruiting of scabs that had gone on, this offer denied the possibility of a peaceful solution to the conflict.

On the evening of the same day, the Sacerdotal Commission of Social Studies made a statement in which it deplored the fact that the strike had not been settled, and called upon the general public ''to collaborate with the religious authorities in taking up a collection for the distressed families.'' On May 1, Mgr. Joseph Charbonneau, Archbishop of Montreal, gave a sermon at Notre Dame Church in Montreal that was of great importance in the history of the strike. He asked the faithful to subscribe to a special fund to aid the strikers and then commented on the statement issued by the Sacerdotal Commission of Social Studies.[1]

On May 2, the Canadian Johns-Manville Co. issued a statement that production in its mines and mill had been resumed for the past two weeks, and claimed that more than seven hundred people were at work on its premises. The communiqué clearly stated that as the number of people at work increased, it would become more and more difficult to guarantee jobs and seniority rights to the striking workers. The strikers should therefore return to work at once if they wanted to keep their privileges. The figure quoted in the statement probably included the office personnel, because S. Sears, head of security for the Company, later revealed that on May 4 there were 348 people at work who were directly concerned with production. The union claimed that only 75 of its members had returned to work. This assertion seemed likely, as a large number of strikebreakers were farmers or manual laborers from the surrounding villages.[2]

On the same day, the City Council was concerned about the problem of the strikebreakers, as is shown by the following resolution passed at the Council meeting: "It is resolved unanimously that the City Council earnestly request the Canadian Johns-Manville Co. to hire its former employees in preference to any person coming from outside the area, in order that the economic situation at Asbestos be affected as little as possible."

Violent incidents became more frequent in the ensuing days. The workers urged the union leaders to take steps to prevent any increase in the number of scabs. Tension mounted rapidly. Deliberations in the union were more and more surrounded by mystery and menace, and a rumour circulated that a new plan was being prepared. The union meeting on May 4 lasted far into the night. It was decided to organize another parade the following day in an attempt to influence the strikebreakers.

6/The days of drama: May 5 to 14

Around six o'clock in the morning of May 5, the unionists gathered in front of the church to organize the demonstration. Meanwhile, the Provincial Policemen were busy on the highways. On the road to Wotton, they arrested a truckload of strikers from Thetford Mines who were on their way to join the demonstration at Asbestos. They forced the strikers to leave the truck. The strikers continued on foot, and a little farther on, they got into a second truck. The policemen also attempted to stop an automobile on the road to Danville. When the driver ignored them, they fired on the car, which sped away.

Meanwhile, the strikers were forming up in parade ranks. Suddenly, from several groups, the cry was heard, "Let's go to the roads." In a short time they had all left their ranks, and in small groups had occupied the various roads into town as well as the entrances to the company premises.

Groups of picketers blocked all the roads leading into town, namely the roads to St. George, Wotton, Danville, and Petit Nicolet. There were several hundred strikers in each group. On the road to St. George, strikebreakers were stopped and turned back; two automobiles were overturned and caught fire. On the road to Danville, the situation was more complicated. Early in the morning, the police had positioned railway cars full of asbestos on the rail line where it crossed the highway. These cars were then moved aside to enable the employees of the Company to enter the town. The strikers had established their picket lines on the far side of the railway line. The strikebreakers, in the face of this, did not approach the picket lines but returned to Danville, where they awaited the moment to return, as rumour had it that the police would soon receive reinforcements and would break the picket lines.

In the city, sizeable groups of picketers occupied the entrances to company property. At the mill entrance, on the other side of the gates, a large troop of policemen armed with submachine guns, revolvers, and grenade launchers kept an eye on the strikers. The fire hoses were made ready. About 7:50 a.m., a procession neared the place: hundreds of women, reciting their rosaries, filed past the gates. About five minutes later, a few strikers slowly approached the gates. When they were within one hundred feet of the entrance, the police fired off tear gas bombs. One striker was hit on the forehead by a missile. The others withdrew, and the wounded man was taken to the city hall.

Late in the afternoon, an automobile filled with plainclothes police drove head-on at the picket line on the road to Danville. The strikers got out of the way, but the car was forced to come to a stop because, on a second line, the road was blocked by trucks and automobiles. The strikers asked the passengers of the car for their identification cards, but the latter did not want to show anything, nor did they want to explain why they had come to Asbestos. A shot was fired. In a few minutes, the occupants of the car were dragged from their seats, and the automobile was pushed into a ten-foot gully.

In a display of sangfroid, the men in charge of the barricade stopped the strikers from molesting the policemen, who were taken to the strike headquarters. A union leader informed the Asbestos police chief of the incident. Chief Bell arrived at the St. Aimé Hall about 12:10 p.m. and urged the strikers not to harm the policemen, whom he ordered to follow him. He took six with him in his car, but there were still two left behind, as a second car of Provincial Police had been stopped shortly after the first. As soon as he arrived at the Iroquois Club, Chief Bell sent Assistant Police Chief Dionne to fetch the two remaining Provincial Policemen. When he arrived at St. Aimé Hall, Mr. Dionne learned that the two policemen had already left on foot with an escort of strikers who were engaged in insulting and even molesting them. Chief Bell then went to the presbytery to take possession of the policemen's guns, which had been placed in safekeeping there. He turned them over to Lieutenant Timlin of the Provincial Police. After dinner, the police chief returned to the presbytery to get the remaining guns.

At this time, the city seemed rather empty. The only centre of activity was the parish hall, which had been transformed into a cafeteria. Women were busy making sandwiches, which were distributed to the picket lines by truck. Donations of chocolate milk and soft drinks were added to the menu. The rest of the population, including women and children, spent the day on the picket lines. Here and there trucks went by, filled with men.

The Provincial Policemen in the city were divided into two groups. One contingent was stationed on the company premises, the other at the Iroquois Club. They did not patrol the streets during the day. The company executives and the office workers went to work as usual, and a few scabs managed to insinuate themselves into the group that was allowed through the gates.

In the evening, the union leaders suggested to the picketers that they return home. The picketers refused, saying that they wanted to stay on the lines all night to make sure that the scabs would be unable to go to work. The picketers were not at all anxious. They chatted and discussed matters among themselves, and spent the evening on the roads at the positions that they had taken up. By now, several of them were armed with clubs. Some strikers who had come back from Danville had reported that the strikebreakers were also armed with clubs, and that they intended to come and dislodge the strikers.

The union leaders became more and more worried. There were rumours of reprisals; a heavy contingent of police was supposed to be coming the following day to take matters in hand. There was even talk of a marshalling of five hundred police at Sherbrooke. About 11 o'clock at night, the chief of the Provincial Police, Hilaire Beauregard, telephoned the strike leaders to inform them that the Riot Act would be read the next day and that any member of an unlawful assembly could thenceforth expect to be severely punished. Around eleven thirty, Beauregard telephoned to Father Camirand and strongly advised him to ask the strikers to go home, lest they be punished as examples after the reading of the Riot Act.

Around midnight, the leaders held a general assembly. In ten minutes, the St. Aimé Hall was filled with strikers. They were not too happy with this recall, because they had got everything ready to spend the night on the roads. Some had even set up tents. The union leaders tried to persuade them to leave the lines and go home, warning them that the police were heavily armed and that they might possibly attack in a force three hundred strong. At that moment, somebody in the hall cried out: ''They may beat us, but they'll have to beat us down first.'' This remark was greeted with much applause, and the strikers left the hall singing, headed for their picket lines. Instead of blocking all the roads, however, they concentrated on the strategic roads to Danville and Wotton.

At about this time, a Provincial Police convoy of around twenty-five cars and a tow-truck departed from Sherbrooke. The policemen were heavily armed and had orders to shoot if necessary. Several telephone calls were made to Asbestos as the convoy proceeded. The union leaders realized the danger, and decided to make one last effort to recall the strikers. Father Camirand himself went along the picket lines, urging the strikers to return to the hall.

The strikers were finally gathered again in the hall by about two a.m. It was quickly explained to them that a great convoy of Provincial Police cars was on the way to Asbestos, that the police were well armed, and that they had been given harsh orders. Under these conditions, a struggle would certainly not be to the advantage of the strikers. All the strikers then dropped the clubs and rocks they were carrying and departed hastily for their homes.

Around four o'clock in the morning, the first cars of the Provincial Police convoy entered Asbestos. The Provincial Police began by sealing off the entrances to the city. Since the policemen knew that the Thetford strikers had not left the city, they then went to the parish hall, where they expected to find them. Most of the Thetford strikers had left to spend the night in various homes in Asbestos, but fifteen of them had stayed behind in the hall, which was in the basement of the church. All of these men were arrested, even on the threshold of the sacristy. Those who had taken refuge in the church were arrested when they came out. Seven of them were beaten by the police in a small room adjoining the main hall, a spectacle that shocked the journalists and photographers who were present.

By about seven o'clock, the city was ''under control'' and the streets were heavily patrolled. At the moment when people were on their way out from mass, Sherbrooke Justice of the Peace H. O'Brady read the Riot Act before a group of fifty people gathered in front of the church. The text of the Act was as follows: ''His Majesty the King charges and commands all persons being assembled immediately to disperse and peaceably to depart to their habitations or to their lawful business upon the pain of being guilty of an offense for which, upon conviction, they may be sentenced to imprisonment for life. GOD SAVE THE KING.'' As soon as the Act had been read, the police placed all the men present under arrest.

The arrests continued in the streets and in the public places: restaurants, billiard halls, stores. Several people did not know why they were being arrested, because not everyone knew about the reading of the Riot Act. The policemen took those arrested to the Iroquois Club. The inhabitants of the city withdrew into their houses as they gradually became aware of what was going on, and in the course of the morning the streets became deserted.

The police then sought out men here and there in the houses. The whole day was devoted to arrests, which continued at a slower pace the next day. The number of people arrested is said to have reached about one hundred eighty. A hundred strikers were released the same day, but fifty-three of them were detained at Sherbrooke and then at Montreal for the weekend.

After their arrest, the strikers were taken to the Iroquois Club to undergo interrogation. Several methods were employed: people were kicked, beaten with truncheons, punched, or shoved against walls. Several of those who were released had swollen faces and bore other marks that testified to the rough treatment they had received. Some policemen threatened to arrest them again unless they returned to work the next day.

Throughout the day, the police maintained a complete control over all activities in the city. The journalists had difficulty doing their job. The reporter from the newspaper *La Presse* was threatened, and Miss Jacqueline Sirois, who had been sent by the *Montreal Star*, was arrested for talking to Father Camirand and for refusing to "circulate" as she had been ordered to do. She was released shortly afterwards.

The police patrolled the entire city all during the night and made a few more arrests. On the following day, May 7, the goings and comings of the people of Asbestos were very limited. The strikers communicated with the union leaders by going to the union office in the house of its secretary, Raymond Pellerin. The house was often filled in the course of the day, but it was emptied periodically to avoid mass arrests.

The churchwardens were the only people to speak up that day, to protest against the acts of profanation the Provincial Police had committed in the Church of St. Aimé. They claimed policemen had pursued and roughed up strikers who had taken refuge in the parish sanctuary. The churchwardens added that foodstuffs stored up for the strikers had been eaten by the policemen.

The Riot Act was "lifted" at 12:45 p.m. on Sunday, May 8. The strikers "recovered" the right of assembly. The inspector still wanted policemen to be present at the union meetings. He withdrew his request when it was pointed out to him that the members of a trade association are perfectly within their rights in holding meetings in camera. A meeting was held that evening, and the discussion centred on the problems created for the union by the recent events. Some strikers who were under arrest had not appeared in court, nor had there been a preliminary hearing into their cases. Their lawyer was unable to communicate with them, and people did not know where things were going.

Two main events occurred on May 9: the representations made by the strikers' lawyers and the evening meeting. All during the weekend Jean Drapeau had tried without success to see his clients. He had even got in touch with the director of the Provincial Police and with the Deputy Attorney General to obtain this permission, but without any better results. On the morning of the 9th, the accused were taken from Montreal to Sherbrooke. There, Drapeau and C. Fortin tried to see them before they were due to appear in court, but the lawyers were able to do so only at the insistence of the judge. On the same day, Drapeau wrote an open letter to the Attorney General, which was published in the newspapers, in which he protested against the fact that he had not been allowed to see his clients and against the fact that the accused had not appeared in court within the period of forty-eight hours stipulated by law.

The union meeting began at nine o'clock in the evening. In addition to the union rank and file, the executive and the chaplains, several journalists were present, including Miss Jacqueline Sirois, Réginald Boisvert, and Gérard Pelletier. Armand Larivée pointed out that even if the policemen had been active, they had left a few strikers at liberty, because the hall was filled. Rodolphe Hamel emphasized the determination the workers had shown to hold out in spite of the attacks upon them. Jean Marchand referred to the activities of the police and their brutality. He asserted that the strikers wanted only to see the strikebreakers stay at home.

On May 10, five strikers accused of threatening (strikebreakers) were condemned to prison terms: W. Chapman, R. Dubé, A. Bossé, L. Bossé, and G. Roux. A sixth accused, E. Richer, was acquitted. The sentences varied from one to two months' imprisonment. The sentences were later appealed and transformed into fines.

On May 11, the Canadian Johns-Manville Co. threatened to shut down its operation and move away because of union demands. It claimed that the union leaders wanted to participate in the administration through control over jobs and promotions and through the right to approve of disciplinary measures. The Company added that it had deposits of asbestos elsewhere, as would be shown by Johns-Manville President L.H. Brown, who was returning by plane that very day from Matheson (in Ontario) with good quality asbestos specimens. Its intention, it said, was to build up production on its Ontario properties while gradually curtailing its operation in Quebec.

In the evening, there was a meeting of the executive of the union with Mgr. Bourassa, the parish priest of Bromptonville, at which the union demands were discussed. The next day, Mgr. Bourassa had an interview with the authorities of the Company. He presented them with a compromise solution which contained provisions for a general wage increase, but which gave the Company certain powers of discrimination. The proposed formula also stipulated that the conditions governing a return to work be discussed only by management representatives and by the officers of the local union. Mr. Picard telephoned the president of the local union to advise him not to accept this offer of mediation, because the leaders of the C.C.C.L. were at that moment in conference with Mgr. Roy, Archbishop of Quebec, on the subject of a possible compromise.

On May 14, Rodolphe Hamel and Armand Larivée were arrested early in the morning by members of the Provincial Police. Although Mr. Hamel was sick, he was dragged from his bed. The arrest warrants held by the police were signed by Judge Aimé Chassé. The union leaders were accused of having conspired and plotted in the company of others during the asbestos strike. These other persons were Daniel Lessard of Thetford, Secretary of the Federation of Mining Industry Employees, René Rocque[3] of Montreal, a C.C.C.L. organizer, and sixteen other miners who were arrested in the course of the day. All these persons were alleged to have committed criminal offenses by participating in unlawful assemblies and by interfering with peace officers in the performance of their duties. Two days later, the accused persons were released, with the exception of Rocque and Charpentier (one of the sixteen strikers), who were already free on bail.

7/The conflict resolved at length: May 17 to July 5
On Tuesday, May 17, Mayor Goudreau of Asbestos, accompanied by several aldermen, had a long interview with the Prime Minister of the province, the Hon. Duplessis, and with the Minister of Labour, the Hon. Barrette. No official statement was made following this interview. On May 20, in the same week, Mr. Picard had talks with the Hon. Barrette in another attempt to find some common grounds for agreement. After the interview, Mr. Picard was supposed to meet with

the members of the union to communicate the proposals of the Minister and to discuss any counter-proposals that might be made. Another interview with the Minister was set for the beginning of the following week. This attempt to come to an understanding also met with failure.

During the weekend of May 21 and 22, the strikers were visited by the officers of a union at one of the biggest Johns-Manville plants, at Manville, New Jersey. The American unionists, who were members of the American Federation of Labour, stressed the fact that the working conditions in the asbestos mines were twenty years behind the times in terms of industrial hygiene. They also emphasized that they had been very warmly welcomed, though they had been told that strangers were regarded with suspicion by the strikers at Asbestos.

About the same time, the Sherbrooke newspaper *Le Messager* published a letter from Mgr. Desranleau, who was in Rome, in which he expressed sympathy for the strikers.[4]

On May 24 four strikers, J.P. Houle, A. Blanchette, J.N. Hamel, and G. Chamberland, initiated actions for damages of $25,000 against the Canadian Johns-Manville Co. for the brutal treatment they had suffered at the hands of Provincial Policemen in a company building.

Two days later, the strikers received considerable aid in the form of seven tons of foodstuffs, which had been collected by the members of the Canadian Brotherhood of Railway Employees.

At Sherbrooke on May 27, a preliminary inquiry was held in the case of the union leaders charged with conspiracy. The court advised them to have nothing more to do with the strike.

At the meeting of June 1, the leaders of the union made it clear that, even after fourteen weeks of strike, there could be no thought of bartering away the basic guarantees demanded by the union. These guarantees were as follows: the renewal of the unions' certification; the assurance that there would be absolutely no discrimination against any of the strikers; the promise of a binding arbitration of such points as were not settled by direct negotiations; the guarantee of an impartial arbitration committee.

On June 12, the central office of the C.C.C.L. made a very important decision, namely that the monthly dues paid in by all the member unions would be turned over to the asbestos strikers, and that the first such money would be dispatched within the week.

The next day, the Archbishop of Quebec, Mgr. Roy, had an interview with Lewis Brown (who had come from New York for the meeting) and Yvan Sabourin, solicitor for the Company. From this moment on, Mgr. Roy became the principal mediator in the asbestos conflict. On several occasions, he got in touch with the Hon. Duplessis and the Hon. Barrette to discuss the conditions of a return to work, as well as the criminal actions which had arisen out of the circumstances of the strike. He also met with Gérard Picard to consider the various formulas of compromise that had been put forward.[5]

On June 17, the Canadian Johns-Manville Co. made a new offer to the union, a compromise solution which was rejected the following day by the strikers: 976 of 1,019 members voting were opposed to the measure.

At Thetford, however, where there was no problem of discrimination, there was progress in the negotiations between the management representatives and Jean Marchand. On June 24, the Asbestos Corporation, the Flintkote Co., and the Johnson Co. accepted the union offer which had been drafted with the help of Mgr. Roy. This proposal contained the basic guarantees demanded by the strikers. At Asbestos, the strikers refused a final offer by the Johns-Manville Co., which was unwilling to rehire twenty of the strikers and wished to give one hundred strikebreakers a job priority over the strikers.

On the first of July at 1:30 a.m., the strike at Asbestos came to an end thanks to the patient mediation of Mgr. Roy. The Johns-Manville Co. granted a wage increase of ten cents per hour and guaranteed work for all of its employees without any discrimination. The return to work took place under the supervision of the Director of the Conciliation and Arbitration Service of the Province of Quebec. Four days later, the first shift of workers passed through the gates to take up the jobs they had left nearly five months before.

The asbestos strike was over, but the differences were not completely resolved. Many further meetings, discussions, and interventions were required before the asbestos companies and the C.C.C.L. unions could sign collective agreements, at the beginning of 1950. The story of these negotiations is told in the following chapter.

III/Conclusion: what was at issue in the strike

The asbestos strike was a stage in the history of the relations between the Canadian Johns-Manville Co. and its employees. Its origins and duration, and the upheaval it caused, are hard to understand if they are viewed apart from this history, or that of Quebec industrial relations in general. The causes of this drama are revealed by the leading actors in it and by some episodes involving them.

The change in the actions and attitudes of labour is a dynamic factor of prime importance in the dispute at Asbestos. For the first time, strong and independent unionism, in full possession of its powers, confronted the Canadian Johns-Mansville Co., which had been operating the asbestos mine in the city for several decades. There had been labour agitation at Asbestos before, over a period of about twenty years, but this was almost the only form of collective action on the part of the workers, and it was merely a discontinuous series of protests against the wage policy and arbitrary powers of the Company.

From about 1936 on, the collective action of the workers at Asbestos became more institutionalized; the union was now the principal weapon of the working class in the struggle for its objectives. Several things prevented this union from becoming effective. It was trying to steer a course between an ideological conception of trade unionism on the one hand and immediate economic tasks on the other. It did not have much economic power, as its membership fluctuated considerably, and the Company was able to keep an iron grip on its labour market because of the instability of the Canadian asbestos industry at the time. Finally, the union had a serious internal weakness in that it was led by people who were attached to a political party whose attitudes were at variance with the deeper significance of the trade union movement. It was seven years after the revival of 1936 before the union members managed to elect leaders who were free of political ties, and these leaders were unable to resort to traditional labour tactics because industrial relations were rigidly controlled by the government until the end of the Second World War.

After the war, the union became the instrument of an institutionalized and permanent labour movement. With its large, active membership and militant leaders, it became the true representative of the workers. The leaders worked tirelessly to develop a strong unionism and to define its objectives. An important factor in the asbestos industry at the time was solidarity among the unions. Negotiations were no longer undertaken between each employer and the union of his employees; rather, the National Federation of Mining Industry Employees acted as negotiator in all the asbestos mines where there was a Catholic union.

This new type of industrial relations first emerged in the discussions that led to the signing of the collective agreement for 1947. These negotiations occurred in a period of strong inflation at a time when the Company could not risk a strike. They were consequently brief; an agreement was soon signed. The real test of power came in the negotiations of 1948, and the strike was the result.

The most important firm in the industry was the Canadian Johns-Manville Co., which employed two thousand persons at Asbestos. This company was a very important element in a prosperous industry, as its American processing plants drew their raw material from the mine at Asbestos. From the economic point of view, the Johns-Manville Co. had managed to survive the most violent economic fluctuations, while its employees had had to put up with great variations in their standard of living and had even suffered poverty and unemployment from time to time. The structure of this firm had always been very authoritarian. Orders were always passed down through the hierarchy, and communication from the bottom to the top of the organization was weak. The authoritarian character of this organization was permanently embodied in the fence and the gates that walled off the properties of the Company, the strict surveillance of comings and goings, and above all the security system, manifested in the constant presence of security guards.

A certain number of facts may have led the Company to adopt the policy of resistance that resulted in the strike. On the ideological level, the Johns-Manville management was made nervous by two schools of thought. The adherents of the social doctrine of the Church (officially that of the union as well) frequently preached the co-partnership and co-determination of enterprises. Secondly, many workers in Asbestos advocated the doctrines of Social Credit, among them state control of the economy based on moral principles, and the exercise of control over the authoritarian tendencies of the social process. The Company restricted its study of currents of social thought to the asbestos region, and was thus not in a position to gauge their importance in relation to ideological trends in the province as a whole.

The Company was also firmly convinced that the union representatives did not want to negotiate and were determined to have their strike at all costs. The union representatives thought the same of the Company. It was a typical case of a very tight deadlock in the relations between an employer and a labour organization. The tactful intervention of a third party might have lessened the resentment between these two and brought them to reconsider their respective positions, but it is unlikely that even this overture would have met with success.

The union demands were revolutionary in the eyes of the Company, as they clearly indicated that the union wanted to exercise some control over both the general policy of the company and its specific decisions regarding hiring, firing, promotions, seniority, and the treatment of grievances. The officers of the Company saw this as an attack upon the traditional structure of the firm, and also felt that the monetary demands were excessive, although in 1947 the Company had granted a basic wage increase of twenty-seven cents per hour (which included the cost of living bonus of ten cents an hour) after brief negotiations.

The declaration of the strike showed how profound this conflict was. Economic theory offers an explanation of the miners' decision: in periods of a rapidly rising cost of living, strikes occur with much greater frequency in order to reduce the spread between cost of living and wages. At this particular time, economic forecasts predicted a considerable recession in the offing for 1949, and one might argue that the strike was perhaps due to nothing more than economic misgivings. However, this hypothesis does not explain why the miners decided on an illegal strike. In similar cases of difficult bargaining, the unions have usually waited until all the legal formalities have been met before declaring a work stoppage.

The theory of the political strike has frequently been invoked. There certainly were tensions at the time between the C.C.C.L. and the provincial government; and the leaders of this confederation of unions had clearly expressed their disapproval of the incumbent government's labour laws. This thesis, however, does not explain the duration and the cohesiveness of the strike, for it lacked some of the essential features of a political strike: the attempt to gain precise political ends and the incorporation of the strike in the strategy of a political party. Because of this, the strike did not have political repercussions except insofar as it was prolonged because of the inflexible attitude of the provincial government.

It has also been maintained that the strike was declared and led by revolutionary union leaders who had imposed it upon the workers. This hypothesis is even weaker than the preceding one. The actions of the leaders were always guided by the traditional aims of trade unionism. Moreover, these leaders had the support of the two thousand unionists at Asbestos and of the three thousand miners at Thetford for more than four months of hardship, in spite of many adverse influences. The workers would not have suffered what they did simply for the pleasure of upholding "revolutionary" leaders, if the aims of the latter had not been identical with those of the union rank and file.

In our opinion, only one hypothesis explains this conflict: a deep resentment on the part of the workers at Asbestos. A class consciousness, heightened by a strong labour movement, accompanied this resentment, which arose at a time when economic conditions favoured the unionists and made possible a long and thoroughgoing conflict. The strike at Asbestos was a power struggle, and was only resolved when the union leadership came to feel that the Company would in future heed the union and respect the will of the workers.

The real issue in this dispute was a radical change in the system of social relations within the Company. The union wished to replace the authoritarian postures of the Company with a more egalitarian scheme in which the union would be officially recognized as the representative of the employees. The strike was aimed at this *real* recognition of unionism, which is not obtained automatically with the return of a certificate by a government agency. The Company, on the other hand, did not want to give up a part of its prerogatives without defending them to the very last. We must consider the dispute in the light of this clash of forces. Moral and legal categories will not help us here. The unionists, even after massive reprisals, accepted no compromises on their principles lest they lose the strike. The Company, to maintain its traditional authoritarian control, tried to preserve its right to reprisals to the very last minute and at great cost.

The asbestos strike also sought recognition of the trade union movement within the French Canadian community. In the postwar period, the labour movement in French Canada was in a state of anticipation, feeling its way towards a role. In earlier times, French Canadians had accepted a locally developed trade unionism as long as it did not try to introduce social goals different from those of the community. The war years saw an increase in the membership of Catholic trade unions and a change of direction as well. The unionists of the Canadian and Catholic Confederation of Labour accepted the aims of modern trade unionism as their own, and once the war was over, bravely undertook to make those economic demands that required the effort of the unions. The asbestos strike offered a unique opportunity to take the measure of unionism's importance in the province and in the country as a whole. The C.C.C.L. members went on strike, but the entire working class participated in the struggle. The approval shown by the Church inspired the collaboration of many groups and many different communities in the province. The C.C.C.L., and with it the trade union movement as a whole, gained official recognition and the support of a segment of public opinion, which were to serve it well in the hard struggles to come. French Canada had just gone through a social transformation of the same type experienced by other modern democratic countries: the working class, long neglected, had acquired a freedom of action and an official status.

Notes on the sources

In a scientific presentation of this historical account, we would have had to give the source of each fact and each assertion in our text, and our account would have become unnecessarily cumbersome.

We have reconstructed this history of the strike at Asbestos by the use of oral evidence and written records. Maître J.P. Geoffroy, who was at Asbestos throughout the entire strike as a representative of the C.C.C.L., has given us invaluable help in our efforts to draw the events together and to grasp the stages in the development of the conflict. Among union leaders, Messrs Hamel, Lessard, Larivée, and Pellerin have helped to corroborate or correct our description of this or that event. Father Camirand went over this history with us and made the necessary corrections. Messrs Picard and Marchand of the C.C.C.L. explained the last stages of the strike to us. We have also met with Mr. McGaw of the Canadian Johns-Manville Co., who gave us some information and added certain details about the first week of the strike. We have also discussed some points with Mr. A. Bell, the police chief of Asbestos.

We have carefully read the news reports and articles in the newspapers *Le Devoir, L'Action catholique, La Tribune, La Presse,* and the *Montreal Star.* We have made particular use of the reports in *Le Devoir, La Tribune,* and *La Presse.* Finally, we have consulted various official documents regarding the strike, such as the statements by the ministers of the provincial government and by the city councils of Asbestos and Thetford, union resolutions, and legal documents.

Notes to Chapter IV

[1]On this subject, see Chapter VI below.

[2]The Company figures are, however, different. (See the chapter by Sauvé under the section: *The strikebreakers*.)

[3]For the consequences of this affair, see Appendix IV at the end of this book.

[4]See chapter VI below.

[5]The details of the negotiations that occurred before the settlement of the strike and of the developments that followed this settlement are not given here, as they form the subject of the following chapter.

Chapter V

History of the Negotiations

Joint authorship

I/Before the strike

At the beginning of December 1948, the National Federation of Mining Industry Employees sent the mining companies at Thetford Mines and Asbestos a list of amendments that its member unions wished to have introduced into the collective agreements then in force. These proposed amendments were as follows:

1— The elimination of asbestos dust both inside and outside the mills.

2— A general wage increase of 15 cents an hour.

3— An 18% raise for the employees paid on the basis of their output (piece or contract work).

4— A bonus of 5 cents per hour for night work.

5— A contribution by the companies to the social security fund of the Federation, to be equal in amount to 3% of the total gross wages.

6— Compulsory payment of union dues ($1.50 per month) by all employees, whether union members or not.

7— Double-time pay for work on Sundays and holidays.

8— Nine paid holidays per year.

9— An increase in holiday pay.

10— The consultation of the union in all cases involving promotion, transfer, or dismissal.

11— The right of employees to accept or reject established rates of production, on an individual basis.

12— An inquiry into work on Sundays, to be conducted by the union.

13— The new agreement at Asbestos to come into effect on
January 1, 1949, one month before the expiry date of the
agreement then in force.

On the other hand one of the firms, the Canadian Johns-Manville
Co., asked the union to accept some amendments to the agreement,
particularly in the clauses regarding the general aims of the contract,
the role of management, and standards of efficiency.

The public relations people attached great importance to the rights
of the employer during the strike. For this reason, we feel we should
cite the clause concerning the "exclusive functions of management"
proposed by the Company:

> The Company retains all the rights, powers and authority which are
> normally exercised by "Management," except in those cases
> where it is specifically laid down in the contract that concessions
> are made in a particular case. This covenant represents a complete
> agreement between the two parties and must be followed to the
> letter.[1]

During the following two and a half months, the two parties tried to
come to an understanding about the terms of the collective agreement,
either by direct negotiation or through an intermediary, the provincial
conciliator. All these attempts met with failure. The spokesmen for
labour stuck to their demands, and the employers would offer no more
than a general increase of five cents per hour, two more paid holidays,
and some improvements in the system of paid vacations. They refused
all the other requests of the workers.

The negotiations with the companies at Thetford Mines proceeded
without incident. At Asbestos, the Canadian Johns-Manville Co. took
action only three days after the first negotiation meeting on December
4, 1948. The Company found that the demands of the miners were
"excessive." Deeming it advisable to say so directly to its employees,
it posted a "progress report" of its own invention in the factory.

Further meetings to undertake negotiations occurred on January 4
and 5, 1949, and once more the Canadian Johns-Manville Co. issued a
progress report. This time, the Federation conferred with its central
body, the Canadian and Catholic Confederation of Labour
(C.C.C.L.), and then formally expressed its opinion to the Company
on this subject: " . . . Seeing that the Union and the Federation are
legally recognized as negotiating agents, and that the present collective agreement sanctions their exclusive right to represent the workers,
they can only view your gesture in insisting on the publication of the
above-mentioned bulletins as a token of no-confidence towards

them ... Consequently, the Federation and the Union are ready to carry on at once with the negotiations that have been undertaken ... but they wish to warn you that if the Company in future publishes any more bulletins about the negotiations, this action will automatically put an end to our direct negotiations. The same applies to any official statement issued by your company which expresses a determination to carry on with the policy which it appears to have adopted in this affair.''[2]

Two days later George K. Foster, a vice-president of the Company, refused to admit that the Company was trying to negotiate directly with its employees by means of the bulletins, writing that '' ... we intend to report the progress of any such negotiations to our employees.'' The next day, January 14, 1949, a new bulletin announced that at the meeting held the previous Monday (January 10), the Federation had broken off the negotiations ''because of our policy of keeping our employees up to date by posting bulletins, after each meeting, on the progress of the negotiations.''

On the following Sunday, January 16, the miners held a general meeting at which they endorsed the positions adopted by the C.C.C.L. and the Federation. The Canadian Johns-Manville Co. interpreted this decision as meaning that the workers no longer intended (''you are unwilling ... '') either to negotiate or to sign a collective agreement with it. On January 24, the Federation again took the offensive, repeating that it intended to continue with the negotiations. It went on to say that the posting of further bulletins would be regarded ''as evidence of bad faith towards the union negotiators.''

The negotiations had been so arduous that the parties to them had not yet had time to discuss wages, paid holidays, etc. In a letter of January 24, the Company stated that it had no intention of changing its policy in any way. On the same day, the Federation appealed to the Conciliation and Arbitration Service of the Province of Quebec.

The Federation asked for the services of a conciliator for the purpose of obtaining a renewal of the collective agreements not only with the Canadian Johns-Manville Co. but also with the companies at Thetford Mines, where the negotiations had made scarcely any headway in two months. In both cases, the statutory periods for direct negotiations had elapsed. The assistant secretary of the Labour Relations Board replied on January 26 ''that before acting on your request, the Board would like to know how many times your Federation has met with the employers or their representatives, the dates of these meetings, the issues discussed by the parties to the dispute, the points on which an agreement has been reached, and those on which it has been impossible to arrive at an understanding.''

The next day, the secretary of the Federation sent a reply to the Board as follows:

I acknowledge receipt of your letter of January 26 last, and am disappointed at the prospect of the delays which will be caused by the Board's requests for information. You may rest assured that our Federation is asking for conciliation because the situation is serious, and we do not want to find ourselves in the same predicament as we did last year, on January 7, 1948.

For your satisfaction, however, we are enclosing the details of our negotiations to date:

1— Wages: Overall increase of fifteen cents ($0.15) per hour; an increase of 18% for workers who are paid on a piece-work or contract basis; five cents ($0.05) more per hour for night work.

2— That the Company make a contribution to the Federation equal to 3% of the total wages paid to its employees, for the financing of a social security fund.

3— A clause in our agreements stipulating the elimination of asbestos dust both inside and outside the mills.

4— A change in our system of vacations. At the present time we receive two weeks' vacation after five years of service; we are asking for two consecutive weeks after two years of service.

5— We are asking for nine paid holidays. At the present time, eight holidays (unpaid) are prescribed in all our agreements, (except that of this number) the Asbestos Corporation and Johnson's Co. (pay their employees for) St. Jean Baptiste Day and for Labour Day.

6— Double time for work on Sundays and holidays.

7— At the Canadian Johns-Manville Co., we are asking for a complete change in the text of the agreement. A copy is attached.

We have had meetings jointly with the Asbestos Corporation Ltd. and Johnson's Co. Ltd. The first of these meetings was held on December 10 and 11, 1948. We later met on December 20 and 21, 1948, and a final time on January 7, 1949.

We met with the Canadian Johns-Manville Co. for the first time on December 24, 1948. A second meeting with the Company was held on January 4 and 5, 1949, and a final meeting on January 10, 1949.

In our many meetings, we have discussed all the issues mentioned above. The Asbestos Corporation and Johnson's Co. have offered us a general increase of five cents per hour, and they have offered to organize a social security fund themselves, on condition that the workers contribute 50% of the cost. The rest of our demands have been refused. The workers who are employed by these two companies have refused these offers, and have requested that all necessary legal steps be taken to ensure that their demands are met.

The negotiations with the Canadian Johns-Manville Co. came to an end on January 10 because the Company has adopted a policy of bad faith towards the representatives of the union and the Federation by publishing reports and commentaries on the negotiations in progress. The evidence of this policy is contained in the correspondence between the Company and the Federation on this matter. (Copies attached.) In addition we feel that, quite apart from the question of the bulletins which the Company is publishing on the negotiations, we will not be able to reach a satisfactory agreement within a reasonable length of time, as stipulated by article 12 of the Act.

We believe that we have given you enough information. We hope that you will expedite matters, and that a conciliator will be sent here as soon as possible, before the workers grow impatient with the delays caused by the Board.

The request for conciliation gave the Canadian Johns-Manville Co. another opportunity to blame the Federation. It expressed its censure in another bulletin addressed to its employees, dated January 28. The bulletin clearly attempts to convince the employees that the Federation is alone responsible for the delays that have occurred in the course of the negotiations, and that it committed an even more serious offense when it infringed upon the rights of the Company by opposing the posting of the bulletins. On the other hand, the Company declares that it is "still ready, at any time, to resume the negotiations on working conditions and on the wage increase it intends to offer for the new labour contract."

At the beginning of February the conciliator, Léopold Rogers, arrived at Asbestos, and spent the next ten days trying to get the two parties to come together. He was not successful, and therefore recommended that they go to arbitration. On the evening of February 13, a general meeting of the strikers at Asbestos was held; their representatives informed them of the results of the negotiations, and then . . . the strike broke out at midnight. *Le Travail,* the official organ of the C.C.C.L., in its special issue of May 1949, summed up the strikers' motives as follows (p. 9):

The miners knew in advance that an arbitration board would not grant them union security and could not assure the establishment of a health care security plan. On February 13, their representatives made a report to them on the progress of the negotiations, during one of their meetings. They decided unanimously to go on strike without waiting for the results of an arbitration that might have gone on for six months.

The next day, the miners at Thetford followed the lead of their fellow-workers at Asbestos, and within a few days, the strike had spread to nearly the whole asbestos industry in the Eastern Townships.

To gain a clear understanding of this spontaneous action on the part of the miners, we must recall the historical context in which it occurred. Among the events which most concerned the miners, we should mention their long struggle to get asbestosis recognized as an industrial disease. In 1949, this struggle had won them only a partial victory, because monetary compensation was still granted only to those whose health had been impaired by asbestos dust for a period of five years or more. We should also emphasize the battles to obtain the recognition of their unions, and the long and exasperating proceedings they had to put up with whenever they negotiated to settle grievances or get collective agreements signed.

If, at least, the government of the Province of Quebec had been able to create a climate of social harmony . . . but quite the contrary was the case. During the fall session of 1948, this government had aroused the indignation of the working class and provoked the opposition of the clergy and a group of employers by bringing a reactionary and anti-union bill before the legislative assembly: a law enacting the Labour Code of the Province of Quebec—known since as Bill 5.

Although the miners had not totally lost confidence in arbitration boards, their memory gave them excellent grounds for being suspicious of government meddling, and for not believing blindly in the impartiality of these boards. They had but recently been victimized by them.

In a first case, the union at Asbestos had had recourse to arbitration in connection with a grievance about the interpretation of the collective agreement which regulated the relations between workers and employers during the year 1948. At that time, the Company extracted asbestos ore by means of electrically operated excavating machines. Four employees were involved in operating one of these machines: a mechanic, an oiler, and two tenders. Their classifications and wage rates had been determined by the application of a job evaluation system which took the responsibilities involved into account. Now, one day the Company decided to eliminate one of the tenders. The union claimed that the task of the remaining tender was thereby increased, and demanded that his wage be adjusted accordingly. In the course of the arbitration, the Company itself admitted that the task of this tender had been increased by 2.4%. The board still handed down a majority decision—the chairman and arbitrator for management being in agreement—which rejected the union request out of hand. At Asbestos, this decision gave rise to much criticism of the employer and the government. We should mention that this decision was handed down on October 22, 1948, just a few months before the strike.

Approximately one year earlier, when they were at the conciliation stage, Johnson's Co. Ltd. and Asbestos Corporation, both of Thetford, had with union consent agreed to commit themselves in advance to abide by the decision of a "private" arbitration board, which was appointed to resolve the problem of union security. There were three people on the board: one representative each of management and the unions, and Georges Lépine, a conciliator who served as chairman. It handed down a majority decision that the "Rand formula" should be applied. Johnson's Co. did not want to accept the judgment of the board; in contempt of its earlier promise, it disputed the decision's legality before the Minister of Labour, who upheld the position of the Company.[3]

It was, then, only after many annoying incidents that the Rand formula made its appearance at Thetford in the contracts that were signed a short while later.

During the first two months of the strike, in spite of offers to mediate on the part of the Minister of Labour and several other overtures of this kind (the intervention, for example, of the city councils of Thetford Mines and Asbestos), it was impossible to get the parties to the dispute to negotiate on anything other than the conditions for a return to work. Every time the labour representatives demanded written guarantees that there would be no reprisals after the return to work, the talks collapsed. The employers invariably refused to make these guarantees.

One of these efforts at mediation produced the suggestion that a single arbitrator be appointed. Jean Marchand, the General Secretary of the C.C.C.L., later expressed regret that "the government objected to the appointment of a single arbitrator, although the proposal was made to it by an intermediary of the highest authority."[4]

About April 22, or nine weeks after the strike had started, the first official negotiations began which offered some real hope of a settlement. Only four people took part in the deliberations: the Minister and Deputy Minister of Labour (Gérard Tremblay), Théodore Lespérance, the legal representative of the unions, and Yvan Sabourin, the lawyer representing the employers. At that time, the Minister of Labour made a statement which we wish to quote here verbatim, because it gives a precise definition of the role of the arbitrators, and because all the guarantees demanded by the strikers are clearly assured:

After successive interviews which I have had with the representatives of the "Canadian Johns-Manville," it was decided that the two interested parties would nominate their arbitrators. When the Minister of Labour has been officially notified as to who have been appointed arbitrators for the unions and for the Company, he will summon both of them to his office on Monday afternoon (April 25) at three o'clock. It has already been agreed that the arbitrators will be appointed, as the Minister has requested, and that they will meet for the purpose of choosing the person who will act as the chairman of the arbitration board.

Once this arbitration board has been set up, the heads of the unions will recommend a return to work, and the employers will hire the workers back *without discrimination on account of the strike, and will not oppose the restoration of certification to the unions.*

Immediately after the return to work, the Minister continued, this arbitration board will study all the clauses of any proposed contract, or all the proposals and counterproposals which have been made, but its decision will be be binding on the two parties, unless they agree otherwise. The board will, in fact, be an ordinary arbitration board, and will perform its function in conformity with the law and established procedure, with this difference that the parties to the dispute must agree on the choice of the chairman when they meet at the Minister's office on Monday afternoon.[5]

The negotiations between the two arbitrators were concerned with the choice of a chairman of the arbitration board and with the conditions for a return to work. On Friday evening, April 29, the talks were broken off. They had not resulted in agreement on any of the points under discussion. According to the arbitrator for the unions, the reason was that the Company intended to take reprisals:

I agreed to act as an arbitrator for the choice of a third arbitrator in the asbestos dispute in the belief—shared by the union representatives who appointed me—that the terms of the return to work would include real guarantees that there would be no reprisals against workers or labour organizations.

In the course of the discussions about the choice of a third arbitrator, on which there was neither definitive agreement nor disagreement, it became clear that the Johns-Manville Company, represented by Yvan Sabourin, Q.C., did not intend to give up the possibility of taking various forms of reprisals. This point became an obstacle, and as it was impossible to clear it up, we were obliged to bring the talks to an end.[6]

The arbitrator for the employers, Yvan Sabourin, simply said:

> I find it very odd that they are refusing to go to arbitration after the offer which we have made. This attitude on the part of the unions is staggering, especially when one bears in mind that the wages paid by the Canadian Johns-Manville Co. assure the workers daily minimum earnings of $7.65 . . . etc.

Then, after speaking of "requests for work which are coming in from all over," to such a degree that by his estimate "the Company will soon no longer be able to meet these demands," he added the frank remark:

> I cannot imagine what motivates the unions, nor what feelings underlie the strikers' behaviour.

II/During the strike

Scarcely two days after the dispute had begun, on the morning of February 16, Quebec's Minister of Labour, the Honourable Antonio Barrette, expressed his official opinion on it. According to him, the strike was illegal because the miners had refused to submit to arbitration. An arbitration board might still be set up, but only after a return to work. The Minister added that if the strikers did not return to work, he would be obliged to notify the Labour Relations Board of the illegality of the strike, and invite it to "consider the withdrawal of certifications."

Barrette's two main themes were the illegality of the strike and the return to work before arbitration. The Prime Minister and Attorney General of the province (the Honourable Maurice Duplessis), the Minister of Labour, and the Canadian Johns-Manville Co. brought them continually to the attention of the public up to the end of April. The Minister of Labour, even when he offered to act as an official mediator—which he did twice in the first month of the strike—did not fail to remind the strikers that they were in the wrong . . . On February 22, the Labour Relations Board, after refusing to listen to the representations made by the labour spokesmen, notified each of the unions at Asbestos and Thetford Mines that it was depriving them of their certificates of recognition because the strikers had not returned to work within the prescribed period: this action on the part of the Board only served to complicate the situation even more from the legal point of view.

By an odd coincidence, the statement of the Minister of Labour also blamed the unions:

> I regret to announce that the Catholic unions, represented by Maître Théodore Lespérance, broke off the negotiations at about 10:15 this evening . . .
>
> I may add that I have spared no efforts in attempting to secure an agreement which would have enabled me to set up the arbitration board I had proposed.

Gérard Picard, the President of the C.C.C.L., emphasized the following points:

> The C.C.C.L., the Federation, and the Unions have tried in vain to reach an understanding which would contain a reasonable minimum of guarantees concerning the most pressing issues . . .
>
> Although the Minister of Labour did help to obtain agreement on one of the points under discussion, it is rather surprising to find him taking the side of the Johns-Manville Company on two issues which vitally concern any settlement of the strike . . .
>
> The responsibility for the collapse of the talks must be borne by the Canadian Johns-Manville Co. Ltd., represented by Maître Yvan Sabourin and supported by the provincial government, which refused to accept the conditions for a return to work which had been agreed upon before the highest religious authorities.[7]

The next day, the newspapers reported the collapse of the negotiations, and also published an urgent appeal from the Sacerdotal Commission of Social Studies, signed by Mgr. J.C. Leclaire, D.P., for aid to families who were suffering hardship because of the strike.[8]

This report was one of the very few which referred to efforts at mediation on behalf of the religious authorities during this period of the strike. This implies that all of these interventions were made unofficially.

One week later, the "disorders" of May 6 occurred at Asbestos, and the strike assumed tragic proportions. People wondered if the parties to the dispute were going to break off negotiations altogether, but on May 17, negotiations were begun again, and the president of the Canadian Johns-Manville Co. himself, Lewis H. Brown, made a new proposal to the unions through the intermediary of Maître Y. Sabourin. The labour representatives found it unsatisfactory, but made a counterproposal, which the employer rejected in turn. The Minister of Labour himself presented them with another plan, a compromise solution which he regarded as a "happy medium."

In the first days of June, however, the Minister of Labour was obliged to inform the public that the negotiations had once more come to an end. He said that since the Company had accepted his proposal in its entirety, the unions were responsible for the breakdown. The parties to the negotiations had not been able to come to an agreement on two of the points under discussion: the guarantees against reprisals and the procedure for arbitration. The president of the C.C.C.L. offered the following explanation:

> The Minister of Labour and the employers wanted to retain the right to take reprisals against those asbestos miners who have been arraigned on various charges. The C.C.C.L. cannot accept this position, because the employees concerned are not people who have committed an offense in the exercise of their ordinary functions or in the course of their usual work, but mainly workers who have been arrested at Asbestos without a warrant following the reading of the Riot Act.
>
> Not only would the employer and the Minister treat them as criminals, but they would also have their union organizations sign a document which presumes their guilt . . .

Another part of his statement shows just how much the labour representatives distrusted the government's involvement in the setting up of the board:

> The unions in the asbestos industry have proposed the setting up of an arbitration board which is guaranteed to be impartial, and have recommended that the decision of the board be final. Neither of these suggestions is incorporated in the proposals made by the employers and the Minister of Labour.
>
> If the decision is not final on the usual matters of negotiation at least, there is likely to be another serious conflict in the near future . . .
>
> The important thing is to find a fair solution to the present dispute, which is a serious one, not to lay traps for this person or that. The appointment of a chairman should be free from political or managerial influence, and the chairman himself should be in a position to hand down a decision which in his opinion is fair and equitable.[9]

The position of the Canadian Johns-Manville Co. was explained by G.K. Foster, a vice-president and local manager:

> The Canadian Johns-Manville Co. has accepted the proposal of the Minister because we sincerely want to do all we can to end this strike . . .

One can only come to the conclusion that the labour leaders do not want the strike to be settled, and that the loss of work and the hardship of the strikers' families will have to continue for the time being . . .

We advise those of our former employees who wish to retain their status and seniority in the Company to report to work as soon as possible, without further delay. Their basic wage will be ten cents per hour more than the rate in force according to the terms of the contract which expired on January 31, 1949. They will have four paid holidays.[10]

While the negotiations with the Canadian Johns-Manville Co. continued to dominate the news in this fashion, other talks were taking place with Nicolet Asbestos Mines, of St. Rémi de Tingwick, a small firm whose 125 employees were also on strike.

On May 24, the representatives of the workers had sent this company a proposal for an agreement on the conditions for a return to work. No publicity was given to these negotiations, which ended on June 6 with the signature of a preliminary agreement which gave this group of strikers an assurance of "the major part of the guarantees" which they were demanding, and "the terms for wages and paid holidays (i.e., an increase of 10 cents per hour and four paid holidays) which have been put into effect by certain asbestos companies since the beginning of the strike." It also stipulated that an arbitration board find a satisfactory solution to those problems which were not settled by subsequent negotiation.[11]

Elsewhere, though, the strike continued unabated. In spite of intimidation, public statements, the attacks of newspapers favourable to the government, and the paid advertisements of the Canadian Johns-Manville Co., the strikers held out. They were undoubtedly encouraged by this first victory, and by the certainty of receiving the increased aid which the bodies affiliated with the C.C.C.L., at their Plenary Council meeting of June 11, had promised them.

Immediately after the agreement was signed with Nicolet Asbestos Mines, the three companies at Thetford made new proposals. Counterproposals followed. The miners of Thetford rejected a management offer by a nearly unanimous vote (1,081 to 91), and the employers then tried to break the strike. On June 24, however, the three companies of Thetford signed a joint agreement containing the following provisions:

1— The companies would not oppose the return of certificates of recognition to the Federation and to the unions whose members were on strike.

2— All the employees would return to work at their old jobs as quickly as possible, with due regard for the requirements of production.

3— No reprisals would be taken against the employees because of their participation in the strike. It was nevertheless agreed to and accepted that this clause would not apply to employees who were guilty of causing damage to the companies' property, or of harming their representatives. Employees convicted on these charges might be dismissed.

4— The parties to the agreement were to negotiate the terms of the collective agreement for 1949 and, if they were unable to reach a settlement in the ten days following the signing of this agreement, all the provisions of the collective agreement would be referred to arbitration "in accordance with the law." If the arbitrators could not agree on the choice of the chairman of the board, Judge Thomas Tremblay of Quebec City would perform this function. The decision of the arbitration board would not be binding on the parties to the agreement.

Meanwhile, new negotiations with the Canadian Johns-Manville Co. began on June 9, when Mgr. M. Roy, on his own initiative, submitted a proposal for an agreement directly to the Company. As always, the union and the employer made counterproposals. On June 20, the miners at Asbestos rejected a management proposal by a vote of 976 to 37, because the employer wanted to retain the right to reprisals against a score of strikers who had been arrested and arraigned. This setback did not, however, put an end to the negotiations, and the Archbishop of Quebec made several further attempts to keep in touch with the Prime Minister and the Minister of Labour of Quebec, the president of the Canadian Johns-Manville Co., and the president of the C.C.C.L.

Finally, towards the end of June, Lewis Brown sent Mgr. Roy a final proposal which had already been signed by two officers of the Company. That very day, the presidents and the secretaries of the Federation and the union also signed it. The "asbestos strike," as it was called, was over.

The text of the agreement is as follows:

1— As soon as the strike is over, the Minister of Labour will recommend to the Labour Relations Board that it restore the certificates of recognition to the union and the Federation whose members are on strike, in the form in which they previously existed.

2— When the strike is over, the personnel will be increased to
include all those employees who were on the payroll of February 12, 1949. These people will return to their former jobs
as soon as possible, according to the requirements of production and with due regard for seniority, under the supervision
of the Director of the Conciliation and Arbitration Service.

3— It is not to be inferred from the fact that the employees have
been rehired that the Company is compromised regarding acts
for which some persons may be judged criminally responsible.

4— In connection with the employees' return to work, neither the
Company nor the union shall show discrimination on account
of the strike.

5— If the employees return to work at once, the Company agrees
to hire back as many men as possible in the mine, mill, and
factory, under efficient working conditions, and to keep production at a high level until the fibre reserves have reached a
normal level.

6— The Company shall also endeavour to enlarge its underground
mining operations, to increase the number of workers by
about one hundred.

7— After the return to work, direct negotiations will be undertaken to arrive at a collective labour agreement. The two
parties shall have recourse to conciliation and arbitration in
accordance with the law. If there is arbitration, it is agreed
that Judge Thomas Tremblay will serve as the chairman of the
arbitration board.

8— As soon as possible after the signing of a new agreement, the
Minister of Labour will intervene with the Company to obtain
an amicable settlement of the civil actions now before the
courts.

9— Within the period when the proposed contract is in force, the
Minister of Labour will call together representatives of the
union and the mining companies to discuss the question of
industrial safety.

10— The Federation and the union at Asbestos recognize property
and management rights, and they agree to include a so-called
management rights clause in the contract.

11— The employees returning to work will have a right to the
existing wage rates and holidays.

The resolution of the strike must have been deeply gratifying to Mgr. Roy, who since his return from Rome in April had laboured tirelessly and ceaselessly to work out a formula for its settlement. What words, though, could express the delight of the strikers, who had not perhaps yet fully realized that they had just fought one of the most important battles in the history of the Quebec trade union movement?

III/After the strike

Less than ten days after the end of the strike at Asbestos, the arbitration proceedings were about to begin. The unions had not, in fact, been able to sign a collective agreement with the companies at Thetford within the period of time prescribed by the agreement on the return to work.

At that moment, a serious incident came near to upsetting all the calculations and dangerously complicating the situation. On July 5, the Labour Relations Board refused to return the certificates of recognition to the unions, in defiance of the agreements signed with the companies, and in spite of the fact that a formal verbal promise had been made to Mgr. Roy and the unions. The Board even wanted to force them to make new applications to obtain this right. It was most fortunate that the Board altered its decision eight days later.

Another development boded ill for the negotiations with the Canadian Johns-Manville Co. A lengthy memorandum signed by the president, Lewis Brown, was published and distributed to the employees of the Company. Using the pretext that all the employees might not have understood the terms of the agreement at the time of the return to work, Mr. Brown took it upon himself to give them an "explanation." At the same time, the employees received a copy of a letter from Mr. Brown to Mgr. Roy, which summed up some of the particulars in the memorandum. Fifteen days later, the president of the C.C.C.L. made a reply to the memorandum, calling it "a unilateral interpretation of the agreement which ended the strike" and dealing in turn with those parts of the memorandum which in his opinion contained "inaccuracies, insinuations detrimental to the truth, and even falsehoods."[12] Fortunately, this incident did not have unhappy consequences.

Meanwhile, the companies and the unions at Thetford nominated their arbitrators, Maître Raymond Caron and Maître Théodore Lespérance. They were joined by Judge Thomas Tremblay, acting as chairman of the arbitration board, as had been agreed. Lawyers J.E.L. Duquette, Lucien Tremblay, and T.R. Ker, of Montreal, were to act for the companies, and Maître Louis Philippe Pigeon, of Quebec City, for the unions.

The parties to the arbitration later agreed among themselves that the board would hear only the case involving the Asbestos Corporation, and that its decision would apply equally to the two other companies. It was also agreed that the Canadian Johns-Manville Co. would wait until the decision was handed down before consenting to it.

From August 2 to October 6, 1949, the arbitration board held a dozen public sittings to hear the evidence, the depositions of witnesses, and the speeches of counsel. The depositions and speeches covered 1,938 pages of shorthand text. The union filed 22 documents in evidence, the Company 96, a total of 188 exhibits. The board did not hand down its decision until December 10, more than five months after the strike had ended.

When the public learned of the majority decision of the board, from which the union arbitrator dissented, it was obliged to recognize that the board had radically amended or rejected almost all the demands of the miners.

The Rand formula, though it had formed part of the agreements of the previous year, was treated as ''a clause at variance with common law, and contrary to the principle of liberty which must serve as a basis for trade unionism. It is also contrary to the dignity of the worker and may even be detrimental to his liberty of conscience. . . .'' Nevertheless, the majority decision granted a binding and voluntary checkoff of union dues (i.e., the employer was obliged to ''deduct'' the amount of the union dues from the pay of any employee who requested it, and to turn that amount over to the union).

The employers did not ask for changes in the clauses on Sunday labour and holidays. The union, to get the employers to reduce the work to a minimum on those days, demanded that it be paid at a double-time rate. The board upheld the position of the Company.

The union requested two weeks of paid vacation after two years of service, while the employer offered 14 days after 5 years. The board granted 12 days after 5 years of service!

In accordance with the law, the union wanted a one-year collective agreement. The board decided that the agreement would remain in force for two years. Article 15 of the Labour Relations Act (since amended), however, formally stipulated:

> No collective agreement shall be made for more than one year, but it may be agreed that it shall be automatically renewed for a similar period, and so on, upon failure by one of the parties to give a written notice to the other party within a delay which shall not be more than sixty days nor less than thirty days prior to the expiration

of each period.

The union would have liked to have a clause in the collective agreement obliging the Company to do everything in its power to eliminate asbestos dust as soon as possible, both inside and outside the mills. This was among the issues most discussed in the course of the strike. The board handed down the following majority decision on this point:

> The Company recognizes that the asbestos dust is harmful. It states that it is prepared to continue the work which it has already begun [to eliminate it] ... This clause may not in any way be interpreted as a contractual obligation on the part of the Company. ...

The board, again by majority decision, granted a wage increase of only $0.10 per hour retroactive to January 1, 1949, which the Nicolet Asbestos Mines had agreed to when its employees returned to work.

The union arbitrator, Maître Théodore Lespérance, offered his evaluation of the decision itself before giving his grounds for dissenting from most of the board's recommendations:

> I must refuse to assent to the report presented by the chairman and the management arbitrator, because this report, in its conclusions and its grounds for them, repudiates Catholic social doctrines, drawing its inspiration from the most blameworthy economic liberalism and from the most individualistic conception of property rights.

On December 16, two days after the decision was handed down, Maurice Duplessis held a press conference on it. His first remarks touched on "the strike which has lasted more than five months and has cost those involved, especially the workers in lost wages, thousands and thousands of dollars,"—"millions," as the *Sherbrooke Daily* and *La Tribune* of Sherbrooke were to report it.

The Prime Minister then went on to mention the workers of East Broughton and of the Bell mine (Thetford) who "refused to go on strike and did not suffer any of the huge losses sustained by the strikers at the other firms." Duplessis ended his press conference with these words:

> Each of the parties to the arbitration has had a portion of its demands granted or rejected. In the interests of the province in general and the municipalities involved in particular, as well as in the interests of the workers and employers, it is imperative that everyone become fully aware of his duty to cooperate in assuring respect for justice and for the legally constituted order. ...

The government of the province will always be glad to do what is reasonably possible, within the bounds of respect for established order and authority, to ensure that everyone obtains justice and that the public interest is safeguarded.[13]

The day after this press conference, A.L. Penhale, President of the Asbestos Corporation, sent a telegram to the Minister of Labour, and to the newspapers as well, in which he announced that his company conditionally accepted the decision of the arbitration board:

Re: Asbestos Corporation Limited and the Union of Asbestos Employees of Asbestos Corporation Limited. We have examined the report concerning this matter which was made by the arbitration committee on December 10 and placed in your hands on December 13, 1949, in conformity with the Quebec Trade Disputes Act. The decision of the majority of arbitrators in many respects goes beyond what seems reasonable to us, considering the evidence submitted. We feel that such a decision can only be justified as an attempt to find a practical solution to a difficult problem, in order to reestablish the good relations which once existed in our industry. In the same spirit, we are prepared to accept the decision of the majority of arbitrators without reserve, provided that this decision is likewise accepted by the union which represents the employees. We are also ready to put into effect the higher rates and retroactive financial adjustments prescribed by this decision, as soon as we receive formal notification of this acceptance by the unions. We are sending a copy of this telegram to the local union and to the Federation.

Before entering upon further negotiations, the unions of Thetford held a big meeting on December 18, in the course of which some 1,500 miners decided "to shelve the report of the board because this board recommends that the two parties act in contravention of labour law." The secretary general of the C.C.C.L., Jean Marchand, stated unequivocally that "the miners will not sign a contract for more than one year."[14]

On December 19, the unions clearly stated their positions at the first session of negotiations with representatives of the three companies at Thetford, which were started after the arbitration. They declared that they were ready to accept the financial arrangements stipulated by the decision for the year 1949 only, and demanded an increase of five cents per hour for the year 1950. All the other decisions of the arbitration board were accepted.[15]

The negotiations which took place on December 19 were "long, but amicable." Nevertheless, the negotiators for the workers decided to bring the problem of the duration of the agreement to the attention of the Minister of Labour:

> The recommendation of the board on this point [wrote D. Lessard, the secretary of the Federation] is contrary to the agreement of June 1949 between the asbestos companies and the unions involved, and contrary to the law. It is clear and manifest, by the terms of this agreement, that the jurisdiction of the arbitration board should have been limited to a study of the agreement of 1949.
>
> I wish to emphasize once more that the unions are ready to conclude an agreement for 1949 on the basis of the majority decision and in conformity with the agreement of June 24. We feel that it is unjust and immoral to make the retroactive payments for 1949 dependent on the signing of the same agreement for 1950, using as grounds a recommendation which could not and should not have been made. The companies are not bound by the decision, but they are bound by their agreement of June 24, 1949.
>
> All the workers in the asbestos industry have benefitted from the increase of 10 cents per hour retroactive to the beginning of the year, except for those who work for the three companies affected by the decision of the arbitration board. These workers need their money, and they are being refused it only because of an unfortunate misunderstanding.
>
> It would surely be advisable to inform the public that the unions are not rejecting the majority decision of the arbitration board, and that it is the companies who are violating their agreement of June 24.

The unions, unable to find an area of agreement with the companies at Thetford, requested the intervention of a conciliator. As the Minister of Labour was away on a trip to Rome, the file landed on the Prime Minister's desk. At an interview which he granted the labour representatives on December 29, he made them a proposal which the unions accepted, on the conditions which we find set forth in the following letter, addressed to Mr. Duplessis by the secretary of the Federation on the same day as the interview:

> The representatives of the asbestos workers, who have had the pleasure of meeting with you this afternoon concerning the disagreement which persists in the asbestos industry, have given careful consideration to your proposal regarding the collective agreement of 1950, which is at present a matter of dispute between the parties involved.
>
> Your proposal is to include a clause in the collective agreement of

1950 which provides for an automatic wage adjustment geared to increases in the cost of living index. After careful consideration of the problem, and in the hope of quickly reaching a definitive agreement on this thorny question, the officers have decided to recommend to the general meeting of the miners that they accept your proposal, and on the following terms:

a) The agreement for the year 1949 will be established on the basis of the majority report of the Hon. Judge Tremblay.

b) As of January 1, 1950, the workers covered by the collective contracts to be signed will receive an increase in their wages equal to 40 cents per week for each point of increase in the cost of living index, taking the index of January 1, 1949, or 159.6, as a base. This index (159.6) is the last one considered by the Hon. Judge Tremblay in his recommendation on wages.

c) It is clearly understood that this clause will not be applied in the event of a decrease, and that it will not have any retroactive effect for the year 1949.

d) The agreement will have to be submitted to the general meeting of the workers for final approval.

We hope, Mr. Prime Minister, that the companies will agree to settle the problem on the basis established above, and that the asbestos miners will be able to receive the money coming to them for the year 1949 as soon as possible, and that they will not have to face further difficulties.

On December 30, the Prime Minister sent his proposal to the companies by telegram, and accompanied it by an urgent request that they accept it:

In the present circumstances, and in conformity with the public interest, since the public is always deeply affected by these problems, the Government is of the opinion that a settlement between the employees and the employers, based upon the above conditions, should be reached as soon as possible. The Government strongly recommends this settlement, which we feel is fair and proper in the circumstances. We expect that the employers will kindly send us a favourable reply to these proposals before 12:30 p.m.

John E.L. Duquette, the Asbestos Corporation attorney, transmitted the companies' reply of acceptance:

I have been instructed by the Asbestos Corporation Limited, and by T.R. Ker, Q.C., the attorney for Johnson's Company Ltd., and Lucien Tremblay, Q.C., the attorney for Flintkote Mines Limited, to advise you that on your personal recommendation and on the grounds expressed in the telegram which you sent me on December thirtieth, and in the sincere desire to cooperate with your efforts to assure a lasting peace in the asbestos industry, the three above-mentioned companies agree to accept in principle the proposals set forth in the above-mentioned telegram for the settlement of the appropriate clauses, in a satisfactory form which is in conformity with our acceptance of these proposals, including our interpretation that no adjustment in the cost of living bonus will be made on the basis of fractional changes in the cost of living index amounting to less than one whole point, and on condition that the majority decision of the arbitrators be wholly accepted in all other respects.[16]

The parties to the negotiations reached a definitive agreement on all the clauses of the collective agreement on January 5. The miners held a general meeting on January 8, at which they accepted the agreement which had been negotiated by their representatives. They had previously rejected all the arguments which the chairman of the arbitration board and the management arbitrator had brought forward in favour of their recommendations. The collective agreements were signed in mid-January.

The negotiations with the Canadian Johns-Manville Co. went on for six more weeks after that. At the beginning of February, the Company took steps to improve its system of dust elimination and air purification, setting aside some $500,000 for the purpose.[17]

On February 16, René Rocque was condemned to 6 months in prison for "conspiracy to commit acts of violence."[18]

On February 21, 1950, a collective agreement was signed with the Canadian Johns-Manville Co.

The negotiations with the asbestos companies, begun in December 1948, had come to an end.

Notes to Chapter V

[1]Canadian Johns-Manville. Letter to its employees, January 8, 1949.

[2]Letter of Mr. Daniel Lessard, secretary of the Federation, January 11, 1949.

[3]Approximately the same thing happened at Flintkote Mines Ltd., of Thetford Mines.

[4]As reported in *Le Devoir,* April 23, 1949. On this matter, see the following chapter.

[5]*Montréal-Matin,* April 25, 1949. (The author's italics.)

[6]*Le Devoir,* April 30, 1949.

[7]*Ibid.*

[8]This appeal is quoted in the text of Chapter VI below.

[9]*Le Devoir,* June 4, 1949.

[10]*Ibid.*

[11]*Le Devoir,* June 6, 1949.

[12]*Le Devoir,* Aug. 6, 1949.

[13]*L'Action catholique,* Dec. 17, 1949.

[14]*La Tribune,* Dec. 19, 1949.

[15]*Le Devoir,* Dec. 20, 1949.

[16]*Le Canada,* Dec. 31, 1949.

[17]*Front ouvrier,* Feb. 4, 1950.

[18]Appendix IV of this book deals with the Rocque trial.

Chapter VI

The Church and the Conflict in the Asbestos Industry

by Gérard Dion

I/The facts

In many respects, the asbestos industry dispute will remain an important event in the history of labour relations in the Province of Quebec. This strike assumed a very peculiar character from the beginning.

Other chapters of this book have noted that the asbestos strike is framed by a sequence of events which, though external to it, had a decisive influence on the climate of labour relations at the time it occurred.

From the beginning, moreover, the provincial government was not content to declare the strike illegal, as it had already done in similar circumstances, but openly and publicly expressed its opinion on each of the union demands (wages, sanitary working conditions, Rand formula), upholding company positions.[1] Such an attitude did nothing to restore the workers' lost confidence in the impartiality of an arbitration system in which the chairman was inevitably appointed by the government. Furthermore, the representative of government attacked the Catholic labour leaders from the floor of the Legislature, insinuating that they were unorthodox in matters of doctrine.[2]

Finally, it is highly significant that the union chaplains, particularly Abbé Camirand and Abbé Poulin, immediately came to the defence of the workers. Statements like that of Father Camirand, "If I were a miner, I would be a striker," were given wide circulation in the whole Canadian press and in American magazines.

In other words this conflict, because of its scale and the confrontation of forces involved, could not remain a conflict "like the others." Since the Catholic Church is an integral part of Quebec society, it is not surprising that it played a role in the dispute, even a role of prime importance. Without its intervention, both the immediate results of this conflict and its long-range consequences would surely have been very different, for the strikers and for the Church itself.

This was not, however, the first occasion on which the Church had intervened in a labour conflict. Mgr. L.N. Bégin had arbitrated the boot and shoe industry dispute at the beginning of the century, and the formula he had suggested for the settlement of labour disputes later enjoyed a great success, serving as a basis of labour legislation in each of the provinces and in Canada as a whole.[3] The workers still had bitter memories of the disappointments they had suffered when Cardinal Villeneuve intervened in the textile industry dispute of 1937.[4] These interventions were exceptional, however, and in spite of their momentary importance, they are of slight significance in comparison with what took place during the asbestos strike.

When people speak of the Catholic Church, they are often inclined to consider the hierarchy exclusively. Catholic laymen, though, as individuals or as members of institutions committed to Catholic doctrine, also represent the Church and its policies. Our study of the asbestos strike must take this fact into account.

In the first place, the people concerned were Catholic workers, belonging to unions which publicly proclaimed their adherence to the social doctrine of the Church and which had chaplains to provide moral guidance. Economic and social organizations act on their own responsibility in the temporal domain. The Church is not involved in their affairs from a legal point of view, but is inevitably present in people's thoughts. The Catholic religion provided considerable moral support to the strikers during the long weeks of idleness and hunger: every day at three o'clock in the afternoon, the workers of Asbestos gathered at the offices of the union and, led by a standard bearer, proceeded to the parish church to tell their beads.

The Catholic Church, then, quite apart from anyone's actual intervention, was implicated in the asbestos strike. Outside the Province of Quebec, the newspapers realized this, and said so.[5]

Union chaplains further involved the Church by their actions: Father Camirand, chaplain of the local union at Asbestos; Abbé Lucien Poulin, chaplain of the Sherbrooke Central Labour Council; Abbé Henri Masson, union chaplain at Thetford; and Abbé Henri Pichette, chaplain of the C.C.C.L. By the very nature of their jobs, they were "dragged into this business" once the strike began. In addition, they publicly expressed encouragement and support of the strikers by their interventions.[6] Because of the official role they played in the striking unions—as long as the religious authorities kept them at their posts —the Church found itself yet more involved, even in an active way. In a talk to the strikers on March 27, the Chaplain General of the C.C.C.L. asked the miners to put their trust in their chaplain, Abbé

Camirand, and added: "He has been appointed by your bishop, who is himself responsible to Rome. If he acts in a manner that is not in conformity with the doctrines of the Church, the authorities will know how to punish him. This is their responsibility alone."[7]

Up to this point, we may look upon the role of the Church in the dispute as perfectly in keeping with its usual behaviour in our society. It is, in sum, the normal course of events, what one ought to expect when there are Catholic unions with chaplains. However, as the situation developed, the dispute assumed major proportions, and the chances of reaching an understanding between the parties to the conflict became more remote. Some influential clergymen then tried to intercede with the government authorities to get them, finally, to play a mediating and conciliating role. For several weeks, Their Excellencies Mgr. Courchesne, Mgr. Garant, Mgr. Papineau, and Mgr. Leclaire, to mention only a few, made repeated attempts of this kind, but in vain. Despite their rank and the relationships they had enjoyed with the top men in the government, they were unable to bring about any change in the situation. The government did not want to intervene, alleging that such a conciliatory gesture was an incitement to break the law, since the strike was, it claimed, illegal. As a necessary condition of any intervention, it insisted that all strikers whom the company was willing to rehire must return to work at once, without any guarantees. The unions could not accept this condition; they had been disappointed by similar experiments in the past. Uppermost in their minds was the textile industry strike of 1937, which they had ended in this fashion. The same political party was now in power. Furthermore, how could the National Federation of Mining Industry Employees trust a government which, from the earliest days of the conflict, had publicly taken a stand against each of the union demands?

Because of political interventions and the great amount of space that was devoted to it in the newspapers, the asbestos strike was no longer a mere dispute between a union and a group of companies. It had acquired a general significance for the entire Catholic trade union movement.

As events pursued their course, the financial resources of the National Federation of Mining Industry Employees, the C.C.C.L., and its affiliates diminished, and the leaders of these organizations found themselves faced with the possibility of an unconditional surrender. Having used up all their lines of credit, they knocked on the doors of a few bishops. Quite independently of the question as to who was in the right in this dispute, it became progressively clearer that the very fate of the C.C.C.L. depended on the outcome. For this reason, certain dioceses decided to advance it some money unobtrusively.

Meanwhile, His Excellency Mgr. Maurice Roy had returned from Rome on April 5, and at the request of both the Canadian Johns-Manville Co. and the unions had made repeated efforts to achieve a settlement of the dispute. At this point the representatives of the strikers were not received by the government. The newspapers had become the medium of communication, and dialogue between the parties to the conflict took place by means of statements to the press. About mid-April, Mgr. Roy was able to submit a proposal for a settlement to the Minister of Labour. The Minister, who seemed interested in resolving the conflict, received him warmly, but the next day he informed the parties to the dispute that the government rejected this proposal because, according to a later statement of Mr. Duplessis, the arbitration formula suggested, calling for a single arbitrator and a decision having the force of law, was not the usual one.

Mgr. Roy continued his mediation between the government and the parties to the dispute. At his suggestion, each nominated an arbitrator to represent it. For four days, from April 25 to 29, these men vainly tried, in the presence of the Minister of Labour, to arrive at a satisfactory formula. On April 29, an important date, they went their separate ways, unable to arrive at a compromise. The union now had no alternative but to throw itself on the mercy of the Company. It was not even sure that the Company would negotiate with it, because the Labour Relations Board had withdrawn its certificate of union recognition. The Company also voiced its determination to take reprisals against a certain number of strikers. This amounted to asking the unions to accept a humiliating and unconditional surrender. The Canadian Johns-Manville Co. had even begun to hire scabs, and the local manager, Mr. Foster, had sent a written eviction notice to each of the strikers who rented accommodation from the Company.[8]

During the previous week, another event had occurred which had a very great effect on public opinion. Since the beginning of the strike, the C.C.C.L. and its leaders had been the object of many denunciations. Circulars had been distributed to the strikers, and some were even sent to the priests of the province. On April 21, 1949, the Semaine religieuse (Symposium on Religious Issues) at Quebec City had published, without commentary, extracts from the writings of Benedict XV in its unofficial section. All the readers of these statements felt that they were intended as a condemnation of the C.C.C.L. Now, on April 22, all the big English- and French-language dailies in the province published a full-page advertisement under the title A Report on the Strike in the Asbestos Mines. The text was signed: Lewis H. Brown, Chairman of the Board, Canadian Johns-Manville Co. This document presented certain facts concerning the strike and

sketched the history of the trade union movement in Quebec. Mr.
Brown recalled that the C.C.C.L. had been created to combat the
radicalism of the American unions.

As is well-known, the population of Quebec is overwhelmingly
Catholic. The Church's influence in the Province is widespread,
important and highly respected. It was natural, therefore, that leaders of the Catholic Church figured prominently in the organization,
promotion and development of these Syndicates.

The Church leaders felt that they had a two-fold responsibility in
encouraging the Syndicates. They wanted to discourage the spread
of radicalism and they considered it their moral and religious duty to
support employees in their efforts to form unions for collective
bargaining on wages, hours and working conditions in order to
improve the standard of living of the worker and his family.

To foster the growth of this movement the Church established a
separate staff organization to encourage and guide the Syndicates.
Over the years the Syndicates grew in strength and entered into an
increasing number of labor contracts under the Quebec Labor Law.

                                   * * *

In the last few years, however, the top leadership of labor groups
with which our local Syndicate is affiliated has undergone a marked
change. It has taken on a more radical aspect.

About a year ago the term "Catholique" was eliminated from the
name of the Syndicate representing Johns-Manville employees.

Today the top Provincial leadership of the Syndicate no longer
confines itself to acting in the interests of the worker through collective bargaining. It is operating on a much broader scale. The welfare of the worker appears to be secondary in the ultimate objectives
of the new leadership. There is now a growing tendency on the part
of the Syndicate leaders to preach a doctrine opposing capitalism
and upholding a philosophy that is more closely akin to communism
or socialism.

The president of the Canadian Johns-Manville Co. passed judgment
not merely on the doctrinal orientation of the C.C.C.L., but also on
the attitude of the priests:

It is surprising and a source of disappointment that some spokesmen in the Church appear to be supporting strike leaders who seem
intent upon usurping the functions of management and thereby unjustly injuring the property rights of thousands of owners who have
invested their savings in the mine, mill and factory.

The present impasse is all the more astonishing because the leaders of the Church, out of the purest motives and devotion, encouraged the formation and growth of the Syndicates in their efforts to combat radicalism. It is strange indeed to find that this sincere anti-radical movement seems now to have transformed itself into something like the alien movement it originally repudiated.[9]

This was an unequivocal denunciation, publicly broadcast everywhere. The text of this report had also been published in a bilingual pamphlet which was distributed both in Canada and in the United States.

Up to this point, apart from those directly involved, the public at large knew little of the actions of the hierarchy. Only the statements of the chaplains, or of the priests in the parishes affected by the strike, had made the rounds of the press. In spite of the repeated condemnations by the government authorities, and the pressures applied by the companies, the workers had stood fast. When the labour leaders informed the workers of the deplorable collapse of the negotiations in the period of April 25 to 29, despair reached the lowest depths. People were completely at the end of their tether; they had neither the financial resources nor the moral courage to carry on the struggle. Three months of sacrifices and anxieties had seemingly been in vain, and the strikers envisaged a return to work accompanied by insecurity and by the disappearance of the union in which they had placed their trust.

The Sacerdotal Commission of Social Studies had followed the development of the dispute stage by stage, and had made representations in an attempt to achieve a settlement. Its members[10] now felt that the situation was so serious that they should take a public stand on the strike. At the request of the religious authorities, and with the approval of the Episcopal Commission on Social Issues,[11] they prepared a statement for the press. This statement, which appeared on April 30,[12] is dated Friday, April 29. It reads as follows:

Let us Help the Asbestos Workers
Since the beginning of the strike which is affecting the industrial area of the asbestos industry, the religious authorities have made a great effort to hasten the settlement of the dispute; they have approached the parties to the conflict repeatedly, inviting them to examine various formulas for a solution. These formulas took into account the legitimate demands of all the parties at issue. Unfortunately, neither their efforts nor the interventions of the civil authority have yet achieved the desired result.

Meanwhile thousands of families are suffering hardships which affect the women and the children. In these circumstances, charity imposes an obligation on everyone, regardless of social class, to show sympathy for the workers and their families in this trying situation, and to give them, if he can, the material assistance that they require more and more. For this reason we are making an urgent appeal to all associations, and we are asking them to cooperate with the religious authorities in the organization of a collection for the stricken families.

All Catholics must urgently pray to God that those who are presently divided by a painful conflict may soon forget the past and enjoy the benefits of a just peace.

For the Sacerdotal Commission of Social Studies (with the approval of the Episcopal Commission on Social Issues),

Mgr. J.C. Leclaire, D.P.,
chairman.

Saint Hyacinth, April 29, 1949.

Two days later, on Sunday, May 1, H.E. Mgr. Joseph Charbonneau, Chairman of the Episcopal Committee on Social Issues and Archbishop of Montreal, delivered a Mother's Day sermon in Notre-Dame Cathedral in Montreal, in which he took a public stand on the strike. The sermon was a spontaneous commentary on the statement of the Sacerdotal Commission. The newspapers which appeared the next day reported his words as follows:

The working class is a victim of a conspiracy which seeks to crush it, and when there is a conspiracy to crush the working class, the Church has a duty to intervene.

We want to have peace in our society, but we do not want to see the working class crushed. We are more attached to man than to capital. This is why the clergy decided to intervene. They want to see that justice and charity are respected, and it is their wish that more attention be paid to human beings than to the interests of money.[13]

In each of the dioceses the bishops, starting with Their Excellencies Mgr. Arthur Douville and Mgr. Maurice Roy, ordered that collections be taken up at the doors of the churches.[14] These collections were taken up every Sunday until the end of the conflict. The amount of these contributions reached the impressive figure of $167,558.24.[15]

The statement of the Sacerdotal Commission calling for collections completely altered the situation. Henceforth the workers could count on the effective sympathy of the public at large except for the people who were completely blinded by political or anti-union prejudice, and they could contemplate the future with greater confidence. The promised financial aid enabled them to bear up under the strain for a little longer, and to hope for a fair and honourable settlement which would provide safeguards for the things that really mattered. The traditional forces of our society were no longer exclusively deployed on one side, in an effort to crush the workers. Without taking a stand on the secondary points at issue, and without directly condemning anyone, the Church gave its effective support to the workers in the name of charity, justice, peace, and social harmony.

H.E. Mgr. Philippe Desranleau, Bishop of Sherbrooke, who was in Rome on a journey *ad limina,* sent a letter to all his diocesans on May 14, asking them to support the strikers:

> Here at Rome, we hear sad news of the asbestos strike. In my opinion, this serious situation has lasted too long; the suffering of the workers, and of their wives and children, has gone beyond all bounds; and their real and natural needs are neither recognized nor safeguarded. Every authority, of whatever kind, has the duty to uphold, support, and aid the weak, those who labour to earn their living.
>
> Like Our Lord, I have pity on the masses; as a bishop, I wholeheartedly support the asbestos workers in their just demands.[16]

The strike lasted for two more long months. H.E. Mgr. Maurice Roy became not only the mediator, but the respected conciliator of the unions and the Canadian Johns-Manville Co. The parties at issue came to his office to state their points of view and to present their proposals for bringing an end to the conflict. With a patience equalled only by his calm and sympathy, the Archbishop of Quebec studied the smallest details with care and made suggestions that he felt might be acceptable to all. An example will illustrate his methods. At one point, the Canadian Johns-Manville Co. was ready to make a settlement, but it refused to rehire immediately some two hundred workers against whom it claimed to have legitimate grievances. Mgr. Roy had the list of workers brought to him, and discussed the case of each one with representatives of the Company. After this exhaustive inquiry, the Company cut the list down to twenty names; a short while later, it agreed to drop this disputed issue altogether.[17]

When the conflict ended, the press was rightly unanimous in its praise of H.E. Mgr. Roy and of the actions taken by the Church. The Washington newspaper *Labor,* in the issue that appeared after the strike, published a large photograph of the Archbishop and commented: "There was dancing in the streets of the little town of Asbestos when one of the most unusual strikes in the history of the Dominion labor movement was settled this week through negotiations personally conducted by Archbishop Maurice Roy of the Roman Catholic church.''[18]

The report of the secretary of the Federation of Mining Industry Employees, presented to the C.C.C.L. convention in September 1949, contained the following remarks:

> This strike, which lasted 114 working days at Thetford and 120 working days at Asbestos, was marked by events which are unique in the history of the trade union movement in the Province of Quebec: ... the Church played an invaluable part through the statement of the Sacerdotal Commission of Social Studies; the categorical statement of Mgr. Charbonneau of Montreal in favour of the miners; the collections taken up for the strikers at the doors of the churches throughout the province, on the recommendation of the bishops of each diocese; the personal intervention in the strike settlement of His Excellency Mgr. Roy, Archbishop of Quebec, and of Mgr. C.O. Garant, Auxiliary Bishop of Quebec City. . . .[19]

Lewis H. Brown sent a letter to Mgr. Roy and revealed its contents to his employees on July 19, 1949. In it he praised Mgr. Roy highly, thanking him for "his services as an intermediary in the settlement of the strike at Asbestos, and for the important role he played in seeing that the men returned to work in an orderly fashion."

II/The causes
The Church accumulated several new grounds for intervening in the asbestos dispute as the strike progressed.

As we have seen, the Church was already implicated in spite of itself by the very fact that Catholic workers and Catholic unions were involved. However, if the conflict had remained nothing more than a routine dispute between companies and workers, the Church would have had no reason to intervene extraordinarily. Of course, the Church can ignore neither the fate of workers nor the claims of justice, but in specific cases it is not easy to pass judgment on the morality of a situation, unless it is manifestly unjust or threatens to disrupt society.

When, however, people try to justify a situation and certain attitudes by appealing to false principles or by passing judgments detrimental to a Catholic institution, the matter becomes serious.

The government authorities and the Canadian Johns-Manville Co. did exactly that. Never in the history of the trade union movement had a strike resulted in so many public statements from important men in authority condemning the C.C.C.L. for failing to observe all the procedures stipulated by the law before calling the strike. People did not merely discuss the illegality of the strike: they even ventured into the realm of morality. Maître Antoine Rivard, a government minister, explicitly referred to the asbestos dispute in a speech he gave to a luncheon meeting of the Jeunesse de l'Union nationale (Young National Unionists). He frankly declared: "The laws of this province, all the laws of this province, are binding, and binding on the conscience; they are binding on everyone because they issue from legitimate authority. They contain nothing which is opposed to divine, natural, or human law. One may express a difference of opinion on their expediency and effectiveness, but one may not deny one's duty to obey them."[20] In the Legislative Assembly, the Minister of Labour commented on the C.C.C.L. leaders: "The chaplains will put up with them until a clean sweep is made, and it will be."[21] Each week the small political papers sang the same tune on the morality of the strike, quoting the theologians of days gone by.[22] The Canadian Johns-Manville Co., which certainly had the right to defend its interests with economic and legal arguments, transferred the problem to the field of morality. We have already mentioned the advertisement that was published in all the newspapers in the province, accusing the C.C.C.L. of departing from its principles and of breaking with the social doctrine of the Church.

A passive attitude on the part of the Church would have been interpreted as an approval of these moral judgments. The government authorities were certainly well aware that the Church did not support these statements, for despite their unequivocal overtures, they had not been able to obtain what they wanted: an official condemnation of the chaplains and of the C.C.C.L. itself.[23] These efforts had some effect on the decision of the Episcopal Committee on Social Issues to approve the statement of the Sacerdotal Commission of Social Studies.

Furthermore, the Church clearly saw that the very survival of the Catholic trade union movement was at stake in this conflict. The consequences of the dispute seemed likely to affect much more than the unions involved and the Federation of Mining Industry Employees. In such a big dispute as this, if the C.C.C.L. could not summon the economic strength to fight for what it deemed the interests of the workers and emerge with honour, its days were plainly numbered. The C.C.C.L.'s failure would have revealed an incapacity to defend effectively the interests of workers in the big companies: the C.C.C.L. would have been unable to keep its membership in future or gain ground in the industries that play an important role in the economy of the province. The Church could not allow an institution it had established and fostered for nearly forty years to be sabotaged in a few months.

The Church advanced money to the C.C.C.L. and ordered collections on its behalf. These actions were neither a canonization of the C.C.C.L. nor an approval of all it had done in the course of the strike. The Church carefully avoided such an endorsement, and did not even pass judgment on the morality of calling the strike, so that those who had made a negative judgment on it might not be embarrassed.

Of all the draft statements prepared by the Sacerdotal Commission of Social Studies, care was taken to choose the one which did not offer any ambiguities on this point. Special attention was given to this problem, because the Church had also been careful to avoid any statements which might be construed as censure of the government authorities for their openly anti-union bias, which they displayed from the very beginning of the dispute. In this respect, the statement pushed goodwill to the very limit.

The Church intervened officially to help the C.C.C.L. financially and to calm the public apprehension about the orthodoxy of C.C.C.L. doctrine. As we can see, its approach was characterized by much caution, wisdom, and tact, but also by much audacity and courage.

The Church also intervened to achieve peace in society. This was the object of the representations it made to the Canadian Johns-Manville Co. and to the government.

Once the strike had been declared, the families of the strikers suffered hardship, and individuals were unjustly hunted down by the police. An atmosphere of hate developed; the prestige of government authority and respect for law were disappearing. In short, the social order was seriously threatened. In the face of calamity, repeated efforts to bring the parties at issue to an understanding had failed. The workers no longer trusted the government authorities, which had decisively sided with the companies.

There remained the possibility of interventions by private individuals. To the equal credit of unions and companies, they were all looking for someone who could reestablish the dialogue that had been broken off by the strike.

H.E. Mgr. Maurice Roy was the man of providence to whom people turned. The Archbishop of Quebec did not seek this role on his own initiative; rather, his reputation for wisdom and sympathy led people to ask him to assume it.

The managers of the mining industry and the president of the Canadian Johns-Manville Co. himself, Lewis H. Brown, who bore a recommendation from H.E. Cardinal Spellman, invited Mgr. Roy to take the matter in hand. Why did they ask Mgr. Roy rather than someone else?

In the first place, the Bishop of Sherbrooke (who had jurisdiction

over Asbestos) was away; secondly, some of the strikers lived within
the boundaries of the Diocese of Quebec City. Mr. Brown himself had
a very particular reason for wanting Mgr. Roy to act as mediator. The
president of the Canadian Johns-Manville Co. had received a military
training, and in his opinion, the administration of a business enterprise
was much like that of an army. He was inclined to have confidence in
someone who was familiar with military structures and organization.
Mr. Brown felt that Mgr. Roy, who had once been an army chaplain,
could understand his way of looking at things better than anyone else.
Finally, Brown, who was not a Catholic, had rather simplistic ideas
about the relationship between the Church authorities and the Catholic
unions. He believed that a bishop could give orders to labour leaders
in any field whatsoever. In war, the soldiers lay down their arms as
soon as the commanders make peace; initially, Brown thought that he
could negotiate with the Archbishop of Quebec. In the course of his
interviews and discussions with Mgr. Roy, he learned that even the
Catholic unions acted on their own responsibility in the temporal
domain. He had, however, found the man who was to succeed in
promoting dialogue and in finding a solution to the conflict.

Of the three members of the Episcopal Committee on Social Issues,
two publicly stated the reasons for the intervention of the Church. We
have already quoted all of the frank commentary by Montreal's Archbishop, H.E. Mgr. Joseph Charbonneau. He spoke of "peace in our
society." He added: "This is why the clergy decided to intervene. They
want to see that justice and charity are respected, and it is their wish that
more attention be paid to human beings than to the interests of
money."[24] H.E. Mgr. Arthur Douville, Bishop of St. Hyacinth and
secretary of the Committee, in the letter he sent to the parish priests of
his diocese calling for collections, expressed himself more soberly, but
hinted at much more than he said: "The Church has always felt sympathy for its suffering children. This ground of charity, apart from many
others which could be advanced, will be enough. . . ."[25]

III/The consequences

What were the consequences of the intervention of the Church in the
asbestos conflict?

Without the timely intervention of the Church, the asbestos strike
would unquestionably have followed a different course, and the unions would not have been able to emerge with honour from the deadlock in which they found themselves. The workers, the unions, and
their leaders benefitted from this intervention.

The very reputation of Catholic trade unionism was enhanced. In
the not so distant past, because of certain rash acts which it had once

committed, and especially because of a deliberately slanderous propaganda, the Catholic trade union movement in Canada had seemed a
second-class trade unionism, a kind of "confraternity" dominated by
the clergy, to those people outside the Province of Quebec whose
acquaintance with it was superficial. As we have seen, the union
chaplains became directly and closely involved in the asbestos strike,
playing a role of considerable importance and even identifying themselves with the strikers' cause on some occasions. Never, though, did
they take the place of the labour leaders. The Church *qua* institution
intervened with much caution and discretion. The course of events,
and certain acts which the Church could certainly not sanction, clearly
showed to all that the Catholic trade unions were truly autonomous
institutions in the economic and social fields, and adhered to principles
of action which could be dynamic. The C.C.C.L. won itself a place of
honour among North America's trade unions.

The priests involved in social work found that their prestige among
the workers was increased and that they had greater opportunities to
engage in apostolic work in their communities. We should note, however, that since the time of the strike these people have suffered
persecution at the hands of other groups, and these persecutions have
not entirely disappeared with the passage of time. H.E. Mgr. Desranleau, the Bishop of Sherbrooke, felt the need to make a statement on
this matter as early as August 22, 1949. The document speaks for
itself:

> For the last fifteen days, in the Diocese of Sherbrooke and in
> several other parts of the Province, a pamphlet has been distributed
> signed by THE PROVINCIAL POLICEMEN concerning *the Pro-
> vincial Police at Asbestos*.
>
> The appearance of this pamphlet, at a time when the employers
> and the workers are making most laudable efforts to reach a
> thoroughgoing agreement, is badly timed. The pamphlet is also an
> affront to decency.
>
> Without going into the accusations made against the workers for
> the moment, we have carefully examined everything that this
> pamphlet says against Abbé Camirand, the parish priest of
> Saint-Aimé at Asbestos; we have questioned several people, the
> parish priests of the region in particular; and we have studied the
> accusations and the actual facts. This inquiry permits us to state that
> the accusations brought by the PROVINCIAL POLICEMEN
> against Abbé Camirand, the parish priest of Saint Aimé at Asbestos,
> are falsehoods.
>
> On the basis of that part of the pamphlet which falsely accuses a

priest of our diocese, leaving aside the improprieties contained in the rest of it, but noting that people have dared to publish the pamphlet in this cool fashion, over a month after the end of the strike and before court decisions have been handed down, in the desire to usurp our function of guardian of truth and morality in the diocese, we protest against these falsehoods, we request all our diocesans to pay no attention to them, and we assert that such a publication explains certain acts on the part on the Provincial Police at Asbestos and deprives the PROVINCIAL POLICEMEN—here, the words must be understood in the same sense and with the same extension which they have in the signature to the pamphlet—of the trust and respect of the citizens. Philippe, Bishop of Sherbrooke.[26]

Abbé Pichette, the Rev. Father Jacques Cousineau, S.J., and nearly all the members of the Sacerdotal Commission of Social Studies were censured and "denounced" before the religious authorities. As nothing resulted here, in Canada, from these attempts, briefs against them were sent to Rome. One of these, bearing the signature CUSTOS,[27] was also secretly distributed in political and management circles in the province. These denunciations to Rome did not come to anything.

In certain circles, people were so gross as to interpret the resignation of H.E. Mgr. Charbonneau from his post as Archbishop of Montreal as a consequence of the stand he had taken on the asbestos strike. The French-language newspapers in Canada had enough decency not to retail this fantasy in public, but the English-language press in Canada and the United States was not so reticent.[28] H.E. the Apostolic Delegate to Canada formally denied such suggestions,[29] and his denial was more than a mere statement of diplomacy: we are well enough acquainted with the personal role played by H.E. Mgr. Antoniutti in this strike to affirm that the resignation of Mgr. Charbonneau was not due to the attitude he adopted towards the asbestos strike. The same people who had wrongly interpreted the resignation of the Archbishop of Montreal had also predicted the same fate for Mgr. Philippe Desranleau of Sherbrooke. Far from being forced to resign, Mgr. Desranleau was promoted to the rank of archbishop in March 1951.

For the Church in Quebec, the period of the asbestos strike was a time of both trial and exaltation.

The Church was made to suffer by the suffering of its children, and by the abuse of its principles to condemn institutions which it had supported and which, in its eyes, had not behaved badly. The Church suffered to see some of its children proclaiming their faith in a loud voice and taking advantage of the prestige conferred on them by high office to denigrate priests and even bishops who were only doing their duty, and to try to obtain their condemnation on the part of the higher authorities in the hierarchy.

In spite of these sufferings, the asbestos strike offered the Church a marvellous opportunity to display its charity towards the needy and to increase its prestige in the eyes of all the workers on the continent, and even in the entire world. It was everywhere recognized that the collections ordered in favour of the strikers' families were a matchless gesture of charity; and they have since been imitated in other countries. Non-Catholics learned that the Church does not allow itself to become a vassal to the powerful men of the day, that it has a social doctrine.

The Church emerged from this conflict magnified by the sympathy it had shown towards the weak and by its concern for promoting an authentic peace in society, based on justice and order.

We should also mention that the bishops of Quebec found, in all that had transpired in the course of the asbestos strike, additional and decisive grounds for offering the faithful a doctrinal synthesis on the labour question. This synthesis was published in the form of a joint pastoral letter issued early in 1950.[30] When people's feelings run high and their immediate interests are at stake, it is extremely difficult and sometimes even unwise for the authorities to remind them of certain principles. They run the risk of being ignored, of being accused of bias, and even of being exploited. By the beginning of February 1950, people had calmed down again, and there were no other conflicts in sight. The bishops therefore felt that the time had come to set forth the moral principles which govern labour relations, and to apply them to the society of Quebec. They passed judgment on all the disputed moral issues that had arisen in the course of the strike: the role of the government authorities, and the respect due them (nos. 160-164); the respect due to the laws (nos. 162, 182-183); the primacy of man over the interests of capital (no. 170); sanitary working conditions (nos. 39, 108-109, 132, 171-173); the right to membership in a union and to collective bargaining (nos. 103, 131, 176); the role of the labour union (nos. 108-110); the legitimacy of union security (no. 112); the arbitration procedure and morality of the strike (nos. 178-181); management rights (nos. 75-77, 110, 133). Now, this letter, which is a unique document in Canadian history, was most highly praised by the authorities in Rome,[31] and was subsequently published in English, Italian, Spanish,[32] and Dutch editions. It contributed substantially to the spread of the social teaching of the Church.

Finally, the asbestos strike and the bishops' joint letter on the labour question later gave rise to many schemes, some of them very subtle, to destroy that unity of feeling and action which the provincial episcopate had revealed in those circumstances. Considering just how profoundly the Church is enmeshed in our social fabric, this need not surprise us. The men at the head of the political system are compelled, to a certain degree, to rely upon the Church as a force in society, while the Church, because of the extent of the works in which it is involved, can scarcely get by without the cooperation of the State, as things are presently constituted. Only in the perspective of history will people be able to estimate all the consequences of the asbestos strike on the relations between Church and State in Quebec, on the development of the social welfare or educational institutions supported by the Church, and on the great trust which the working class has placed in the Church in Quebec.

Notes to Chapter VI

[1]These statements of the government attitude were repeated several times in the course of the conflict: in a speech of Mr. Barrette at the Legislative Assembly on February 23, 1949; in a statement to *Montréal Matin,* February 26, 1949; in *Le Devoir,* March 28, 1949; in a speech by Mr. Barrette on the radio, *Le Devoir,* March 19, 1949.

[2]Speech of Mr. Barrette in the Legislative Assembly, February 23, 1949.

[3]Everywhere else in the world, conciliation and arbitration boards consist of a single person, but in Canada such bodies are made up of a chairman and two other members, of which one is nominated at the suggestion of the firm, the other on the recommendation of the union.

[4]After several months of a severe strike which affected the entire textile industry in the province, the workers who had requested the intervention of the Archbishop of Quebec returned to work without any guarantee from the company either of union recognition or of collective bargaining. The government of the day, instead of forcing the parties at issue to come to the negotiating table, made a decree establishing a minimum wage in the industry.

[5]See "The Catholic Church and Quebec Labour," *Financial Post,* June 4, 1949; *Ibid.,* May 28, 1949.

[6]It is impossible to mention all the interventions on the part of the chaplains. Several times a week, the press reported statements made by them to the union members at Asbestos, Thetford, or elsewhere. We shall note only a few of them.

In an interview granted to *La Presse,* and reproduced in *Le Devoir* of March 23, Abbé Camirand stated: "It is my duty as pastor to teach the practice of all the virtues, and I do not have the right to ignore the virtue of justice. I also feel that it is my imperative duty not only to forbid my parishioners to act unjustly, but to come to their defence when they are victims of injustice, as is presently the case. I know the miners at Asbestos well, for I am their union chaplain. In the past, they have been extremely patient and docile; they still are. They have not temporarily deprived themselves of a livelihood for themselves and their children for the fun of it, but because they have been driven to act this way by unspeakable tactics of provocation. If I were a miner, I would be on strike myself and, in the present circumstances, I would have a clear conscience. I may add that though I am not a miner, I am with them all the way, and they know it . . . I regard the strikers as the Zouaves of the Papacy. In 1870, the Zouaves defended the Holy See, which was directly attacked. Today, I glory in the fact that the miners at

Asbestos are helping to defend, not the Pope in person, but his social teachings." *(La Presse,* March 21, 1949.)

On April 3 Abbé Roland Frigon, the assistant to the chaplain general of the C.C.C.L., made the statement: "The workers of the province are pleased with the struggle, which is being carried on energetically but peacefully . . . You are working for the Christian renewal of Society, in accordance with the teachings of all the popes, from the great Leo XIII, called the workers' pope, to Pius XII, whose fiftieth anniversary of ordination as a priest is currently being celebrated." *(Le Devoir,* April 5, 1949.)

On April 5 Jules Lockwell, Chaplain of the National Federation of Pulp and Paper Workers, addressed the members of the Quebec City Central Labour Council. He said that in spite of all the statements made by the government ministers on the illegality of the strike, no adherents of the Church's social doctrine could be deprived of the right to feel anguish at the sight of the hungry multitude, and to join together to help their brothers. "The entire soul of the Church is present in each member who suffers," he said. "In the present situation, the entire C.C.C.L. is suffering with the strikers in the asbestos industry. To help them, each of its members must share not only his surplus, but his very necessities." *(Le Devoir,* April 6, 1949.)

On April 11, the Reverend Father Jacques Cousineau, S.J., accompanied a group of students from the universities of Montreal and McGill on a trip to Asbestos. They were bringing money that had come in from a collection they had taken up. On this occasion, Rev. Cousineau said: "This action marks a turning point. When organized labour learned of Bill 5, it wondered how professional people, graduates of our colleges and universities, could have drafted a bill which took so little heed of, and was so harmful to, the interests of the workers. Here, though, are young people who have a completely different outlook. You see before you the representatives of a generation of professionals who will place social justice above legality." *(Le Devoir,* April 12, 1949.)

To these remarks by union chaplains, we wish to add a statement by a well-known member of the clergy.

On April 20, Canon Groulx made a newspaper appeal in favour of the strikers in the asbestos industry. "Why," he said, "don't we take up a collection in aid of the asbestos strikers at the national level, and start a prayer campaign to get the stubborn people responsible for the strike to relent. These strikers—and this point has not been emphasized enough—are not like other strikers. They are not fighting merely for food and wages. They are fighting, in fact, for their lives and for the lives of their sons and daughters, workers in a murderous industry. They are fighting against companies which, as far as one knows, have never undertaken, clearly and honestly, to remedy the abominable evil which they have long been spreading. The evil is too serious. The time has come to make an appeal to the entire population. The whole province has a duty to see that this undeserved misery is ended. People talk of legality. This would be the time to cry: 'Legality, O what crimes are committed in thy name!' If people happened to find out that a communist from the bacterial warfare squad had infected our halls of justice or our parliaments, how much attention would be paid to the question of legality by lawyers, judges, and members of the legislature who were called upon to plead their cases or sit in parliament without waiting for the disinfection? Some people are claiming that the workers took a long time to realize the dangers of asbestos dust, and that they might well be patient for a while. Who displays such heroic patience in the face of sickness and death? Is not the patience of an entire generation enough for our casuists? It is more than time to bring an end to a strike which has brought complete disgrace on the Province of Quebec. . . ." *(Le Devoir,* April 20, 1949.)

[7]*Le Devoir,* March 28, 1949.

[8]This threat was never carried out.

[9]All the newspapers carried this announcement on April 22. We are quoting from the *Toronto Star*.

[10]Mgr. J. Charles Leclaire, chairman, Vicar-General of the Diocese of St. Hyacinth; the Rev. Father Jacques Cousineau, S.J., moral advisor to the Montreal Central Labour Council; Abbé Henri Pichette, Chaplain-General of the C.C.C.L.; Abbé Gérard Dion, assistant chairman of the Department of Industrial Relations, Laval University, and moral advisor to the employers' associations of the Diocese of Quebec; Abbé Omer Genest, moral advisor to the national unions of the Diocese of Chicoutimi; Paul Emile Bolté, P.S.S., Professor of Social Sciences at the Faculty of Theology of the University of Montreal. The Rev. Father Emile Bouvier, S.J., Chairman of the Department of Industrial Relations of the University of Montreal, was a member of the Commission at that time, but he did not come to the meetings.

[11]In the statement, it was carefully pointed out that it was issued "with the approval of the Episcopal Commission on Social Issues" because, after the statement of the Sacerdotal Commission on Bill 5 (a Labour Code) the previous January 26, the Prime Minister of the province, in a discussion in the Legislature, had clearly insinuated that the Sacerdotal Commission did not in any way represent the thinking of the bishops. See *La Presse, L'Action catholique, La Patrie,* February 25, 1949.

The Episcopal Commission had the following members: His Excellency Mgr. Joseph Charbonneau, Archbishop of Montreal, chairman; H.E. Mgr. Arthur Douville, Bishop of St. Hyacinth, secretary; H.E. Mgr. Charles-Omer Garant, Auxiliary Bishop of Quebec City, member.

[12]*L'Action catholique,* April 30, 1949.

[13]*Le Devoir,* May 2, 1949.

[14]The letter of H.E. Mgr. Douville, Bishop of St. Hyacinth, read as follows: "Gentlemen and dear collaborators, the Bishop of Saint Hyacinth endorses the statement of the Sacerdotal Commission of Social Studies. He is himself a member of the Episcopal Commission on Social Issues. To make this charitable appeal effective, he is asking all the parishes of the diocese to organize their own collection of money, and a collection of foodstuffs as well (sugar, vegetables, peas, beans, etc., biscuits, meat, all kinds of tinned goods, etc.) . . . The money will be gathered through a collection either in the church itself or on the church steps, following Sunday mass. The collection of foodstuffs will take place during the week; a door-to-door canvass will assure its success. The collaboration of all your parish organizations (trade unions, Catholic Farmers' Union, Catholic action movements, Sacred Heart League, St. Jean Baptiste societies, Knights of Columbus, etc.) will help you to answer this appeal both in gathering foodstuffs and in the collection of money, if you decide to collect money only after the mass. The Church has always felt sympathy for its suffering children. This ground of charity, apart from many others which could be advanced, will be enough to ensure that you take all the necessary steps to make this appeal successful and to provide the impetus for a generous response on the part of all the faithful of the diocese. . . . (*Le Devoir,* May 4, 1949.)

The text of the letter of H.E. Mgr. Maurice Roy was as follows: "Father, Charity urges us to request that a collection be taken up in our archdiocese to help the asbestos workers. To achieve this, I ask you to do as follows: 1. Next Sunday, May 8, and on each successive Sunday until further notice, take up a collection at the door of the church, at all masses, for the workers' families in Thetford Mines and the surrounding area; 2. At each mass on the coming Sunday, you will kindly read the bulletin from the Sacerdotal Commission, which is enclosed, and announce the collection which will be taken up at the door of the church, without further commentary; 3. Where there is no

Catholic union to see to this collection, it may be made by the members of a parish organization or such other persons as you may choose to nominate; 4. The sums collected will be given to the parish priest after each mass, and then sent by cheque to the procurator of the Archdiocese each Monday. I expect that you will give your full attention to this work of Christian charity. Faithfully yours in Jesus and Mary." (*L'Action catholique,* May 5, 1949.)

[15]The following sums were raised in collections taken up at the doors of parish churches, by diocese: St. Hyacinth, $10,015.42; Montreal, $54,407.80; Joliette, $7,843.35; Three Rivers, $6,345.00; Nicolet, $3,353.84; Sherbrooke, $11,122.71; Valleyfield, $2,000.00; Mount Laurier, $1,105.12; Saint John's, $2,800.00; Quebec City, $50,000.00; Chicoutimi, $15,000.00; Rimouski, $3,565.00. (For more details on the aid sent to the strikers, see Chapter IX below.)

[16]*Le Devoir,* May 25, 1949.

[17]The company reverted to this question after work had begun again: see the chapter by Sauvé below, II, 2c.

[18]*Labor,* July 3, 1949. See also the press review published on this occasion by *Le Devoir,* July 9, 1949.

[19]Minutes of the 28th annual convention of the C.C.C.L., Montreal, 1949, pp. 263-264; *Ibid,* p. 95; pp. 70-71.

[20]See *L'Action catholique,* April 8, 1949; *Le Devoir,* April 8, 1949.

[21]See the newspapers of February 25, 1949.

[22]See *Le Moraliste,* Montreal, April 2, 1949. This National Union paper was even distributed to all the strikers.

[23]On May 21, 1949, the Catholic weekly *The Ensign* stated: "Premier Duplessis even sent emissaries to see some of the highest Church authorities and approached other bishops in the hope of obtaining withdrawal of Church interest. He failed to find any attitude other than that taken in Montreal and Quebec. His efforts to have a bishop take the matter up with the Vatican direct were equally futile. Government pressure has also been brought 'to have certain priests silenced' for pleading aid to the striking families but all such efforts were rejected." Nobody has ever denied these assertions.

[24]*Le Devoir,* May 2, 1949.

[25]*Le Devoir,* May 4, 1949.

[26]*Le Messager Saint-Michel,* the official publication of the diocese of Sherbrooke, August 27, 1949.

[27]*Receuil de documents sur la grève de l'amiante 1949* (Collection of documents concerning the asbestos strike of 1949), Vol. 1, a mimeographed volume of 184 pages. In the foreword to this work, it is stated that it has been prepared by "a group of Catholic militants." Nevertheless, the authorship of it has been attributed to Rev. Father Emile Bouvier, S.J., by several people, including Gérard Picard in the newspaper *Le Travail,* March 2, 1951, and March 16, 1951. Picard compared many passages of this report with those of a book later published under the name of Rev. Father Bouvier and entitled *Patrons et Ouvriers (Employers and Workers),* Vol. 1, 208 pp., Industrial Relations Department, University of Montreal, 1951. The passages agree with one another perfectly. No attempts have been made to deny the allegation of Mr. Picard. (See also Appendix II of this book).

[28]*The Montreal Daily Star,* Feb. 11, 1950; *The Standard,* Montreal, Feb. 11, 1950; *Time Magazine,* Feb. 20, 1950, p. 18.

[29]The following is the text of the telegram sent to *Time,* with a copy to the Canadian Press: "I am commanded by His Excellency Archbishop Antoniutti, Apostolic Delegate to Canada, to deny categorically, with reference to *Time* magazine, February 20th, that he ever asked Archbishop Charbonneau to draw back from his pro-labor stand, since he has, on the contrary, always approved and encouraged the very charitable attitude of Archbishop Charbonneau towards all victims of war, of strikes and of social injustice. The Reverend William Aquin Carew, Secretary of the Apostolic Delegate to Canada." (*Le Devoir,* Feb. 21, 1950.)

[30]*Le problème ouvrier en regard de la doctrine sociale de l'Eglise* (The Labour Question and the Social Doctrine of the Church), a joint pastoral letter from Their Excellencies the Archbishops and Bishops of the Civil Province of Quebec. Extramural service of popular education, Laval University, Quebec, 1950.

[31]In a letter which he sent to H.E. Mgr. Ildegrando Antoniutti, Apostolic Delegate, on May 20, 1950, H.E. Cardinal Piazza, the Secretary of the Sacred Consistorial Congregation, wrote as follows:

" . . . I have the pleasure of informing Your Most Reverend Excellency that the Joint Pastoral Letter of the Episcopate of the Civil Province of Quebec on the Labour Question has been attentively examined by this Sacred Congregation.

This document, concrete evidence of the vigilant concern of the Pastors of souls, even in the social field, is a credit to those who wrote it, for the august teachings of the Pontiffs, set forth as a well-organized whole, could not find a more profitable application than to the present economic and social conditions in Canada.

Seeing that the problems of labour, studied and resolved with care and watchful experience in this pastoral letter, are substantially the same as those which are arising today throughout the Catholic world, we are pleased to note that the words of these Pastors of souls in this case go beyond the limits of their dioceses and their country to assume a universal value.

I therefore offer my warm congratulations to all the Most Excellent Colleagues in the Episcopate for their considerable labours and for their paternal concern in the field of social apostleship. I am also sure that the publication of this Pastoral Letter would be very useful to the clergy and the Christian population of every nation, and I am asking this Episcopate, through the intermediary of Your Excellency, for the authorization to prepare an Italian edition of it. . . ."

[32]There were two editions in Spanish, one published in Spain, the other in Argentina.

Chapter VII

The Strike and Our Judicial System

by Charles A. Lussier

I/Introduction

Illegal acts were committed before, during, and after the asbestos strike, in their chronological order, by the Canadian Johns-Manville Company Limited, by the union members, by the Labour Relations Board of the Province of Quebec, and by the provincial Minister of Labour. We will consider the judicial character of each one of these illegal acts.[1] We regard those of the Company and the union as the violation of a law, and those of the Board and the Minister as the denial of a right.

To assist the reader, we will quote from texts of law as we require.

II/Illegal acts of the parties to the conflict
1/The Canadian Johns-Manville Company Limited

Article Four of the Quebec Labour Relations Act stipulates that: "Every employer shall be bound to recognize as the collective representative of his employees the representatives of any association comprising sixty percent of his said employees and to negotiate with them, in good faith, a collective labour agreement."

From the very beginning of negotiations between the union representatives and the officers of the Canadian Johns-Manville Co., the latter defied the provisions of the Act by addressing themselves directly to the employees by means of commentaries posted on the bulletin boards. In vain, the union reminded the Company of the aforementioned text, and of the following one which occurs at Article Twenty of the same Act: "No employer... shall seek by any means to dominate or to hinder... the activities of an association of wage-earners."

The Company paid no attention and, on January 14, 1949, posted a notice to the effect that the union no longer wished to negotiate.

Though the Canadian Johns-Manville Co. admitted as of that date that the negotiations had been broken off, it was still subject to the provisions of the Act. The legal remedy available to it was set forth in Article Twelve: "If ... either party believes that they [the negotiations] will not be completed within a reasonable time, each party may so notify the Board. ..."

As we have seen in the preceding chapters, all the asbestos workers in the region followed the negotiations with the Canadian Johns-Manville Co. attentively; the breakdown of these talks was a spark to the powder-keg. The illegal actions of the officers of the Canadian Johns-Manville Co. were, from a psychological point of view, seen as the work of the managerial class as a whole.

2/The unionists

The unionists, on the other hand, did not respect the time limits fixed by the Act at Article Twenty-Four: "Any strike ... is prohibited ... so long as ... fourteen days have not elapsed since the receipt by the Minister of Labour of a report of the council of arbitration upon the dispute." While the parties were still at a stage intermediate between conciliation and arbitration,[2] the members of the union at Asbestos decided, on February 13, 1949, to go on strike at once.

The illegal acts of the Canadian Johns-Manville Co. and of the members of the union at Asbestos do not imply that they systematically opposed the Labour Relations Act. The parties to the dispute, on the contrary, remained submissive to this Act, the main purpose of which is to guarantee parity of means between the contracting parties, one of which has economic, the other numerical force.

In their dealings with one another, in their condition as legal persons, the parties to the dispute had adhered to this Act. Their derogations did not constitute a stubborn and systematic refusal to comply with the orders of the legislator, but were merely the result of ill-considered actions by one party, and spontaneous gestures by the other.

The Company, by its infractions of the letter of the Act, had at the very least made itself liable to a fine, as laid down by Article Forty-Two: "Every employer ... who fails ... to negotiate in good faith a collective labour agreement with them [the union representatives] shall be liable, for the first offense, to a fine of one hundred to five hundred dollars and for any subsequent offense to a fine of two hundred to one thousand dollars. ..."

It was most clearly in the interest of the union to be submissive to the Act. The Labour Relations Act had been created much more with the intention of forcing the employers to reach a compromise with the trade unions than with the aim of giving the latter more duties towards the former. The rights and duties that had formerly been reciprocal by nature were now made so in law. The trade union movement, in virtue of this new legislation, enjoyed a greatly improved judicial status. Once a mere numerical force, it acquired the powers of an organization, the activities of which occur within the legal framework of society.

When the unionists called the strike before they had met all the provisions of the law, they did not place themselves completely beyond it. They had merely taken a shortcut. The strike, in our legislation, is a weapon, the use of which is controlled. In particular, attempts have been made to prolong the steps which lead to it. The legislator has passed laws concerning the means that are naturally at the disposal of each party, among them the strike and the lockout, which are no longer regarded as illegitimate means. The legislator does not prohibit their use, but regulates it. The unionists, in not going through all the steps prescribed by the law before calling the strike, did not oppose the Act as a whole, but only one of its provisions.

The legislator upheld these elementary principles of law when he passed Article Forty-Three of the Act, which authorizes the courts to deal severely with, but never to annihilate, those who are found guilty of such derogations. The text is as follows: "Any person declaring or instigating a strike . . . contrary to the provisions of this act, or participating therein, shall be liable . . . to a fine of not less than one hundred and not more than one thousand dollars for each day or part of a day during which such strike . . . exists. . . ." We have minutely examined the Labour Relations Act as it existed in 1949, but have not been able to find the jurisdiction that would have permitted the Labour Relations Board to deprive of legal existence—by absolute authority and in the absence of any accused persons—those associations which hearsay had made guilty of an illegal strike.

III/Illegal acts of the public administration
1/The Labour Relations Board
Even at this stage, we can appreciate the seriousness of the illegal acts committed by the Labour Relations Board. In addition to going beyond the bounds of its jurisdiction, it lost sight of the principal aims of the Act, although it was commissioned to supervise its application.

a) Abuse of jurisdiction
Had the Board begun by forgetting the limits or the scope of its jurisdiction when, on February 17, 1949, it ordered the strikers to return to work at once in the following telegram: "Labour Relations

Board, informed that the strike now in progress at the Canadian
Johns-Manville Co. is illegal in the meaning of Paragraph One, Article Twenty-Four of the Labour Relations Act, *orders*[3] an immediate
return to work; otherwise it will cancel the certificate of union recognition for all legal purposes... which entails the prescribed penalties
and the loss of your rights...''?

To assure the application of the Act, especially in the case of a
violation of it, Article Thirty-Six of the Act granted the Board ''all the
powers, immunities and privileges of commissioners appointed under
the Public Inquiry Commissions Act.''

By *ordering,* the Board turned its powers of inquiry into executive
powers. This was no longer a mere abuse, but rather a usurpation, of
power.

The Board does not have the right to order anyone to do something
that he refuses to do in the exercise of his rights. As a Commission of
Inquiry, the Board may summon anyone to appear before it, and the
refusal to comply with this order makes one liable to a prison sentence
for contempt of court. For this reason, it is imperative that the Board
give orders only within the bounds of its jurisdiction.

The Board, in 1949, was unable to distinguish between the quasi-
judicial powers that belong to it and the executive powers that belong
to the Minister of Labour.

Apart from its right to summon people before it for questioning, the
Board does not have any authority to issue orders. When it orders a
vote by secret ballot, it is initiating an inquiry. Its inspectors, elected
by the voters, are delegated only to take testimony from the wage
earner. All the orders issued by the Board are directly or indirectly
connected with its jurisdiction of inquiry. When it recognizes a union,
it does not compel the employer to negotiate with the union's agents:
the Act itself makes provision for this. The Board merely informs the
employer and the public of the legal existence of the union in question.

b) Absence of jurisdiction

While giving orders that went beyond its jurisdiction, the Board itself
also avoided this jurisdiction, by not making an inquiry before passing
judgment on the illegality of the strike. The telegram of February 17,
1949, confirms this: ''Board... informed that the strike... is illegal....''

As the unions had not been summoned before it, the Board had
done no more than ratify the opinion of the third parties who supplied
it with information. Although the Board was justified in believing that
there was *circumstantial* evidence for the responsibility of the strikers,
it still did not have the jurisdiction to pass its judgment unless the

parties accused were at least summoned to testify to the facts of the case. The Board did more than judge the strikers in advance; it condemned them in advance.

The Supreme Court of Canada has clearly expressed its opinion on the status of the Labour Relations Board in stating that it is a quasi-judicial tribunal. As such, this tribunal no longer has any jurisdiction when it elects to hold a sitting without hearing the parties to the dispute. In judging those actions that the Act entrusts to its powers of inquiry, the Board cannot elude the fundamental principles inherent in the legal system. Each time in future that it repeats the same mistake, it will be acting without jurisdiction and will consequently act illegally, handing down decisions that are illegal and without legal significance.

c) Confusion
Having confirmed the illegality of the strike and presumed the responsibility of the strikers, as we have seen, the Board, on February 21, 1949, handed down a decision that is a judicial absurdity. By cancelling the certificates of union recognition, the Board disputed the validity of the Labour Relations Act.

The Board explained its decision as follows: "Considering the summons addressed to the unions concerned on the 17th instant and completed on February 19, to return to work at the latest on Monday, February 21, 1949, on pain of the prescribed penalties and of the loss of their rights in accordance with the provisions of the Act. . . ."

In the first place, by the use of the term "summons" the Board is referring to its order to return to work which we have discussed above.

Secondly, the words "and completed on February 19." The Board, which had taken the liberty of telegraphing its order to the unions, felt that it was adhering more closely to procedure in confirming its telegram by a letter. The Act from which it receives its jurisdiction, however, likens it to a commission of inquiry. To our knowledge, there is no legal procedure other than the summons which authorizes the Board members to issue orders. These summonses are served through the agency of bailiffs or other persons serving as such. It should be remembered, then, that this order of a return to work, even if it had been valid in itself, was never legally transmitted to the unions.

We believe that it is advisable to draw attention to such irregularities, because they give rise to many subsequent injustices, and above all because our silence on this subject enhances the climate of comfortable impunity which increasingly envelops the senior officials of the province.

The words "on pain of the prescribed penalties" bring us back to the Act. In Section VII, the so-called penalties section, there was nothing[4] that authorized the Board to cancel a certificate following a strike declared "contrary to the provisions of this Act." Article Forty-Three, mentioned by the Board, certainly does deal with penalties to which is liable "anyone who declares a strike contrary to the provisions of this Act." This text is straightforward, and if the Board had not chosen to ignore the Labour Relations Act and exceed the bounds of its jurisdiction, it might have found grounds for a prosecution in accordance with the Summary Convictions Act of Quebec, on the basis of Article Forty-Nine.

In presenting further grounds, the Board refers us to Article Forty-One of the Act: "The Board may, for cause, revise or cancel any decision or order rendered by it, or any certificate issued by it."

Article Forty-One appears at the end of Section VI of the Act, the section that deals with the Board properly speaking, its functions, and its powers. Penalties are not discussed. What, then, is the meaning of the phrase "for cause"? In the first place, we know for a fact that the Board has the power to revise and cancel its decisions.

The legislator, however, has not given the Board discretionary powers to reconsider its decisions, but has imposed a condition: "for cause." Studied in their precise context, where a withdrawal of a certificate is concerned, these words refer to the indispensable conditions for the existence of a union.

When a union makes a request for a certificate of union recognition, has come before the Board, and has met all the requirements of the Act regarding its actual existence and its right to representation, the role of the Board is to issue a certificate to it. When a request is made to obtain a certificate, the Board does not exercise absolute discretion. Its discretion is limited to an appraisal of the indispensable conditions for the existence of a right to recognition. Here again the Act is clear, as is shown by Article Seven: "The Board shall assure itself of the representative character of the association and of its right to be recognized. . . ." Article Nine is also entirely in agreement with this interpretation. Once the union has submitted its proofs, the Article places the Board under an obligation: "The Board shall issue to every recognized association, a certificate. . . ."

The Board has the power to make inquiries; it has the duty to issue a certificate to a union that has proved its right to be recognized. The union is recognized "for cause." If at some time the "cause" should prove to be lacking (e.g., through the union's loss of its majority), the Board may withdraw the certificate. Here we see that there is a world of difference between a "cause" and an "offense": the difference between the death of the organization and a fine.

Such was the intention of the legislator. Having completed the chapter on the powers and duties of the Board with the article referring to the withdrawal of certificates "for cause," he went on to enact a separate chapter on penalties. These are penalties established for infractions of the Act. The second infringement mentioned in this chapter consists of declaring a strike outside the legally prescribed time limits.

In spite of the provisions of the Act, the clear meaning of its articles, and its manifest aims, the Board revoked all the certificates on February 21, 1949.

One of the most unmistakable aims of the Act is to establish "orderly relations" between employers and wage earners. The legislator established the Board to assure the enforcement of this Act. The only function of the Board is to clarify matters. It is a body that has the means to set things in order. It makes inquiries into the right of association, but it does not have any jurisdiction over the right itself. It clarifies the rights of all, but grants none.

When the Board withdraws a certificate as the result of an infraction, does it thereby help to maintain or restore order or to clarify the situation? Quite the contrary, it poisons relations between employer and union. By its unwarranted action, it creates confusion, because in spite of the cancellation, the labour association has a right to negotiate (Article 18),[5] and the employer is compelled to enter into these negotiations (Article 4).[6]

The legislator has tried to establish an equilibrium between two forces. The Board, by usurping an *omnibus* jurisdiction in virtue of Article Forty-One, has destroyed this equilibrium.

2/The provincial Minister of Labour

All the incidents we have described involving the Labour Relations Board could not have so occurred except at the instigation and with the support of the highest official in the Department of Labour. The facts bear out this assertion.

a) Improper intervention

On February 15, 1949, the provincial Minister of Labour sent the following telegram to the strikers: "... if the situation continues, it will become even more necessary for us to advise the Labour Relations Board of the illegality of this strike, and to ask it to consider the withdrawal of certification. ..." The Minister is not a tribunal. Even if he were, he would not have the right to declare acts involving the responsibility of persons illegal without summoning these persons before him and permitting them to testify. No text of law could authorize him to "advise" a tribunal of the illegality of an act. In the case we are considering, he would at most be entitled to order the Board to make an inquiry into the illegality of the strike.

The Minister is not the legislator, but the man who puts his provisions into effect. Since the Act has established a Board of Inquiry to judge the responsibilities of persons involved in such disputes, the Minister has no jurisdiction enabling him to take the place of the Board, or even to exempt it from its duty to make an inquiry.

When the Minister, in addition, asked the Board "to consider the withdrawal of certification," he thereby misled it, as is shown by what we have said above about the withdrawal of certification "for cause."

On the specific point of his "asking," the Minister must be accused of performing an illegal act. The administrative law that authorizes him to order the Board to inquire into a given matter strictly forbade him to make any reference prejudicial to the accused persons. His executive function in the Department of Labour lends a prejudicial character to his words, and even suggests a course of action, when he asks the Labour Relations Board "to consider the withdrawal...." From this moment on, there is no assurance that the tribunal of inquiry will be objective in handing down its decision.

b) Breach of executive duties

In the same telegram, the Minister replied to the unions that were asking for an arbitration board: ".... We are prepared to set up an arbitration board, but this board will not be formed until the employees have submitted to the Law by returning to work...." Is this the position the Law ordered the Minister to take?

The text of the Department of Labour Act states: "He [the Minister] has charge of the carrying out of any acts respecting ... disputes between employers and employees...." In this case, we undoubtedly have a dispute. The stage of direct negotiations, and even of conciliation, had been passed. At this point, what was the role of the Minister? Article Fourteen of the Labour Relations Act spelled it out for him in these terms: "If the report [of the conciliation officer] shows that agreement has been impossible, the Minister shall appoint a council of arbitration pursuant to the Quebec Trade Disputes Act, the report of the conciliation officer taking the place of the application contemplated in the said act." In the case we are considering there was, in addition to the conciliation officer's report, the application for arbitration on the part of the unions which is referred to in the Act just quoted.

The Minister, whose duty it was to see that the Act was enforced, did not appoint an arbitration board and prevented the Act from taking its course. He thereby committed a serious breach of his executive duties.

By a failure to understand the Act, similar to the failure of the Board, the Minister classified the withdrawal of the certificate of union recognition as a punishment, and believed that he had the power to impose this pseudo-penalty. He also forgot that he did not have the competence to inflict penalties, because Article Forty-Nine of the Act specifies: "No penal prosecution may be taken under this act without the written authorization of the Board or the consent of the Attorney General."

Just like the Board, the Minister had made a judicial aberration, confusing the conditions for the existence of a natural right to union recognition with the conditions entailing the infliction of a penalty. Instead of assuring respect for the Act, the Minister of Labour contributed to the Board's misunderstanding of it. Such contempt for natural law, combined with a like disrespect for actual statutes, amounts to a disturbance of the social order from the top, especially when directed against the working class.

3/Procedures employed in the renewal of certification

One last document of the Board deserves our attention: "The Labour Relations Board, sitting at Montreal on July 13, 1949, having been informed of the written agreement between the union and the management parties and of the spirit of this agreement, and having taken into consideration the return to work and the formal promise made by the Honourable Minister of Labour in this connection, with the sole purpose of not interfering, of cooperating and of not in any way harming the future good relations between the parties, decides to cancel its decision, wholly in conformity with the Act, handed down on July 5, 1949, concerning the issuing of a certificate of union recognition, and also decides to cancel its decision to revoke the certficate of union recognition, handed down on February 21, 1949." Let us consider some of these phrases.

"The Board . . . having been informed . . . of the spirit of this agreement . . ." We wonder how the spirit of an agreement between management and labour might affect the latter's right to union recognition.

". . . having taken into consideration the return to work and the formal promise made by the Honourable Minister of Labour in this connection . . ." What is expressed by such an admission? The Board, then, is not afraid to state publicly that the Minister of Labour no longer exercises a mere right of inspection (which would already be illegal), but rather a peremptory power over the decisions to be handed down following the inquiry. The Minister has a duty to supervise the proceedings of inquiries conducted by the Board. Administrative law never grants him the power to influence a decision. In the case we are considering, the Board has acknowledged that it is bound by a formal promise of the Minister. We find, within the Department, a disturbing confusion of powers. We are also witnessing, in our time, the progressive enslavement of the Boards of Inquiry to political power. These are phenomena which, in our province, dispute the honour of undermining the authority and the prestige of our high officials.

". . . decides to cancel its decision, wholly in conformity with the Act, handed down on July 5, 1949 . . ." The Board first tells us that it has handed down a decision wholly in conformity with the Act. If this first decision was wholly in conformity with the Act, that which is substituted for it is not entirely so.

". . . and also decides to cancel its decision to revoke the certificate of union recognition, handed down on February 21, 1949." Are we still on quasi-judicial ground, or are we not rather astride a legal seesaw? The certificate was revoked on February 21. On July 5, it was decided not to rescind the revocation. On July 15, it was decided to revoke the non-revocation of the revocation. Result: a return to the point of departure. This war of words which the Board has allowed us to witness is called a quasi-judicial decision. And people are surprised that the public no longer puts its faith in provincial commissions of inquiry.

On July 15, 1949, the Board returned to the unions concerned all the certificates that it had taken away from them on February 21 of the same year. It reestablished the status quo, implicitly admitting, by its last decision, that the deprivation of the right to union recognition, imposed from February 21 to July 15, was arbitrary. In fact, no procedure, i.e., no petition, was necessary, in the opinion of the Board, for the unions to recover their certificate of union recognition. Since such certificates can only be obtained by petition (Article 6),[7] we are obliged to conclude that, from the legal point of view, the unions had never lost them.

During this whole intervening period, of capital importance for the unions, the Board had politically taken the side of the companies, erroneously leading them to believe that they no longer needed to pay any attention to the union representatives, because the certificates had been cancelled. There was, however, a clear conflict between the Board on the one hand, which was withdrawing the certificates, and the Act on the other, which by virtue of its Article Four, quoted above, still placed the employers under the obligation to recognize the union representatives. It is obvious that, in this situation, the only purpose of the Board's intervention was to do harm. The Board confirms this in its decision of July 15, testifying that it is now acting with the intention "of not in any way harming the future good relations between the parties. . . ."

Aberrations, inconsistencies, judicial antinomies, and a deviation towards a political role: such is the record of the interventions of the Labour Relations Board in the asbestos strike.

Notes to Chapter VII

[1]The question of the unconstitutionality of the Labour Relations Act itself was brought up several times before our courts, notably by Maîtres Théodore Lespérance and Jacques Perrault. This question has not, however, ever been the principal object of a litigation, and the courts have not yet had to pass judgment upon it. We will not consider it here.

[2]In our Act, conciliation and arbitration are virtually synonymous, as arbitration legally results only in recommendations. The second stage is no more than a multiple of the first, in the sense that it increases the waiting period four times and more often ten times, which then becomes a period of exasperation.

[3]My italics.

[4]Bill 19, passed in 1954, could not be taken into account at the time. This new law permits the withdrawal of a union certificate if the union has called an illegal strike.

[5]"Nothing in this act shall prevent an unrecognized association from entering into a collective agreement. . . ."

[6]"Every employer shall be bound to recognize as the collective representative of his employees the representatives of an association comprising sixty percent of his said employees and to negotiate with them in good faith, a collective agreement."

[7]"Every association desiring to be recognized . . . *shall* apply by petition in writing to the Board. . . ."

Chapter VIII

The Strike and the Press

by Gérard Pelletier

I/General introduction

In my opinion, the asbestos strike marked the beginning of a new era in the relations between the Quebec press and the labour movement. Until the conflict of 1949, most of our newspapers viewed the battles between management and labour as isolated phenomena, foreign to the French Canadian social context.

Strikes were treated in the newspapers in a very superficial way. The facts were offered through the publication of agency dispatches, but no serious effort was made to obtain a deeper understanding of them, nor did the press try to give the public anything better in the way of information. The press also affected a lukewarm attitude towards the strikers. In dealing with the funeral rites of a Member of Parliament, a reporter could refer to "these fine people of Valleyfield," but when the strike was in progress the same people were labelled "the members of the labour organization involved"; in other words, a group of virtual delinquents who were no longer recognized as members of the family.

In short, the press did not acknowledge the validity of the actions taken by the labour movement.

Press editorials made little effort to study the profound causes of strikes and to assess their objectives. They were either denounced outright as subversive action or else ignored. It was very unusual to come across a serious editorial dealing with a strike.

The asbestos strike did not change these habits of thought overnight. With the rapid increase in the number of union members during the last war, the judgments of public opinion had begun to change. The unionists were no longer regarded as a small minority inhabiting the lower depths of society; through the growth in their numbers, they gradually acquired a greater influence. Public opinion began to react to

239

this new social ferment.

Nevertheless, the asbestos strike, occurring at the moment it did, marks the beginning of a new and decisive phase in this evolution of public opinion.

This labour conflict, because of its scope, its duration, its style, and the peculiar nature of its aims, forced the entire press, even the smaller local papers, to take a stand. For the first time, it became impossible to adopt an attitude of polite indifference. Public opinion was profoundly affected by the strike, and those who made a profession of expressing this opinion (while also "guiding" it) had to get down to serious work.

For the first time, the members of the press were confronted with a social problem, not in the form of a fleshless abstraction, but as a terribly urgent and very specific situation. This essay is dedicated to revealing, as clearly as possible, the singular lessons this new experience held for the press.

II/The "opinions" of the press

A folder of press clippings on the asbestos strike is sitting on my table. There are more than one thousand items for the five-month period of the conflict, all of them taken from newspapers published in the Province of Quebec. Articles and reports on the strike in Canadian newspapers in other provinces and in foreign periodicals would bring the number up to over two thousand.

This is the material we propose to examine, but how are we to analyze it? I felt, after careful consideration, that my most important task was to give the opinions expressed by the most representative newspapers, and this is what I have done in this section of this chapter. In the following part, I will examine the *news policy* of the papers in relation to the events of the strike and add a few brief comments about the radio as a source of information. Then it will be time to draw conclusions.

1/A preliminary classification

It is well known that the diversity of the Quebec press is largely determined by the interest groups that control its various sectors. In order to understand the situation, we must make a preliminary classification. Here, then, is the cast in order of appearance, an order I shall follow scrupulously in my analysis of the editorials.

a) *Le Devoir,* an independent newspaper, is a unique case, and in this analysis seems to deserve a section all to itself. I do not, however, wish to imply that *Le Devoir* operates with complete and unfettered liberty. Working in a definite social and religious context, *Le Devoir* must observe certain limits of action, like all the other newspapers. Still, it does not depend on any financial power (even its own, which is nonexistent!), and it is not bound by any church allegiance (except for the *personal* religious obedience of its editors) or political affiliation (nationalism has demonstrated its own impotence at the polls). This unique situation of *Le Devoir* among our newspapers demands special treatment. The part played by this daily in the strike is also of great importance, as we shall see.

b) For the purposes of this study, it also seems natural to group together the newspapers that represent the various political parties. On the government side, *Montréal-Matin* and the *Montreal Gazette* were the standard-bearers for a whole host of small weeklies that supported the National Union. *Le Canada* voiced the opinions of the Liberal opposition, and was poorly seconded by a more unruly group of small weeklies.

c) *L'Action catholique*, as the chief spokesman for the opinions of the Church, has always played an important part in the press in Quebec, as has *The Ensign*, the weekly of the minority of English-speaking Catholics. In the particular case which concerns us here, *Le Messager* of Sherbrooke, the newspaper of the diocese where the main events of the strike occurred, played a role of exceptional importance, as did *Le Front ouvrier*, a weekly which has since disappeared, but which was then at the peak of its career as the representative of the opinions of the Catholic labour movement.

We will leave to part III of this chapter ("The information provided") our treatment of large-circulation newspapers which are really "press enterprises" in the capitalist sense of the term: *La Presse, The Montreal Star, The Standard, The Herald, La Tribune* of Sherbrooke and other dailies of the Nicol chain, etc.

2/Le Devoir, a precursor

Those who like to look for secret forces at work in history have not failed to discover a plot in the origins of the asbestos strike. It may be said by way of excusing them that the course of events at the beginning of 1949 lends itself to this kind of interpretation.

On January 12, *Le Devoir* published a study by Burton LeDoux entitled: "Asbestosis at East Broughton—A Village of 3,000 Suffocated by Dust." The article made a violent attack on the asbestos industry in the Province of Quebec. We do not have the space to summarize an indictment that filled several full pages of the newspaper. Let us merely note here that, following upon the same investigator's exposé of the scandal of silicosis the previous year,[1] his condemnation of the health conditions in some of the asbestos mines at once aroused a great deal of feeling.

The editors of *Le Devoir* made no secret of the fact that they were embarked on an energetic, indeed a violent campaign against the attitude of employers and government towards industrial hygiene. Between January 12 and February 14, hardly a day passed when *Le Devoir* did not return to the subject of asbestosis, either to add a new piece of information to that already collected or to offer further editorial comment.

The attack was maintained with such vigour that the people under fire seemed at a loss to reply, and more than a month went by before they attempted to make a defence.

Meanwhile, an event of great importance totally altered the situation: five thousand asbestos miners went on strike. Up to that time, Burton LeDoux's indictment of the industry was merely an article which had been published and endorsed by *Le Devoir*;[2] after the declaration of the strike, the unexpected publicity brought it to the attention of a public that was now keenly interested in the situation in the asbestos industry.

With even a modicum of imagination and prejudice, people were easily led to regard this chain of events as evidence for a cunning strategy devised by editors of *Le Devoir* and the leaders of the Canadian and Catholic Confederation of Labour. Such an interpretation could find support in the fact that Gérard Picard, the president of the C.C.C.L., was on the board of directors of *Le Devoir*.

This very plausible suspicion was groundless. I can bear witness to the fact, because I was very closely involved with the publication of LeDoux's article. When the management of *Le Devoir* first considered publishing it, it was much more interested in undertaking a logical continuation of the campaign for industrial hygiene, begun the previous year with the report on silicosis, than in promoting the cause of trade unionism in any way. Furthermore, there had been no suggestion that a strike would take place at the time the article was written. We did not learn that a strike was about to break out at Asbestos until the first rumours of it were published in the Canadian newspapers, on February 7. The relationship between *Le Devoir* and the C.C.C.L. was so tenuous at that time that we were worried about whether or not the unions were aware of the problem of asbestosis. I myself was sent by the paper to the union members at Asbestos to give them some information on the subject.

There is one single but important fact that in itself should have been enough to discredit the conspiracy theory: the workers of East Broughton, who particularly worried Burton LeDoux and who were preeminently the victims of asbestosis, were the only unionists of the organization who never went out on strike...

The above remarks are intended to refute a false report about LeDoux's article on asbestosis. This indictment did, however, have a significant effect on the course of events, and put *Le Devoir* in the camp of the strikers. The social outlook of the newspaper had been expressed before, in 1947 for example, when a special correspondent was sent to Lachute at the time of the strike against the Ayers Company. *Le Devoir*'s concern with labour disputes antedated the outbreak of the asbestos strike.

Still, *Le Devoir* created a precedent both in its own history and in the history of the daily French-language press in Canada by devoting, in this five-month period, more reports, commentaries, editorials, and dispatches to a strike than to any other current issue.

As Grace Morey McKenzie notes in her book on the strike:[3] ''The French-language daily, *Le Devoir* of Montreal, was the only newspaper to give complete coverage of the Asbestos strike. It sent its special correspondent, M. Gérard Pelletier, to the strike-field the day the strike started. M. Pelletier was there continuously until the conclusion of the strike....'' Miss McKenzie, in her documentation on the strike, includes over three hundred different documents regarding the struggle which were published in *Le Devoir* between February 14 and August 17.

This newspaper, in other words, not only took the side of the striking workers, but conducted a systematic campaign on their behalf throughout the course of the conflict. It would be easy to show that the news offered by *Le Devoir* was always more plentiful, more detailed, and more up-to-the-minute than that of the other newspapers.

Of even greater importance was the continuous series of editorials the newspaper published in the course of the strike. Every aspect of the strike was taken into consideration. The editorial writers had time to reflect upon the events and to develop a clear understanding of the social philosophy behind this strike. They were in a better position to do so than the labour leaders, who were busy with the day-to-day developments and who were forced to move about constantly.

To make even a brief summary of the offensive and defensive activities of the newspaper during these months, we would have to repeat here a considerable part of the history of the strike which other collaborators have already given in detail.

Accordingly, I shall merely quote a few of the more significant passages that sum up, in the main, the position taken by the newspaper. The following straightforward paragraphs, for example, are taken from an editorial of April 2, 1949, signed by Gérard Filion:

Because *Le Devoir* has recently expressed firm support of the workers who are *illegally* on strike, some people have come to the general conclusion that we advocate violation of the law, and are therefore anarchists. In view of this, it is not a bad idea to express our own opinions on this subject.

First of all, we wish to draw attention to the fact that we have never recommended the strike as a means of regulating industrial disputes. At the most, we recognize that this trial by force is at times the last method available to the workers in their search for justice. Moreover, we have never urged any group of workers, manual or intellectual, to resort to a strike. We have always tried to advocate conciliation.

When a strike is declared, however, the problem changes completely. A new situation is created, and different forces confront one another. The public has the right to an explanation of the causes of the dispute, so that it may understand the grievances of the workers and the defences made by the employers.

Anybody with the slightest knowledge of philosophy knows that a strike is permissible under the following conditions: a just and serious cause to uphold, and the use of fair means to attain one's goals.

This is fine in theory, but who can tell us in practice, in a given concrete situation, whether the cause upheld by a group of striking workers is just and serious, and whether the means employed are fair?

To the moralist comfortably ensconced in his armchair, who weighs the opinions of the learned with scales of great precision, the asbestos strike, for example, might well seem illegal. But how can we explain this to the miner who has been suffocating in asbestos dust for ten or twenty years? He would send us packing.

In the Province of Quebec, our working class is long-suffering, habituated to order, and innately respectful of the law. There is thus presumptive proof, in general, that strikes occur for good and serious reasons. We should not forget that the worker who goes on strike is risking the welfare of his family, his goods, sometimes his future and his job, while the employer is threatened only with a loss of profits.

The two parties to the conflict should not, then, be regarded as on an equal footing: what one finds secondary often seems essential to the other. A few more cents an hour do not, perhaps, mean much to the company, while to the worker they may represent the difference between poverty and a modest degree of comfort.

Strikes, then, are like specific cases before the law, which must be judged individually on their merits. This is what we have done for the last two years. We have upheld the workers, except in a couple of cases where we felt that they were wrong, in the meat packing strike, for example. This is because we felt that justice was on their side. . . .

There remains the case of the so-called illegal strikes, which are so designated either because the conditions laid down by the law have not been fulfilled, or because the law formally prohibits certain categories of workers from going on strike.

In this case as well, we must not consider the matter in the abstract, without taking the concrete realities sufficiently into account.

In the first place, labour law is in the process of evolution. It is not, like the Civil Code, a prescriptive system that has been tested by centuries of experience. The laws pertaining to labour are full of anomalies, and are being modified every year. . . .

Because of this provisional nature of labour laws, they do not carry the same degree of obligation as the common law . . . They have the power to command obedience only as long as they are neither ridiculous nor unjust. . . .

Furthermore, society is gravely menaced when people constantly invoke legality to sanction injustice. Such a policy eventually leads people to think that the law and injustice go together, and that the only way to obtain social justice is to break the law. . . .

I ask the reader's indulgence for the length of this quotation. I felt that it was needed to make him familiar with the tone of the editorials that *Le Devoir* published during the strike. The impressive thing about most of these texts is that they almost always go beyond the limits of the specific strike in question to consider the whole problem of French Canadian society. On April 23, for example, in commenting on a refusal of the Rector of Laval University (who prohibited his students, on pain of expulsion, from undertaking a planned visit to the miners of Thetford), Gérard Filion attacked the whole social position of our universities:

Our universities have an eminent role to play in the social field. For who will teach the doctrine of the Church and find practical applications for it, if not the Catholic universities?

They must expect opposition, however. One can already sense it. We hear it said with growing frequency that some of the heavy contributors to our university treasuries frown whenever people speak of social sciences, social service, of training trade union leaders, etc. There is no miserly attitude towards the faculties that turn out professional gentlemen, but those that are intended to help the people are considered very expensive.

One week later, the same editorial writer offered similar comment on the attitude of the "people of standing" who had joined forces against those who, "having tasted political democracy, now aim at economic democracy." On May 9, André Laurendeau, assistant to the editor-in-chief, published an "Open Letter to the Ambassador of the United States," to whom he confided the problem of the asbestos miners:

> Will you permit the moneymen to ruin your reputation in Canada as a great and civilized people? Are you willing to take the chance that, at international assemblies, the adversaries who are on the lookout for your weaknesses will be able to produce overwhelming evidence against certain American [employers]? Will you have it said that for the United States, neither democracy, humanity, nor justice are export products—not even for a neighbour of the white race?

On May 25, Mr. Filion resumed the role of prosecutor in considering the problem of our natural resources, which are leased out to foreign capital. He stated in an editorial:

> It is not xenophobia to demand that the natural wealth of our province be placed under the majority control of Canadian stock-holders and administrators: it is no more than a mark of self-respect and a sense of good order.

On June 6, Laurendeau, in dealing with certain incidents in the courts concerning the asbestos strike, considered the whole problem of the political use of the judicial system. In his editorial, he excoriated certain magistrates who were using the bench as a speaker's platform.

These passages show the general position adopted by *Le Devoir* throughout the course of the strike. The last paragraph of an editorial by Gérard Filion, published on July 6, or one week after the conflict had been resolved, may round out our anthology:

> The asbestos strike was a great misfortune, but it was far from useless: the social climate of Quebec is no longer what it was six months ago. Today, we are beginning to acquire a social conscience. Good can sometimes come of evil.

I feel that this final remark reveals the originality of the press campaign waged by *Le Devoir* during the asbestos strike: the Montreal daily had chosen combat on the social level. Throughout the period, it remained attached to its own nationalist propensities, but without allowing them to overshadow the fundamental aspects of the problem.

I shall not describe all the effects of *Le Devoir*'s campaign. One is more striking than all the others: by its display of courage, this daily showed just how aggressive, tenacious, and determined it could be, and forced the other newspapers to define their own attitudes. We are not engaging in idle speculation here. For example, the party newspapers would have acted differently if the attitude of *Le Devoir* had not obliged them to join in a debate that was not to their advantage.

3/The political newspapers, or the impossible silence

The most striking thing about the political papers is their reluctance to get involved in the dispute, a reluctance which is first revealed by their inexplicable delays in dealing with the strike.

The strike began on February 13. By March 14, one month later, neither *Montréal-Matin* nor *The Gazette* nor *Le Clairon* had offered the slightest commentary on it. Everyone will agree, I am sure, that these three newspapers, with the addition of *Le Canada*, offer a fair sample of the party-oriented press in Quebec at the time.[4] The first editorial in *Montréal-Matin* concerning the strike is dated March 18, and the first treatment of it by *The Gazette* (with the exception of a vague allusion on March 29) appeared on May 6. The evidence suggests that there was no rush to deal with the subject, even though the men in power, during these few weeks, were experiencing the most forceful and direct attacks that they had known in their entire careers.

One might think that the official opposition at least, trounced at the elections of the previous summer and reduced to an insignificant minority in Parliament, would have taken advantage of the situation created by the strike to influence public opinion. Such was not the case. So our disappointment in their performance is even greater, and their silence arouses even more profound suspicions.

A careful reading of all the editorials published by the party newspapers reveals that the commentators maintained an almost total silence about the reasons advanced by the strikers to justify their dispute. Nowhere do we find a frank discussion of this topic in the editorial pages of the party newspapers. One looks in vain for a presentation of the strikers' demands, or for an overall criticism of them. Here and there, one encounters a vague allusion to ''the complaints voiced by the miners'' *(Montréal-Matin)* or an attempt to discredit their aims *(The Gazette)*.

There was, however, nothing obscure about the union demands. The strikers presented their claims in a very clear fashion, regarding both wages and working conditions. It would have been easy to examine each of their demands and to assess whether they were timely or not. The defenders of the government never attempted to write in this way, not even to add their own arguments to Barrette's and Duplessis's defences of the government position in the Legislative Assembly or in press conferences.

A few typical quotations from these four newspapers will give us some idea of their positions on the strike.

a) Montréal-Matin

On March 18, when the strike was already five weeks old, Roger Duhamel, an editorial writer for *Montréal-Matin*, published some reflections on "Practising Lack of Foresight" (such was the title of his article). Duhamel first summed up the declaration of the strike and Barrette's two offers of conciliation in nine lines. He then went on to state:

> Meanwhile, tension is increasing. The exalted spirits of the first few days are waning. After these weeks of inactivity, it is only natural that the workers are becoming bitter and can no longer view their problems calmly. Resentment is gradually replacing the legitimate claim to certain rights which have been allegedly violated. [This is the only sentence in the article which refers to the causes of the strike, and to the demands of the miners.] In every group that places itself outside the limits of the law, there is an inevitable growth in rancour and animosity, which can even lead to acts of violence. [An allusion to the illegality of the strike.] So, there has been a dynamiting, and it has been reported that a peaceful engineer, because he did not share the views of the strikers, has been beaten up by a number of individuals who believe in "striking" arguments. If the present situation continues, we can expect further brawls. When people are stirred up, it is almost impossible to make them listen to reason.
>
> We must emphasize that all this is most unfortunate. We are seeing the concrete results of a constant incitement to riot, undertaken by certain irresponsible individuals who invoke the hypocritical pretext of social justice. Their activity is leading to the disorganization of society and the undermining of the foundations of order. What does it matter to them, after all, as long as they attain their ends? The anarchists in detachable collars go resolutely about their task, in the hope that the upheaval they so earnestly pray for will enable them to emerge from the obscurity in which they whine away their days.
>
> It rarely happens that truth is found exclusively on one side of a dispute; life does not lend itself much to such oversimplification. It is remarkable that the people who keep labour relations in a state of

instability have never had the slightest criticism to make of the
workers, and on the other hand, have never been able to see any
merit in the viewpoints espoused by the companies or by the employers. The latter are a wretched lot, who have no rights that deserve respect and who are laden with every sin. We know perfectly
well that this is how the communists explain the capitalist world,
but we are justifiably astonished to find that earnest students of the
papal encyclicals are using the same kind of language and performing such reprehensible acts.

The article ends with a prophecy: incidents will occur at Asbestos,
the Provincial Police will intervene, and certain members of the press
"will devote themselves to denouncing the use of truncheons." The
last sentence reads: "The strike, what a godsend for the fishers in
troubled waters!"

Three weeks later, in other words not until April 7, *Montréal-Matin*
took up the subject again, but in a very indirect way. It published the
conclusions of a "sacerdotal study group" regarding the following
problem: is the strike legitimate? The text is vague, involved, and
incomplete, ending with the words TO BE CONTINUED. The sequel,
however, was never published . . .

On the eighteenth, *Montréal-Matin* published an anonymous letter
from a "Veteran of Thetford Mines," preceded by an Editor's Note
which was very hostile to the strikers and to "the muddle-headed
people, clergy or laymen." It is a pity that we cannot reproduce here
the complete text of this document, which is too long for this purpose.
It admirably reveals a certain "right-thinking" attitude towards the
strike. Needless to say, the reproach of illegality is exploited at great
length, and all the acts of violence that had occurred in the strike up to
that point are brought forth and severely condemned. These are arguments, however, which we will find used elsewhere, better formulated
and more effectively used.

I will quote here, then, those passages of the letter that are unique in
their paternalistic flavour and right-thinking attitudes:

> It was no child's firecracker, but a stick of dynamite that was
> hurled at the home of Mr. Andrew Johnson. What worker's family,
> what poor person, what woman in distress can honestly say that Mr.
> Johnson, Mrs. Johnson, or Miss Johnson [the family that owned the
> most important mine in Thetford] have let a poor person, a mother
> of a family depart without giving them not a penny, not five cents,
> but five dollars or more each time?
> . . .
> At the present time, humorists are inveighing against the mayor

of Thetford, the Hon. Minister Tancrède Labbé.

I lived at Thetford during the unemployment crisis of 1929, 1930 . . . What working man out of a job ever went to the home of Mr. Labbé without leaving with a sack of flour, coupons for bread and milk, etc? And what did today's false friends of the working man give at that time? Where were they then?

. . .

Who allowed the Guards of St. Alphonse, whose uniforms were for the most part paid for by Mr. Andrew Johnson, to head up the parade of the strikers, carrying signs which called upon the citizens to riot and to express their contempt for the employers?

On April 28, *Montréal-Matin* published an editorial signed by Duhamel which took it for granted that the strike was all but settled: "When Things Have Returned to Normal." The editorial writer emphasizes the "salutary lessons" to be learned from "this episode in the social war." He finds that these lessons are three in number, which I summarize in order not to overburden a text that already contains many quotations: a) the workers must be "extremely careful about choosing their leaders"; b) "The political parties, as one might have expected, have not made the distinction" between the citizens who were favourably disposed towards the strikers and those who condemned their actions. "The members of the National Union have blamed the illegality of this work stoppage, which is evident and recognized by all; the Liberals have not dared to approve the attitude of the strike leaders, even if they were eager to embarrass the provincial government"; c) those "who have preached illegality and revelled in it" are therefore: the strikers themselves, good people who were not well informed of the situation, and "closet revolutionaries"; d) finally, the strike has taught us "that Christian values are poorly served by those who claim to be their traditional defenders."

On April 27, *Montréal-Matin* published, without commentary, a long document of Benedict XV, taken from the letter *Intelliximus* (1920). The following passage was regarded by the editors of the newspaper as of capital importance:

My dear Sons and Venerable Brothers, you must make a zealous effort to assure that the people resolve their conflicts only by peaceful means . . . The clergy must not become involved in agitations, and especially not it seditions; they must rather strive, through giving better counsel by both word and example, to allay when necessary the excitement of those who have become overwrought.

On April 28, the former inhabitant of Thetford published a new letter in *Montréal-Matin*. The anonymous author reprimanded the chaplain of the Quebec City Central Labour Council, Abbé Ouellette, "who has been born, it seems, to implement the social doctrine of the Church." His accusations against the labour leaders now took a new tack: he insinuated, by the use of rhetorical questions, that the union management was dishonest:

> Why does he [the worker] not have access to the books of the unions? What happens to the dues paid by the unionists? What are the salaries and the travel expenses of the union officials? Who controls and distributes the money that has been collected to help the strikers? What control does the worker have over these funds, which should go to him exclusively? Are political organizations secretly giving financial support to this dispute, which seems to be becoming more and more an essentially political struggle? There are so many unfathomable mysteries. . . .

Before the publication of the last, and particularly significant, document discussed below, three more editorials on the strike appeared in *Montréal-Matin*. In the first of these, on April 30, Duhamel vigorously attacked your humble servant for his report of an incident that implicated Laval's Rector, Mgr. Ferdinand Vandry. This was *Montréal-Matin's* first explicit reference to me, though it had previously made a number of vaguer references to a journalist from *Le Devoir*. Duhamel spoke of "the shameful slanders of an obscure pen-pusher" and of "the insignificant young man, a haughty admirer of anarchism, whom *Le Devoir* [named for the first time] has for the past weeks assigned on a regular basis to Asbestos and Thetford." (We may note in passing that *Montréal-Matin* had special correspondents only at the courts which were considering incidents related to the strike.)

On May 2 Joseph Bourdon, another editor of *Montréal-Matin*, wrote an editorial on the high cost of the strike and the many months that the strikers would require to make up their wage losses. On May 9 Duhamel commented on the violent acts that had been committed on the sixth, and alluded directly to the influence of the extreme left. He beclouded his utterances with figures of rhetoric, to discourage attempts to sue for defamation of character:

> It has been noted that the strikers have received much outside support, especially from Montreal. Communist agents would have indeed been foolish to let slip such a golden opportunity. We are convinced that the great majority of asbestos workers are sincerely opposed to any collusion with the communists. As always, they are

being manipulated by agitators who are experts in the technique of violence and the coup d'etat.

Such were the main features of *Montréal-Matin*'s editorial policy on the strike. It ignored the basic issues in the dispute, emphasized the illegality of the strike, and identified the adversary with the communists (even though to do this, it had to reveal a somewhat right-wing anti-clerical tendency). *Montréal-Matin* discredited the union leaders, represented itself as the upholder of law and order, and by quoting from Benedict XV or some other deceased pope, tried to refute the arguments in favour of social justice.

In view of all this, Duhamel's "closing" editorial of July 5, on the (now final) strike settlement, comes as a surprise. It is a profession of faith in trade unionism, rather unexpected of course, and rather theoretical as well, as this support is offered after the settlement of the dispute. It is, however, unequivocal. Duhamel had realized that trade unionism was no longer a negligible force:

> On this occasion [the final settlement of the dispute] it is timely to recall the principles that should be followed in troubles of this kind.
>
> In the first place, trade unionism is here to stay and it would be both futile and dangerous to try to destroy it; such an attempt would fail, thereby running the risk of starting a class struggle which would cause great harm to the prestige and well-being of the province. It is of vital importance that recalcitrant capitalists, if there still are any in 1949, take this undeniable truth to heart. They will gain nothing, and may lose everything, if they try to obtain, by guile or force, excessive advantages which will not be tolerated by present-day public opinion. The workers have become aware of their collective power. . . .

b) *The Gazette*

Allowing for the fact that *The Gazette* is an English-language newspaper addressed to an English-speaking population, the "line" it adopted is very similar to that of *Montréal-Matin*. Its orientation implies a certain aloofness, a somewhat superior tone, and an ignorance of the facts affected with the greatest elegance.

To give an example, *The Gazette* finally decided to end the silence of its editorial pages on May 6, two and a half months after the strike had begun. It did so to deplore the violence which had occurred at Asbestos and to make the frank comment:

> There is still no clearly defined statement as to just what the strikers demand or what their grievances are.

The Gazette added, as if it were talking about some event that had occurred in Africa:

> Appraisal of the true inwardness of the situation is made more difficult by reason of the partial indoctrination of many of the people of the district with the dogma that it is possible to get rich quick by methods of "funny money," and the attitude of certain of the clergy, apparently in opposition to the position of provincial authorities.

In the six editorials that *The Gazette* devoted to the strike, this same tone of haughty aloofness is maintained to the very last line. Ten days later, *The Gazette* claimed, without the slightest reference to wage scales or to the problems of industrial hygiene, that the C.C.C.L. was really waging war on the international unions at Asbestos, "by trying to prove that it can make effective use of the same techniques as these unions"! On June 3, the editorial writer was content to deplore the failure of the conciliation proposed by Barrette, and blamed the union for it. Finally, on June 24, *The Gazette* offered a solemn commentary on the announcement by the president of the Johns-Manville Co. that the firm intended to transfer its mining operations to Ontario. The editorial criticized Jean Marchand for ridiculing the pretensions of Mr. Brown, and insisted that this displacement would mean a serious loss to Quebec. The title of the piece indicates *The Gazette*'s position clearly enough: "Threat to Quebec's Economic Progress." (*The Financial Times,* on July 8, spoke of this threat as a tall tale—a "hot weather story." The financial paper reported the reaction of a number of businessmen who were asked what they thought of the statement by Mr. Brown. A typical reply: "HE said that?" Another: "He should not have made such a statement." The article suggested that, generally speaking, nobody took this threat seriously.)

c) Le Canada

The Gazette's comments on the strike reveal an astonishing poverty of thought and a complete failure to consider the economic facts and the human side of the strike. They raise serious doubts about the reputation which *The Gazette* enjoys among businessmen as a "great newspaper." The attitude of the Liberal press towards the strike is even more revealing.

Let us briefly recall the political situation in the first few months of 1949. The provincial Liberal Party had not yet recovered from its almost total defeat in the summer of 1948. It had only eight members in the provincial legislature. None of these men were politicians of distinction, with the exception of George Marler, who represented the interests of high finance. In other respects, a strong Quebec government had never before had to confront such powerful forces of opposition, though these forces were not to be found in the legislature. Bill 5 was defeated from without: not a single serious speech on the subject was delivered in Parliament. The coalition of unions, achieved at last, was responsible for this defeat; after Bill 5 had been rejected, the coalition continued to exist, and was given new life by the asbestos strike.

The time seemed ripe for the Liberal Party to regain some lost ground by taking advantage of these currents of opinion. The party had a press, the few seats in Parliament that were not held by Mr. Duplessis, and political·experience. The discontented unionists were not yet fully conscious of the nature of their feelings. With a bit of adroit manipulation by the party, all this social unrest could have been profitably exploited by the Liberals. The party could have immediately launched the whole propaganda campaign which it later undertook in the elections of 1952; it would have been much more effective in 1949.

The Liberal Party, however, was paralyzed. Was this inaction due to the causes assigned by Mr. Duhamel, which we have examined above? Did the "powerful friends" of the Liberals secretly approve of the attitude of the Duplessis government? Did they have nightmares in which the strikers at Asbestos established the dictatorship of the proletariat?

Ten days passed before the editorial writer of *Le Canada* chose to recognize the fact that the asbestos miners were on strike. Then, every ten days or so, a few very timid editorials discussed some of the secondary aspects of the strike. There was not one in-depth article on the issues involved, but only a series of feeble protests against the improprieties and brutality of the police. *Le Canada* devoted itself, for the most part, to pointing out the blunders of the government, and at the same time was very careful not to support the strikers' cause. The paper took a malicious pleasure in emphasizing the differences of opinion that existed between the provincial cabinet and some men of the Church.

For example, in reply to the National Union spokesman, who was complaining of the "nonsense" spoken about the strike (and against Mr. Duplessis), *Le Canada* quoted the Archbishop of Montreal (May 24):

> The working class is the victim of a conspiracy which seeks to crush it, and when there is a conspiracy to crush the working class, the Church has a duty to intervene.

That was all that *Le Canada* had to say on the subject. It then remained silent for over a month, until June 25, when it published an editorial dealing with the statement of Lewis Brown. The writer of the editorial (who had also been taken in by Mr. Brown's announcement, it seems) said that if the Johns-Manville Co. changed its location, this would not be the fault of the asbestos strikers but of the Duplessis government, which had unduly prolonged the strike by its stubborn attitude.

On July 4, *Le Canada* offered a final commentary, a jejune piece on the settlement of the strike. Here is the most significant sentence from it:

> The various repercussions of this persistent labour dispute had created, in our society, an unhealthy climate of distrust towards certain capitalist institutions.

d) Le Clairon (The Bugle)

Does this explain the incredible apathy we find in some of the articles in *Le Clairon*? As is well known, Senator T.D. Bouchard was not without influence among the Liberals. In their hour of crushing defeat (on the provincial level, of course), the senator from St. Hyacinth appeared to be a solid bastion.

Senator Bouchard was not merely a Liberal; he was above all a capitalist. How, then, could his newspaper have been expected to defend the position of the strikers, who had brought the activities of a great American company to a halt, and who had been encouraged to do so by a whole section of the clergy? The few articles (e.g., of July 1) of Georges Lasnier on the miners' struggle are completely unfavourable. For Mr. Lasnier, the strike was nothing more than a nationalist plot which had been hatched by the unions in connivance with *Le Devoir*. One of the people who were deceived by Lewis Brown's little hoax, he wrote in all seriousness:

> The nationalist publication [*Le Devoir*] immediately denounced the statement as a piece of intimidation, a bluff. But if, as seems to be the case, Mr. Brown is sincere [sic], and the company plans to put its new mine into operation before the end of the year, we wonder where *Le Devoir* is going to find work for the hundreds of miners who will find themselves permanently out of a job.

This passage, I feel, takes the measure of *Le Clairon*'s efforts to participate in the discussions about the strike. The paper never made even the most superficial attempt to understand the problem. The editorial writers of *Le Clairon* were interested only in using the occasion of the strike to satisfy old and well-known prejudices.

One could certainly make some fruitful observations here on the inability of the old bourgeois parties to grasp the true nature of a given social problem, but I shall leave this task to others.

I shall mention, however, that the newspapers of the weak parties (C.C.F., Social Credit) made a much more careful study of the facts, although they had far fewer means to do so. The limited effect of their writings precludes an analysis of them within the framework of our study.

4/The Catholic newspapers: caution and sympathy

a) The nature of the problem

In the last weeks of the strike, when the conflict seemed to have reached a stalemate, the financial papers attempted to interpret the facts for their English-speaking public, which understood nothing about the strike but which was greatly worked up about it. On May 14, 1949, *The Financial Post* of Toronto explained the astonishing facts, and saw the heart of the problem, in the following terms:

> The most surprising thing to many Canadians is that these disorders should have occurred in an entirely Catholic community and that the union involved is a Catholic syndicate which heretofore has never been involved in serious conflicts.
>
> The attitude of the Roman Catholic church raises a number of questions to which there are as yet no clear answers.
>
> * * *
>
> The Quebec church had seemed to be on the extreme right wing and some liberalizing of its thought was welcomed. But the Asbestos disorders have raised important questions as to how far the swing is going to go, and how representative of church opinion the current attitude toward the Asbestos disorder is.

It is easy to see to what precise facts the *Post* is referring here: the collections taken up at the doors of the churches, the declaration of Mgr. Desranleau, the sermon of Mgr. Charbonneau at Notre-Dame, the attitude of the "Catholic" press.

In this study, we designate as "Catholic newspapers" all those publications that are tied to the clergy through their administration: *L'Action catholique* of Quebec, *Notre Temps* and *Le Front ouvrier* of Montreal, *Le Messager* of Sherbrooke, and, in the English-speaking community, *The Ensign* of Montreal. A brief survey of editorials in these six publications is enough to show the attitude of the Catholic press towards the strike.[5]

b) L'Action catholique

It is not the "style" of this Quebec daily to take a violent stand for or against a provincial government. We should not expect here the kind of lively remarks we find in the pages of *Le Devoir,* but in the light of *L'Action catholique*'s habitual attitudes, the following quotations clearly show that it abandoned its usual practices at the time of the asbestos strike.

Ten days after the work stoppage, on February 25, 1949, André Roy, then an editor of *L'Action catholique*, published an editorial containing allusions which, vague in appearance, were in fact clear to all:

> Organized labour in our province is going through an unprec-
> edented crisis. This is understandable. It was a vanguard in the
> movement to demand more for the working class, and was thus in a
> position to receive the most forceful blows as soon as there was a
> chance to impede the progress which it has made in the last few
> years.

A month later, on March 24, the editor-in-chief, Louis Philippe Roy, took up the pen. He began by insisting that the newspaper was not taking anybody's side in the conflict, but the following paragraph shows that this was not true:

> Considering the situation as it exists today, and taking into ac-
> count some regrettable incidents that have occurred, and for which
> both parties are perhaps responsible, we feel that the official
> mediator[the Minister of Labour] should not insist that the strikers
> return to work without offering them some guarantees. The conflict
> has become so bitter that the strikers cannot now go back to work
> without certain assurances, regardless of the errors that they have
> committed, if indeed they have committed any.

In spite of the wariness and the great caution with which Mr. Roy expresses himself in this short editorial, and in spite of the long silence that preceded this statement, one very important point is made: *L'Action catholique* supports the idea, against the government's posi-tion, that an "illegal" strike does not deprive the strikers of the right to demand "certain" assurances before returning to work. This is hardly an assault on law and order, but those who are familiar with the usual behaviour of *L'Action catholique* and of its editor-in-chief have reason to be astonished at these words. One might well expect to read other interesting articles in the pages of *L'Action* as the conflict pro-gressed.

They were not long in coming.

On March 30, André Roy began a series of editorials on the strike. "Is this not the right time," he wrote in the first of these articles, "to ignore the purely legal aspect of this dispute, and to consider the demands of the unions which, after all, are the reason for the present strike?'' True to his resolve, Mr. Roy offered four successive analyses (on March 30 and 31, April 4 and 5) of the principal union demands: better wages, improved industrial hygiene, social security, and union security.

These articles, though they were well documented and measured in tone, still concluded that the miners were justified in making all their major demands. With the exception of *Le Devoir*, *L'Action catholique* thus became the first daily to discuss the basic issues involved in the strike, to bring out the disputed points, and to make an unequivocal judgment, not on the government's antagonistic attitude, the technical illegality of the strike, or the violent acts resulting from it, but on the essential matter of the dispute.

The newspaper adhered firmly to this position to the very end. Certain reservations were expressed from time to time (especially in the editorials of L.P. Roy, who does not seem to have been always at ease in his role as an ally of the strikers), but the fundamental attitude did not change.

On May 5, *L'Action catholique* published an appeal to the farmers signed by Abbé Louis Marois, entitled "Will We Let Them Be Crushed?" It included the following lines:

> Farmers, your brothers the workers need your help and are short of food. The Church, your mother and theirs, begs you to come to their assistance. We know that you will heed this call.

On May 10, L.P. Roy protested against the police repression after the May 5 incidents. On the twelfth, he refuted a number of statements by Lewis Brown, President of the Johns-Manville Co., denying him ''the necessary competence to judge the doctrine of the Church and its application by the Catholic unions.'' He stated explicitly that profit-sharing and co-determination cannot be treated as communist policies. (''We do not wish to judge the asbestos strike in itself'' is the sentence which introduces the article, a rather strange remark in view of the fact that the position adopted by *L'Action catholique* was made perfectly clear by the publication of the four editorials of André Roy.)

Finally, on July 4, the editor-in-chief of *L'Action catholique* entitled his last article on the strike as follows: ''The Strike Is Over, *Deo Gratias!*'' The editorial is a eulogy of Mgr. Roy for his activity as a mediator, and a plea in favour of Catholic trade unionism, which we should ''carry forward to its ultimate perfection: corporatism.'' The whole piece was a *Te Deum* to mark the end of a ''critical'' situation.

c) Le Front ouvrier (The Labour Front)

The attitude of *L'Action catholique* to the strike was astonishing, given its prestige, its direct ties to the Church, and its traditional moderation. The position adopted by *Le Front ouvrier*, the official organ of the Catholic Labour League, is still more significant. Less cautious, less "inhibited" regarding "left-wing" ideas, and also more in touch with the aspirations of labour, this weekly gives us a better idea of the changes in the social and even religious thought of Quebec which resulted from the memorable months of early 1949.

In the first place, *L'Action catholique* never sent a special reporter either to Asbestos or to Thetford. On March 5, on the contrary, *Le Front ouvrier* reported the impressions of an "impartial observer" who "has just spent a few days" at Thetford among the asbestos strikers. The report is entitled: "The Asbestos Strikers Are at Peace with Themselves." The following are two short extracts from this article:

> The serene faces of the strikers and dignified tone which prevails everywhere oblige one to recognize that these people are at peace with themselves. The action which they have undertaken gives them no qualms of conscience. Some people may accuse them of making an illegal strike, but there is a virtue which is greater than some of the laws governing strikes: justice, in whose name they are acting in these circumstances.
>
> The justice demanded by the miners now on strike consists of a better and more humane treatment: better wages, a social security fund, and the elimination of the asbestos dust which inexorably kills them off.
>
> When the apostles replied to the Sanhedrin that it was better for them to obey God than man, they . . . implicitly supported the principle that the human person is of supreme importance. The person must realize himself fully in order to attain his end, which transcends all other realities, whether they be the State, Finance, or Capital.

These statements of doctrine may seem, perhaps, a bit naive, but they still represent a liberation of thought, and show that abstract belief has finally made contact with a specific, and very concrete, situation. To compare these statements with their complete antithesis, one need merely read any one of thousands of doctrinally impeccable speeches on the social doctrine of the Church . . .

Le Front ouvrier had no intention of becoming bogged down in doctrinal arguments. On March 26 Réginald Boisvert, the editor of the newspaper, signed a perfectly documented photographic report. The reporter had visited the homes of the strikers; he had interviewed the parish priest of Asbestos, and various other men and women; he had noted the paradoxical behaviour of the strikers, who were somewhat outside the law in the eyes of the public, but who said their rosaries every day at the parish church and went on a pilgrimage with their priest heading up the procession. The words of the parish priest concluded the report:

> You should have heard the parish priest, Father Camirand, declare that in this conflict, the strikers are the new defenders of the doctrine of the Popes, and advise them to go all the way with the worthy and competent leaders they have been given.

On April 2 the editor-in-chief of the newspaper, Fernand Bourret, considered the problem of the strike in an editorial entitled "Human Laws and the Rights of Man":

> The fact that the asbestos strike is technically illegal is no excuse for not supporting the miners, who are striking to obtain just demands: better wages, more humane working conditions. These are the things that we ought to be concerned about before condemning the strike, and not the question of whether or not all the legal procedures have been duly followed.

These few quotations are enough to show the line of thinking that was represented by *Le Front ouvrier,* for the newspaper did not alter its stance throughout the entire course of the strike.

d) Le Messager

Le Messager Saint-Michel, a property of the bishopric of Sherbrooke, also offers us a great insight into the attitude of the religious authorities of the diocese in which the most important events of the strike took place. (Asbestos is located in the diocese of Sherbrooke.) This weekly, which is normally of no more than purely local interest, became extremely important at the time of the strike because it unofficially expressed the views of His Excellency Mgr. Desranleau, the bishop of the diocese.

On March 12, when Mgr. Desranleau, on a trip to Rome, had not yet made any comment in the strike, *Le Messager* published an unsigned editorial containing the following important paragraphs:

> The trade union movement was founded to promote and defend the interests of wage earners. This defence concerns the living standards of the workers and the establishment of adequate and humane working conditions. This is why there is justification for the clauses guaranteeing union security which are written into collec-

tive agreements.

The promotion of workers' interests demands that, in the course of time, they should share in business enterprise, professional life, public life, and the national economy. Only in this way will the proletariat disappear.

Slavery and serfdom did not disappear painlessly. Catholic workers, in their struggles to emerge from the proletariat, must expect to encounter, from every stratum of society, lack of understanding, opposition, persecution.

In spite of these difficulties, they will win out: they have truth, justice, and right on their side, even if the powerful and the rich, armed with the narrow formulas of the law, are opposed to them.

This is certainly the strongest statement of its kind, because of the historical perspective in which it grounds its analysis and because of the absence of the rhetorical precautions which usually flourished in this kind of literature. In the atmosphere of those months of trouble, the terms "the powerful" and "the rich" were transparently clear.

One is almost tempted to say that in this case we are not dealing with a newspaper but only with a man, the Bishop of Sherbrooke, whose ideas on society had been well known for a long time.

Having noted that the weekly *Notre Temps*, of Montreal, followed substantially the same line as *L'Action catholique* of Quebec City (and also published the excellent articles of Jean T. Larochelle on the economic aspect of the conflict), we will end this review as we began it, by studying the attitude of an English-language weekly.

e) The Ensign

The Financial Post is the unofficial publication of high finance; *The Ensign* is the national weekly of Canada's English-speaking Catholics. It is not, however, completely incongruous to discuss the two newspapers together. *The Ensign* frequently replied to statements of the *Post* in a large-scale effort to give English Canada an explanation of the Church's stand on social issues.

This was no easy task. *The Financial Post* was not alone in situating the Quebec Catholic Church at the extreme right of the political spectrum. This view of the Church was the usual one among English-speaking people; one can thus imagine the shock that must have resulted from the selections we have just read. Public opinion in English-speaking Canada tends to assume that French Canadian society is unchanging, and that the Catholic Church upholds monolithic conservatism. The events at Asbestos were an affront to these prejudices.

The Ensign's refutations give us a clearer idea of the degree of shock experienced by English Canada. Under the title "The Church and Business in Quebec," an editorial of May 7 took issue with certain statements of Lewis Brown, the President of the Johns-Manville Co., which had enjoyed considerable success in the English-language press:

If we want to avoid the repetition of disastrous strikes like the one which is paralyzing the Canadian asbestos industry, we must, among other measures, dispel any confusion that exists about the nature and the purpose of the Catholic labour unions in Quebec.

That this subject is misunderstood in some quarters is clearly shown by the text of an advertisement published by one of the companies involved, the Canadian Johns-Manville Co., and signed by its president, Mr. Lewis Brown.

Mr. Brown begins by praising the influence of the Church in the Province of Quebec, and adds that the Church authorities have favoured the development of Catholic trade unions, with the double intention of putting a check to the forces of radicalism and improving the living conditions of the workers.

Nevertheless, if one is to believe the statements of Mr. Brown, the unions have abandoned the designation "Catholic" in the last few years, have fallen into the hands of "radicals," and have devoted themselves "to preaching a doctrine which has more in common with communism and socialism."

To lend an air of plausibility to this last accusation, which has a familiar ring to it, Mr. Brown states that the union leaders have "tried to secure for themselves certain controls over managerial policy."

Then Mr. Brown adds: "Some of the spokesmen for the Church seem to be supporting the strike leaders. This is both astonishing and disappointing."

It is clear from his remarks that Mr. Brown regards the Catholic Church as a force for social conservatism, eager to support the capitalist social order which is dominant at the present time, and inclined to leave the workers to their fate as ordinary "labourers" as long as they are paid a tolerable wage. It is also evident that Mr. Brown looks upon the leaders of the Catholic trade unions as people who have abandoned the path of true doctrine.

We must reply to Mr. Brown that the dropping of the designation "Catholic" does not in any way imply that the unions have stopped conforming to the ethical and religious principles of Catholicism. The unions still have chaplains, and the chaplains agree that Catholicism has not been abandoned.

It is also untrue that the teachings of the Church with regard to social questions are conservative. Catholicism is radical in the true sense of the term and in no way supports capitalism in the form in which it has developed. The property that the Church defends is a property that is fairly distributed and accompanied by responsibilities, not the large and often irresponsible concentrations of power that have been brought about by the managerial revolution.

Moreover, if the present leaders of the trade union movement attempted to change what has up to now been only a simple contract between wage-earners, and to alter it into some other form of association, they would be doing no more than following the directives which have been laid down by the Pope.

The leaders of the Catholic trade unions have perhaps been wrong to carry out their negotiations as they did, and perhaps they have been right to do so. In any case, it is neither proper nor useful for an employer to cast doubt upon the orthodoxy of their fundamental convictions.

On May 28, *The Ensign* took up the subject again in an article called "The Facts of the Asbestos Strike." It contained a very vigorous attack on the labour legislation in Quebec, a "defence and illustration" of the union positions, a very sober explanation of the violent acts that had occurred, and a restatement of the facts surrounding them.

III/The information provided

I deeply regret that the limits of my study do not permit me to make a minute analysis of our press as a source of information, because I had personal experience of the strike before I read about it in the newspaper reports.

In the troubled months of 1949, when I followed the press from day to day, comparing the reports with the events which were occurring before my very eyes, I was struck by the imperfect, schematic, and occasionally grotesque reflection of these events in the press. Today, when I compare the facts as a whole with the mass of press clippings, the shock I feel is even greater. One cannot but feel a touch of disenchantment when one looks in vain, in the great majority of newspapers, for a description that corresponds more or less to the events, or for a commentary that includes even a crude consideration of the facts of the case.

It must be understood that a detailed study of the press reports (which would fill several thick volumes of fine print) is impossible here. I will simply make a few sample studies and report a few significant incidents.

1/The news-gathering effort

The first subject of our examination is the effort made by each newspaper to provide its readers with adequate information on the strike.

I have already mentioned that from the beginning of the conflict, *Le Devoir* kept a special reporter at the scene of the strike. One of the so-called "news" papers, *La Tribune* of Sherbrooke, also had its own reporter on location. The other newspapers, for a period of over a month, were content with the dispatches sent by the "Canadian Press" agency, which cannibalized the reports of *La Tribune*.

On March 21, Montreal's *La Presse* sent its labour reporter, Roger Mathieu, to Asbestos. Mr. Mathieu conducted an investigation and then published a report in which he gave the points of view of the various persons involved in the dispute: union leaders, the manager of the Company, the town councillors, the parish priest, members of the Provincial Police, etc. This report is one of the finest documents published during the strike. Each time that new and significant developments occurred either at Thetford or at Asbestos, the newspaper again sent its reporter to cover them.

It was not until April 16 that another representative of the "news-gathering press" appeared on the scene. *The Standard* (now *Picture Magazine*) of Montreal sent Miss Jacqueline Sirois and the photographer Sperling to Asbestos on that date. They produced a report of high quality, a comprehensive study which gave the uninitiated reader a good understanding of the strike, and enabled him to form his own opinions about it.

At about the same time, the other dailies began to take a more serious interest in the strike. *The Gazette* published some dispatches which were sent in by a district correspondent, and *The Herald* used the telephone to fill out the overly meagre reports of the Canadian Press. *The Montreal Star* sent its reporter, Fred Kaufman, to Asbestos, who sent back some rather lackluster dispatches. (If I remember rightly, Mr. Kaufman had only a skimpy knowledge of French, a fact which would explain his lack of success.)

On May 5 and 6, when the mass picketing and the police repression occurred, I myself counted 32 special press envoys in Asbestos, not including the reporter from the *Toronto Star,* who was flying over the town in an airplane!

The course of these developments suggests that the "news-gathering press" was loath to fulfill its mission until it was forced into action by the pressure of public curiosity. We could easily show that it is much more attentive to sports events, for example.

I would not be happy with myself if I did not mention, before closing these remarks, the strange inertia of the Canadian Press news agency. It did not send its own special correspondent until the last minute, in spite of the evident interest that its member newspapers were taking in the strike. And what a reporter he was! He spent his time getting a good night's sleep, and the next day questioned his fellow reporters to find out what had happened since the previous evening, flaunted his ignorance of all that had preceded the strike, and even had the bad taste to quote the opinion of a reporter from *The Standard* in one of his dispatches without giving his own!

I might also mention the conduct of the labour reporter from *The Gazette,* Karl Gerhard, who entered the city incognito (although the strikers extended a welcome to all the journalists). He first became an investigator, then an informer for the Provincial Police. I should also note the on-the-spot report of Ron Williams, of *The Financial Post*, which proved to contain so many errors of fact that his newspaper, without retracting anything, still had to publish a number of corrections . . . The prize effort was without doubt the offer made by some reporters from Toronto (from *The Toronto Star*), who wanted to put false bandages on the head of a striker who was perfectly unhurt, in order to get some "documents."

Such were the shabby efforts of the so-called "objective" press, of these great "news" papers which have the reputation of being respectable! Still, they had never before spent so much money to cover a strike in Quebec. It seems plausible that they were at first prepared to ignore the strike, and we have seen that the so-called "journals of opinion" outdistanced them and forced them to pay attention. They seem, however, to have learned their lesson. Their attitude towards the strikes at Louiseville (1952-1953) and at Rouyn (1953)[6] reveals that definite progress has been made.

2/The "audacities" of the press

Two secondary incidents will show how the strike enabled the French-language newspapers to adopt an irreverent tone that was out of keeping with their usual behaviour.

The March 21 edition of *La Tribune,* for example, contained a rather remarkable account entitled "Yesterday's Sermon in the Two Parishes of Asbestos."

The newspaper gave, without comment, a "substantial summary" of the two sermons. The confrontation of the two documents revealed a fundamental contradiction, of which the following extracts give a good idea.

I have also been told that others are spreading the idea that there is no need to pay rent in times of a strike. Where does this doctrine come from? The catechism has never taught that. Debt must always be paid. Some people are claiming that the civil laws allow them not to pay rent. I do not believe that these laws exist, and if they did, they would only apply to a legal strike. The government, however, has declared that this strike is illegal, and it does not fall within my competence to discuss the legality or illegality of this strike.

There are 50 or 60 families which, fifteen days from now, will find themselves in the street with no roof over their heads because they are unable to pay their rent. I ask, for pity's sake, that the landlords who are able to wait for their money have mercy upon those who are in difficult financial circumstances.

Asbestos has never known as tragic a time as this. I know what I am talking about, for I am well informed about the present state of things. Some people's eyes will be dry from weeping at the present situation. It do not tell you this to frighten you, but to ask you to reflect upon these circumstances. One should not wait until misfortunes have passed to think about them.

If I could see some help for you, I would tell you. There is, however, but one person who can help you to emerge from your present difficulties, namely God. Pray to God, ask Him to help you. Believe in His infinite power, that He may pardon the public blasphemies. Have people not had the misfortune of saying in public: "If we lose, there will be no more religion?"

Pray that He will bring back happy circumstances for you, and that He will save you quickly from the abominable misfortunes with which you find yourselves surrounded!

(Abbé Alphonse Deslandes, priest of the parish at St. Isaac-Jogues.)

                                *   *   *

The priest of the St. Aimé parish did not make any personal comments on the asbestos strike which enters its sixth week today. He simply read passages from the encyclical and from the short address mentioned above. Here is what he read:

Extracts from the encyclical *Divini Redemptoris:* "The wage-earner is not to receive as alms what is his due in justice. And let no one attempt with trifling charitable donations to exempt himself from the great duties imposed by justice. Both justice and charity often dictate obligations touching on the same subject-matter, but under different aspects; and the very dignity of the workingman makes him justly and acutely sensitive to the duties of others in his regard."

Father Camirand then read an excerpt from the encyclical in

which Pope Pius XI urged the priests to go to the workingman, and went on to quote extensively from a short address given by Mgr. Desranleau at Sherbrooke on September 5, 1938:

"The first thing that the Church recommends," said Mgr. Desranleau, "is a return to the Christian spirit. If the workers return to it, the employers will eventually return to it as well, and when all the workers demand their rights in a spirit of justice and of charity, the employers will meet these demands and everything will return to order."

For those familiar with the habitual discretion of French Canadian newspapers regarding any aspect of internal disagreements among clergymen, such a report clearly shows the exceptional interest the public was taking in anything connected with the strike, and the audacity this curiosity inspired in the press. Another indication of this development was the zeal of the big dailies when Mgr. Ferdinand Vandry, Rector of Laval, delivered his diatribe against *Le Devoir*. The incident has been mentioned above; we shall merely note here that *La Presse,* for example, having faithfully reported the "denunciations" of the Rector (in a speech at Three Rivers), then published, prominently and at length, a letter by two students offering a version of the facts in flat contradiction to the statements of Mgr. Vandry. This document appeared in a newspaper that still uses the expression "a forty-two-year-old bachelor" to refer to a priest brought before the criminal court: it is highly revealing of the social climate of Quebec in those days.

3/The radio news

Finally, I wish to say a few words about the radio, about its very poor efforts to inform the public, and about the role it refused to play.

Ever since 1949, I have distrusted the radio as a source of information. Its methods have no doubt improved since then, but at the time they were deplorable. Of all the organizations involved in broadcasting news on the strike, the radio stations were the only ones, if I am not mistaken, which did not send a representative to the scene at any time. For their information, they depended in part on the news agencies, and in part on whoever took a notion to telephone their compilers of half-baked stories.

The CBC had a well-established policy that it would not broadcast any dispatch which had not been sent in through the news agencies. It received very little information from them, and what there was was sent in late, so that the CBC broadcast anemic news bulletins, pale and mostly incomplete reflections of what had already appeared in the daily papers.

The private radio stations went too far in the opposite direction. Because they had no way of verifying the news they received, and were also unprepared to leave their listeners' hunger for information unsatisfied, they broadcast to all and sundry any news that came their way, from whatever source. Any rumour was grist for their mill, the wilder the better. While I was drinking a cup of coffee in a restaurant in Asbestos, for example, I learned that I had been run out of town and would not be allowed to return until the strike was over! On five or six occasions, Montreal radio stations claimed (quite wrongly) to offer their listeners a news scoop that the dispute had been settled by a "definitive" agreement. The most fantastic statements by management on the number of desertions from the ranks of the strikers were broadcast without comment.

In all fairness let us note that later on, thanks to the teams of reporters which they now had at their disposal, both the publicly-owned and the private radio stations were able to do a better job, except in the field of rapid news reporting.

When I spoke above of the role the radio refused to play, I was thinking of the function of commentator. In the five-month period of the strike, the CBC did not once make the slightest effort to offer the public an explanation of a problem that left it in a state of perplexity. One can imagine a hundred ways to comment on the situation without running the risk of repercussions (a confrontation between the employers and the union, a press conference, a public forum, etc.), but none of these was attempted. While the most insignificant newspaper, the least important rag (including the *Revue eucharistique du clergé*)[7] risked a commentary, the powerful CBC remained silent.

The honour, but only the honour, of the private radio stations was preserved. Two commentators of CKAC (René Garneau and Jean-Pierre Houle, financed by the Galeries N.G. Valiquette) attempted to explain the situation. The only other radio commentaries on the strike were: a speech broadcast by the Minister of Labour and an account of the situation by the president of the C.C.C.L. (both delivered in paid time slots, on April 18 and May 13). This inertia clearly shows that at the time of the strike, radio had not yet accepted its responsibilities in the editorial field, especially on social issues.

One could fairly sum up developments in radio since the strike by saying that the private radio stations have hardly improved at all in providing commentaries on current issues, while the French-language branch of the CBC has taken a number of important steps forward with the development of its talk shows, the creation of programs like *La Vie économique* (Economic Life) and *La Vie ouvrière* (Working People's Life), and the institution of television broadcasts like

Conférence de Presse (Press Conference).

IV/Conclusion
I have presented such involved clusters of fact that I would not feel I had done a good job if I ignored this complexity and drew oversimplified conclusions. Throughout the course of the preceding pages, I have tried to show the press at work without attempting to conceal either its faults or its merits, its industry or its sloth. Here, too, I do not claim to be drawing all the conclusions that could be extracted from the facts, nor to be explaining all the "singular lessons" I spoke of at the beginning of this chapter. Let us say, rather, that at this point I take my place among my readers and, having asked them to consider the significance of the presented facts for themselves, I am the first to obey this command. What follows, then, represents only the reflections of one man who in no way pretends that he has exhausted all the conclusions that can be drawn from the preceding pages.

In my opinion, four general observations may serve to synthesize the detailed impressions, while remaining broad enough to include the apparent contradictions in these impressions.

1/A temporary state of grace
The first thing that strikes me is that the state of crisis induced by the strike occurred in conjunction with a certain "state of grace" exhibited by some newspapers. The "Church" publications offer the best example of this phenomenon. I do not have to repeat here what has been said about the unaccustomed courage and audacity displayed by *L'Action catholique,* for example, or by *Notre Temps,* not to mention *Relations* and *The Ensign.*

I speak of this state of grace as temporary because I am also struck by the unaffected facility and ease with which these newspapers returned to their habitual posture—mistrustful conservatism—once the crisis was over. Their attitude at the time of the Louiseville strike (1952-53) showed clearly that "order" had been completely reestablished, in other words, that a deep-seated distrust of trade unionism was once more the ruling spirit. *L'Action catholique* published denunciations of the "class struggle" because the C.C.C.L. had spoken of a general protest strike. The editor-in-chief of this daily spoke in an equivocal way of the "unfortunate affair of Louiseville." *Notre Temps* offered its readers the comments of the Rev. Father Bernardin, O.F.M., who called the union leaders "foreigners" even though they were directing a strike in an area within their jurisdiction.

I would not want to say that all the windows opened in 1949 have now been closed again. I believe, though, that very few of them are still open, as one might well have expected.

The astonishing fact remains that this state of grace existed for the few months of the strike, and the departure from habitual attitudes of caution is surprising. It seems to me that there is only one explanation for this departure: the men who run this press found themselves prisoners of their own principles. The asbestos strike broke out with such suddenness that they were unable to seek refuge in procrastinations and periphrases. The strikers' cause was too just and too clear-cut, their actions too decisive; the miners had poured the wine, but it still had to be drunk; the full weight of the facts was thrust upon the journalists. Had they refused to support the strikers, who had not awaited this help before acting, they would have had to repudiate too many articles and to withdraw from reality in plain sight of all. It was also felt, in those days, that to break with the asbestos strikers was tantamount to denying the cause of labour, to abandoning the mass of industrial workers.

Helped along by certain newspapers that were not afraid of putting themselves in an awkward position and encouraged by the brave attitude of some bishops, the Church press discovered a valour that it doubtless did not know it had.

2/The search for objectivity

My second conclusion might be called "the search for objectivity." It is particularly concerned with the political press and the large newspapers.

Some of the papers included in the second of these categories were also affected at times by the state of grace. I have referred in passing to the remarkable articles by Roger Mathieu which appeared in *La Presse,* and those by Jacqueline Sirois which were published in *The Standard.* I would also like to express my esteem for the *Montreal Star* which, in the course of the strike, protested against the travesties of justice that were acted out in some of our courts.

Nevertheless, both in news reporting and editorials most big newspapers, for the most part, did no more than serve up their prejudices, skilfully masked by an impeccably objective style. Is objectivity, i.e., "fidelity to the object," reconcilable with a refusal to take a position on the very basis for such a debate? We are told that the major newspapers limit themselves to presenting the "news," but not a day goes by that their readers are not glutted with hymns in praise of capitalism and private enterprise, and with denunciations of communism and socialism. This so-called "news" press is engaged in vigorous warfare on all fronts, which it carries out both through its news dispatches and on its editorial pages. It is a militant press. What meaning, then, must we assign to its pretended neutrality, its dearly bought objectivity in a situation like the asbestos strike? Consider, for example, the statement of the manager of the Canadian Johns-Manville plant: "The strike leaders themselves can find nothing wrong either with our wages or our working conditions. All they are looking for is an increase in their personal power." This declaration was published by *The Gazette* on May 7 without any comment whatsoever. What became, then, of its objectivity?

The strikers, at least, were not taken in. A *Gazette* reporter himself bears witness to the fact in a dispatch published May 18, in which he says that Rodolphe Hamel refused to grant him an interview with the words: "We do not care for your presence here. Everybody knows that you represent high finance."

3/The real nature of our problems
My third observation aims at showing that the asbestos strike produced a perceptible change in the terms of the debate in which the Quebec newspapers are perpetually involved. During the months of the strike, the lines separating the parties, even the demarcation between the confirmed nationalists and the militant adherents of a *bonne entente,* were no longer of great importance. For once, the centre stage was yielded to the problem of Quebec society.

We have referred in passing to the inertia of the Liberal newspapers, which had, at the time of the strike, a unique opportunity to regain influence with the electorate after their humiliating defeat the previous summer. To describe their attitude, the phrase "opportunity refused" would be more appropriate than "opportunity lost." The big supporters of the party, the financiers and the big-business men, were just as worried about this revival of the labour movement, and about the support it was gaining in public opinion, as were the Conservatives in power.

It seems as if the Liberals hoped that the miners would be defeated, and silently endorsed the police repression, while remaining ready to blame Mr. Duplessis for it later on in order to win votes. At the time of the strike, the main thing was to defend the interests at stake. Political rivalry only entered the picture later, in the elections of 1952.

It is no less remarkable that nationalism did not play any part in the strike. On only one occasion, at the meeting in the Palais Montcalm,[8] a few of the union speakers attacked the Johns-Manville Co. by referring to its foreign origin. Even at *Le Devoir,* the struggle was simply and frankly situated in the realm of social problems; thereafter it was waged almost unceasingly within these limits. The dispute was not envisaged as a conflict between "the English" and "the French Canadians,'' but rather as one between an employer and his workers. The realities of the situation were not camouflaged by the traditional disguises, nor was the indignation of the people channelled in the wrong direction. This is one of the reasons why the strike is of such importance in Quebec history. Through it, the social realities of our community revealed their true nature, and had to be faced.

4/Violence and sympathy

A final remark will deal with a strange correlation which could be observed, in the course of the strike, between occasional acts of violence and the behaviour of public opinion.

On several occasions, at meetings of the strikers, I heard speakers for the workers warn their audiences against resorting to violence. Among the arguments employed to persuade the strikers to refrain from ''direct action,'' a reference to public opinion always had a place of honour, towards the end of the speech. ''Today,'' the speakers were wont to say, ''you have the support of decent people. The population is behind you, but beware of violent incidents. If they occur, public opinion will turn against you.''

The analysis of the facts seems to reveal that the course of events does not justify these warnings. Let us consider three graphs: *a)* violent incidents, *b)* press articles in favour of the strikers, *c)* aid sent to the striking miners by different groups within the population. The peaks of these three graphs coincide with one another, within a matter of a few days. In other words, to each incident of violence there corresponds a new wave of sympathy, or rather an increase in the number of people who sympathized with the strikers. This increase revealed itself by a greater number of statements in the press that were favourable to the strikers, and by the dispatch of greater quantities of aid.

We must be very cautious about interpreting these coincidences. I am not trying to make out a case for violence. In other circumstances (the absence of provocations by the police, premeditated violence, etc.) violence might have had the opposite effect. I wish to emphasize the coincidences in this case because they reveal, in my opinion, a remarkable stability in public opinion. Once they were in possession of the facts, the great majority of those who sympathized with the strikers were not easily shocked, and remained favourably disposed towards them in spite of the many efforts by a certain sector of the press to frighten decent people. Does this not tend to show that public opinion in Quebec is neither so timid nor so affected by emotion as people are accustomed to think? In my opinion, its behaviour at the time of the strike is a sign of maturity.

. . . Were the press, then, to play its part in our society in a freer and more honest way, social conflicts would no doubt be resolved more rapidly, and in a fairer manner.

Notes to Chapter VIII

[1]See the review *Relations* (Institut social populaire, Montreal), March 1948, and the Montreal press in the ensuing months. The report concerned a factory at St. Rémi d'Amherst. Several workers contracted silicosis there and died of it. Burton LeDoux's denunciation of the company created a scandal at the time.

[2]We shall also mention the editorials of *L'action nationale, Notre Temps,* and *Vers Demain,* which drew attention to the article by LeDoux and called for a reply on the part of the government.

[3]*The Asbestos Strike: The Press and Public Opinion,* by Grace Morey McKenzie. Unpublished M.A. thesis, University of Toronto, 1951, p. 24.

[4]*Montréal-Matin* and *The Gazette* are Conservative dailies of Montreal. *Le Canada,* a Montreal daily, and *Le Clairon-Montréal,* a weekly, both representatives of the Liberal point of view, have since ceased publication.

[5]We have not been able to add to this chapter, which is already very long as it is, an analysis of the articles on the strike in the Ottawa daily *Le Droit.* Since *Le Droit* is not strictly speaking a Quebec newspaper, we feel that the omission is justified. Still, we have carefully compiled the 15 articles and short mentions regarding the strike that appeared on the editorial page of this newspaper: they reveal a very strong sympathy for the strikers. Some of the writings of H. Lessard and C.H. Daigneault are among the fairest and most insightful which have been published on the subject.

[6]In this last case, in particular, the reporting of the Canadian Press, written by John Leblanc in six consecutive articles, is a remarkable attempt to provide honest and objective news: *Canadian Press,* September 29, 1953.

[7]*Revue eucharistique du clergé,* March 1949, "Grève illégale... licite?" (An illegal... or lawful strike?).

[8]A union rally held at Quebec City, April 24, 1949.

Chapter IX

Six Years Later

by Maurice Sauvé

I/Introduction

At its general meeting of December 5, 1948, the National Union of Asbestos Employees of Asbestos, Inc., denounced the collective agreement it had signed with the Canadian Johns-Manville Company Limited, an agreement which was valid until January 31, 1949. The National Federation of Mining Industry Employees was subsequently asked to negotiate a new labour contract for 1949 with the Company, in the name of the union.

On December 14, 1948, the secretary of the Federation presented the Company with a list of the amendments proposed by the union for the renewal of the collective agreement. (The terms of these amendments are given at the beginning of Chapter V above.)

Direct negotiations were carried out between December 24, 1948, and January 14, 1949. The two parties were unable to reach an agreement, and at the beginning of February a mediator was sent to the scene from the office of the Minister of Labour of the Province of Quebec. His efforts, however, did not meet with success, and he withdrew on February 10. On the thirteenth, the members of the union at Asbestos decided to go on strike, starting at midnight.

This memorable strike lasted until June 30, 1949, although an agreement was reached on June 27 between the representatives of the Canadian Johns-Manville Co. and the leaders of the National Federation of Mining Industry Employees. The strike lasted 134 days.

In analyzing the results of the strike in the asbestos industry, I shall try to show the consequences for the workers. My study began with the question: did this strike prove to be advantageous for the asbestos workers?

In the first part of this chapter, I examine the relations between the union and the Company, concentrating on the conditions of work laid down in the collective agreement of 1952, in comparison with the union demands of December 1948. By choosing the collective agreement of 1952, I am able to observe the results of the strike at a certain distance. I shall then consider the settlement of the difficulties that arose out of the strike itself, and the attitudes towards one another of the parties to these disputes. In the second part of my analysis, I will examine the worker's relations with his union, and the present situation of the union at Asbestos. Finally, I shall conclude the chapter with a study of the economic consequences of the 1949 strike for the worker who participated in it.

Throughout this study, I shall refer to a collective agreement and to statistics, the discussion and presentation of which will necessarily be dry and disjointed. The terminology used derives from the wording of a collective agreement, as I have felt it would be unwise to stray too far from it.

My study is particularly concerned with the National Union of Asbestos Employees of Asbestos, Inc., the Canadian Johns-Manville Co. Ltd., and the workers and population of Asbestos. Activities connected with the strike were more intense in the municipality of Asbestos, due to the following factors, which did not affect the situation at Thetford Mines:

1. At Asbestos, there is only one employer, the Canadian Johns-Manville Co. This firm alone employs almost half of all the asbestos miners.

2. The Canadian Johns-Manville Co. is the largest of the seven asbestos producers in the Eastern Townships region, and thus the leader of the industry.

3. The asbestos strike was directed by a committee that convened at Asbestos.

4. Abbé Camirand, sympathetic chaplain of the union and priest of the St. Aimé parish.

5. The activities of the Provincial Police, which established its headquarters in the hotel belonging to the Johns-Manville Co.

6. The riot of May 1949, which resulted from the Canadian Johns-Manville Co.'s policy of employing scabs.

7. A much smaller and more homogeneous population than at Thetford Mines.

8. The homogeneity of labour organization at Asbestos; at Thetford Mines, a rival union was led by Paul Emile Marquette.

From time to time, I shall compare the situation in the two mining centres, although the conditions of work and wages, as they are described in the collective agreements, are very nearly identical.

II/Relations between the union and the employer
1/The present situation in relation to the demands of December 1948

The strike settlement of June 27, 1949, did not consider the demands presented to the Company in December 1948. Consequently, direct negotiations on the union demands had to be renewed. Clause 7 of the above-mentioned settlement provided for conciliation and arbitration under the chairmanship of Judge Thomas Tremblay if the parties involved were unable to reach an agreement. In fact, they were not able to do so.

The arbitration, however, took place at Thetford Mines, between the National Union of Asbestos Employees of Asbestos Corporation, and the Asbestos Corporation. As has been explained in Chapter V above, it was agreed that, to facilitate negotiation procedures, this arbitration would serve as a basis for a settlement between all the companies and unions of the region.

The (majority) decision of the arbitration board, handed down by Judge Thomas Tremblay on December 10, 1949, was accepted by the unions and employers of Asbestos and Thetford Mines. The unions accepted it with the reservation that it should apply only to the year 1949. Of the 17 demands made by the union, only one was accepted, and nine were refused. A compromise was reached on five of the remaining demands; two of them were accepted by the arbitration board, but only as suggestions to the employer. Of the 17 demands made by the employers, the committee accepted 13, refused no demand outright, and compromised on four of them.

The details of the majority decision were as follows:

A— Union demands:

    a) Accepted:

        1. Good Friday was added to the list of unpaid holidays. (Article 10a of the collective agreement of the Asbestos Corporation, for the year 1948.)

    b) Refused:

        1. Double-time pay for Sundays and holidays. (Article 7c.)

        2. Time and a half pay for baggers after a regular working day. (Article 7e.)

        3. Double-time pay on Sundays and holidays for the employees on piece or contract work. (Article 7f.)

    4. Double time after 8 hours of work on Sundays and holidays. (Article 7i.)

    5. An employee paid by the hour will not be forced to accept payment on the basis of a contract. (Article 17.)

    6. Weekly payment of wages in cash. (Article 19.)

    7. A premium of 5c per hour for night work.

    8. A premium of 2c per hour for loading fibre.

    9. A premium of 10c per hour for bagging with used sacks.

  c) *The following compromises were reached:*

    1. A change of wording in the clause on the regular working day. (Article 7a.)

    2. Four regular paid holidays instead of the nine demanded. (Article 10b.)

    3. Three weeks of vacation after 25 years of service instead of after 20 years, as demanded. (Article 22.)

    4. A change of wording in the clause on conciliation and arbitration. (Article 22.)

    5. An increase of 10c per hour, instead of 15c.

  d) *Suggestions made to the employer:*

    1. Concerning the elimination of asbestos dust.

    2. For the formation of a committee to study the demand for a system of social security.

B— *Demands by the employers:*

  a) *Accepted:*

    1. The prohibition of union activities on company property during hours of work. (Article 1e.)

    2. The cancellation of the Rand formula where it was in force (Asbestos Corporation, Johnson's, and Flintkote).[1]

    3. Time and a half on Sundays and holidays. (Article 7c.)

    4. Cancellation of the secondary clause on pay. (Article 7d.)

    5-8. Changes in wording. (Articles 7e, 7f, 7i, 8b.)

    9. Seniority clause: family status to have priority over union status. (Article 12.)

    10. Elimination of the clause protecting the hourly paid employee regarding contract work. (Article 17.)

    11. Weekly payment of wages by cheque. (Article 19.)

    12. A whistle to announce the end of a shift (accepted by the union).

    13. A rewording of the no-strike and lockout clause. (Article 23.)

b) *The following compromises were granted:*
1. A change in the wording of the clause on the regular working day. (Article 7a.)
2. Four regular paid holidays instead of the two offered. (Article 20b.)
3. Three weeks of vacation granted after 25 years of service, and two weeks after 5 years. (Article 11.)
4. A change in the wording of the clause on conciliation and arbitration. (Article 22.)

New contracts, more or less the same for all the companies, were later negotiated for the years 1951 and 1952-54. By an analysis of this latter contract, signed on February 25, 1952,[2] and valid for two years, I will show the advantages the union obtained by the strike, taking into consideration its demands of December 1948.

a) The elimination of asbestos dust
Since the strike, the companies of Thetford Mines and Asbestos have incurred considerable expenses to eliminate dust in the asbestos mines and mills. Although the companies have not been completely successful in their efforts, the union has not pressed for a clause stipulating the elimination of asbestos dust. Although this request did not appear on the list of official demands, it was frequently discussed, especially with the companies of Thetford Mines.

b) A general wage increase of 15c per hour
In December 1948, the hourly wage of a laborer working in the asbestos mines at Thetford or at Asbestos was 85c. The union asked for an increase of 15c per hour to bring the hourly rate to $1.00. The Tremblay arbitration board recommended an increase of 10c, and the new rate of 95c per hour was finally accepted by all the parties to the negotiations, with a provision for a cost of living bonus. (See Chapter V.) In the negotiations of December 1950, the hourly wage of a laborer was raised to $1.09, a new increase of 14c per hour. On September 1, 1952, the hourly rate was set at $1.51 (including the cost of living bonus), a further increase of 42c per hour. On February 1, 1954, this basic rate was raised to $1.53, and a year later to $1.54 per hour. Finally, in the spring of 1956, new contracts were signed in the asbestos industry, bringing the basic wage up to $1.64 per hour.

From December 1948 to September 1952, then, the hourly wage of a laborer went from 85c to $1.51 per hour, an increase of 66c per hour. This represents a substantial improvement.

It is very difficult to attribute this increase to a single cause. The rise in the cost of living, the increase in the selling price of asbestos and in the profits of the companies, and a possible improvement in productivity could all have contributed to this increase in wages. My information on these matters does not enable me to pursue my inquiry very far in this direction.

The wages of asbestos workers, in comparison with those of workers in the mining industry as a whole, increased rapidly after the 1949 strike. I believe that this rise in wages in the asbestos industry is principally due to the strike. There seems no other adequate explanation for such a considerable increase, in this industry in particular, and in such a short period. (See Table 1.)

Table I

Year	1 Basic hourly wage–asbestos industry	2 Average hourly earnings–asbestos industry	3 Average hourly earnings–Canadian mining industry
	(yearly average)		
1939	.35		
1940	.37		
1941	.39		
1942	.43		
1943	.46		
1944	.53	.63	
1945	.53	.63	.85
1946	.58	.68	.87
1947	.65	.76	.98
1948	.85	1.01	1.11
1949	.95	1.08	1.17
1950	1.00	1.16	1.21
1951	1.19	1.39	1.33
1952	1.51	1.63	1.47

Remarks: 1.   Hourly wage, including the bonus for a laborer.
2. Includes: hourly rate and overtime for the workers as a whole. Source: 1 and 2—The Canadian Johns-Manville Co., Asbestos.
3. Source: *Canadian Statistical Review*, 1953 Supplement, Bureau of Statistics, Ottawa, p. 44.

A comparison of the average hourly earnings in the asbestos industry (column 2) with the average hourly earnings in the Canadian mining industry as a whole (column 3), whose employees are, moreover, organized into powerful unions, suggests that the events of 1949 were an important factor in the rapid increase of wages at Asbestos and Thetford Mines since that time. An examination of the wage scale in the Canadian mining industry as a whole reveals that the asbestos miners earned, in 1948, 10c per hour less on the average than workers in other mines. In 1952, they earned an average 16c per hour more. In other words, from 1948 to 1952, the average increase for the asbestos miners as a whole was 62c per hour, while wages went up only by an average 36c per hour for the workers in the Canadian mining industry as a whole (column 3).

The asbestos strike of 1949 thus had a considerable success. The increases that were not obtained when the strike was settled were granted in the ensuing years, and we may be sure that they resulted from energetic and disciplined union action on the part of the miners at Asbestos and Thetford Mines.

c) A 5c premium for night work
The union was not able to obtain most of its demands for the workers on the afternoon and night shifts until the collective agreements negotiations of 1954. At that time, the Company agreed to pay an additional 3c per hour for workers on the afternoon shift, and 5c per hour for workers on the night shift.

d) 3% of total wages to be paid into a social security fund organized by the union
In spite of repeated negotiations, this demand has still not been met.

e) The Rand formula
Three mining companies in the area, The Asbestos Corporation Limited, Johnson's Company Limited, and Flintkote Mines Limited, had accepted this formula before the strike occurred. It provides for payroll deductions in favour of the union, and requires every employee covered by the agreement, whether he belongs to the union or not, to make a monthly contribution to the union equal to the amount paid by the members of the union. Since the strike, these three companies have abided by the so-called irrevocable checkoff formula. By the terms of this formula, once an employee *who is a member of the union* has signed an authorization to deduct the union dues from his pay, this deduction must continue to be made as long as the collective agreement is in force, even if the employee quits the union.

The Rand formula has not yet been accepted by any of the employers in the area (except for the Bell mine, where the workers belong to a union led by Paul Emile Marquette), and all the unions in the asbestos industry are still trying to win acceptance for it. In this respect, the strike was a complete failure.

f) Double-time pay on Sundays and holidays
The situation has not changed. Time and a half is paid, as in 1948, for work on Sundays and holidays. Furthermore, the union has not been able to have an inquiry started into the necessity of working on Sundays.

g) Nine paid holidays
Before the strike, Johnson's and the Asbestos Corporation, of Thetford Mines, gave their employees two paid holidays. The Canadian Johns-Manville Co. did not give any paid holidays at all.

In 1954, the employees of all the companies in the region received eight paid holidays per year.

h) Improvement of the vacation plan
In the amendments to the collective agreement proposed in 1948, the union requested two weeks of paid vacation after two years of service and three weeks after twenty years of service. On this particular issue, the negotiations have been only partially successful, although the present plan is more favourable than the one in force before the strike, which allowed only two weeks of paid vacation, after five years of service. In 1954, the employees in the asbestos industry received two weeks of paid vacation after three years of service and three weeks after twenty years of service.

i) Submission to the union of all cases of promotion, transfer, or dismissal.
The union has never obtained full satisfaction on this point, although a new clause (Article VI: COMPLAINTS AND GRIEVANCES) has been added to the collective agreement that was signed after the strike. In virtue of this clause, the union may attempt to obtain what it has not been directly granted, by submitting grievances regarding cases of promotion, transfer, or dismissal, on the grounds that such measures were undertaken in contravention of the collective agreement.

j) The right of employees to accept or refuse, on an individual basis, the rates set for standards of production
On this point, the union managed to have a regulation included in Article VII of the collective agreement which establishes a procedure for dealing with these disputes. Any grievance concerning the standards of production is submitted to an industrial engineer who does not belong to the company hierarchy and who judges the case as the sole arbiter. This is a significant improvement in the collective agreement, and reveals an effort to come to terms with a very complex problem.

2/The settlement of grievances arising from the strike

By the time the strike was over, the union and the Company had a number of grievances against one another which were a serious obstacle to the establishment of harmonious relations between them. These grievances fell into four major categories:

a) The civil actions initiated by the Company

During the strike, the Company obtained an injunction, based on a $500,000.00 suit for damages, against the National Union of Asbestos Employees of Asbestos, Inc., the National Federation of Mining Industry Employees, and the Canadian and Catholic Confederation of Labour. This injunction implicated not only the striking asbestos workers, but the whole membership of the C.C.C.L. as well. When the collective agreement which followed the settlement of the strike was signed in February 1950, the Company waived this injunction.

b) The laying of criminal charges against strikers

During the strike, 173 strikers were arrested, on the charges which appear in Table II.

Table II

Charge	Arrests	Pleaded guilty	Found guilty	Acquitted	Charges withdrawn	Suspended
1. Vagrancy	22	20				2
2. Unlawful assembly	100					100
3. Aggravated assault	14		2	4		8
4. Assaulting a police officer	2					2
5. Drunk driving	1					1
6. Conspiracy to commit a felony	4					4
7. Intimidation	8		5	2	1	
8. Obstructing a police officer	5		3	2		
9. Conspiracy	17		1		3	13
Total	173	20	11	7	5	130

Thirty-one of the accused pleaded guilty or were found guilty. In July 1954, one hundred and thirty of the accused had not yet stood trial, five years after the strike had been settled. The strikers accused of misdemeanours were at liberty, for the most part on bail. The posting of bail had not resulted in the withdrawal of the charges, although the department of the Attorney General was not going ahead with the prosecutions.

Finally, in the spring of 1955, all the suspended accusations were withdrawn. This occurred a few months after the Superior Court had dismissed the suits for damages which some of the former strikers had brought against certain members of the Provincial Police. (See Appendix III.)

c) The strikers who were not rehired

At the time of the settlement of the strike, the Company refused to rehire nineteen strikers who had been accused of serious criminal offenses. This action seemed to contravene paragraphs 2 and 3 of the settlement which ended the strike. On June 30, 1949, the Company announced that these nineteen employees would be laid off for three weeks. At the end of this period, nine strikers were rehired; the remaining ten were later rehired one by one. The nineteenth striker in question did not return to work at the factory until January 1952.

Paragraph 4 of the settlement which ended the strike specified that the return to work would take place "without any discrimination on account of the strike. . . ." However, seventy former strikers were never rehired by the Company, on the grounds that their records were unsatisfactory. This clumsy excuse puzzled the union leaders, who claimed that if the Company had kept these seventy people in its employ up to the time of the strike, their output must have been satisfactory, and for that reason the Company should have rehired them once the strike was over. If their work had been unsatisfactory as far as the Company was concerned, why had they not been dismissed before the dispute began? The union leaders are convinced that the Company has made an effort here to eliminate some of the overly zealous adherents of trade unionism. Who can judge the situation fairly?

d) The strikers who were not rehired in their former positions

In June 1949, when the strikers returned to work in the mill, 610 scabs were working at jobs that had been held by the strikers before the dispute began. The strikers wanted their old jobs back. Since there were normally 2,000 people working at the mill, 1,400 workers could theoretically have returned to their former positions. On the contrary, the strikebreakers were given preferential treatment: 285 of them, who had already been working for the Company before the strike, were maintained in *new* jobs, and 325 new employees of the Company simply took over jobs formerly held by strikers. The strikers had to be satisfied with the remaining positions.

The attempt to settle this thorny question dragged on from June 27, 1949, to February 25, 1952, when the Company signed an agreement resolving this serious problem in a satisfactory manner. The text of this agreement is as follows:

In supplement to the collective agreement concluded this day at Asbestos, it is agreed that:

1. All the jobs held by workers who were hired, promoted, or transferred during the strike of 1949 are declared vacant and a list of such jobs will be posted within one week of the signing of this agreement, so that the workers who deem that they have a right to these jobs may offer themselves as candidates.

2. At the request of the union, the Company undertakes to advertise any job which is not included in Paragraph 1 of this contract, of which an employee deems that he has been deprived because of the strike, provided that the position is presently filled by a worker who continued to work for the Company during the strike. Claims of this type must be submitted within two months following the signing of this contract.

3. In the fifteen days following the advertisement of these positions, the Company undertakes to carry out all transfers, promotions, or demotions resulting from this contract.

4. In assigning these jobs or occupations, preference will be shown to those workers who deem that if there had not been a strike, these jobs or occupations would have been given to them in the normal course of things. The same procedure will be applied in the case of employees who are in the normal line for promotion to these jobs.

5. The employees who worked during the strike and whose jobs are advertised will be assigned to jobs which they would have held if there had not been a strike.

6. The employees who are displaced in virtue of this contract will not have the right to appeal to the seniority clause of the collective labour agreement in order to dispute the rights of those employees who deem that they have been deprived of the enjoyment of these rights because of the strike.

7. The application of this contract will not in any way affect the rights and privileges granted to the parties to the dispute in virtue of the collective agreement.

8. The purpose of this contract is to bring about the elimination of any prejudice which may have arisen against certain employees

as a result of the strike of 1949.

3/The present attitudes of the union and the Company

The officers of the union and the representatives of the Company are unanimous in their desire to forget the period of the strike and the difficulties that were created by this conflict. The Company admits that those who acted on its behalf at the time of the strike did not always behave in a diplomatic manner, and is pleased with the harmonious relations which presently exist between the two parties, although it is still worried by the attitude of some of the union leaders.

The union, which has the same officers as at the time of the strike, is satisfied with the attitude of the Company and of its chief representatives: it is often remarked that they are more understanding than their predecessors. Each of them, it seems, is working to improve the relations between union and management which, after a fierce struggle, have become almost cordial.

III/The union itself
1/The attitude of the members

A union that undergoes that trial of force known as a strike is in serious danger of seeing a decline in its activity once the conflict is settled. Having given of their best during the time of trouble, the members may be inclined to take less interest in the activities of the union, which may seem dull when things are quiet. The union at Asbestos, however, through some interior dynamism that eludes analysis, is still very active, and its members are among the most ardent defenders of trade unionism. Instead of exhausting the union's strength, the strike seems to have nourished and greatly increased it.

The attendance at the regular meetings of the union is the same as before the strike. The workers have come to realize, through concrete experience, that trade unions are necessary. It goes without saying that the improvements in wages and working conditions that have been obtained since the strike help to maintain confidence in the trade union movement.

In a struggle like the one at Asbestos, it would be perfectly understandable if, because of conflicts arising between men at a time of tension, some of the higher officers of the union became the victims of their own success; if the union members hastened to reproach them for inevitable errors; or if the unionists were afraid that over-excited militants might involve them in further exhausting conflicts. On the contrary, the members of the union display an unwavering confidence in their chief officers, a confidence that is revealed at the annual union elections. The president, vice-president, and secretary of the union at

Asbestos hold the same positions today as they did before and during the strike. The same situation exists at Thetford Mines and in the National Federation of Mining Industry Employees. The reelection of officers has certainly helped to increase the prestige of the trade union movement in the region.

When labour disputes have affected other sectors of Canadian industry, the workers—whether they are affiliated with the C.C.C.L. or some other central labour body—have been able to count on the unqualified support of the former strikers in the asbestos industry, who always contribute most generously to strike funds. The asbestos workers are obviously very aware of the duties imposed on them by trade union solidarity.

The asbestos workers may still be confirmed unionists, but are they always content with their federation's affiliation with the C.C.C.L.? During the strike and since, it has been rumoured that they would have preferred affiliation with some other central labour body. This rumour is completely unfounded. Although the unionists in the asbestos industry are very grateful for the generous help they received at the time of the strike from unions affiliated with the Canadian Congress of Labour and the Canadian Trades and Labour Congress, they have no intention of renouncing their ties with the C.C.C.L. Furthermore, the two central labour bodies mentioned above have never tried to organize the miners of Asbestos in an effort to persuade them to choose other affiliations.

The same cannot be said of Paul Emile Marquette, President of the Canadian Labour Association, who has unsuccessfully tried to recruit members at Asbestos and Thetford in an attempt to break the near-monopoly of the C.C.C.L. in the unions of the asbestos industry, and to increase the membership in his association, which in the asbestos region is restricted to the Bell mine. It is significant that the management of this mine, which is well-disposed towards Mr. Marquette, has granted him, among other concessions, the Rand formula.

2/The union's situation

a) Number of members

There is always a danger that the ordeal of a strike will weaken a union, even if it is settled to the union's advantage. The union at Asbestos was no exception to this general rule.

Table III shows the changes in union strength in relation to the total number of employees eligible for membership.

Table III

Membership in the Union at Asbestos

1	2	3	
Year	*Members*	*Hourly paid employees*	*Percentage*
	(monthly average)		
47-48	1,090	1,931	56
48-49	1,570	2,036	77
49-50	1,251	2,021	62
50-51	1,390	1,992	70
51-52	1,494	2,101	71
52-53	1,764	2,167	81

Remarks: Column 1— The union's fiscal year begins on June 1 and ends on May 31, except for the year 1948-49, when it ended on July 31,1949, and for the year 1949-50, when it began on August 1 and ended on May 31, 1950. This was the year of the strike.

Column 2— According to the audited records of income derived from union dues. We may add that at the time the strike was called in February 1949, the union had 1,700 members.

Column 3— Figures provided by the Company.

In June 1947, the membership of the union at Asbestos did not include more than 50% of the workers in the mine and mill, and the annual average was 56%. At the end of the fiscal year 1947-48, there was a trend towards greater membership, which is reflected in the average for the following year, 77%. Union statistics show that 734 new members joined during this period. This was due to a recruiting drive, in which the workers at Asbestos clearly showed that they wished to support the union. During the period 1947-48-49, the union enrolled 844 new members. [3]

The above table shows that the union membership decreased after the strike. The percentage of workers belonging to the union, in relation to the number eligible to join, actually dropped by 15%. This decrease, however, was due to the exclusion from the union of a number of strikebreakers (225 former members), and to the loss of 80 employees who, for one reason or another, did not return to (or remain at) work.

During the year 1950-51, the former scabs were allowed to join the union again as new members, and membership increased to 70% of the workers in the mine and mill. Finally, in 1952-53, union membership climbed to 81%, a percentage which had never been obtained in the history of the trade union movement at Asbestos. Where the development of the union's power is concerned, as in the acquisition of economic advantages, the results of the strike did not become apparent until some years later. The present situation of the union at Asbestos confirms the fact that the strike was beneficial to it.

b) The strikebreakers

From the moment they returned to work in July 1949, the unionized workers were faced with the problem of the scabs who were employed in the mill. How could one readmit to the union those workers who, by their betrayal, had almost caused the defeat of a strike that had demanded so many kinds of sacrifice? While the unionists were living on strike aid and exposing themselves to the danger of reprisals by the Company and the police, the strikebreakers were making a good living in contempt of workers' solidarity.[4] The officers of the union tried to get the former strikers to stop thinking about this complex issue: they managed to get a resolution passed by the general assembly, proposing that the scabs who wanted to belong to the union be readmitted. The resolution, voted into effect on December 2, 1951, reads as follows:

> The General Assembly has decided to readmit the scabs to the union on an equal footing with the other members.
> They will be considered as new members and a) will have to pay an entry fee of $2.00 like any other new member; b) will have to be initiated into the union.

This resolution, recommended by the union executive, has not been able to expunge completely, from the minds of the unionists, the memory of the scabs' reprehensible deeds. Workers' solidarity is one of the fundamental requirements of trade unionism, and a worker who breaks it is marked by his betrayal. Strikebreaking is one of the things that workers find hardest to forgive.

The Company did all it could to help solve this problem. At the beginning of July 1949, it dismissed all the new strikebreakers who had started work after May 1, 1949, and rehired an equal number of strikers to replace them. The number of workers dismissed amounted to 260. Of the 65 new scabs who remained in the employ of the Company, many were subsequently fired. Practically the only ones who were kept on were those who were regarded as people who had been hired because of a need to increase the personnel of the Company. The 285 former union members who had worked as scabs were kept on in their former jobs, relinquishing the new positions they had filled during the strike.

The leaders of the union at Asbestos, when asked about the reason for the defection of the 285 strikebreakers, attributed it not to the financial difficulties of the members but to their fear of losing their seniority rights (which had nonetheless been recognized through union action) and their right to a share of the pension fund. Some of them were also at odds with the leaders of the union.

c) The union's finances
A strike affecting 2,000 employees and their families could not be entirely supported by the financial resources of the local union. During the course of the strike, the union at Asbestos received the sum of $211,215.00 from various sources, and distributed $228,907.00 to its members. The local union contributed the difference, $17,692.00, from its own fund.[5]

In addition, the union lent a total of $48,127.00 to 627 members, mostly for the repayment of debts contracted before the strike.

From the financial point of view, the strike "cost" the union at Asbestos:

in direct financial aid $17,692.00
in loans to members 48,127.00
in loss of dues which were not levied during
    the strike 9,420.00

Total $75,239.00

The direct financial aid and the loss of dues were absorbed by the previous income of the union. The loans were made after the union had borrowed $50,000.00. The union had fully repaid this debt by May 31, 1955. At that time, the union members themselves still owed the union the sum of $18,650.00. I shall return to this problem later.

If the union had not borrowed $50,000.00 to make loans to its members, its finances would be in good shape. The annual surpluses accumulated from August 1, 1949, to May 31, 1953, amounted to $23,707.00. To meet its financial obligations, the union increased its monthly dues to $2.00 as of January 1, 1952. They had formerly been set at $1.50.

IV/The economic consequences of the strike
My study of this problem will be concerned only with the economic consequences of the strike for a worker who returned to his job in July 1949. The general economic consequences of the strike and the situation of the Company following it do not fall within the framework of this analysis.

1/Incomes

The 2,000 workers of the Canadian Johns-Manville Co. were on strike
for a little less than twenty weeks. The gross average loss of wages for
each of them amounted to $1,066.00, and the net loss to about
$880.00 as is shown in Table IV.

Table IV

Wage earnings and losses (in round figures)

1. *Wage losses:* 20 weeks at 48 hours per week at an
   average hourly wage of $1.11 .... Total $1,066.00
   Note: This $1.11 is made up of the average
           hourly wage (see Table I of this chap-
           ter) in the asbestos industry in 1948,
           the year preceding the declaration of
           the strike, plus the 10c per hour that
           the Company offered its employees
           from the beginning of the strike.
2. *Aid:* in money $229,000.00
          in kind ....∴.   40,000.00
   retroactive payment of wages (in
   virtue of the collective
   agreement of Feb. 1950) .... $ 66,000.00
                                       Total: $335,000.00
3. *Workers on strike* 2,000
4. *Workers who remained at or returned to work
   during the strike,* monthly average for the
   whole 134-day period of the strike 200
5. *Number of workers to whom aid was effectively
   given* (item 3 less item 4) 1,800
6. *Average aid distributed per striker* (item 2
   divided by item 5) $186.00
7. *Net loss* (item 1 less item 6) $880.00

We should note, however, that this sum of $880.00 is not strictly
speaking a loss so much as a deficiency in earnings and expenditures.
During the strike, the loss of income was always counter balanced by
a reduction in the standard of living of the strikers and their families.

In other words, the 20 weeks of the strike at Asbestos represented
20 weeks of privations for the population, but do not mean that had
there been no strike, every worker would have had $880.00 more in
his bank account in July 1949. Almost all of these wages would have
been spent, as is normally the case, to maintain a standard of living

that does not permit the average working-class family to save much.

Furthermore, the temporary privations of a strike are often regarded by strikers as a risk which they are taking in the hope of assuring themselves a greater income in the future. This was particularly true of the strikers in the asbestos industry. As I have mentioned above, in connection with Table I, this strike was followed by much more rapid wage increases in the asbestos industry than in the Canadian mining industry as a whole.

From 1945 to 1948, the wages in the asbestos industry were actually $0.10 to $0.22 per hour less than the average for the mining industry, while from 1949 to 1952, this lag was transformed into an advance of $0.16 per hour, in favour of the asbestos workers. A good part of these relative advantages may be attributed to the fact that the strike had considerably increased the negotiating power of the asbestos unions.

It is, moreover, dangerous to judge a strike solely on the basis of the economic advantages it wins for the strikers. The strike is a powerful defensive weapon for the working class. It is an affirmation of the force of labour, and it may just as well be used to support the principle of union recognition as to obtain increases in wages. The striker makes a social gesture whose repercussions are felt by all workers. He goes on strike to gain advantages for himself, no doubt, but his act influences the whole working class.

If the strike had not occurred at Asbestos and at Thetford, would there still be unions there, and what would be the wages and working conditions? . . . We should ask ourselves such questions when we try to assess the effects of the strike.

2/Debts

a) Owing to the union

We have seen above that during the strike, the union at Asbestos lent a total of $48,127.00 to its members: 627 strikers borrowed money on their personal notes, and they all undertook to repay the union one year after the date of the loan.

Many of the loans were made to union members who, before the strike began, had bought a car, furniture, or household goods on credit. In these cases, the union paid the finance company directly, and thus kept the article in question from being repossessed. Other loans were made for the payment of rent or for monthly mortgage payments.

On July 1, 1952, 191 of the 627 borrowers had completely repaid their loans. Three years after the strike, there were thus 436 borrowers who still owed the union $37,306.00.

How can we explain this lack of responsibility on the part of some of the former strikers? In any case, it does not redound to their credit. The union at Asbestos estimates that the majority of those who have not yet paid their debt do not want to pay it. Many are convinced that the union will never ask them for the money. It goes without saying that such an attitude operates to the detriment of the members of the union as a whole. These people are getting others to pay for money which they alone have enjoyed. Several of those who refuse to pay their debts claim that the money that was lent to them came from the gifts received during the strike. The $50,000.00 lent by the union during the strike came, however, from loans which were taken out by the union at Asbestos with the episcopal corporations of St. Hyacinth, Sherbrooke, and Montreal.

Because the union had to meet its obligations towards its creditors and, in all justice, towards its own members, the following decision had to be taken at the general meeting of the union on November 29, 1953:

A— The borrowers who returned to work in July 1949 will be sued for the repayment of outstanding debts.

B—The borrowers who did not return to work in July 1949 will receive a credit equivalent to the weekly aid distributed during the strike for each week that they were not working after the settlement of the strike.

C— The borrowers of category B who have paid off their note will be reimbursed for the deductible part.

D— The strikers who were maltreated at the hands of the police will be forgiven their outstanding debts.

E— The borrowers who are sued will be required to pay both the capital and the interest.

Because of this decision, the union treasury had to absorb a loss of $16,000.00. The union recovered a total of $18,500.00 from its debtors. Had it not done so, the people who had borrowed nothing from the union during the strike would have been very poorly compensated for their sacrifices.

b) Debts owing to the Caisse populaire (Co-operative People's Bank)
Although there are two banking institutions at Asbestos, most of the workers do their business with the local Caisse populaire (Co-operative People's Bank). The pattern of savings and loans from 1946 to 1953 will give us a better idea of the economic consequences of the strike as far as the financial situation of the strikers is concerned. Table V describes this pattern.

Table V

Year	Total savings	Number of savers	Average deposit per saver	Total capital of the society	Number of members	Average capital per member	Total borrow-ings	Number of bor-rowers	Average amount per bor-rower
1946	$ 485,865	1,765	$275.37	$15,486	1,765	$8.77	$156,900	146	$1,074.65
1947	571,456	1,911	299.03	20,249	1,911	10.59	242,500	138	1,757.20
1948	726,589	2,119	342,89	20,549	2,300	8.93	163,900	169	969.80
1949	763,600	2,260	337.87	21,380	2,347	9.10	286,600	208	1,377.70
1950	855,100	2,443	345.92	29,654	2,360	12.56	328,500	323	1,017.
1951	910,534	2,667	341.78	39,822	2,600	15.31	182,200	295	617.60
1952	1,153,877	2,964	389.29	43,771	2,821	15.51	267,000	309	864.
1953	1,341,954	3,162	424.40	49,754	3,127	15.91	388,000	307	1,264.

The above table shows the effects of the strike. In 1949, there was a slight decrease in the average savings in comparison with 1948, the average amount of society capital per member went up by only $0.17, and the average amount borrowed increased to $1,377.70. In 1953, the amount of money saved and the amount of society capital reached a maximum. The miners benefit more and more from the good effects of the strike.

3/Wages

The wages paid in the asbestos industry have been given in Table I above. Our study would be more complete if these wages were considered in relation to the wage pattern in the different mining industries. Table VI shows this pattern of change. (Unfortunately, the statistics are not complete and go back only as far as 1945.)

Table VI

Average hourly earnings in Canada	1945	1946	1947	1948	1949	1950	1951	1952
	c.	c.	c.	c.	c.	c.	c.	c.
1. Mining, including milling	85.0	87.3	98.0	111.1	117.2	121.4	133.4	147.1
2. Metals	85.0	87.4	99.4	110.2	115.9	121.1	134.8	148.2
3. Gold							121.6	130.1
4. Other metals							145.4	160.7
5. Mineral fuels							139.0	151.5
6. Coal	93.8	95.9	110.4	123.5	128.3	130.1	136.7	148.6
7. Crude petroleum and natural gas							147.8	161.4
8. Non-metals, except fuels							116.3	134.0
9. Asbestos— Asbestos and Thetford	63.	68.	76.	101.	108.	116.	139.	163.

Source: *Annual Review of Man-Hours and Hourly Earnings 1945-53*, Dominion Bureau of Statistics, Ottawa, page 10.

The asbestos industry is classified, for statistical purposes, among the "non-metallic minerals" (line 8). In this category, the wages have always been the lowest in the entire Canadian mining industry.

The wages paid at Asbestos from 1945 to 1950 have, according to the table, always been lower than the wages paid in the other sectors of the mining industry. In 1952, the average hourly earnings at Asbestos were $1.63 per hour. This average was higher than the average wage paid in each of the other categories of the Canadian mining industry. The workers on the oil wells, who are generally well paid, received average hourly earnings that were lower than those of the asbestos workers.

This brief comparison is enough to show how the trade union movement in the asbestos region has made great strides in improving the material situation of the miners.

Notes to Chapter IX

[1]Here is the decision of the arbitration board on this point, handed down by Judge Thomas Tremblay:

"We believe that this clause goes beyond the bounds set by common law, that it is contrary to the principle of liberty which must be basic to trade unionism. It is also contrary to the dignity of the worker, and is even capable on infringing on his liberty of conscience."

One year earlier, the same Judge Tremblay had declared, in a unanimous arbitration board decision handed down on November 27, 1948, in the dispute between the Traverse de Lévis (Levis Ferry Service) and the employees of the Traverse:

"With regard to union security, we have considered it just to grant the obligatory wage deduction for union purposes, called the Rand formula. All the employees affected by the agreement benefit from the work of the union as negotiator. Why should a minority have the right to escape the contributions while enjoying the advantages? Let it be noted that this measure will in no way have the effect of making the employees subservient to the present union. Should they wish to change their affiliation at a later date, the Labour Relations Act would enable them to have some other organization recognized at the appropriate time, as a representative either of the workers as a whole, or of some group which is deemed appropriate. By this fact alone, the clause would be revoked (Labour Relations Act, Article 16)." (Excerpt from bulletin 309, Quebec Department of Labour).

[2]On May 20, 1954, the Canadian Johns-Manville Co. and the union signed a two-year collective agreement, valid until January 31, 1956. For the most part, it contained changes in the monetary arrangements only, which we will indicate as the occasion arises.

[3]New members:

1947-48:	734	1949-50:	3	1951-52:	275
1948-49:	110	1950-51:	175	1952-53:	84

[4]Employees at work during the strike (these figures are provided by the Company):

March 1949	— 122
April	— 252, including 65 new employees
May	— 455, including 212 new employees
June	— 610, including 325 new employees

⁵Cost of the asbestos strike and the source of funds, according to the official figures of the C.C.C.L. (Minutes of the 28th annual convention of the C.C.C.L., Montreal, 1949, p. 72).

Collections taken up at the doors of churches in the
    province $167,558.24
Contributions of the C.C.C.L. and its affiliates 300,014.52
Individual and other contributions 27,708.61
Unions affiliated with the Canadian Congress of
    Labour 7,683.00
Unions affiliated with the Trades and Labour Congress,
    railway and police brotherhoods, teachers, etc 6,413.41
Total $509,377.78
Value of foodstuffs sent to Thetford and Asbestos 75,000.00
Grand total $584,377.78
Of this amount, not including foodstuffs, the union members of Asbestos received $228,907, those of Thetford $280,470.

Chapter X

The Strike and the Labour Movement

by Réginald Boisvert

I/Introduction

To what extent are the three great labour movements of Quebec, affiliated either to the Canadian Congress of Labour, the Canadian Trades and Labour Congress,[1] or the Canadian and Catholic Confederation of Labour, capable of developing a joint program of action, and of uniting their forces in the pursuit of common objectives? Today, this is a question of capital importance. From the political point of view, it is even *the* question. The political future in our province undoubtedly belongs to the party which will be able, within the framework of a general platform, to work out a social and labour policy which will win the votes of the working masses. Depending on the degree of agreement in thought and action among the various forces in the labour movement, this program will be better or more poorly adapted to the real needs of the workers, and will be implemented with greater or lesser efficiency.

Our best guide to this subject is the asbestos strike. This strike, in fact, represents a high point in inter-union collaboration in our province. The Quebec labour movements as a whole had never before made such an effective attempt to help a group of workers in a precise set of circumstances, and the attempt has not been repeated since.

It must be said that in the spring of 1949, labour solidarity was very much a part of the social climate of the province. On the very eve of the asbestos strike, the Duplessis government, by the introduction of Bill 5, had threatened the very existence of every one of the labour unions, regardless of the movement to which they belonged.[2] In the presence of this common danger, the labour leaders had felt it necessary to forget their differences and create an inter-union conference,[3] which led a vigorous campaign against the proposed legislation, with the result that Bill 5 was withdrawn.

The asbestos strike, though not the biggest to occur in our province, had by far the greatest impact on the imagination of the working classes. The victory over Bill 5 had given rise to a spirit of solidarity among the workers, and the asbestos strike, occurring when it did, gave them a new opportunity to oppose the labour policy of the government.

How great was the general sympathy aroused by the strikers? What does this action tell us about the state of inter-union relations at this time? To what extent has the collaboration which then existed been maintained among the central labour bodies? At the present time, what are the possibilities of a unified action on the part of the unions? These are the questions I shall attempt to answer by an examination of the facts.

II/Inter-union action during the strike

The strike started at Asbestos on February 13 at midnight, and at Thetford on the following day. These strikes were illegal, as far as labour relations law was concerned. Nevertheless, the C.C.C.L. decided that they were justified and gave its full support to the miners. On February 17, the secretary of the C.C.C.L., Jean Marchand, made a public statement on the attitude of his labour organization towards the strike: "The workers are not opposed to arbitration, but their daily experience has taught them that the application of this law is nearly always unfavourable to them. Arbitration has become a weapon which is used by the employers to treat the workers unjustly."

"We are supporters," he said, "of legality. We are firmly devoted to the respect of the laws, but we must examine what laws we are dealing with, and above all the manner in which they are applied."

At first, the asbestos strike attracted no more public attention than most other strikes. It was much less interesting to the workers than certain recent strikes, for example the strike of the workers in the meat packing plants. However, the Prime Minister himself soon embittered the conflict and gave it an unprecedented importance. Shortly after his dispatch of the Provincial Police to Asbestos (when the miners occupied the offices of the Canadian Johns-Manville Co., an incident which is reported in the chapter by Beausoleil), the Prime Minister made virulent public attacks on the leaders of the C.C.C.L. [4]

1/The Joint Conference of Organized Labour

The C.C.C.L. hardly deigned to reply to the remarks by the Prime Minister. It protested against the "lease-lend" of the Provincial Police to the Company, and some of its regional councils expressed their confidence in the leaders who had been attacked. Its response, however, consisted mainly of acts. It immediately made an urgent appeal to its unions and to their members, and referred the conflict to the inter-union conference, which was still in session. The labour leaders reacted in a unanimous way. We should offer here verbatim the statement they made to the newspapers on March 17:

> The Joint Conference of Organized Labour of the Province of Quebec, an organization which represents, in the province, the 250,000 members of the Fédération Provinciale du Travail (Provincial Federation of Labour, P.F.L.), the Canadian Congress of Labour (C.C.L.) and the Canadian and Catholic Confederation of Labour (C.C.C.L.), has been informed of the facts and circumstances which have led to the strike in the asbestos industry.
>
> The Conference wishes to state, in connection with the dispute:
>
> a) that it gives its full support to the unionized miners of the asbestos industry and hopes that they will obtain a satisfactory settlement of the present difficulties;
>
> b) that it does not accept the principle that the legality or the illegality of a strike be determined either by the Prime Minister and the Attorney General, by the Minister of Labour, or by the Labour Relations Board;
>
> c) that it protests most vigorously against the abuses which the Provincial Police has committed at Asbestos;
>
> d) that it will examine without delay the best methods for providing effective aid to the unionized miners of the asbestos industry.

This masterly statement, which is unique in the annals of the Quebec labour movement, was signed, on behalf of the P.F.L., by Elphège Beaudoin and Marcel Francq; on behalf of the C.C.L., by Philippe Vaillancourt and W.J. Smith; on behalf of the C.C.C.L., by Gérard Picard and Jean Marchand.[5] This unanimity on the provincial level had significant repercussions in the world of organized labour from one end of Canada to the other. Thus the Canadian Congress of Labour, which includes 200 unions and more than 350,000 members, from the Atlantic to the Pacific, assured the C.C.C.L. of its moral and financial support. It denounced the attitude of the government and the asbestos companies, and called upon all its affiliated unions to contribute to the strike fund.

The Trades and Labour Congress decided not to intervene, although a certain number of its unions gave moral and financial support to the strikers.

The asbestos strike had, meanwhile, become a matter of national importance, and even had repercussions on the floor of the House of Commons, where a member who represented the interests of labour, Clarie Gillis (C.C.F., Cape Breton South), demanded that the federal Minister of Labour intervene in the conflict.[6]

In the meantime, at the behest of the Joint Conference and the C.C.L., a great number of unions of all sorts, from the Maritimes to the Pacific Coast, sent aid to the miners.

2/The efforts of the C.C.C.L.

It goes without saying that the members of the Catholic unions had not awaited these appeals to come to the aid of their fellow workers in the asbestos industry. However, until the hiring of scabs and the intervention of the Attorney General had destroyed any prospect of a settlement, the aid which was sent was hardly more than the amount of money which is generally contributed by the members of any labour organization whatsoever when a strike of some importance occurs. The strikers in the asbestos industry soon found themselves in a desperate situation, and much more substantial aid had to be collected. At this point, Gérard Picard, the President of the C.C.C.L., hit upon an ingenious method for organizing this aid which, in addition to providing the strikers with the necessary help, caught the imagination of the workers in an unprecedented way. Instead of sending their contributions individually, the unions made a group effort. They loaded trucks with footstuffs of every kind and drove them to the strike-bound villages.

The first of these trucks, carrying 8,000 pounds of foodstuffs valued at $1,500, reached Thetford Mines on March 18. This aid was paid for by contributions raised by the Quebec City Central Labour Council (C.C.C.L.). From that time onward, to the very end of the strike, unions from every part of the country answered the appeals of their councils, and through their efforts the people of Asbestos and Thetford Mines were supplied by a virtual provisioning service. In the records which were scrupulously kept by the secretaries of the two locals, it is noted, for example, that between March 18 and May 18, union members from the Quebec region alone sent the strikers aid valued at more than $9,000. Gradually, veritable caravans were formed. For example, a delegation organized at Sherbrooke arrived at Asbestos laden with gifts from the workers of Bromptonville, Windsor Mills, Richmond, and Danville. In this atmosphere of enthusiasm and emulation, the smallest union was moved to make its contribution, and all the resources of the labour movement were gradually deployed in the effort to help the miners. On April 9, the Plenary Council of the C.C.C.L., in an extraordinary meeting at Montreal,[7] voted a contribution of $25,000 to the strikers' fund, and announced that it was taking the necessary measures to establish a strike fund of $100,000.

The tremendous effort of the C.C.C.L. is shown by the fact that by August 29, 1949, its unions and their members had contributed approximately $300,000 worth of aid.

3/The support given by other labour organizations

The "international" unions, whether affiliated to the C.C.L. or the T.L.C., did not offer nearly so much help as the "national" unions, although many urgent appeals were made to them. The Quebec leaders of these organizations repeatedly called on them for help, and their appeals produced concrete results of some importance. Many international unions decided to send their own truckloads of provisions. The workers in the meat packing industry, who were affiliated with the C.C.L., had recently fallen victim to the truncheons of the Duplessis regime; they took a malicious delight in sending 1,000 pounds of margarine to the strikers, at a time when the Quebec government had just prohibited the sale, or even the consumption, of this product.

Cash donations amounted to $7,700 from the C.C.L. unions, and $6,500 from the T.L.C. unions (and their associates). These figures do not give an accurate idea of the relative amount of effort made by the two groups, because in 1949 the T.L.C. in Quebec had three times the membership of the C.C.L. All the organizations in the C.C.L. made contributions, but only a fraction of the T.L.C. unions helped the strikers. The firemen, truck drivers, and brewery workers of the T.L.C. were among the more important contributors.

Some people have made much of the idea that the strikers obtained a great deal of support from the communists. Of the $509,377 received from all sources as of August 29, however, only $558 came from unions known to be dominated by communists, namely the Mine, Mill, and Smelter Workers and the United Electrical Workers. We should add that at this time, the American divisions of these two unions were still members in good standing of the C.I.O., and the Labour Relations Board recognized their Quebec branches as legitimate labour organizations.

One further aspect of the help given to the strikers by the international unions deserves to be mentioned. On May 21 and 22, three American labour leaders paid a visit to the strikers. They represented the workers at the Johns-Manville plant in New Jersey, and were members of the American Federation of Labour. They declared that they were shocked at the working conditions in the mines in the Eastern Townships, told the strikers that their cause was a just one, and advised them to fight to the end. One of these men, E. Macko, even spoke at a meeting of the strikers, telling them that they should put their trust in their leaders, who in his opinion were excellent. The American labour leaders also assured the strikers that they could count on the support of their fellow workers south of the border, who were ready to endure all the consequences of the strike, and who would not do anything to put an end to it, even if it brought about a work stoppage in their own plants.

4/The independent unions

Mention must be made here of the effect of the strike on the independent unions. Two of them are of particular importance in this connection: the Montreal Catholic Teachers' Association and the Canadian Labour Association, respectively headed by Léo Guindon and Paul Marquette.

The teachers' association quickly came to the aid of the strikers. It had had to endure a difficult strike against an employer supported by the government, and it readily understood the plight of the asbestos workers. On March 25, the newspapers carried the story that one hundred teachers, men and women, had made up parcels for the strikers. At this time, the teachers had also contributed $500 in cash.

The attitude of the Canadian Labour Association was completely different. It had always had a cordial relationship with the government, even at the time of Bill 5. On March 8, a union affiliated with this labour body signed a labour contract with Bell Asbestos, of Thetford Mines. This agreement specified that the workers would receive an overall increase of 10 cents per hour, and contained the assurance that they would receive additional raises to equal any amount won by the strikers at the end of the dispute. Shortly afterwards, Mr. Marquette declared that he intended to intervene in the conflict by forming a new association of miners. Marquette no doubt made this move to see what effect it might have among the ranks of the miners; his trial balloon collapsed, and Mr. Marquette kept his mouth shut thereafter.

5/The labour press

A study of the labour press in relation to the asbestos strike yields few results. In the first place, there were only three official labour publications of some importance in our province at the time: Le Travail, a C.C.C.L. organ; Les Nouvelles ouvrières, published by the Quebec branch of the C.C.L.; and Le Monde ouvrier, representing the Provincial Federation of Labour (T.L.C.).

We do not propose to discuss Le Front ouvrier, published by the Catholic Labour League and the Catholic Labour Youth (J.O.C.): it should be considered in a study of the labour press. We also feel that it is best to leave Le Travail out of account: during the course of the strike, it always reflected the official policy of the C.C.C.L., and the readers of this book would gain no new insights from an analysis of its positions.

Les Nouvelles ouvrières and *Le Monde ouvrier* naturally echoed the views adopted by the Joint Conference of Organized Labour. *Le Monde ouvrier,* however, deserves a special mention for its moving praise of the asbestos strikers, which appeared in its April 30 edition. The following are some extracts from that article:

> Five thousand asbestos workers are now in the line of fire—let us remember that we may be the next target of the forces opposed to labour—*noblesse oblige* . . . [These workers] have taken it upon themselves to go on strike without recourse to arbitration, which might well last 12 or 15 months (this is what is happening in the streetcar strike, and what has happened at Shawinigan) . . . they have remained very calm for three months in the face of provocations both from their inhuman company and from a vicious government and its goons . . . they no longer have the slightest confidence in the dictatorial and anti-labour government of Quebec . . .
>
> Five thousand asbestos workers who in struggling for their own cause are fighting for the future of the entire working class in the Province of Quebec . . . who are the first martyrs of Bill 5 . . . who are giving the entire working class the noblest of examples of solidarity and perseverance . . . who are writing one of the most important pages in the history of Quebec society and the Quebec labour movement. . . .

Elsewhere in the same issue, the publication of the Provincial Federation of Labour flays the government unmercifully for its attitude:

> . . . Our Minister of Labour, in refusing to do anything to settle this conflict, has been trying to work both sides of the street. Like his boss, who is very intelligent but who is also imbued with medieval ideas, he has confined himself to noting that the strike is illegal . . . This is nothing but a smokescreen to hide the government's real game; it has sworn that it will destroy organized labour in the province . . . The asbestos strike (and other strikes) is illegal because the government wanted it that way, through its adoption of compulsory arbitration, with its delays and financial sacrifices. . . .

Some English-language Canadian labour newspapers published a concise report of the situation in the asbestos industry and repeated the C.C.L.'s appeal to its member unions. On the other hand, *The Labour Review,* a "labour" journal which offered a management viewpoint, jeered at the strikers and castigated their leaders.

Several communist publications carried articles on the asbestos strike. As a general rule, these articles tried to establish a parallel between it and the Canadian Seamen's Union strike, then in progress.

The strike had some echoes in the American labour press. *The Labor Leader,* a publication of the Association of Catholic Trade Unionists, carried articles on the asbestos strike on May 30 and June 30. This paper embraced the cause of the strikers, denounced the government and the Company, noted the many collections taken up for the miners at the behest of the bishops of Quebec, and invited its readers to make their own contributions.

On July 9 the newspaper *Labor,* the weekly organ of the American railway brotherhoods, published an account which was very favourably disposed towards the strikers. It emphasized the unusual aspects of the dispute, especially the role played in the settlement of the strike by Mgr. Roy, the Archbishop of Quebec.

III/New inter-union relations

The Canadian labour movement was made up of three groups which had long been divided among themselves: this fact must be clearly grasped if one is to understand just how it was affected by the asbestos strike. These divisions were particularly deep in our province, where the mutual contempt existing between the C.C.L. and the T.L.C. was only surpassed by their common contempt of the C.C.C.L., and by the latter's mistrust of the two other organizations. Many of the officers of the international unions who were the most devoted to the cause of the asbestos workers, among them some important figures, had long held the view that the national unions were little more than pro-management organizations. In some circles, this animosity degenerated into an incurable hatred. When one of the three organizations was involved in a difficult strike, the two others thought only of how to supplant it.

1/The C.C.C.L. in a new light

The cause of the asbestos miners aroused an unprecedented interest and created great enthusiasm, winning considerable support for the C.C.C.L. These developments were due to the extraordinary vigour shown by the C.C.C.L. at that time, which took the world of labour by surprise. Some union people, especially in the C.C.L., had already realized that the C.C.C.L. militants were inspired by a new dynamism, and were warmly sympathetic towards them. Most of those in the labour movement, however, did not think that the Catholic unions were ready to engage in such a desperate struggle, nor did they believe that they were capable of carrying it on to the very end.

This was no more than justifiable scepticism. The C.C.C.L. was founded and nurtured in a society which was still largely made up of peasants, where the city worker was little more than an artisan. In its thirty years of existence, the C.C.C.L. had shown little dynamism and, like most of the institutions in French Canada, it had been created to achieve a purely negative goal: to protect the workers of Quebec against foreign influences, against the virus of modern ideas. It is hard to conceive of such an attitude today, but it is readily understandable in the light of social conditions prevailing at the time. Strongly attached to their ancestral traditions, which they regarded as their sole means of survival, the French Canadians were almost fatally bound to see all their problems in terms of Quebec nationalism. Everything had to contribute to the safeguarding of French culture. Pretending to make language the servant of our faith, we often made our faith the servitor of language. The trade union movement was not exempt from these tendencies of Quebec thought. So it happened that at the very time when Catholics in the United States were placing the broadest possible interpretation on the social encyclicals, and were going out among the working masses, into the heart of the non-denominational labour movement, to promote a resolutely modern conception of Christian humanism, the same encyclicals were interpreted in our province in their most restricted sense, and our bishops promoted the creation of French Canadian labour unions, which were intended to organize French Canadian Catholics in the interests of the French Canadian conception of Catholicism.

It soon became clear, however, that this formal nationalism was unable to cope with the problems which arose in French Canadian society with the advent of a phenomenon of great significance, the modern industrial world. The nationalist ideology gradually came to recommend the adoption of certain American methods to French Canadian businessmen and industrialists, so that they might gain control of economic life, and accumulate enough capital to make us, as a group, the masters of our own natural riches. On the other hand, this same ideology feared that the group would become a prey to the social struggles and labour conflicts which had broken out in all societies in the process of industrialization. In the name of national survival, the embryo proletariat had to be hedged in. It had to be advised against the use of force, and every form of violence had to be presented to it as anathema. A strong nationalist mystique had to be preserved, and if necessary instilled, in the hearts of these proletarians. In the name of this mystique, the workers were supposed to soft-pedal their demands and look to the French Canadian employers for any improvement of their lot.

We may note, in defence of the nationalists of the era, that they were almost totally unaware of the concrete problems that were soon to be created in our society by the industrial revolution. It still cannot be denied that for all practical purposes, the workers were expected to pay, all by themselves, the enormous price at which the survival of our traditional society might be bought.

It is not surprising that the workers of Quebec were not overjoyed with the role they were called on to play. Through their daily experience, they soon came to sense the human drama which lies at the heart of our American capitalism: the profound insecurity of the modern worker. For this reason, they turned in great numbers to the American unions, who had the advantage over the C.C.C.L. of stating a primarily economic problem in economic terms (for which they were accused of being materialists), and thus of proposing more effective courses of action. In spite of the repeated warnings of our clergy and our nationalist elite against the "materialism," "neutralism," "internationalism," and "radicalism" of the American labour movement, it still managed to gain a foothold in our province, especially in the cities, where our people have been turned into proletarians at an accelerated pace. Accordingly, on the eve of the last war, after nearly twenty years of existence, the C.C.C.L. was still marking time. Unable to formulate a purely modern problem in modern terms, it had won only feeble gains for its members. It easily became the butt of the international unionists, and did not inspire much confidence among the workers in the large industrial centres. In other words, in creating a trade union movement based on a profound internal contradiction, our nationalism brought about its own ruin, in labour as in other fields.

Our economy was rapidly becoming a vassal of the U.S. economy; the workers of Quebec had experienced a brutal awakening during the Thirties; beyond the frontiers of our province, the Congress of Industrial Organizations (C.I.O.) cut a dynamic figure in the field of organized labour. All these developments led people to think that the C.C.C.L. would eventually disappear from the arena of organized labour, and that the workers of Quebec would be irresistibly drawn into the orbit of the big American unions.

Contrary to every expectation, the C.C.C.L., far from disappearing, has acquired a new lease on life in the last ten years. Today, its membership compares favourably with that of the two other central provincial labour bodies. According to a University of Laval survey, the C.C.C.L. had 90,000 members at the end of 1954, while the C.C.L. had 45,000, and the T.L.C. about 130,000.

For the most part, the C.C.C.L. owes its renewed vigour to the new direction it took about ten years ago, when a new group of leaders took the helm. The doctrine of social conservatism, the essence of a certain kind of nationalism, had not been able to achieve results. The C.C.C.L. was able to do so by developing a dynamic doctrine which ignored neither the changing patterns of our lives nor the economic and social characteristics of a modern industrial society. The C.C.C.L. had to become aware of the fact that the capitalist world, through the inhuman structures it creates, weighs upon the human person with all the heaviness of the machine; that the proper function of the trade union movement is precisely to liberate this individual and to place the machine at his service; and that only then, men will begin to acquire again, gradually, the character of human beings, and the society that they create will be worthy of the name. To save society, the individual had to be given priority over society. In raising French Canadian society to the level of an absolute, our nationalism had tried to abase the person, and had thus unwittingly become the accomplice of those very forces which, through the oppression of the individual, were undermining the foundations of society.

These momentous changes in the thinking of the C.C.C.L. necessarily brought it into closer contact with the outside world and broke down the overly restrictive barriers of Quebec nationalism. Towards the end of the last war, the C.C.C.L. began to take an interest in international problems, and to look at the problems of union action in a more and more universal perspective. On the national and provincial levels, its new orientation led it to work with the international labour movements from time to time, in dealing with specific problems affecting the whole of the working class. Internally, this change of direction removed some of the barriers that had been set up by nationalism, and the C.C.C.L. began to welcome Canadian workers regardless of race or religion, as long as they agreed to abide by the constitution and the established rules. The C.C.C.L. is thus no longer a denominational movement in the sense intended by the great social encyclicals.

At the same time, the new orientation of the C.C.C.L. led it to place the greatest emphasis on industrial unionism. Up to that time, it had enjoyed particular success in organizing the so-called craft unions, which grouped only the practitioners of the same trade, or in organizing the employees of small industries which were more or less based on the labour of the craftsman. In other words, the C.C.C.L. had been mainly concerned with workers who were still imbued with the traditions of the artisan and the villager. From this time onwards, the C.C.C.L. made much more serious efforts to penetrate the world of big modern industry and to create industrial unions there, bringing all the workers in the same industry into one union. This type of organization is much more suited to the structures of the modern world, and to a much more personalist and communal mode of thought.

It is true that, in the past, the C.C.C.L. had organized a few industrial unions, but for the most part it had not "digested" them. It had not been able to use these unions as an effective instrument for achieving the liberation of the workers. These previously existing industrial unions did not fully understand their mission until the C.C.C.L. acquired its new orientation and its revitalized leadership. Until that time, many of them had been little more than company unions.

The C.C.C.L., for example, was the first to organize the shipyard workers. Later on, however, it lost them when this field was invaded by the international labour movement, which was more dynamic and more realistic. Then, a few years ago, the C.C.C.L. in turn outdistanced the international trade unions ideologically: it regained control of the shipyards by offering the workers an industrial unionism.

The international labour organizations remained virtually unaware of the new spirit, the revitalization of the C.C.C.L., right up to 1949. Their blindness was above all due to the fact that they were not in the habit of taking the national unions seriously, and did not take the trouble to reflect upon the changes that were taking place in the C.C.C.L. They felt that they had had the last word on the organization in saying that it lacked the maturity, realism, fighting spirit, and material resources required to conduct an effective union campaign.

The asbestos strike showed clearly that quite the opposite was true, and many officers of the international unions came to realize this. The C.C.C.L. showed at once that it was capable of assuming a fighting stance. In the context of the opposition to Bill 5, the struggle of the asbestos miners became a symbol of the struggle of the entire labour movement. Within the inter-union conference, the leaders of the C.C.C.L. proved to be men of undoubted effectiveness in the field of legislative action. The asbestos strike revealed the C.C.C.L.'s dynamism, ingenuity, and endurance on the purely union level, and earned it the unwavering respect of the other labour movements.

Labour's change of attitude towards the C.C.C.L. is particularly well brought out by an incident that occurred during the strike. The newspapers had wrongly stated that Rodolphe Hamel, the President of the National Federation of Mining Industry Employees, intended to transfer his allegiance to the C.C.L. as a last resort. Pat Conroy, the National Secretary of the C.C.L., replied publicly that the miners should stay in the ranks of the C.C.C.L., in their own interest: "We want you to win this strike," he said.

On the other hand, the asbestos strike gave the international unions the opportunity of exonerating themselves from certain accusations which had often hindered them in their work in our province. Very often, in the midst of their organizing efforts, the international unions were accused either of anticlericalism or of communism. These accusations were usually made by the members of the clergy, and the organizers of the national unions were not about to refute them.[8] Thanks to the moral and material support which the international unions gave to the asbestos miners, the C.C.L. and the T.L.C. acquired a respectability which they had never enjoyed before.

Accordingly, when the asbestos strike was over, the general atmosphere in the labour movement was one of mutual confidence, and everything seemed to suggest a new era, in which the workers, by cooperative effort in dealing with their common concerns, would gradually obtain that place in society that was their due. The three central labour bodies had come to an understanding on a certain number of points. They were unanimous, for example, in declaring that the labour laws were inane and that they had to be changed. The problem of housing had been discussed in common. Inter-union meetings were held to lay the groundwork for the creation of a Labour College. In the face of the avowed hostility of the Duplessis government and the apathy of the Liberal opposition towards labour problems, it even seemed that there might be joint labour action in the political sphere.

The whole working class was in a state of great expectation, to such a degree that a manifesto of the Catholic Labour League, published at the same time, made an urgent appeal for inter-union collaboration and for the promotion of the common interests of all workers.

2/The changing pattern of union relations
Later developments showed just how illusory this optimistic outlook was. By the end of the summer of 1949, the Duplessis government had managed to make a breach in the common front. At its annual conference, the Provincial Federation of Labour, forgetful of the opinions it had expressed a few months previously, heaped praises on the provincial Minister of Labour, the Honourable Antonio Barrette. Soon afterwards Elphège Beaudoin, the President of the Federation, accepted a seat on the Labour Relations Board, a post he had earlier refused. His tenure was to be taken by Marcel Francq, who had succeeded him as president of the Federation. The arena of labour struggles was thus deserted by two men who had signed the statement of March 17 by which the organ of the Federation had denounced the "medieval conceptions" of Mr. Duplessis and Mr. Barrette, and had unmasked "the game of a government which has sworn to destroy the trade union movement in the province."

From this time on, the relationship between the P.F.L. and the other labour movements in the province, especially the C.C.C.L., gradually deteriorated. Attempts to promote the joint action of the unions became less and less frequent. In the ensuing years, however, the three labour bodies made several joint statements in favour of the Catholic Teachers' Association of Montreal. At the end of 1949, they even made a combined effort on the national level to have the federal rent control maintained, but this plan failed when the Duplessis government declared its intention of establishing provincial rent control. On February 20, 1951, the T.L.C., the C.C.L., and the C.C.C.L. presented a joint brief on price controls to the federal government. The railway brotherhoods also created a joint legislative committee. Finally, in the spring of 1952, a union belonging to the C.C.C.L. declared a strike against the Dupuis Frères store in Montreal, and here again the three labour bodies were brought together on the same platform, and indeed on the same picket line. A few months later, however, at its Hull convention in June, the Provincial Federation of Labour belied this show of solidarity: its delegates adopted a resolution denouncing the revolutionary mentality of the national unions, which the Federation claimed was akin to that of the communists. This time, the Duplessis group had succeeded in making deep divisions in the Quebec labour movement. This resolution, which was adopted on the eve of the provincial election of 1952, helped to mitigate the electoral defeat of Duplessis's men in the industrial centres.

The Provincial Federation of Labour claimed that its policy of collaboration with the government enabled it to obtain more for the workers than might be gained by a combative stance, like that adopted by the C.C.C.L. and the C.C.L. It did manage to win some minor advantages (for example, some amendments to the provincial Regulation of Rentals Act), but it was not able to obtain a single important concession from the government.[9] The Labour Relations Act, which all the central labour bodies denounced both for the way it was framed and for the way it was applied, was never modified to eliminate its anti-union aspects. None of its ambiguities—the delight of management lawyers—were clarified. Even more significant is the fact that the government never renounced its intention of getting the measures proposed in Bill 5 adopted into law. This is shown by Bill 60, passed in 1949, which deprived the employees of school and municipal corporations of their right to strike; and by Bills 19 and 20, enacted in 1954, which gave the Industrial Relations Board the right to withdraw the certificates of union recognition from those unions which had made an illegal strike, or which had officers who were communists. The last two laws were retroactive, and provided the government with what amounted to powers of blackmail over some labour unions.

These two bills were violently denounced by the C.C.C.L. and by the new Quebec Industrial Unions Federation (a provincial federation which held its charter from the C.C.L.). They provoked a certain reaction among the members of the Provincial Federation of Labour, but it was no more than a short-lived return to consciousness in a movement that was becoming more and more lethargic.

The relations between the C.C.C.L. and the C.C.L. developed in another direction. These two movements did not agree completely in their opinions, nor had they even achieved a close understanding on matters of thought and action. On the contrary, they remained sharply distinct from one another. Different outlooks shaped their infancy, and they are still deeply imbued with the peculiar spirit which engendered them. They may share, for example, the same point of view regarding labour legislation, and their attitude towards the Duplessis government may be substantially the same, but they do not have the same ideas about the labour movement's political role. Since 1943, the C.C.L. "recognizes the C.C.F. Party as the political arm of Labour in Canada."[10] The C.C.C.L., on the other hand, shied away from politics for a long time, and today seems to favour, at least as an ideal, the eventual establishment of a new political organization, better adapted to the needs and mentality of our province. Meanwhile, the C.C.C.L. decided, in the elections of 1952, to support those Liberal candidates who were in favour of the reforms which it recommended. At the present time, however, some of its bolder militants are drawing close to the C.C.F., the Quebec wing of which has taken the name of Parti social démocratique (Social Democratic Party).

In general, the relations between the C.C.L. and the C.C.C.L. since 1949 have been courteous, indeed cordial, and the two organizations have taken every opportunity for joint action, where their views coincided on a specific issue. At the end of 1952, for example, the member unions of the C.C.L. gave their moral and material support to the strikers at Louiseville, who were affiliated with the C.C.C.L., and in 1953 specialists from the C.C.C.L. were active in a labour education institute established by the United Steel Workers of America (C.C.L.-C.I.O.), for the benefit of the striking miners of Rouyn-Noranda.

The strike at Rouyn-Noranda showed what a profound effect the asbestos conflict had had on the imagination of people in some sectors of the international labour movement. Five years after the asbestos strike, the miners of Abitibi were filled with the same spirit that had animated the workers at Asbestos and Thetford Mines. They even retained the services of René Rocque for the duration of their strike;

Rocque was a former organizer of the C.C.C.L., and his name is indissolubly linked with the events of 1949. Jean Marchand and Rodolphe Hamel, of the C.C.C.L., were invited to address a meeting of the strikers, and they were vigorously applauded.

A certain rivalry continued to exist in spite of the new spirit of cooperation, but this rivalry was of a more normal kind. It frequently served the interests of the workers, because of the emulation which it created among the unions. The two bodies have been involved in several hard-fought struggles against one another. The most remarkable of these occurred in the summer of 1950, when the United Steel Workers of America made an unsuccessful attempt to supplant the C.C.C.L. union in the aluminum industry at Arvida. Both sides put up a stiff fight, but a fair one. Instead of accusing one another of scabbing and communism in their usual pre-1949 style, the two groups duelled with more reasoned arguments. The United Mine Workers emphasized the numerical and financial weakness of the C.C.C.L. from a continental point of view, and showed off their own vast resources which could be used to ensure that the rights of labour were respected. The C.C.C.L. denounced the United Mine Workers as an international union, and stressed the fact that among the rank and file many of the decisions affecting its internal policies largely depended on American leaders. The C.C.C.L. also drew attention to the advantages of an autonomous Canadian organization, and thereby managed to retain the confidence of the mine workers of Arvida. We should add, however, that without the intervention of the clergy, things might have turned out quite differently . . .

Since the asbestos strike, the relations between the C.C.C.L. and the C.C.L.-Q.I.U.F. (Quebec Industrial Unions Federation) group have remained within the limits of armed truce, courteous rivalry, and occasional joint effort. Their collaboration included a joint denunciation, by the Montreal Labour Councils of these two organizations, of the preferential treatment which the Labour Relations Board gave to the Montreal Association of Catholic Educators, at the expense of the Montreal Catholic Teachers' Association, headed by Léo Guindon. The two bodies also organized a march on Quebec City in 1954, to protest against Bills 19 and 20. The high point of this march was a mass meeting held at the Palais Montcalm in Quebec City, which was attended by labour representatives from every corner of the province.[11] This joint campaign of protest was subsequently carried on at the provincial level.

Many officers of the C.C.L.-Q.I.U.F. were eager to establish good relations with their opposite numbers in the C.C.C.L., as is shown by the following incident. The president of the Montreal Labour Council

(C.C.L.-Q.I.U.F.), who was attempting to establish closer ties with the so-called international organizations as a means of combatting the C.C.C.L., made an attack on Gérard Picard, its president. He only succeeded in arousing the indignation of his fellow members against himself, and was ousted from his presidency of the Council shortly afterwards.

The asbestos strike was thus a turning point in the relationship between the C.C.C.L. and the C.C.L. The C.C.L. (which plays approximately the same role in Canada as the C.I.O. in the United States) was born of the Depression, founded on a totally new conception of labour action, and dedicated by its very nature to organizing industrial unions. It was thus deeply concerned for the well-being of the individual person,[12] and was prepared to understand the new outlook of the C.C.C.L. as soon as it revealed itself.

As we have seen, the strike initiated a complete change in the relationship between the C.C.C.L. and the T.L.C. (a kind of Canadian counterpart of the A.F.L.). Prior to 1949, the T.L.C. in Quebec (the Provincial Federation of Labour, P.F.L.) readily accused the C.C.C.L. of making deals with the employers and government. The C.C.C.L. usually replied by asserting that the T.L.C. was communist. Today the situation is completely altered. The P.F.L. now attacks the C.C.C.L. for its revolutionary intrigues, and the C.C.C.L. accuses the P.F.L. of entering into collusion with the employers and with the government.[13]

In our province, the relations between the C.C.L. and the T.L.C. have always been characterized by that difference of opinion which led a group of American leaders of the A.F.L. to break away some fifteen years ago and create a new labour organization for the American worker, the C.I.O. The dispute between the two groups set the adherents of craft unions (A.F.L.) against the supporters of industrial unions (C.I.O.). In the course of time, this quarrel subsided as the A.F.L. came more and more to recognize that industrial unions were a necessary development,[14] and the C.I.O. was led to assign more importance to the wage differential between skilled and unskilled workers in framing its agreements with the employers. The A.F.L. was still heavily influenced by a whole slew of craft unions, which divided up a very large part of its membership into small compartments. The C.I.O. still criticized the A.F.L. for continuing to put up with this obsolete formula, which enabled union officers to barricade themselves within their craft union and to ignore the fate of their fellows, even though they were affiliated with the same organization.[15] The same kind of strong animosities existed in Canada between the C.C.L.-Q.I.U.F. group and the T.L.C.-P.F.L. group. In our prov-

ince, there were incidents like the Gaspé Copper affair, in which a
P.F.L. union took advantage of a sympathetic attitude on the part of
employers and government to supplant a union belonging to the
Q.I.U.F. Such incidents did not further the cause of reconciliation.

As we have seen above, the C.C.L.-Q.I.U.F. group worked closely
with the C.C.C.L. in the legislative and political spheres to bring
about a defeat of government policies, while the T.L.C.-P.F.L. group
openly courted the Duplessis machine.

The events that occurred in our province since 1949 made it clear
that the future of inter-union relations was to be sought in the sympathetic feeling which grew up at that time between the C.C.C.L. and
the C.C.L.-Q.I.U.F., and which grew stronger with each passing day.
From 1949 to the present time, the relations between these two groups
have steadily improved as they came to have a deeper understanding
of their common interests, and as they acquired a better insight into the
nature of their respective roles, and were thus able to define the
character of their coexistence, and to note both the points on which
they differed and the areas in which they were prepared to collaborate.
Unless they were able to win over the members of the third federation
(T.L.C.-P.F.L.), however, the C.C.C.L. and the C.C.L.-Q.I.U.F.
could not hope to achieve decisive political results in a short space of
time. In particular, it seemed unlikely that political action on the part
of the labour movement would rapidly attain its goals as long as the
Provincial Federation continued to be a rather docile ally of the Duplessis government.

Now that the international labour bodies have decided to merge, all
of these problems must be looked at in a new light. These last developments are discussed below.

IV/Perspectives for the future

We can gain some idea of the future development of inter-union relations in our province by looking at the directions that the various
labour movements are taking, and the positions that they occupy with
respect to one another. These data would in themselves be sufficient to
analyze the problem if Quebec were truly autonomous, but this is not
the case. The economy of our province is becoming more and more
dovetailed into the structure of the North American economy as a
whole, and whether we like it or not, we have to consider the problems
of business, and therefore the problems of unionism, in a continental
context. We can only exercise a limited influence over our destiny. If
we confine our thinking to a single province, and look at the problem
of trade unionism in provincial terms, we are condemning ourselves to
a state of ignorance about our present situation and our future pros-

pects; allowing ourselves to be lulled by illusions; and, assuredly, making ourselves the playthings of unknown, and therefore invincible, forces.

We should not, of course, lose sight of the trends in the labour movement in our province. They are of great importance, because our social and labour legislation originates, for the most part, with a provincial government. We must, however, consider this local problem within the framework of the overall problem, and examine the inter-union relations in our province in the light of the inter-union relations which exist on the North American continent as a whole.

1/The problem of amalgamation

While people in our province were still weighing the chances of a unified action on the part of the unions, an event of great importance occurred in the United States. This development suddenly confronted the world of labour with a new problem: the question now facing unionists was no longer whether there would be joint action among the labour bodies, but whether there would be a pure and simple unification of the labour movement. The two great labour bodies, the C.I.O. and the A.F.L., decided to amalgamate.

This decision, which was taken in the United States, necessarily set in motion a similar attempt in Canada on the part of the T.L.C. and the C.C.L. Meetings were in fact held on the national level, and the executives of the two bodies came to an agreement which was subsequently ratified at their respective annual conferences in 1955. In this way, the amalgamation of the T.L.C. and the C.C.L. in April 1956 gave birth to a new central labour body, the Canadian Labour Congress.

How, then, did the creation of this Congress affect the C.C.C.L.?

Although the C.C.C.L. draws almost its entire membership from Quebec, it is still recognized as a national movement. Because of its numerical importance, it presents a brief to the federal government every year in which it outlines the legislative demands of its members, just like the T.L.C. and the C.C.L. It is thus directly affected by the question of amalgamation, but up to the present has not expressed its point of view on this issue. It has not yet been formally invited to join the new amalgamation, but the "amalgamation agreement" specifies that "all the other union organizations in Canada, whether local, provincial, national or international, may become members" of the new Canadian Labour Congress.

At first glance, it is hard to see how the C.C.C.L., which regards strictly Canadian union autonomy as one of its basic principles, could become affiliated to a Congress which, though insisting on its constitutional autonomy, groups unions which, for the most part, are Canadian branches of international unions dominated by an American leadership. The present international situation should also give the C.C.C.L. cause to adhere to its principles of autonomy. Everybody knows that the views of the great American labour body on international issues are roughly identical to those of the government in Washington. To a certain extent, it disseminates these ideas to both its American and Canadian members through the distribution of papers like the *C.I.O. News,* the *A.F.L. News,* etc. The C.C.C.L. does not fully endorse the foreign policy of Washington—far from it.

This does not imply that the senior officials of the C.C.C.L. are hostile to the American labour movement. They are aware of the considerable debt that we owe to the A.F.L. and the C.I.O. in the United States, and to the T.L.C. and the C.C.L. in Canada; they have been largely responsible for making us aware of the need for trade unionism. These organizations have devoted a great amount of time and money to the development of our own labour movement, especially when it was in its infancy, and the C.C.C.L. itself gained much from the lessons offered by the development of the American labour movement. The C.C.C.L. is not concerned with denying the indebtedness of the Canadian labour movement to the mother organization, but rather with repaying this debt in the manner of every self-respecting son who repays his debt to his parents: by leaving them to establish his own home.

2/Possible solutions

Some of the international unions have proposed the following solution. Within the groupings of both the C.C.L. and the T.L.C., there were a certain number of purely Canadian unions which coexisted with the unions affiliated to organizations in the United States. These internationals believe that the new Canadian Labour Congress could develop a basically pluralist formula of organization, which would enable the C.C.C.L. to join the new group without sacrificing its principles. Several of the large American federations already grant their Canadian affiliates a considerable measure of autonomy, both in the management of their internal affairs and on the level of national policy. It is, moreover, undeniable that the T.L.C., under the direction of Percy Bengough, has become more and more independent of its American connections. As for the C.C.L., it has always guaranteed its international affiliates that they would have autonomy vis-à-vis the American sector. A case in point would be the United Mine Workers, which have always been affiliated with the C.C.L. in Canada, while in the United States the American branches of this union were affiliated with the C.I.O., then transferred their affiliation to the A.F.L., and later transferred it back again to the C.I.O.

In short, there already exists a powerful tendency towards autonomy within the "international" unions, much stronger than most people imagine. The C.L.C. expressly defines itself as "a completely autonomous central labour body," and it is possible that its impulse towards independence would be unaffected by the decision of the C.C.C.L. to join or not to join it.

In any case, it is unlikely that the C.C.C.L. would agree to join the rest of the Canadian labour movement unless it obtained a number of important guarantees. Up to now, its complete autonomy has enabled it to pursue its own ideals, and it is not likely that it would agree to an amalgamation if this fusion threatened to hinder its freedom of action and weaken its influence over its members.

What would become of the C.C.C.L. if the new Canadian Congress of Labour were not able to make these guarantees? The growth of the C.C.C.L. is due, in part, to the divisions which existed among the international unions. If the other central labour bodies succeed in resolving their differences and in undertaking a large-scale organizing campaign, the C.C.C.L. could find itself in a very awkward predicament. The least one can say is that it would have to sustain assaults which would threaten its own survival, and consequently the survival of the values which it embodies.

profound aspirations to a united labour movement, merely for the pleasure of obtaining more quickly an independence which they feel is already within their grasp, or which, perhaps, they feel they already have to a sufficient degree. Moreover, the idea of joining a new central labour body, to be dominated by French Canadians from the start, would be repugnant to most of these unions.

3/The principles of effective action

The C.C.C.L. may decide purely and simply to remain apart, to amalgamate with the other Canadian organizations, or to found a new Canadian labour congress. In any case, it is clear that it must adopt a very open and positive attitude if it is to fulfill its specific mission and effectively serve the principles which inspire it. The history of the C.C.C.L. amply demonstrates the fact that its progress is intimately associated with the realism of its thought, which is indispensable to a dynamic course of action.

One fact should retain the attention of those who choose to speculate on the future course of events. The leaders of the C.C.C.L. made a vigorous attempt to rectify its ideology, and were so successful that it was able win a respectable place in the world of organized labour.

This new realism, however, has yet to make a profound impression on the rank and file. The C.C.C.L. still has a great number of unions in its membership, especially in the smaller centres, which have hardly advanced beyond the outlook which prevailed when they were founded, and which still adhere, practically speaking, to the narrow nationalist principles of yore. These elements constitute a wing of the C.C.C.L. which has enough coherence within itself to place considerable limits on these new directions.

In the present state of affairs, these reactionary elements are a serious menace to the survival of the C.C.C.L. Wherever they have had the upper hand, they have done little to meet the real needs of the workers, and have gravely compromised the position of their movement in the eyes of the other groups. One can imagine what would happen if a conservative wing of the C.C.C.L., committed to nationalism and denominationalism at all costs, managed to exert its influence over a substantial part of the membership; went on to denounce all open-mindedness as cowardice, and every honourable compromise as an abdication; and succeeded in discrediting any new directions in thought which aimed at bringing the actions of the C.C.C.L., in one way or another, more into line with the activities of the Canadian labour movement as a whole. The effectiveness of this labour movement would be destroyed for a long time to come.

The amalgamation of the T.L.C. and the C.C.L. has created serious problems for the C.C.C.L. on the national level, but it has given rise to no less serious difficulties on the provincial level for the two federations which are directly involved in the merger, the Provincial Federation of Labour (T.L.C.) and the Quebec Industrial Unions Federation (C.C.L.). As we have seen above, these two groups in Quebec have found themselves at opposite ends of the spectrum in the last few years, both in matters of principle and in collective action. The Q.I.U.F. took a firm stand against the labour and social policies of the Duplessis government, while the P.F.L. paid court to the government. One wonders how these two attitudes could be reconciled within the framework of one and the same provincial federation. It is not easy to see, for example, how the C.C.L., in the name of trade union unity, could abandon its principles for others which are radically opposed to them. In spite of these difficulties, the two groups seem to have decided to attempt a reconciliation. This tentative step has, to say the least, an uncertain future. An understanding, if it is achieved, will not be arrived at smoothly.

It seems evident, then, that the effectiveness of the labour movement in our province depends upon a more intensive pursuit of the dialogue which has already begun between the C.C.C.L. and the present members of the C.C.L. This development offers the best chances for a course of action on the part of labour which will lead to an improvement of the social and labour legislation in our province, and a more effective application of these laws. The workers in our province have everything to gain from a situation in which these two groups acquire a growing understanding of their common interests, and are able to define, through a steadily increasing grasp of their respective roles, the manner of their life together, and to specify the points on which they differ, as well as the areas in which they may undertake joint action.

It is interesting to note how, in the course of time, these two groups have drawn progressively closer to one another in their thinking. The Q.I.U.F., for example, which is dominated by international unions, was at one time fiercely opposed to any form of Quebec nationalism. In March 1954, however, it presented a brief to the Tremblay Commission in which it recommended a fiscal policy which would recon-

The C.C.C.L. might well propose another solution: it could put forward, at the appropriate moment, the idea of a labour congress comprising those unions that are exclusively Canadian. Its program would be designed to attract the other non-international unions, and perhaps even some of the international unions, if they could be persuaded to separate from their American sections.

The most important argument against breaking off the American affiliations is that the Canadian workers are economically stronger, for making their demands, if they belong to unions that have hundreds of thousands of members in the United States. There is some truth in this argument, but perhaps not as much as is claimed. There is a limit to the amount of money, collected for the most part in the form of American dues, that the American unions can afford to do without in order to help the Canadian workers. For all practical purposes, these amounts cannot indefinitely exceed the contributions of Canadian members to the central American bodies.

The C.C.C.L. has also shown that a purely Canadian labour movement can not only survive, but can pursue a course of effective action. There is nothing terribly frightening about the fact that the financial resources of this organization are rather limited, once the course of action has been set in motion, as is actually the case. The attempt to establish an exclusively Canadian congress of labour might well involve its founders in a few financial difficulties, but we should not forget that the central American labour bodies have their financial troubles as well, and their needs are a match for their large income.

This solution is, however, a rather theoretical one, and if people tried to put it into practice, it would probably fail. It is, in fact, extremely unlikely that the unions which belong to the new C.L.C. would be attracted by the prospect of a change of allegiance which would be so radical and so expensive, and which would frustrate their cile the concern for provincial autonomy with the requirements of a federal control of the Canadian economy. The C.C.C.L., on the other hand, was founded in a nationalist spirit, and yet did not hesitate, a few years ago, to call a strike against the Dupuis Frères stores of Montreal, which had long been known as a distinguished bastion of nationalism. More recently, in the conflict between the newspaper *Le Devoir* and the Union typographique Jacques-Cartier (Jacques Cartier Printers' Union, T.L.C.), the C.C.C.L. took a straightforward stand in favour of the typographers, and advised the members of its affiliates not to cross the picket line.

We see, then, how the C.C.L.-Q.I.U.F. group developed an awareness of the peculiar problems of French Canadian society without giving up its basic principles, and how the C.C.C.L., while also remaining true to its fundamental principles, did not hesitate to violate the taboos of nationalism when these taboos would have required it to inhibit its own practical effectiveness. In other words, these two organizations are finding more and more common ground, and their cooperative effort might well give birth to a political and social action which could have a decisive effect on our society. A prerequisite of this dialogue, once more, is that the C.C.C.L. as a whole decide to follow a positive course of action once and for all, and that it free itself of its heavy incrustations of doctrine. In this way, it will be able to enter the real world of today's trade unionism.

4/Conclusions
As we have seen, the spirit expressed by the Quebec labour movement in its declaration of March 17, 1949, the seeds of life which the asbestos strike either sowed itself or revealed in our society, have not yet yielded the expected harvest. The history of the last few years has shown that there was much self-deception and naive idealism in the expressions of mutual goodwill which were made at the time. The important thing, however, is that this spirit has not vanished completely, but has slowly but surely gained ground. It has refined itself to the point where the labour movement has been able to use it as a basis for more and more concrete, realistic, and reasoned collective actions.

The first thing on a list of priorities is the last to be achieved in practice. We should never lose sight of the fact that the labour movement is forever in the process of becoming, and that in those areas precisely where it has enjoyed the greatest and most complete development, it is still far from achieving the goals which were set for it by its founders and prophets. Nevertheless, in this twentieth century of ours, in spite of its errors and setbacks, it is the movement which *is making* History, and which will leave the deepest imprint on the society that is coming into being before our eyes. The basic principle common to all the labour movements worthy of the name is the promotion of the interests of the working class through the collective and democratic actions of the workers. Starting from this fundamental principle, the movement will be carried forward irresistibly by its internal logic. For this reason, we are justified in regarding the future of inter-union relations in our province with optimism.

Addenda

Since we wrote this chapter (summer 1955), the optimism we then expressed has grown stronger for a number of good reasons. As we write these lines (April 1956), a Canadian Press dispatch informs us that Gérard Picard and Jean Marchand, the President and the Secretary of the C.C.C.L. respectively, will soon meet with Claude Jodoin, the President of the T.L.C., and Donald McDonald, Secretary of the C.C.L., to discuss the possibility of affiliating the C.C.C.L. to the new Canadian Labour Congress.

Of the three solutions available in the face of union amalgamation, the C.C.C.L. has, after mature reflection and several months of deliberations, chosen that which will bring it into closest contact with the realities of North American trade unionism. The C.C.C.L., however, does not intend to join the new, unified organization unless it is admitted "as an organic whole," in other words, with due respect for its own spirit and its own structures.

The productive dialogue established between the C.C.L. and the C.C.C.L. has once more borne fruit. If the C.C.C.L. is accepted into the C.L.C. on such conditions, the credit for this development must largely go to the reciprocal understanding which exists between the two groups. We learned quite recently, for example, that the Montreal Labour Council (C.C.L.) is making a detailed study of the problem of the C.C.C.L. affiliation, and that most of the executives of this group, who represent a very important part of C.C.L. opinion in Quebec, declared themselves in favour of admitting the C.C.C.L. Their point of view, in essence, is that 100,000 workers should not be set aside for "technical" reasons.

All the indications suggest, then, that the Canadian labour movement will soon pass through a decisive stage on the road to full maturity. In a country like ours, such a maturity necessarily implies the ability to reconcile the pursuit of unity with respect for valid differences. This pluralist vision is an essential element of our destiny.

It was present, in an embryonic form, in the federation principle which has given birth to modern Canada. It is comforting to note that this principle seems likely to go beyond the purely legal and constitutional limits within which it was confined for so long, and to become embodied at last in popular movements (like the cooperative and trade union movements), through which the Canadian people eminently expresses its real diversity.

This militant people is at last acquiring a face of its own, and finding its own voice. In the next stage of its development, it must find a politics which gives expression to its collective personality, and which answers its real needs. Everything leads us to believe that this new politics is gestating, and that we may now announce the decline, sooner or later, of the political parties which are governed by an "aristocracy" and financed by the big corporations. The future of politics in Canada belongs to those movements which will draw their support, both financial and ideological, from active memberships which are directly representative of the dynamic groupings of the electorate, and which are educated to act within the framework of democratic movements.

Notes to Chapter X

[1]At the time that this chapter was written, the integration of these two central bodies had been accepted by their respective general meetings, but was not due to take effect until April 1956. We will discuss this question in Part IV of this chapter. In the meantime, it is useful to consider these movements as separate, for even if the merger becomes a fact in law, it will not alter the characters and the intelligence of individual men. The destiny of the new Congress will depend on the forces which we should examine at work in the separate Congresses.

[2]Let us recall briefly that Bill 5 proposed a labour code, in other words it combined in a single piece of legislation the laws which formerly governed industrial relations, to which it added a certain number of amendments.

It goes without saying that the labour movement was not consulted on the framing of the new bill. It has ever been said that the Minister of Labour, the Honourable Antonio Barrette, had not received any communication from the labour movement before the final draft of the bill was written. The labour movement, which considered that the former laws were already too restrictive, was violently opposed to the proposed amendments, which would have hindered its action even more.

We will see later on that although the actions of the central labour bodies forced the government to withdraw its bill, Prime Minister Duplessis was still able, in the ensuing years, to obtain the adoption of the majority of the above measures, through Bills 60 (in 1949), 19 and 20 (in 1954). On the other hand, another projected labour code, which was prepared with the collaboration of representatives of management, labour, and government, aided by sociologists, and including a certain number of compromises considered acceptable both by employers and employees, has spent several years languishing in governmental files.

[3]This inter-union conference was a real improvisation. Bill 5 was presented to the legislative assembly as a surprise, and the officers of the unions did not have the time to give a precise structure to their coalition. The inter-union conference was created in the face of the absolute necessity of making a common front against the assaults of the Duplessis government. Accordingly, it was not an organization in the strict sense of the term. Under normal conditions, it should have ceased to exist once Bill 5 was withdrawn, but as we shall see later on, this establishment of contacts between labour organizations enjoyed an unexpectedly new lease on life.

[4]On February 23, during a debate in Parliament on Bill 60, Mr. Duplessis directly attacked the leaders of the C.C.C.L. who were involved in the strike. *La Tribune*

325

reported the following day: "In speaking of the labour leaders, the Prime Minister said that some of them live by the worker instead of living for the worker." *Le Soleil,* on the same day, reported the words of the Prime Minister as follows: "Several leaders of the Catholic unions are saboteurs rather than labour leaders." Mr. Barrette took it upon himself to reply to a question by René Chaloult, then a member from Lothinière: "The chaplains are putting up with the situation, but they are sorry about what is happening. They have informed us that they will endure the present state of things until affairs are settled, and believe me they will be!"

On February 25, the chaplains of the C.C.C.L. and all the chaplains of the dioceses and of the Federation replied to Mr. Barrette that in their opinion the C.C.C.L. was on the whole applying "the social thought of the Church in a very satisfactory way" and that it was "competently guided in this direction by its present leaders."

[5]It may be said *in general* that the Provincial Federation of Labour (P.F.L.) includes the Quebec locals of labour unions which, on the national level, are affiliated with the Trades and Labour Congress (T.L.C.), and which in the United States are affiliated with the American Federation of Labour (A.F.L.).

To simplify matters in a similar way, it can also be said that the Quebec Industrial Unions Federation (Q.I.U.F.)—founded only in 1952—includes the Quebec locals of those unions which on the national level are affiliated to the Canadian Congress of Labour (C.C.L.), and which in the United States are affiliated with the Congress of Industrial Organizations (C.I.O.). For this reason, in the Province of Quebec, these unions are usually referred to as "international unions," and their members as "internationals," in contrast to the unions and union members of the Canadian and Catholic Confederation of Labour (C.C.C.L.), which includes only unions which are strictly Canadian, which are almost entirely located in the Province of Quebec; they are frequently referred to as "national unions."

We should add that there are a number of unions affiliated with the T.L.C. or the C.C.L. which are strictly Canadian in the sense that they are not tied in any way to unions in the United States.

[6]We may note in passing that the C.C.F. Party sent gifts to the strikers having a total value of approximately $200. The other parties, though they were much richer than the C.C.F., did not follow this example.

[7]This was the first time in the history of the C.C.C.L. that such a meeting was held.

[8]There were even cases of flagrant abuse of spiritual power, like the recruiting drives of the C.C.C.L., where parish priests threatened the wives of workers with a denial of the sacraments if their husbands joined the international unions.

[9]The Federation certainly claimed that the provincial rent control act was passed as a result of its efforts. In fact, the Duplessis government had not consulted the Federation in any way before it passed this law.

[10]Let us mention here that the slogans of the C.C.L. in favour of the C.C.F. in Quebec have had little effect. For this reason, many Quebec militants seem to have come gradually to favour the regrouping of union forces in a political movement which is better adapted to the mentality of the people of Quebec. Some people have even spoken in terms of creating a new political party in Quebec, in collaboration with the C.C.C.L. if possible, and with the leftist elements now in existence.

[11]The Provincial Federation of Labour decided not to participate in this demonstration. Prime Minister Duplessis congratulated it publicly on its abstention, and it managed to have a few minor changes made in the proposed bills. These amendments did not have any substantial effect on the anti-union aspects of these laws, which were in effect the same measures that the Federation had denounced in 1949, at the time when Bill 5 was

proposed.

[12]The last words of Philip Murray, president of the C.I.O. and the United Steel Workers of America, are instructive in this regard. A few hours before his death, Murray addressed a group of union organizers, warning them of the danger of losing sight of individual persons in an organization as vast as the C.I.O. "Stay close to the man in the shop," he said. President Harry Truman referred to him in public as "the Christian gentleman."

[13]There is some justification for this accusation. A few years ago, for example, the C.C.C.L. and the P.F.L. were engaged in a battle for the control of the Canadian Vickers plant in Montreal. On this occasion, the P.F.L. did not hesitate to accept the support of the employers in its struggle against the C.C.C.L. In spite of this aid, the P.F.L. managed to retain control of only a few craft unions in the plant, while the majority of workers joined the C.C.C.L.

As regards the P.F.L.'s criticisms of the C.C.C.L., we may note that the leaders of the national unions readily denounce the present structures of capitalist enterprise, and the stamp which these structures place on our society; they also state clearly that they firmly intend to work for a change in the present system of values. No person of sense would claim, however, that these officials are planning to overthrow the institutions of our society, even the bad ones, by violent means.

[14]We should point out that the A.F.L. had always contained a certain number of industrial unions, notably the International Ladies' Garment Workers' Union.

[15]It has even been noted that this excessive independence of the craft union favours the creation of real union "rackets"; the case of the longshoremen of New York, which inspired the film *On the Waterfront,* was a famous example of this. We should add that the longshoremen were expelled from the A.F.L. some years ago.

Epilogue
by Pierre Elliott Trudeau

The curtain has fallen at the theatre of the asbestos strike, but a host of images still crowds our minds.

The events were played out against the backdrop of an industrialized province; there can be no doubt of that. Those in charge of the spectacle, however, had taken pains to coach the players only in the declamation of pretty pastorals and patriotic harangues. They were not prepared, nor had they prepared us, for anything more than another entertainment to please our masters.

To our surprise, the three raps which introduced the play resounded through our province like a dynamite explosion.[1] The actors, a nervy bunch, suddenly improvised a proletarian drama. The audience grew impassioned, and divided into troubled factions. The stage was even invaded by a turbulent crowd of spectators who wanted to participate in a dramatic action which, they felt, affected their own liberties. Several of them must have been carried away by the collective enthusiasm, for having given some thought to the meaning of their commitment, they suddenly jumped down from the boards and were never seen there again. Henceforth, they made common cause with those who call for a return to the theatre of the bosses.

For many people, however, the drama at Asbestos was a violent announcement that a new era had begun. For this reason, the authors of this book wanted to write its history. For them, the asbestos strike means more than the memory of events which they witnessed or participated in, and more than an episode in their intellectual development or their social experience. For them, this strike is a turning point in the entire religious, political, social, and economic history of the Province of Quebec.

By way of an epilogue, then, I want to invite the reader to derive, from the mass of information we have provided, some lessons on the past, some reflections on the present, and some prospects on the future.

I/The past

I must confess that I am only interested in the past as a means of acting upon the future, in the sense that Gide understood it when he wrote: "The present would contain all futures if the past did not already project a history upon it."

We, the French Canadians, have a social history rich in errors which we must not repeat. The first chapter in this book has been especially devoted to pointing them out. The following chapters offered us a minutely detailed description of a crucial conflict of forces: they have enabled us to see how a present event can compel forces emerging from the past to make fundamental choices, and how pitilessly it renders obsolete whatever is incompatible with the future course of things.

The lessons contained in these chapters are self-evident, and I need not repeat them here. I would also have preferred not to deal again with the questions of the legality or illegality, and the morality or immorality of the asbestos strike, and would rather not waste my time making futile judgments on "those who were truly responsible" for the whole business. However, there are still so many people, in the so-called enlightened circles, who unhesitatingly make summary, and usually unjust, assertions about strikes, that I would like to take the opportunity, in dealing with a famous one, to emphasize, at least, the complexity of events which are too often judged as if they were simple.

1/Illegality

According to the terms of the Labour Relations Act, the asbestos strike was illegal. Lussier in his chapter, however, has provided us with a wealth of information showing that this illegality had been directly provoked, and subsequently followed, by all kinds of other illegalities which originated in government and management circles.

An analogous treatment could easily have brought to light a host of iniquities committed by government and management over a long period of years.

The employers in the asbestos industry had made several attempts to break the trade union movement, although it was recognized by the law. Dumont's chapter has made us familiar with some of their procedures: intimidation, delays, dismissal of unionized workers, lockouts, the fostering of company unions, negotiations with "workers' committees," etc. The president of the Canadian Johns-Manville Co. had an "employers' creed" of which he had a very high opinion, and which he boasted of applying.[2] In it, he displays a perfect contempt for trade unionism. In the light of his comments, his quotations from encyclicals seem the product of cynicism, like his claim: "We who have abided entirely by the law. ..."[3]

Dumont has also shown us the equivocal attitude of the federal government agencies in dealing with the unionists in the asbestos industry: the acceptance of the idea of "workers' committees," a lockout treated as an illegal strike, the arbitrary and contradictory decisions of the National War Labour Board, etc. In spite of all this, the federal Minister of Labour had the audacity, in the course of the strike, to wash his hands of the whole business by lecturing the parties to the dispute on vigilance, honesty, and justice ... (See the chapter by Beausoleil.)

The illegalities committed by provincial government agencies were legion. In addition to the farcical arbitrations which victimized the workers before the strike (see Chapter V) and the illegal acts denounced by Lussier, let us recall for the record all the incidents connected with the Riot Act. In law, the reading of this Act is an emergency measure, the purpose of which is to achieve *the immediate dispersal of a rioting crowd*. The Provincial Police authorities announced the reading of the Act *on the previous day*; they *assembled* people in front of the church to read them the Act; they arrested these people, who were *in no way in a state of riot, without giving them the time or the opportunity to disperse*; they also arrested other people *who were not even assembled,* but who were simply present in restaurants, in their houses, or on the sidewalks; and they had the nerve to *leave the Act in effect* for 53 hours! (See the account of Beausoleil.)

Criminal acts were also committed by policemen who beat up prisoners (see Appendix III); lawyers were forbidden to speak with their clients; citizens in jail were kept from appearing in court within the time limits prescribed by the law. A judicial comedy was played out by a Deputy Attorney General who, at a session of the Court in Sherbrooke in May 1949, had an arraignment of strikers preceded by an *ex parte* inquest into the good conduct of the policemen, not only in contravention of every rule of criminal and civil procedure, but with the goodwill of the presiding judge. We should also note the hateful discrimination of which René Rocque was a victim, not only during his detention (see *René Rocque, political prisoner,* quoted in Appendix I), but also at the time of his arraignment.[4]

Under these conditions, the provincial government's claim to be the benefactor of the asbestos workers must be regarded as an example of black humour.[5]

Still, the unionists in the asbestos industry went on strike illegally, did they not? Of course, and they were at fault in other ways as well. Who among their adversaries, though, is the one just man who is entitled to cast the first stone at them?

2/Responsibilities

The question of illegality is closely connected with that of responsibility.

Obviously the miners were responsible for the strike, in the sense that they decided to call it themselves, without waiting for the length of time demanded by the representative of the C.C.C.L. It is also evident, though, that the employers and governments which forced them into this extreme position are responsible as well. The asbestos miners went on strike so spontaneously in February 1949 because they had learned, by long and painful experience, that governments and employers alike regarded justice as nothing more than a by-product of force. Dumont has shown that the recourse to direct action is a theme which runs through the whole history of labour relations in the asbestos industry. There was a strike or lockout (sometimes several in the same year) in 1915, 1916, 1920, 1921, 1923, 1937, and 1938; in addition, there were many occasions on which people came to blows, and there were also the expulsions *manu civili*[6] of the managers: McNutt of Thetford in 1923, and Shoemaker of Asbestos in 1937. In the years immediately preceding the strike of 1949, when the exercise of the right to strike was more closely regulated, the workers still had to resort to it on several occasions: a strike (and two lockouts) at East Broughton in 1942, because an employer refused to sign a collective agreement with the union; a strike at Thetford in 1945, to get the National Wartime Labour Relations Board to stop beating around the bush and order that a vote on representation be taken; strikes at Asbestos and at Thetford in 1946, which forced the National War Labour Board to revoke its arbitrary decisions; strikes at Thetford in 1948 to obtain the Rand formula for the assessment of union dues, which was needed because certain employers seemed to be favouring pro-management unions.

It is important to emphasize that a very large number of these strikes were called, not to support excessive demands, but to obtain recognition of the pure and simple fact of trade unionism. (We have even seen that some strikes were pre- or para-union demonstrations which had been started instinctively by a proletariat at its wits' end.) This fact explains the touchiness of the unionists (which non-specialist readers might, perhaps, have judged excessive) regarding the employers' tactic of bypassing the union and addressing the workers directly, during the negotiations of December 1948 and January 1949.

For these reasons, I agree with the conclusions of Beausoleil, who sees the strike of 1949 as a decisive struggle for recognition. This opinion is corroborated by the course of events, which clearly shows that the managerial and government authorities did not fully recognize trade unionism: the Prime Minister of the province, for example, refused to receive the strikers' delegation on February 23, because its makeup did not appeal to him; and the president of the Canadian Johns-Manville Co. declared in May 1949 "that we prefer to come to terms with a *local* Catholic union,"[7] thereby setting aside the National Federation of Mining Industry Employees and the C.C.C.L., which had resources more likely to ensure that there would be equality between the parties to the negotiations.

Whatever may be thought of the responsibility for *starting* the strike, there remains the further accusation that the union leaders deliberately aggravated and prolonged it, through stubbornness or dishonesty.[8]

These assertions are contrary to the facts, as is clear to anyone who will recall the spirit in which the strike was called and the circumstances in which it was prolonged.

The asbestos workers believed that the strike of 1949—like the many strikes they had had before—would be of short duration. They were accustomed to walking out to show their discontent; the dispute would then be settled for better or worse, and they would return to work.

This illusion also explains the atmosphere of festivity and unconcern which characterized the first few days. This misapprehension as to the length of the strike did not take into account two new factors:

a) The managerial class in Quebec felt that it was about time to put a stop to the ambitions of the workers, once and for all. These ambitions had grown considerably in the euphoric social and economic climate of the postwar years. In 1949, however, the financial community began to fear that the halcyon days, when wages and profits could increase at the same rate, were over: it became a matter of urgent necessity to slow down the rate of wage increases. The asbestos companies also claimed that they had a special reason to be afraid: "It seemed certain that the strike was, in essence, not concerned with wages or working conditions, but was an attempt on the part of the labour leaders to deprive the proprietors of our companies of the use of them, unless we granted these labour leaders the right to dictate the way in which the proprietors may use their own companies, and *who* will administer them."[9]

b) The second new factor to affect the strike of 1949 was the desire of the provincial government to break the back of the militant trade union movement once and for all. Months before, the party of Duplessis had been returned to power by 51% of the vote, due especially to the rural voters. In spite of the fact that it held 81 seats out of a total of 91, this government was unable to get its inept and reactionary Labour Code (Bill 5) enacted, because public opinion had been alerted. It was therefore looking for a chance to avenge itself on the working class for this bitter humiliation; the illegality of the asbestos strike gave it its chance.

Without realizing it, the unionists in the asbestos industry—and the entire labour movement with them—were thus getting involved in a fight to the finish with adversaries in management and government who were determined to join forces and play a cautious game. In this juncture of circumstances, the strikers at Asbestos made a mistake when they occupied the offices of the Canadian Johns-Manville Co. on February 18. From the purely tactical point of view, it gave the Company the chance to make a request for the intervention of the Provincial Police, and the government the opportunity to grant it. This protection, which was not directly enjoyed by the rival companies in Thetford, seems to have whetted the greed of the Canadian Johns-Manville directors,[10] because from that time on this company (and this company alone) attempted to start up production again by using scabs, and drew freely on the classic repertoire of anti-union procedures, known by the infamous name of The Mohawk Valley Formula.

In the final analysis, this strategy was detrimental to the cause of management, for in creating this ever-explosive mixture of strikers, strikebreakers, and hostile policemen, it focussed the attention of union forces in the province, and even in the country, on Asbestos. In the meantime the asbestos unions, the National Federation of Mining Industry Employees, and the C.C.C.L. had come to realize what a trap they were in, and at a very early date they seem to have been prepared to end the strike providing simply that there was a return to the status quo. The companies and the government, on the contrary, seemed determined to press their advantage by refusing to accept anything less than an unconditional surrender. In Chapter V, and in the chapters of Beausoleil and Abbé Dion, we have learned that in the very first weeks of the strike the negotiations for settlement had begun to collapse because the government and the employers refused to agree that the return to work be accompanied by the usual guarantees against reprisals.

Many people believe that it is the *summum* of the art of war to annihilate the enemy. And weren't the employers and the government guilty of this intention? They wanted to take advantage of the opportunity which the battlefields of Asbestos seemed to offer them, to reduce the entire trade union movement to a state of servitude...

I am not, however, concerned with this question, but only with examining the accusation levelled against the union leaders, that they intentionally prolonged and aggravated the strike. It seems that this accusation loses its validity before the evidence that the unions were ready to accept defeat very early on, not on condition that they receive the honours of battle, as some people claim, but only that they escape with their lives. This fact is also plainly attested by the conditions that enabled the Nicolet Asbestos Mine to conclude an early settlement on June 6, and emerges even more clearly from the history of the negotiations undertaken in the last week of April (see the account of them in chapters V and VI). On this occasion, the unionists were prepared to give in all along the line, go back to work without any gains and without a contract, because the provincial Minister of Labour had promised that "the employers will rehire the workers without any discrimination based on their activities during the strike"... These negotiations were broken off on April 29 because, according to Maître Lespérance, representing the union, "it became clear that the Johns-Manville Company, represented by Maître Yvan Sabourin, Q.C., actually intended to reserve the option of using various forms of reprisal." Neither Maître Sabourin nor the Minister of Labour denies this assertion, but the president of the Canadian Johns-Manville Co. implied that it was false.[11] What is the truth of the matter?

Here again, the later course of events enables us to see the truth in retrospect. On June 27, in fact, the Company announced that its former workers "will be given back their old jobs as rapidly as possible in accordance with the requirements of production, and taking seniority into account"; and that this return to work "will take place without any discrimination based on activities during the strike." Now, on each of these points, as Sauvé's chapter has shown, the Company broke its word to a serious degree. After the fact, then, it revealed the attitude which it must have had at the time of the negotiations about the return to work, which took place during the preceding months.

Feeling the need to clear himself, the president of the Canadian Johns-Manville Co. had an "Explanation of the Agreement for the Settlement of the Strike" distributed. A sociologist described this explanation as preferring "mental reservations to a literal interpretation."[12] For example, to justify himself for not having given the strikers back their old jobs as he had promised, Mr. Brown explained in his pamphlet that "their occupation" meant any job whatsoever, and that "his" definition of seniority included "the demands of the job, the competence of the individual, the length of his service, and his family responsibilities, considered in that order." Finally, we have seen that it was not until February 25, 1952, that the Company agreed to put an end to its mental reservations. (The text of this agreement is quoted by Sauvé.)

In the light of these facts, we might well ask whether those who accuse the strikers, and especially their leaders, of having maliciously prolonged the strike, are not involved in a case of mistaken identity . . .

II/The present

One ought really to translate the famous saying of Clausewitz on war into the language of industrial disputes, and say: "The strike is no more than the continuation of negotiations by other means."

In the present state of society, in fact, it is the *possibility* of the strike which enables workers to negotiate with their employers on terms of approximate equality. It is wrong to think that the unions are in themselves able to secure this equality. If the right to strike is suppressed, or seriously limited, the trade union movement becomes nothing more than one institution among many in the service of capitalism: a convenient organization for disciplining the workers, occupying their leisure time, and ensuring their profitability for business.

Just as Capital can say: "Unless I make an acceptable profit in such and such a business, I will withdraw (by lockout or by withdrawing my investment) and operations will cease," so Labour should be able to say: "Unless I enjoy acceptable working conditions in such and such an enterprise, I will withdraw *and operations will cease.*" In other words, if Labour and Capital (taken as a whole on the level at which the negotiations take place: business, industry, region, etc.) are not in a position to determine themselves the *sine qua non* of their collaboration with one another,[13] negotiations do not take place between two free and equal contracting parties. Instead, one of the two parties imposes its will on the other, and this will is limited only by its own benevolence and by the prevailing economic environment. In such a situation, it is clear that a contingency is introduced into the guarantees of justice. It is, moreover, a fundamental axiom, though it is often not recognized as such, that every system of contract law as a provider of justice is based on the assumption of equality of status of the two parties to the contract:[14] without this equality, justice—if indeed there is any justice present—*never* proceeds from the contract.

From all this it follows that in industrial relations justice presupposes equality, which presupposes the right to strike, which presupposes that the workers have the right to "protect" their strike. Justifying scabs in the name of the freedom of individual workers is the act of ignorance, and for the most part of hypocrisy: of course the worker must be able to express his disagreement with the union by withdrawing and by seeking work where there is no strike in progress, just as the stockholder who is displeased with the management may transfer his capital elsewhere by a stock market transaction. On the other hand, just as it is impossible for a group of stockholders (old or new) to set themselves up as "lockout breakers" by the partial restoration of operations in a factory where the company is having a lockout, so it should be impossible for a group of workers to assure the operation of a factory as long as a strike is in progress there.

Several corollaries derive from these principles: 1—A law which justifies itself for limiting strikes by claiming that it limits lockouts in the same way is based on a sophistry, because the management can get around both the law and the collective agreement by calling its lockout by another name ("reduction" of investment, the closing of "unprofitable" shops, "innovations" in the techniques of production, etc.), while the union can never organize a concerted work stoppage without having it recognized as a strike.[15]

2—The objections which are raised against the different forms of union security (closed shop, preferential shop, etc.) and of assessing union dues (Rand formula, voluntary check-offs, etc.) tend in fact to prevent the workers from negotiating with the employers on terms of equality; these objections would be valid only if, at the same time, the capitalists' liberty was protected by allowing them to invest money in an enterprise in such a way that their funds would not be bound by the decisions of the management, in other words, if the capital of a business were divided up in the same way that people are trying to divide up labour.

3—Even if we assume the existence of a fair employment practices act and a state of perfect security for the unions, the strike is always more difficult to use than the lockout. The technical organization of a business is essentially authoritarian; notwithstanding the possibility of discord among partners or stockholders, the management still has, in the final analysis, complete control over the capital invested in the firm. The union, on the other hand, is essentially and always subject to the requirements of direct democracy. Those who suspect union leaders of calling strikes against the will of the members have never spent a week trying to go to the picket lines with workers who are cold and hungry, and who for the most part did not want to stop work.

4—The strike is an irksome weapon to those who use it, moreover, and negotiations between unionists and management are often conducted without the exercise of this equalizing device against the employers. As a matter of fact, the two parties do not run the same risk when a strike is in the offing, and they cannot both bluff with the same facility. By its very nature, Capital is led to "take a chance." Speculation and investment consist, precisely, in gambling with savings (which are almost always superfluous) in the hope of winning profits; moreover, the budgets (and the warehouses) of many firms contain reserves which tend to damp the effects of these risks. On the other hand, the union that plans a strike must call upon the workers to take a chance not with the superfluous, but with the essential: for them, the strike does not conjure up the possibility of less profits, but of more poverty (if not the truncheons of the police . . .) Both Capital and Labour can thus look upon the strike as a loss of consumption or as an investment for future gains, but the worker wagers with the food on his table, the employer with his bank account and his income tax. The two parties not only make considerably different wagers, but stake very different things as well. When a union loses a strike, it does not always disappear, but at the least it loses more or less all its vital forces, and the employer enters into the conflict with this end in view. When the management loses a strike (or lockout), however, its vitality is not essentially impaired: the workers cannot adopt the strategy of ruining the firm, since they depend on it for their livelihood.[16]

These theoretical considerations enable us to get a better grasp of the manner and extent of the change effected by the asbestos strike in introducing a new measure of equality and justice into industrial relations.

The chapters by Gérin-Lajoie and Dumont have shown us how Capital and Labour, each in its own way, were long involved in their own internal problems. We have also seen, though, especially in Gérin-Lajoie's chapter, how the interaction of these two factors simplified these problems: the companies were *obliged* to strengthen their financial policies *because* the trade union movement was growing stronger, and *vice versa*.

These creative tensions were not at work in the asbestos industry alone, but in the development of capitalist and trade union organizations throughout the province (see Chapter I). Economic history, in dealing with our society as elsewhere, has not sufficiently understood how indispensable the aggressive attitude of trade unionism was to the rise of industrialization. Those who rebuke the workers "for never being satisfied" forget that their very insatiability, as much as that of the capitalists, is responsible for the prodigious progress of the modern world in the fields of technology and material well-being.

The distribution of the fruits of this progress between the two equally "greedy" groups, however, involves problems which are never solved on more than a temporary basis. Fluctuations in the political, social, and economic spheres have as much effect as technological progress in making it necessary to reopen "negotiations" periodically and therefore to reevaluate the status of the negotiators. The first task of the labour movement is thus to ensure that, in the midst of this process and these fluctuations, it never loses its status as an egalitarian movement; this status is a condition of social justice.

In this sense, the asbestos strike has had a two-fold effect:

1—Short-term: it buttressed the negotiating power of the labour movement in the province, at the very moment when the business cycle was leading the employers to assert the primacy of capital. In this way, the impetus given to the trade union movement in the post-war years was prolonged for a number of years.

2—Long-term: it offered a proof in the Province of Quebec, for the first time and once and for all, that a *united* labour movement need not back down in the face of any combination of forces, whatever they might be, and however deep their roots in tradition, or great their support by the prevailing mores. In this way, a new and contemporary power asserted its control over our destinies, the demons that bedevilled the course of history in our province were exorcised, the spell cast on our present by our past was broken, and a host of creative powers were unleashed in all fields.

Let us reflect a moment on these two ideas.

The short-term effect, contained by a given institutional framework regarded as stable, becomes clear if we consider the decade which began with the war. Between 1939 and 1945, the peoples of the earth became more oriented towards the left, in other words, towards a more egalitarian distribution of the fruits of progress. In this period, in fact, "the people had to be given true pledges of its sovereignty to ensure that its enrolment in the machinery of total war would be effective. Governments suddenly paid unwonted attention to the 'plebs,' to such a degree that it became the object of much solicitude: the man of the people was the one who, finally, bore the burden of war, created the prosperity of nations, invested rulers with their power and the laws with their authority . . . In the course of time, however, the propertied classes, who controlled the means of communication, found they had a less urgent interest in devoting the man of the people to the task of saving the nation, and no longer reminded him of his rights and of his omnipotence. They began to hint to him that his extravagant demands had brought about inflation, and that industrial disputes benefitted nobody but the demagogues."[17]

1949 was precisely the year of change. In the business world, exuberance was replaced by caution, and economic conditions began to take a turn for the worse: the Korean War had not yet arrived to revive the sinking hearts of Wall Street and St. James Street. At this time, the people in the trade union movement were confronted with the choice of either stopping short in the face of stiffer resistance from the capitalists or of meeting their opposition head-on, and thereby asserting their ideal of social progress with increased vigour.

We have seen what the response was in the Province of Quebec. When the struggle began in the asbestos industry against the combined forces of management and government, all the people in the trade union movement—who had recently been united in the fight against Bill 5—felt an urgent need to throw themselves into the fray: they realized instinctively that here a struggle for equality was taking place which would determine the future course of industrial relations in the entire province. In actual fact, the labour movement showed a tenacity on this occasion which considerably enhanced its prestige at the negotiating tables for some years to come. Eventually, the oscillations of influence began again, once the course of events had modified the status of the negotiators. In 1952, as Boisvert has pointed out in his chapter, the unity of the labour movement was broken, and since that time defeats for unionism, like that at Louiseville, have given the employers renewed assurance that the labour movement is not invincible. These developments have had a manifest effect on negotiations.

The short-term effects, important as they are, are still of limited consequence; as we have seen, gains and losses can succeed one another rather rapidly. The asbestos strike, too, assumes the character of a turning point in our history especially on account of its long-term effects (i.e., those which do not recognize any institutional framework as unchangeable). In this sense, the stakes involved in the conflict of 1949 were immense.

For fifty years, the phenomenon of the Industrial Revolution had been creating problems in the Province of Quebec which had never really been faced, and the conservatism which imbued our social ideologies was equally typical of official attitudes towards all the problems created by a new order of things in the fields of thought, religious experience, artistic expression, economic structures, political reforms, etc.

It is true that "special" experiments had been made in various fields on a sporadic basis; on each occasion, though, the innovators either had to sacrifice any chance of influencing the community as a whole (e.g., Olivar Asselin, who saw his newspapers banned by the Church), or had to identify themselves, finally, with the traditional doctrines (e.g., Paul Gouin, who let himself be absorbed into the

National Union).

Nevertheless, the Second World War, that interrupter of tradition, produced the new awareness which has been discussed above. In various parts of the population and in several branches of human activity, groups or individuals were busy creating new structures. They did not, however, manage to coordinate their efforts, and there was a great danger that the end of the postwar period would see their scattered forces once more submerged in a relentless return to tradition. At this moment, a social disturbance on a large scale, but coming from within Quebec society itself, broke down the isolation of these groups, and provided them with a rallying point. The asbestos miners' revolt against an authoritarian company and government, at the very moment when the traditional reflexes should have resulted in obedience and submission to these acknowledged symbols of authority, seemed to be a matter which concerned everybody who believed that his hopes for the future should be grounded in liberty. The struggle in the asbestos industry arrived on the scene like a sliver of crystal in a supersaturated liquid: the Province of Quebec emerged from it clothed in new structures.

Clearly, and by definition, the long-term effects appeared only little by little. For this reason, we had to go back somewhat in time to realize just how far the upheaval of 1949 went beyond the social context in which it had arisen, and how, by overstepping the bounds of the institutions of the day, it forced them to readjust themselves to it. This explains why many men came to abjure their commitment of '49: they only realized later on just where the logic of their gesture was leading them.

Union militants, for example, who had felt it a matter of urgent necessity to assert the equality of working people *within* a conventional social framework, became worried as soon as they saw that the impetus for emancipation begun in '49 had to a great extent passed beyond the horizons of the known world. They lacked the courage to go forward with their membership towards an unexplored future: this explains why the Joint Conference of Organized Labour disintegrated, and how the contradictory directions analyzed by Boisvert arose.

Another example is furnished by those nationalist or clerical circles which had courageously supported the C.C.C.L. in 1949, but which afterwards realized that this movement had changed direction, and in its march to justice was striding beyond certain denominational and ethnocentric conceptions of equality. For this reason, they were quick to abandon their "state of grace" and to return to their usual level, as Pelletier has shown in his chapter.

An epilogue does not permit a detailed account of the social changes which have taken place within the Province of Quebec since 1949. However, I wish to add three paragraphs to the remarks of Boisvert and Pelletier, to give a sketch of where the trade union movement now stands in relation to the three institutions of our society which have been traditionally the most important.

Today, the Church in Quebec seems to us very divided. Among laymen, accusations of "reactionary" and "progressive" are vigorously bandied about. Among the clergy, the "resignation for reasons of health" on the part of Mgr. Charbonneau and the sudden death of Mgr. Desranleau have removed the two main pillars of the cause of labour from the scene. There remains, it is true, a brave and dynamic wing of the "young" clergy; a recent inquiry, though, has shown that while one scarcely now encounters union chaplains who speak contemptuously of "the mob" and who get involved in hiring scabs (as in the heroic age of Thetford described by Dumont), it is no less true that the trade union movement still suffers from the deep misunderstanding which prevails in clerical circles. "This general lack of understanding runs the whole gamut from apathy through distrust, fear, and sympathy to pity."[18]

The nationalist school appears to be a little less divided than the Church, perhaps because where social issues are concerned, it enlists scarcely any support from modern-minded people these days, and is taking progressively more conservative stances. The proof of this emerges from a brief examination of the two nationalist publications which displayed the greatest militancy at the time of Asbestos. On December 1, 1953, the editor of Le Devoir still thought that the ideal aim of the proletarian movement should be "to integrate itself into middle-class society"; a year and a half later, as Boisvert has mentioned, he put an end to negotiations with the workers on the newspaper by means of a lockout. This tactic was approved by all the "senior" editors of the newspaper, and on September 7, 1955, a political editor endorsed an opinion to the effect that "the strike is obsolete." As for L'action nationale, May 1951 saw Mr. Esdras Minville still writing in that publication, on the subject of businessmen, that "the present changes in society are due to them, and the society of the future will be to a great extent what they have been able to make it."[19] In September 1953, J.M. Léger created a major scandal in the League which controlled the review by bringing the solutions offered by socialism to the attention of his readers. Such a rigid attitude towards social issues is all the more unfortunate in view of the fact that these very publications show remarkable lucidity in their treatment of international politics, and that in the sphere of domestic politics, they have been almost alone in their courageous denunciations of the scabrous politicking of the old parties. It is this courage and lucidity in certain fields which inspire the occasional hope that some of these nationalists will one day come to realize that they will only be able to make the transition from the past to the future by means of social radicalism.[20]

As far as the State in Quebec is concerned, the present has done no more than reinforce its past anti-union attitudes. At the beginning of 1954, the Duplessis majority in the provincial Parliament took advantage of the dissension among unionists in the province to enact Bills 19 and 20, which embody the most reactionary aspects of Bill 5 (defeated at the time of the Joint Conference of Organized Labour). On this occasion, most of the members who belonged to the Liberal opposition tried once more to outdo one another in having the least to say.[21] As at the time of the asbestos strike, their watchword seemed to be: above all, no trouble with the bosses. This experience had at least the great merit of proving beyond the slightest doubt that where labour disputes were concerned, the categories of legality and illegality no longer had—under the regime of the day—any significance whatsoever, because in virtue of Bill 20, which was passed by the provincial Parliament on January 28, 1952, the legislator conferred *legality and retroactive effect* on an anti-union action on the part of the Labour Relations Board, an action which had been judged *illegal* and *invalid* by the highest court in the land![22] The union militants were thus confirmed in their belief that they should take a more and more active part in politics, and that unless they did so, the dice in the political crap game could always be loaded against them. In this field as well, the asbestos strike was a point of departure. At its convention in 1949, the C.C.C.L. struck its first civic action committee, which was transformed the next year into a political action committee; this orientation has been maintained since that time, much to the horror of the masters of orthodox thought. The Quebec Industrial Unions Federation (C.L.C.), which had formerly given a purely verbal and ineffectual support to the C.C.F. Party, moved towards a more effective political action at its 1954 convention, and the most dynamic elements in this movement came to advocate that the progressive political forces be brought together in the bosom of a new Left.

Our society, then, is in a state of unstable equilibrium, based on a present state of things which is torn between opposing lines of force. Since the asbestos strike, these lines have emerged in contradiction to one another with ever greater clarity and vigour.

Where can such a situation lead us?

III/The future

A social upheaval like the asbestos strike creates more problems than it resolves. It is true that at the time, our labour movement showed that it was capable of producing new structures, but we do not yet know how it will make use of this power. The foundations of Quebec society were shaken at Asbestos: what do people intend to use to replace them?

Of course, such question marks are no bother to those who, like the character in the *Soulier de Satin* (The Satin Pump), want the new, but resemble the old in every way. Behind the solid ramparts of the police and a certain theology, the propertied class is cleverly working to adorn the old system of ownership with new and less provocative finery. New schools of industrial sociology, for example, like that of Elton Mayo, have made enormous strides in overcoming the industrial worker's feelings of frustration and his anxieties of insecurity by giving him the impression that he is participating in the life of the firm for which he works. Very often, of course, the employers adopt these innovations more out of a desire to increase the productivity of their workers than from respect for their dignity as free men, but they still represent a real progress, and have at least the merit of putting the relations between management and unions on a different footing than the law of the jungle.

Such reforms, at Asbestos, have resulted in a steady improvement in industrial relations since 1949. The principle of seniority, for example, is now applied by the Canadian Johns-Manville Co. with an almost scrupulous respect for the rights of the workers. So, too, praiseworthy efforts have been made to improve the system of communications between ruling and subordinate groups, both in social and professional life.

Among trade unionists things were also getting better, as Sauvé has shown. The workers, feeling that they enjoy the respect of their employer, are less hostile towards him, and they can channel their creative energies in new directions. The unionists have thus taken an active part in the election of the mayor and aldermen, and now have control over the municipal administration. Of much greater significance is the fact that at the time of the provincial elections of 1952, the unionists obliged the Liberal machine to accept their candidate, whom they then elected to the Legislative Assembly. In short, the whole working class at Asbestos seems to possess an unprecedented self-confidence.

Is there not a danger, though, that the working class is heading down a blind alley even darker than the old, having lost the means to force the issues? A generation is growing up which has not lived through the heroic struggles of the trade union movement, and everything conspires to make it forget them. Because of the high salaries which are now paid in that city and the preference which is given to hiring local labour, the young people have little interest in continuing with their studies or in seeking wider horizons than the hills of Asbestos. The provincial MPP was elected, but thanks to a party which is completely indifferent to furthering the cause of labour. The working class "controls" the municipal council, but this council does not have a profound effect on the course of community life, and only participates in municipal affairs as the poor cousin. It is revealing, in this connection, that the Civic Centre—which entered the planning stages in 1950 and which will require a great amount of money for its construction—is the work of the Canadian Johns-Manville public relations committee. Furthermore, the executive of this Centre consists of twelve representatives of every stripe, of whom only *one* is a member of the municipal council![23]

In short, the society of Asbestos continues to develop within an authoritarian system. The machine is, of course, better oiled and the wheels do not squeak as much. It is an absolute monarchy in which the subjects eat cake and enjoy the high life, but still remain subjects and not princes. The union at Asbestos seems ill equipped to solve these problems, and yet are they not a sample in microcosm of the problems which, with variations from place to place, will confront, indeed are already confronting, the whole of Quebec society?

A great number of people, even among the working class, will say that these are the remarks of a man who likes to break up dancing in the round[24] (and I would agree with them if we lived in a static world, a world which moved precisely in the patterns of the round dance, where past successes assured future progress). In these circles, people will recall the enormous progress which has been made in the emancipation of the Quebec working class since the war. They will speak of a period of consolidation, of a modus vivendi with the political and financial powers based on mutual respect and understanding . . .

What sort of rubbish is this! After fifty years of servile and stupefied silence, have the mass of industrial workers but recently acquired the right to speak, only to hold their tongues with greater eloquence? At the very moment when Quebec society feels that it may catch up after generations of backwardness, are the gains of recent progress to be converted into a sterile conservatism, or into the traditional "je me souviens"? It is a matter of urgent necessity that we reject these counsels of quietude. We no longer live in a static world: we must go forward with the caravan of humanity or perish in the desert of time past. The current developments in technology and politics herald a future social and industrial revolution in comparison with which the previous one will seem but child's play. It is more vital than ever that we determine for ourselves what our place will be as men in this future world.

I will not say that our very lives are at stake, because men will manage to live whatever the cost; the things that change and die are faith, language, culture, the collective will to live, even dignity...

I shall not claim, either, that our tranquillity will be disturbed. Since Quebec is not sealed off from the rest of the world, we would likely be able to continue to rely on external influences in working out our actual destiny, and would not be forced into a bloody revolution against outmoded superstructures, as in nationalistic and Catholic countries like Spain, Mexico, Argentina, etc.: we have a safety-valve in a continental economy and in a federal constitution, where pragmatism, secularism, and an awareness of change are the predominant attitudes.

The only things at stake, then, are the values which we cherish to a certain degree, as individuals or collectively. The future will either thrust itself upon us, imposing its own standards, or we will win ourselves a place in this future with the values that we cherish. Because it concerns the society of Quebec, this dilemma is especially acute for those who defend a culture which insists on being specifically Christian and French Canadian.

The first chapter of this book emphasized how little these values contributed to the actual determination of our economic and social destiny. The following chapters have described a key episode in a history of social emancipation, which could have occurred solely as a result of forces arising from the industrial world, without any deviations caused by nationalism or denominationalism. This struggle had already begun in 1947, moreover, when the Quebec workers in the meat packing industry showed more solidarity with their fellow workers in the Protestant and English-speaking provinces than concern for the exhortations to autonomy voiced by *Le Devoir* and the provincial government.[25] The same battle was continued in 1952, when (French Canadian) workers called a strike against the bastion of nationalist employers (Dupuis Frères strike), and when (Catholic) workers accepted, as leaders, people who were said to be notorious communists (the Dominion Textile strike at Valleyfield).[26]

Such phenomena have occurred in relatively recent times in Quebec, but they are an inevitable part of the logic of trade unionism's development,[27] and they will appear in the future with ever greater frequency. Many people have already concluded from these events that the trade union movement is essentially materialistic, and that it lacks patriotism and a moral sense. It is therefore not inappropriate to reply that a culture is not necessarily oriented towards spiritual values simply because it pretends to be. A French Jesuit recently said that a civilization may boast many monks and priests, but if people do not have houses to live in, it is unworthy of our support.[28] It does not merit our support either, if the indigent cannot find a place in the hospitals, if the poor have no access to higher education, if men cannot find work, and if all the citizens cannot live as free men and equals before the law. It does not merit our support if it shows that it is not capable of introducing Christianity into the context of the new humanism of the technological age, but forces us instead to live in what the great Catholic historian H.I. Marrou has called "the Catholic ghetto."

Since the epithet of "materialists" is hurled at the union militants, we should also see who—in the course of social history in the Province of Quebec—has deserved this accusation. Is it those who have fought with all their heart to improve the condition and enhance the dignity of a proletariat bogged down in material problems; or the men of property who have preached the honour of doctrine and the palms of apostleship, while casting out trade unionism from the Church and the Nation?

Whose patriotism should be praised: the patriotism of the propagandists for the correct use of French, the apostles of the Achat chez nous program, and the missionaries for the return to the land; or the patriotism of obscure working-class families who have suffered countless hardships to ensure that our ethnic group might ride out the storm of the industrial age? Who was more patriotic, those who advocated reforms in the abstract, or those who created the tools by which the majority of the people might not only ennoble their condition, but eventually gain possession of their natural wealth and their financial and political institutions?

We might likewise ask: where were the upholders of spiritual values at Asbestos? On the side of a management which was quite willing to let the worker earn his daily steak as long as he did not aspire to deal with the forces of money on equal terms; or on the side of a trade union movement which naively believed that the time had come to go beyond purely material demands and lay the foundations for an egalitarian society?

As we can see, there are several ideas in our traditional scale of values which need revision, because many of them have a very debilitating effect on our capacity to adapt ourselves to the transformations of the future, and to become the masters of it.

Our social philosophy, for example, (which nevertheless associates the "right to manage" only with the right of property) recognizes as proprietors only those who—today the holders of a stock—will trade it tomorrow on the stock exchange; on the other hand, the workers who have invested the best years of their lives, their greatest efforts, and their finest hopes in a job or a profession, are not to have any property rights over this occupation, and may find themselves *expropriated without compensation* with the onset of a strike, a lockout, a business recession, or simply old age.

In the same way, our small-time moralists deplore the loss of "respect for authority" among the unionists who—refusing to accept the dichotomy between those who give and those who receive orders as inalterable—are doing all they can to broaden the base of this authority by giving the workers a share in management. These very learned doctors are not satisfied with opposing *industrial* democracy—they look with great disfavour upon any desire of the working class to play an effective role, at last, in *political* democracy by electing governments which no longer rule the majority of citizens against their will and without their consent.

In this way, theologians continue to defend the relatively recent system of private ownership of natural resources in the name of eternal values; they also condemn as socialist programs which aim only at making some of this wealth part of the common patrimony once more.

Clearly, when the revolution produced by automation, cybernetics, and nuclear energy has completely altered the foundations of the present regime of property and authority; when a certain amount of state planning has become an absolute necessity for controlling the chaotic conditions of the period of transition; and when the nationalization of the principal means of production has become an established fact, there will still be clerics around to proclaim, with an old text of Pius XI in hand, that the social doctrine of the Church has never ceased to be avant-garde. Perhaps there will still be some survivors of the "Survival" doctrine to dust off some forgotten text and make the same claims for nationalism.[29] In the meantime, however, these theorists will have done everything in their power to make the necessary transformations impossible, to discredit those who are preparing the way for them, and to give a bad conscience to those who support them.

Let us bear clearly in mind that there is no question here of proclaiming a new regime of industrial liberty, nor of advocating socialism, still less of sketching an economic theory of plenty for all. It is simply a matter of prosaically applying the lessons of the last fifty years to the present. If we refuse to base "the honour of doctrine" on a profound appreciation of reality, it we persist in condemning every new solution ex cathedra and without an impartial examination; if we withdraw into the realm of the a priori and the unreal; if we remain content with the present-day state of things and practice a systematic cult of the past; if we refuse to examine the rich alternatives offered by the future; if, finally, we continually identify Catholicism with conservatism and patriotism with the refusal of progress, we will lose by default the game now played by all cultures, and the concept of "French Canadian," along with the Catholicism which is intimately associated with it, will ultimately prove to be a thing of slight importance.

A whole generation hesitates on the brink of commitment. We hope that this work has offered it some basic principles to assist it in making its decision. Let me add this: in our joint effort to produce this book, my comrades and I have not fallen victim to that malady which a cynical turn of thought is beginning to call *the opium of the intellectuals*. Though "our heart is with those who work in the mine," we are neither fascinated by this or that proletarian messianism, nor subject to the hallucinations of some revolutionary mystique. *At the present conjuncture of events in Quebec,* however, we are clearly aware of the fact that the only powerful medium of renewal is industrialization; we are also aware that this medium will not provide us with liberty and justice unless it is subject to the forces of an enlightened and powerful trade union movement. Who will reproach us because we still believe, with the labour movement as a whole, in the promise: Blessed are those who hunger and thirst for righteousness, for they shall be satisfied?

Notes to Epilogue

[1]*Translator's note:* A French theatrical representation is customarily introduced by three raps of a staff upon the stage.

[2]Lewis H. Brown, *La grève d'Asbestos, 1949,* pp. 3, 4, and 18. (My pagination).

[3]*Ibid.,* p. 8.

[4]If what it says is true, the Custos report (discussed in Appendix II) gives us a remarkable insight into the choice of a scapegoat who would not overawe the jury: "The Court had decided to arrest Abbé Camirand and . . . it was only because of a personal intervention on the part of Prime Minister Duplessis that this arrest did not take place" (Custos report, p. 37).

[5]P. Bouchard, *L'administration de la province de Québec sous les trois gouvernements de Maurice Duplessis,* Vol. 3 (Quebec City: Organisation de l'Union nationale), pp. 72-73: "The leader of the National Union Party is responsible for the fact that the minimum hourly rate in the asbestos industry has been substantially increased since January 1950. The Duplessis settlement of 1949, in fact, stipulated a cost-of-living bonus of 40 cents per week instead of 25 cents, as was formerly the case . . . the average wage . . . has more than doubled since the National Union has been in power."

[6]*Translator's note:* The phrase is Latin for "by a body of citizens."

[7]Lewis H. Brown, *La grève d'Asbestos,* p. 9. My italics.

[8]Pelletier has discussed the unspeakable public opinion on this subject in his chapter. Among other sources, see the explanation offered by the Canadian Johns-Manville Co. for the breaking off of negotiations in late April (Lewis H. Brown, *op cit.,* p. 8), and the insinuation of the Provincial Policemen that the strike was prolonged to help the Liberals in the federal elections of June 1949 ("The Provincial Policemen," on the last page of the pamphlet quoted in Appendix I). See also the Custos report, p. 51, under the title "Machinations to Keep the Strike Going," where P.E. Marquette is invoked as an authority; and p. 76, where Custos speaks of the strategems intended to assure "a swing to the left of the labour vote." See, finally, the declaration of Mr. Foster (the Manager of the Canadian Johns-Manville Co. plant) as reported in *Le Devoir,* June 4, 1949, and quoted in Chapter V above.

[9]Lewis H. Brown, *op. cit.,* p. 5. Beausoleil has emphasized the somewhat puerile character of this fear, which regarded the propensity of certain professors of "social doctrine" for idealistic speculation, notably on questions of joint ownership, as a

definite program of action. Margaret E. Shay, an American sociologist, in a thesis honestly and intelligently aimed at supporting the employers' cause, has also noted that the management rights issue was not as important as the Company had thought (M.E. Shay, *A Preliminary Review of the Asbestos Strike: A Study in the Dynamics of Social Change*. Ph.D. thesis. New York: Fordham University Archives, 1950, p. 103. This thesis is cited in Appendix I). It may be added that even before the strike, union members and employers seem to have already come to an agreement on the terms of the famous clause on management rights: see the statement of the president of the C.C.C.L. in *Le Travail*, August 1949.

[10]M.E. Shay, *op. cit.,* p. 67, could write: "Thirst for production was so insatiable as to cause [those in charge] to rationalize their decision to use strike replacements solely on the ground of expediency. The company heads at Thetford reasoned somewhat differently, and as a result [sic], had to contend with far less animosity."

[11]Lewis H. Brown, *op. cit.,* p. 8.

[12]M.E. Shay, *op. cit.,* p. 188.

[13]In some cases, theorists justify themselves for limiting this liberty by subordinating the impulses of Capital and Labour towards profits and wages to the requirements of the common good; a case in point would be the absolutely indispensable public services. This problem is far too complex to be discussed here, and we shall merely note that such restrictions on liberty could not be considered except in a political and social context where the State would guarantee the equality of the parties to the labour contract by an unequivocal *impartiality*. Now, it is probable that were such a social context to come into existence, the State would be less interested in limiting the right to strike and to lock out than in eliminating the injustices which make the exercise of these rights necessary.

[14]The sociology of law has already studied the transition from status to contract. For a recent application, see H. Lévy-Bruhl, "Le mythe de l'égalité juridique," *Cahiers internationaux de sociologie,* N.S. 2, January-June 1953, pp. 7-16, especially pp. 9-10.

[15]In June 1955, workers of the Consolidated Paper Co. at Shawinigan and at Grand-Mère planned to send individual letters of resignation to their employer, all at once... This tactic created a certain amount of excitement in management and government circles, where there was even more talk of illegal strikes than usual.

[16]I am wholly leaving out of this analysis the general, or political, strike, which aims at a radical alteration of social relations, all at once, and at the national level.

[17]See P.E. Trudeau, "L'élection fédérale du 10 août 1953: prodromes et conjectures," *Cité libre,* no. 8, November 1953, pp. 1-10, especially pp. 1-3. A similar situation arose after the First World War; for an enumeration of the strikes in Quebec at that time by Jacques Guilbault, see *La Revue du Barreau de la province de Québec,* Vol. 11, 1951, pp. 277-297, especially p. 277. For the situation in Canada as a whole, see A. Andras, *Labour Unions in Canada* (Ottawa: Woodsworth House Publishers, 1948), p. 31: "In 1919, strikes in Canada resulted in a time-loss of 3,400,942 man working days, a figure which was not exceeded until the first peacetime year after another war. In 1946, the strike figure shot up to a new high of 4,520,424 man working days lost." On the changes in public opinion regarding unions in certain postwar years, see the Gallup polls in the *Montreal Star,* October 25 and 29, 1952.

[18]*Ad usum sacerdotum* (a bulletin published under the editorial supervision of Abbé Gérard Dion), March-May 1955, pp. 137-138.

[19]This quotation, and the two preceding ones, are taken from articles by Pierre Vadboncoeur (in *Cité libre;* see Chapter I, note 42), in which he regards the nationalists as "the honest wing of the middle-class party." ("Critique de notre psychologie de l'action,"

Cité libre, no. 8, November 1953, p. 21.)

[20]On this subject, see P.E. Trudeau, "L'élection fédérale du 10 août 1953: prodromes et conjectures," *Cité libre,* no. 8, November 1953, p. 9, and the references given there. As this book is about to go to press (April 1956), the nationalist school seems more divided than I suggested in the above paragraph, which was written in October 1955. A proof of this is the great "Alas!" expressed by Léopold Richer, who in *Notre temps,* April 14 and 21, deplored the fact that Jacques Perrault, Gérard Filion and André Laurendeau—each, moreover, with very different degrees of enthusiasm—had had favourable things to say about the Social Democratic Party (C.C.F.).

[21]It is true that some of the Liberals in the Legislative Council voted against the bills, but it is still to the discredit of the Liberal Party that it did not use the majority it enjoyed in this second chamber to obtain the rejection of these laws, which were pernicious for the labour movement, as it had assured the rejection, a few years previously, of a law which would have been detrimental to certain financial interests . . .

[22]On this subject, see "Conflit de droits," *Cité libre,* no. 9, March 1954, pp. 10-14 (the Editors).

[23]Several of the remarks in the two preceding paragraphs are based on a sociological inquiry made by Fernand Cadieux at Asbestos in 1954, for the National Film Board. This work is cited in Appendix I below.

[24]*Translator's note:* The man who likes to break up dancing in the round is a French version of the proverbial "wet blanket."

[25]I am stating a fact, not judging the constitutional implications of that fact.

[26]See the report by F. Dansereau, "Les travailleurs accouchent d'une conscience de classe" (The Workers Acquire a Class Consciousness), *Le Devoir,* April 27, 1953.

[27]For a penetrating study of analogous problems in France, see Paul Vignaux, *Traditionalisme et syndicalisme* (New York: Editions de la Maison française, 1943).

[28]Father Daniélou, at the Semaine des intellectuels catholiques de France (Symposium of French Catholic Intellectuals), Paris, November 13, 1955.

[29]In 1931, the papal encylcical *Quadragesimo anno* affirmed that "Certain forms of property must be reserved to the State, since they carry with them an opportunity of domination too great to be left to private individuals without injury to the community at large." Georges Pelletier, "Les obstacles économiques à l'indépendance du Canada français," *l'Action française,* Vol. 7, August 1922, p. 70, called for the exploitation of the riches of Ungava for the benefit of the nation.

Appendix I

Bibliographical Notice

We have felt that it was not necessary to make this book even bigger by adding a complete bibliography on the asbestos strike.

Those readers who want to pursue their study of the strike in greater depth would perhaps be grateful to us if we showed them some of the paths to follow. As the proverb has it, half of science is knowing where science is . . .

As far as we know, no book has been published on the asbestos strike before ours. However, several Canadian and American universities have accepted this strike as a subject for theses: the archivists of the C.C.C.L. and various union members have had occasion to reply to their requests for information more than once. Among the theses which have been brought to our attention, we wish to mention the following in particular:

1. Margaret E. Shay, *A Preliminary Review of the Asbestos Strike: A Study in the Dynamics of Social Change,* Doctoral thesis, in the archives of Fordham University, New York, 1950.
2. Grace M. McKenzie, *The Asbestos Strike: The Press and Public Opinion,* M.A. thesis, in the University of Toronto archives, 1950.

In addition, various studies have been made for special purposes, and have not been made available to the public. We know of two:

1. The Custos report, intended "for the attention of the clergy only," which is the subject of Appendix II below.
2. A sociological inquiry by Fernand Cadieux, made in 1954 for the National Film Board, and which—by drawing its observations from different levels—brings out with striking clarity the problems faced by a society which has recently emerged from a profound upheaval.

A novel by Jean-Jules Richard, *Le Feu* (The Fire), which takes the strike as its central theme, was published in serial form in the news-paper *Combat,* a weekly publication of the Quebec Labour Progressive Party, at the beginning of 1955.[1]

A certain number of booklets, or rather pamphlets, were written by people who wanted to publicize *their* version of the strike, or of events connected with it. The three following publications, by people of rather disparate interests, are characteristic:

1. Lewis H. Brown (President of the Canadian Johns-Manville Co.), *La grève d'Asbestos,* May 11, 1949.
2. *The Provincial Police at Asbestos,* a pamphlet which is signed "The Provincial Policemen" and which bears the date "May 1949," but which was not distributed until August 12, 1949.
3. Anon., *René Rocque, prisonnier politique?,* published by the C.C.C.L. in April 1951.

These three publications, as well as Chapter IV of this book, take note of the brutalities which occurred during "the dramatic days of the strike." The reader who wishes to have what may be regarded as reliable information on this subject may refer to a judgment handed down by the Superior Court, of which certain passages are quoted in Appendix III below.

Finally, there were a number of magazine articles on the strike in addition to an extraordinary number of reports and editorials in the newspapers. The interested reader may go over them by consulting an "index of magazine articles, editorials, and other newspaper reports concerning the strike" in the archives of the C.C.C.L., which was compiled by Louis L. Hardy. One of these articles, which is particularly remarkable for its detailed scrutiny of our social structures, and which concerns an essential but little studied aspect of the strike, was published by the review *Cité libre;* we felt that we should reprint this piece by J.P. Geoffroy in Appendix IV below.

---

[1]This novel has just been published by the author in book form under the title *Le feu dans l'amiante* (Fire in the asbestos industry).

Appendix II

The Custos Report

This mimeographed work of 184 pages does not bear a date, but it was distributed as early as the month of December, 1949. Its title page has the following information: "Collection of documents.—*On the asbestos strike* (1949) assembled by the Canadian and Catholic Confederation of Labour.—For the attention of the clergy only."

No author's name is given, but at the bottom of the last page, in place of a signature, the Latin word CUSTOS (guardian) designates the individual, or group of individuals, who made the collection of documents (authentic for the most part), and generously interlarded them with defamations and warnings which are directed against certain members of the clergy (from top to bottom of the hierarchy), the leaders of the C.C.C.L., and—for good measure—some third parties.

As a result of certain "indiscretions," the work circulated a bit outside the exclusive circle of "the members of the clergy," and it soon became known as "the Custos report." Various attempts were made to identify the author, and the most interesting one was discussed in the newspaper *Le Travail* (G. Picard, March 2, 1951, and March 15, 1951). However, no completely certain conclusions emerged from these efforts. (On this subject, see note 27 to Chapter IV of this book.)

The report, which is said to have been brought to the attention of Rome, both by ministers of the Duplessis government and by members of the Quebec episcopate, was followed, in February 1950, by the resignation "for reasons of health" of Mgr. Charbonneau, the Archbishop of Montreal.

It is vain to speculate on the possible causal connection between these two events; it would even be an insult to the intelligence of the Vatican administration to believe that it could be influenced by such a partisan dossier. What is certain is that the Custos report was written to serve as a weapon of war for one group of Catholics against another which had different ideas on society.

Because we believe that anonymous denunciations and secret reports are not likely to create that climate of tolerance and frankness which can prevent political and social disputes from degenerating into a religious vendetta, we do not have the slightest qualms about violating the "confidential" character of the Custos report. Because this report clearly shows the tendencies which set official thought in Quebec against the "people of the Left" (others would say, which opposed "reactionaries" to "progressives"), we publish long extracts from it below. We preface these extracts ironically with the sentence which Custos inscribed at the beginning of his study (p.6): "It is no more, in sum, than a collection of important documents, to which we have added a commentary which reflects all the objectivity of which one is capable when one is in the grip of emotions provoked by the scandalous behaviour of certain people."

The book begins with a "schematic account" (p.7):

There are probably secret leaders and several categories of people who are responsible [for the strike]; let us make clear, then, that we are not accusing the Christian union leaders and the chaplains implicated in this affair, a priori, of being the agents of Moscow. But... [to the] question: has this strike played into the hands of Moscow, we reply with an unqualified "yes"...

Here, then, Custos offers his thesis: everybody who was implicated in the strike was either the unwitting dupe of Moscow or its perfidious agent. Nobody is above suspicion, for according to Custos, "the permanent [sic] doctrine of the Comintern" teaches, among other things, that (p.18):

The Catholic unions must be infiltrated by communist agents who, disguised as good Catholics, will attempt to win control over them.

Where, then, has Custos obtained his knowledge of the "permanent doctrine of the Comintern"? From statements of Lenin which are poorly digested, and as raw as dogma. This is an example (p.16):

The unions are in truth the school of communism...

Custos draws his knowledge above all from the supposed teachings of Canadian communist leaders. He asserts that he is familiar with this teaching through "the stenographic notes taken during a course on tactics" by a communist, who has since converted. There is no doubt that these "notes" have been completely fabricated, either by Custos or by some imbecile who duped Custos magnificently. The most elementary internal criticism demonstrates that the inventor of this supposed teaching could only be a blinkered anti-communist whose knowledge of communism is restricted to his own nightmares. To show this, these pages would be worth quoting in their entirety, and would make a lasting monument to the stupidity of the "Right," but a few paragraphs will suffice.

Let us hear, then, how (according to Custos) a communist leader, and a member of Parliament as well, Fred Rose, addresses communist militants, praising the greatness of the encyclicals, lauding the virtue of those who put them into practice, fighting against the spiritual leadership of the confessional, laughing at open-minded people, making ironic comments about the "dear" unionists, and in the final analysis refusing to recognize the makings of true communists except among the ignorant, naive priests, the proud and ambitious, and opportunists (p. 10-11)!

"Though it is relatively easy to spread our ideas in liberal and socialist labour circles, which are all partly won over to Marxism [sic] already, the situation was not the same when we made our early efforts to propagandize among the Catholic proletariat. The social teachings of the Pope are the most dangerous to our cause because they make it possible to resolve social issues without revolution, and therefore without the disorder which alone permits us to appropriate their property for ourselves, without which we cannot continue the revolution. The solution to social problems which is offered by the encyclicals is not, however, capable of achieving happiness for the worker unless it is realized on the basis of a perfect Christianity. It requires of the two antagonists, employers and workers, self-sacrifice, abandonment of their excessive ambitions, rectitude of conscience, absolute loyalty, and perfect charity, qualities which each Catholic may achieve by putting his religious principles into practice.

"Fortunately, our leaders were very quick to realize that our communist revolutionaries might be exposed to great danger from the Catholic trade union movement if it remained in the hands of the Church, and of upright and conscientiously idealistic leaders. For this reason, they established two aims for thwarting the success of the encyclicals:

1. Set up communist cells within the Catholic trade unions by infiltrating some of our men, or by pushing ambitious, bitter or compromised men into the highest positions, whom we might influence or manipulate through the mass, while maintaining an

apparent respect for the religious convictions of the workers.

2. Combat religion in order to diminish its ascendancy over man. We have therefore supported all movements which are likely to separate man from his conscience, i.e., from the spiritual leadership of the confessional: *seclarism*,[1] which holds that religion is a personal affair of each individual and ought not to be taken into consideration in public affairs; *liberalism*, which claims that all religions and all convictions are good and respectable, by means of which we have deprived the priests of the privilege of the authority to distinguish between good and evil; *popular democracy*, which places political and social issues in the front rank of the individual's concerns, and relegates religion to the status of a subordinate interest. All of these movements are, in fact, valuable auxiliaries for the revolution.

"The past fifty years have shown the effectiveness of this method. Secularism has produced anticlericalism, liberalism has produced freedom of thought, and little by little the Catholic worker has fallen away from the strict observance of the laws: he has become tolerant, "open-minded" as they say. He believes, above all, that he is more clear-sighted and independent, but in proportion as he escapes from the priests and religion, he draws closer to new leaders, to *our* leaders... Of course, he still goes to mass, it's a custom which one does not give up readily. He still listens to the sermons, but he only takes them to heart when they are in conformity with his material interests. From time to time, he is pleased to hear the preachers deliver the same revolutionary and socialist language from the pulpit as his dear fellow union members. He can scarcely be aware that these are our ideas which are thus spread by ignorant people or by priests of good will, blinded by an excess of charitable zeal, or again by demagogy.

"*Then:* we can rely on two sorts of accomplices within this Catholic tribe: the *deliberate accomplices*, those who through pride, ambition, opportunism become our own spokesmen; and the *unwitting accomplices*, who spread our revolutionary ideas in all good faith, attacking established authority, discrediting the prestige of employers and managers, and thus pushing the proletarians into our arms.

"These accomplices are indispensable to us, because they alone enable us to make first our ideas, and then our men known in circles which have formerly resisted our attempts to penetrate them. They are particularly indispensable to us for the most important task

---

[1] We are making Custos responsible for his spelling, syntax, and italics.

which we have been assigned in the bourgeois countries where the party cannot act openly: to demolish authority, all the authorities.''

A little further on, the same ''communist leader'' sets a sheep-like people against a respectable bourgeois authority; he sets the scene for the great twilight which he calls the great day; and he promises that it will be followed by brisk liquidations (p.12):

''Once the labouring masses have realized that they can defy authority with impunity, it is enough to repeat illegal strikes a certain number of times, until the perfect and permanent mentality of revolution and insurrection is created, which we need for the great day.

''Then the union ringleaders of whom we are not completely sure will be eliminated first of all, and the sheep-like masses will allow themselves to be led by a handful of determined and energetic men; this, comrades, is the role for which we are preparing you.''

Further on, the same document (published in 1949, but conveniently dated back to 1945) allows Custos to locate the ''subversive'' tendencies of militant trade unionism well back in the past. We may note in passing that the professor of communist tactics (a Jewish Marxist of Polish origin) uses the word ''reactionary'' in the sense of ''radical'' or ''avant-garde,'' a barbarism peculiar to French Canadians (p.12):

''Our cells at McGill University and the University of Montreal should not have any apparent link with the organizations in which cells have been established by our agents. As you know, we can already rely on the certain collaboration of members of the teaching profession, and progressive ideas have already made great progress among the members of the Catholic Teachers' Association. The results achieved by our ideas in reactionary [sic] circles are as important as those gained by our cells.''

Still further on, the same Marxist identifies communism's arrival in power with the destruction of the perceptive individuals in the working class, treats the open-minded attitude of the young priests as demagogy, pays homage to the subversive character of the Christian democrats, and promises that further liquidations will eventually eliminate a part of the sheep-like (a favourite word of his) and lazy masses (p. 13):

''We must be careful to conceal the fact that certain Christian agitators, certain chaplains and certain newspapers are playing into our hands, and we must not express public approval of their behaviour, because those Christian workers who have not yet been entirely won over to materialism would realize that their union favours communism, or that their leaders or chaplains are in other words preaching a doctrine, and thereby preparing the way for our arrival in power . . . and their own destruction. In such a case, our fortunes could take a fatal turn for the worse. In the Province of Quebec especially, the worker is quite willing to do what he's told and play the rebel, as long as he feels that the parish priest is on his side, but he does not want to be accused of communism. We must respect this tendency for the moment, and not show our hand too early. Here and there our friends are working in other fields to win over more chaplains and priests to our ideas. In the face of our fostering and promoting anticlericalism among the workers, the clergy will tend to embrace the causes of labour—our causes—to remain in their good graces. This natural tendency towards demagogy is particularly marked among the young clergy, and it is contributing greatly to the advance of the Christian labour unions. May they not forget that what matters to us is the final goal, insurrection, nor that we will not be able to win the proletarian masses over to this idea by a direct action which would frighten them. Let us, then, leave the Christian unions to propagate our ideas, and to adopt our tactics and our methods for the overthrow of authority, under the direction of their own leaders and with the blessing of their chaplains.

"First in Russia, then in Poland, Hungary, etc. the Christian democrats have been the first to overthrow the established authorities. Once this work was done, it was easy for us to eliminate our accomplices among the democrats on one pretext or another, and to establish ourselves in their place. When we have eliminated the democratic leaders from the scene and have replaced them with our own leaders, the sheep-like masses will obediently follow those who immediately offer them more wages for less work. As for those who do not wish to go along with us, they will quickly disappear, as we have seen in the U.S.S.R. and elsewhere."

This is enough to give us a good idea of what Custos has understood of "the permanent doctrine of the Comintern." Let us take a brief look at how he arrives at the conclusion that "there no longer seems to be a shadow of a doubt that the Comintern played an active part in the strike at Asbestos" (p. 20). A communist newspaper is said to have urged its readers to send aid *directly* to the union at Asbestos; here is what Custos concludes from this information (p. 19):

One might suppose that the leaders of the Canadian Communist Party are convinced that their militants no longer run any risk in frequenting Christian unionist circles, and consider that the rev-

olutionary spirit of the latter is sufficiently developed at this point
so that contact with these circles no longer threatens the fidelity of
communist militants to the cause of Marxism. Must one not suppose, too, that this appeal was not published without first obtaining
the consent of leaders of the Christian unions, and thus having
contact with them beforehand? To our knowledge, neither the
Catholic unions nor the C.C.C.L. have expressed disapproval of
this communist appeal.

Nevertheless, the same communist newspaper complains that "the
union man in charge . . . deliberately lied" when he did not publicly
acknowledge receipt of the aid which arrived . . . (p. 23). Custos,
however, passes lightly over such contradictions in his "documents."
He prefers to quote an appeal on the part of the communist leaders, in
which they ask their militants to protest against the police brutalities at
Asbestos. Now *it just so happens* that *Le Devoir* and the union at
Asbestos protest against these brutalities. Therefore, they are communist (p. 25):

> The instructions of the communist leaders were immediately fol-
> lowed by . . . *Le Devoir* which published . . . a scathing article
> . . . As for the telegram of protest . . . it was sent . . . in the name of
> the National Union of Asbestos Employees.

This then, is enough to give us a good idea of the dialectical powers
of Custos. Let us examine his methods of denunciation. Sometimes he
resorts to known authorities (and what aurhorities!) to accuse the
strikers, their leaders, their chaplains, and *Le Devoir* of "criminal
acts" and of "sins against God" (p. 26):

> A report published by the Provincial Police of Montreal gives an
> overall view of these matters. Since the police have been systemati-
> cally denigrated and their testimony placed in doubt, we will not
> make use of this report. We publish it merely as a source of infor-
> mation.

Then, "as a source of information," and refusing to "make use of
this report," Custos fills ten pages with the nauseating remarks
spewed forth by the Provincial Police. It is true, he admits, that Mgr.
Desranleau, the Bishop of Sherbrooke, decided after careful inquiry to
denounce the pamphlet of the Provincial Police in unequivocal terms
(p. 37):

> "We protest against these falsehoods, we ask our diocesans to
> accept none of them, and we affirm that such a publication . . .
> deprives the Provincial Policemen (signatories . . .) of the respect

and trust of the citizens."

This statement owes nothing to the faith and to the encyclicals, Custos replies: the bishop is talking through his hat (p. 37):

It is clear that Monsignor Desranleau, who was in Rome throughout the course of the strike and who therefore remained unaware of certain facts, was not familiar with the sworn testimonies which were taken at the inquiry.

Having thus imperiously demolished the authority of a bishop, Custos quickly annihilates the small fry: chaplains and laymen. He no longer needs to find definite accusers: rumours are sufficient for his purpose (p. 50):

Rumour has it, though we have not been able to obtain written proof, that the witnesses who were called to testify at the inquiry, before going to the Hall of Justice, had received instructions from their chaplain concerning mental reservations and other subtleties which enable one to swear an oath on the Bible without being thereby obliged to tell the truth. One need merely read over the cross-examinations ... to come to the conclusion that the rumour must have some foundation.

But who needs rumours? Do not gratuitous assertions (that a man is a communist, for example) have a validity of their own (p. 77)?

Mr. Marcel Francq, the Secretary-treasurer of the Provincial Federation of Labour, who supported the strike at Asbestos along with the Christian unions, and whose Marxist tendencies are well known...

Unfortunately for the "truth" as Custos sees it, Mr. Francq was appointed to the Labour Relations Board soon afterward by Mr. Duplessis, a man little enamoured of "Marxist tendencies."—It is true that the communists and the fascists do come to terms with one another on some points of doctrine ... Similarly, but on another subject altogether, Custos reveals "one of the threads which connect communism almost directly to Christian socialism" (p. 80):

Is not the recent establishment of the French Canadian Communist Party, alongside the Labour Progressive Party of Canada, a sop to the national socialists, former admirers of Hitler, of the neo-modernist school at *Le Devoir*?

But let us return—to have done with it—to the system of denunciations used by Custos (p. 58):

Here, then, are chaplains who are real revolutionary leaders, and make no bones about it. They have *descended* [Custos's italics] to the people, and the vulgarity of their behaviour is shown by the fact that the workers no longer address them as "Abbé so-and-so" but as "Curé so-and-so" . . .

To back up his statement, Custos invokes the testimony of Mr. Gerhard (that intrepid reporter who describes how he spent an entire night discussing "new ways of getting information from the barricades, without running too many risks," p. 138). According to Custos, this is how the workers spoke of the parish priest Father Camirand:

Camirand told us . . .

An examination of the testimony offered by Mr. Gerhard himself shows that Custos, in quoting him, has abridged the original text in the right place. Mr. Gerhard, in fact, reported (p. 147) that the workers had said:

Father Camirand told us . . .

Custos must have realized, though, that his "proofs," weak enough to begin with, were becoming progressively more feeble, for as a final flourish, he leads us into the realm of the "true doctrine." Here a swarm of theologians is found, whose discussion topics all but touch on the sex of angels. One of them comes forward to recount the unjust deeds of the union members and asks himself: in the case of a strike against "a manifestly unjust situation which is developing to the common detriment of the workers," may the union exercise a moral pressure against the strikebreakers "by expelling them from the association, for example, without causing them harm?" In other words, may the union say to its members: "If you try to break the strike you will no longer be members of the union"? The learned doctor gives a firm and clear answer in five words (p. 84):

"The matter is perhaps debatable."

In reply to Abbé Masson, who is alleged to have said to a journalist: "We are revolutionaries and we are not ashamed of it," Custos invokes this fulgurating theological authority (p. 88):

"The term 'revolutionary,' in the French language, has a bad meaning. 'Good' and 'revolutionary' are terms which clash with one another; it's a little as though one were to say: a saintly demon. 'Revolutionize' may express good things if need be, but only in profane matters, and it smacks unpleasantly of revolution . . . It is,

in truth, a way of speaking which does not belong in the language of
the apostolate, a way of educating young people which must not be
adopted. Let us speak French, and a Christian French at that.''

To refute the supposed statement of Mgr. Desranleau: "Capitalism
is inalterable and incorrigible," Custos offers a reply of his own,
which reflects both anti-Semitism and nationalism (p. 115):

> The Holy Father has never condemned capitalism as an economic
> system, but only that form of exploitative and oppressive capitalism
> which is unfortunately practised here by the Jews and the Anglo-
> Saxons. The Catholic and socially responsible employers, who have
> recently been encouraged by the Holy Father, are shocked to find
> themselves placed on the same level as the enemies of the Church.

This conception of the social doctrine of the Church, which seeks to
make it the ally of "French Canadian Catholic" capitalists in their
battles against heretical competitors and militant trade unionists, has
already been sketched by Custos in his introduction (p. 5):

> We know of Catholic "capitalist" firms where the Sacred Heart
> is enthroned, in an atmosphere free of bigotry, both in the shop and
> in the president's office, where a sincere and cordial spirit of coop-
> eration daily improves the harmony between employer and workers.
> In such firms, the company union has gone beyond the phase of
> merely making demands, and has become corporative in its out-
> look. The employer must defend himself constantly against
> agitators and troublemakers sent by ... the Confederation of
> Catholic Unions.

Anti-Semitism reappears in the conclusions of the Custos report.
Having brilliantly explained the popularity of communism due to "the
conspiracy of silence" on the part of the world press, Custos asks us to
believe that the great capitalist press deliberately maintains a "silence
about subversive activities in general," so that the poison of communism may seep into the social body almost undetected ... and Custos, who is "in the grip of emotions," cries out (p. 126):

> This explains many things, the fact, for example, that the press in
> Canada has had virtually nothing to say about an article published
> by the Fides Agency [of the Vatican] on the horrible acts committed
> by the Jews in the holy places, which brands Zionism as worse than
> Nazism, and as the carrier of communism in the Middle East, a
> doctrine which finds it impossible to tolerate the expression of the
> doctrine of Christ on "his" earth in some [sic] form whatever

(Catholic Documentation of 22-5-49). A religious review, *Les carnets de Saint Viateur,* has carried cynicism to such lengths as to publish an article exalting the role of Zionism under the title: *Israël porte la civilisation et la démocratie dans le Proche-Orient* (Israel Is the Bearer of Civilization and Democracy in the Near East), while bluntly refusing to publish the article by the Fides Agency, and asserting that it would, on the contrary, continue to show sympathy for the Jews. These are the depths to which some people have sunk!

The utter vileness of this two-bit scoundrel, Custos, cannot be revealed without quoting the whole of his report, which is "written . . . with the intention of . . . broadcasting the social doctrine of the Church in a more extensive and authentic way, as the Holy Father has asked us to do" (p. 129). Still, has the reader not read enough to see that it is not enough to appeal to the Holy Ghost to be inspired by it?

Appendix III

Opinions on the Police Brutalities and Extracts from a Judgment of the Superior Court[1]

At Asbestos, on May 6, 1949, workers and even old men were arrested without a warrant by the Provincial Police, while they were in the streets, in restaurants, in the basement of the St. Aimé Church, or in their homes. They were taken to a building belonging to the Canadian Johns-Manville Co. where they were kept in isolation, interrogated, and savagely beaten.

Lewis H. Brown, President of the Canadian Johns-Manville Co., said nothing about these events in his account of the strike. His pamphlet (cited in Appendix I), which lingers over the strikers' excesses on May 5, merely adds the laconic statement that on the morning of May 6,

> the Provincial Police burst into the city... In a few hours, order was reestablished and all violence had been ended... Now that peace and order had been reestablished, the workers returned the next morning to their work at the mine, the mill and the factory.

Custos, while quick to accuse people of being bolsheviks or gestapo agents (see Appendix II), is understanding itself where brutal police repression is concerned (p. 45):

> One will also understand [sic] how at the time that the riot was put down, the policemen who were so scoffed at, tortured, and insulted treated the rioters roughly. Their exasperation was a human failing, although one cannot, for this reason, excuse certain brutal methods of questioning which are used by all the police forces of the world, and which one must energetically condemn.

The Provincial Police itself thought it more advisable to deny the

---

[1]Superior Court, St. Francis District, Province of Quebec (no. 7725).

367

facts. In its pamphlet (cited in Appendix I) we read:

> When we examine the people on both sides of the battle, we find that the ones who are seriously injured are all from the same camp: that of the Provincial Police. Let us ask, in particular, why it is that if the strikers have been maltreated, no charge has been laid in criminal court against the perpetrators of these assaults. The reply to this is simple: no one dares to confront the courts.

This reply is simple indeed, but it is also ridiculous. The truth of the matter is that the workers did not "dare" to confront the courts because *their lawyers* had no hope of obtaining justice from them. To procure the condemnation of the policemen of the provincial government, they would have had to obtain arrest warrants from a judge appointed by the provincial government. Then—assuming that this first obstacle was overcome—the cases would have been taken out of the hands of the lawyers and conducted by a crown attorney appointed by the provincial government. Finally, the trials would have taken place before a judge appointed by the provincial government.

Now, the strikers' lawyers had unfortunately learned to their cost that, in trials with political repercussions, the separation of executive and judicial powers did not have even the status of a fiction in the eyes of the government in power; English Canadian newspapers, though hostile to the strikers, had even shown some embarrassment at this fact.

For these reasons, "no charge has been laid in *criminal* court" by the strikers; they did not act in this way because their slashed faces, their stitches, their headaches, and their nervous breakdowns had caused them to doubt the fact that they had been "roughly" treated (as Custos put it).

On the other hand, the strikers decided to bring their assailants before the *civil* courts. The attempts to identify the defendants would certainly be subject to the hazards of the victims' uncertain memory, and the perjuries of the men who had beaten them, but at least the trial would be conducted by the strikers' own lawyers, and before a judge appointed by the *federal* government (which has nothing to do with the Provincial Police in Quebec).

Accordingly, six men who fell victim on May 6, and who hoped to be able to identify their assailants, brought actions for damages against eight Provincial Policemen, alleging that these policemen had "participated with other members of the Provincial Police in the organization and implementation of an illegal system of intimidation and of physical and mental violence. . . ."

The trial was not heard until the end of the spring of 1953. In the opinion of the Court, the plaintiffs did not meet their obligation to identify the precise authors of these brutalities in an adequate way. This is not surprising when one recalls that these acts had been perpetrated four years previously. *For this reason,* the plaintiffs' suits were dismissed. In his judgment, however, the Honourable Judge Antonio Garneau did not leave any doubt as to the fact of the brutalities. The most significant extracts in this regard are as follows:

> On the one hand, the plaintiffs and their witnesses have described the circumstances in which they were arrested by members of the Provincial Police force, detained by them in the male nurses' house,[2] and subjected to brutal treatment until they agreed to sign a statement concerning the events which had occurred the previous day.
>
> On the other hand the defendants, who have argued that while the plaintiffs were victims of brutality, this was due to the fact that they not only offered resistance, but even attacked the policemen who were detaining them, have yet not offered any proof of these allegations, except in the case of the defendant Labbé, who has produced evidence tending to show that an assault was committed by the plaintiff Chamberland. In all the other cases, and in spite of the fact that it has been definitely proven that the plaintiffs suffered brutal treatment at the hands of the policemen who were detaining them in the male nurses' residence, the defendants have not seen fit to offer proof of the allegations that resistance was offered to Provincial Policemen and that they were personally assaulted.
>
> ... The result of this manner of proceeding by the parties [to the action] is that except for the case of the defendant Labbé, the Court, in those matters referring to the brutalities suffered by the plaintiffs in the course of their detention by the Provincial Police, finds itself confronted with evidence which has not been denied by the defendants.

The judge then examined the evidence brought forward by each plaintiff, and concluded that it was not sufficient to identify the defendants in the action beyond any doubt. He adds:

> The Court also concludes that the facts introduced in evidence do not permit the establishment of sufficiently serious, precise, and concordant circumstantial evidence of the existence of a conspiracy on the part of the defendants to obtain incriminating statements from the plaintiffs by violent means.

---

[2]Translator's note: Apparently part of a clinic adjoining the hotel used by the Provincial Police as a headquarters.

The principal grounds on which this decision is based are first of all the fact that the evidence does not permit the identification of the policemen who assaulted the plaintiffs . . .

On the question of the collective responsibility of the defendants, the Court concludes that there is no convincing and conclusive evidence of *the participation of the defendants in the offenses committed by their fellow Provincial Policemen* [our italics] and that it is not even possible, in the present circumstances, to use the theory of probabilities to support the defendants' cause . . .

It is, moreover, a matter of common knowledge—and ever more numerous judgments of our courts in this matter attest the fact—that in police circles recourse is sometimes had, to get a prisoner to make a confession, to methods of persuasion which violate the most basic rights of the human person. This is unfortunate from several points of view. First of all, it is scandalous that the law should be flouted by the very people whose job it is to enforce that law. Secondly, the confessions obtained by these means are devoid of value and may not be introduced in evidence. Though one must take it for granted that the policeman who is trying to get a confession is motivated by a desire to see that justice is done, the conclusion must still be drawn that in using physical or psychological violence, he harms rather than serves the cause of justice. Those who have control over the police forces, and who are thus responsible for their professional training, would do well to be troubled at such abuses, and to take the necessary measures to ensure that they come to an end. . . .

Appendix IV

The Rocque Trial: A Case of Judicial Oversimplification

(An article by Jean-Paul Geoffroy, published in **Cité libre**, May 1951.)

René Rocque, the C.C.C.L.'s assistant director of organization, is in prison. The original judgment, upheld by the Court of Appeal, found him guilty of conspiring, between May 1 and 6, 1949, to prevent certain people from doing what they had the right to do by the use of violence or the threat of violence. On May 5, in fact, strikers had taken up positions in large numbers on the roads leading into Asbestos. In the course of the day, incidents occurred in which some policemen and strikebreakers were molested.

Rocque's trial caused a great deal of amazement. The asbestos strike had raised so many problems and reached such proportions that once Rocque had been sentenced, his trial seemed a late and disproportionate conclusion to it. An anxious public opinion sought enlightenment on the causes of the strike, and on the reasons for the behaviour of the parties involved. Even the most detailed examination of the incidents which occurred between May 1 and 5 could not hope to satisfy this desire.

The strike broke out, rather unexpectedly, at the beginning of February 1949. It affected two centres especially, Thetford Mines and Asbestos. The conflict became exceptionally severe in Asbestos, where the Canadian Johns-Manville Co. was determined to carry on its activities despite the opposition of its regular employees. In the first week, the government declared the strike illegal and demanded that the workers return to work before their complaints were considered. The Labour Relations Board deprived the union of its certificate of recognition. The Company obtained an injunction against the union from the courts, and received a large contingent of police from the government. These policemen remained on the scene during the whole period of the strike. The miners were convinced the conflict would not last long. A recent experience of arbitration had made them suspicious of this institution; moreover, they had become exasperated at the unbending attitude of the Company, which had been made that much worse by the use of pressure tactics which they regarded as illegal. When they were placed under the obligation to resort to arbitration once more, they refused; and, spontaneously, contrary to the counsels of their advisors, they declared a strike. In their opinion, this was the only way to draw the attention of the authorities, and to induce them to correct a situation which had become intolerable. They insisted on guarantees before returning to work; all of these guarantees were refused.

All the inhabitants of Asbestos, or about 8,000 persons, were directly affected by the strike, as the mine was the only place where the able-bodied men in the population could find work. In addition, the strike had a very special character from the start; it did not, as is usually the case, affect a local group only, but rather the population as a whole; it was something which took possession of the city, brought people together, and entered into the minds of all, replacing their usual preoccupations by new fears and hopes. The strike became progressively more insistent and demanding as the work stoppage continued.

The Company sent a first letter to the strikers. It explained to them that, as a result of a decision handed down by the Labour Relations Board, it could not discuss the conditions for a return to work with the union. Other letters followed: the Company suggested that it might stop paying its share of the workers' insurance premiums, with the result that the policies would be cancelled; that the employees might lose their seniority rights, be regarded as new arrivals, and given jobs other than the ones they had formerly held; that those who lived in houses owned by the Company might be evicted from them; that the operations might be started up again with the help of labour brought in from outside.

The period of waiting became more and more burdensome. Men no longer ate more than one meal a day. Rents went unpaid; the tradesmen, laden with a heavy burden of credit, were close to bankruptcy. Scabs, recruited in the surrounding towns, arrived in the morning and left again in the evening, under Provincial Police escort. It was impossible to meet with them, to explain one's position to them. At the end of April, the strikers gave up all their demands, and insisted only on a single guarantee: that when the return to work occurred, nobody would suffer reprisals for his participation in the strike. This guarantee, which is normally a part of any strike settlement, was refused.

In the same period of time, the Company announced that as a result of the great influx of workers from outside, the operations at the mine, the mills, and the factory would soon return to normal. The 2,000 workers on strike were confronted with the following alternative: either starve to death or leave the city to find work elsewhere. Obviously, nobody was willing to starve. But what about leaving the city? They had lived in it for ten, twenty, or thirty years. They had built it. They had left their land and abandoned other occupations to come and settle there, and to run the risk of hitching their fortunes to the destiny of the Company. They had dug a mine, constructed mills and a factory, and worked every day to increase the power of a company which had declared a profit of 15 million dollars for the preceding year.

It is May 5. Early in the morning, the miners head out for the roads which lead into Asbestos. They want to make contact with the strikebreakers from out of town and explain the situation to them.

* * *

Rocque's trial took place in an orderly fashion. It was conducted with great dignity and an evident concern to show impartiality. Each party to the trial was able to use all the means at its disposal. The jury returned a unanimous verdict of guilty. The trial was very long, lasting over a month. The strike itself, and the events which preceded it, were never taken into consideration. Nothing was said of the Company's efforts to break the strike, nor of the presence of strikebreakers, nor of the consequences which the strike might have on the life of the inhabitants of Asbestos. The bill of indictment specifically stated "between May 1 and May 6." Did the workers at Asbestos have the right to strike? Had they not, perhaps, been provoked into striking? Why had the strike lasted so long? What had led these people to go out on the roads on the morning of May 5? . . .

The trial was concerned with Rocque alone, not with the people of Asbestos, nor with the Company, nor with the authorities responsible for the common good. By the use of legal techniques, it was possible to separate an incident from earlier events which had produced the conditions for it, and then expound it and pass judgment on it in isolation. And yet, from the beginning of the negotiations up to the fifth of May, the events connected with the strike form a continuous chain; to isolate one of the links in this chain was to gain a false perspective on it, and to run the risk of misunderstanding it completely. The trial, though adhering to the rules laid down for it, could disregard a social environment subject to all kinds of influences, and limit its inquiry to a particular situation. From another point of view, one might ask how the judicial system could proceed otherwise once the incidents of the strike had been referred to it. From the standpoint of the Criminal Code, these incidents were nothing more than drunken quarrels.

By refusing to take the origins of the conflict into consideration, the law kept the Court in ignorance of one of the most important factors in the events of May 1 to May 6: a collective approach to a conception of justice. The working class is particularly susceptible to the allurements of justice: it has always suffered injustice, its very status is the result of injustice. An idea of justice underlies all its collective demonstrations, particularly when a work stoppage occurs. This is why a striker is willing to suffer hardships which are out of proportion to the personal advantages that he will obtain from the strike: his sense of group solidarity is based upon a collective conception of justice. Throughout the course of the trial, the strike, and the idea of justice which it was intended to symbolize, seemed alien to the law. The actions undertaken by the strikers, deprived of their significance by judicial technique, were unrecognizable. The law refused to see them as they had really been. There was a gap between judicial fact and social fact.

Incidents similar to those which took place at Asbestos have already occurred elsewhere. More are yet to come. In every strike, because of the status which is given it, there is an appeal to violence. The right to strike is recognized by the law, but this recognition remains in reality nominal, because the law does not provide the strikers with any protection. The only way in which workers can protect their strike is by picketing their place of work. As this form of protection is not recognized in law, however, the employer, who has recognized rights and the legal means of protecting them, can easily obtain an injunction prohibiting the strikers from picketing his plant. At this point, he may demand the assistance of the police to enforce this order of the Court. The picketers would then be obliged to disperse, and the plant would start up again with the help of strikebreakers. The law—and the police would be there to enforce it—would require the strikers to watch the new arrivals take their place without making a move against them.

The law does not make any distinction between a scab, who has been brought to the work place from outside, and an employee on strike who has worked ten, fifteen, or twenty-five years for a firm. And yet, the wages he has earned are often ridiculously small in comparison with what the striker has contributed to the plant. He has provided his physical strength, and applied his intelligence to the methods of production, which he has often renovated completely. Because of his diligent application to his task, and his total involvement in the movements and rhythm required by his job, he has had to make a considerable effort of adaptation; he has become tied to the firm, and has acquired almost property rights over his position. In the name of the freedom to work, the law will protect the strikebreaker. The slightest gesture on the part of a striker, in these circumstances, will be regarded as an act of intimidation or a threat.

The deficiencies of the law weigh heavily upon a community on strike. Deprived of legal status, and reduced to a passive role, the group will try to protect itself. It will have but one means at its disposal: force.

* * *

Rocque is in prison. Nobody thinks of disputing the trial itself. However, when it is looked at in the light of the strike, the problems to which it gave rise, and the responsibilities which it involved, the trial seems to have been no more than a cunning and facile means of pigeonholing an event. For many years, the laws have been made for the protection of industry. The nucleus of the law, which was created at a time when big industry hardly existed, and by people who did not believe that it would develop in the future, does not show much consideration for the working class. It ignores its existence. It happens that this class feels ill at ease in its legal straitjacket. It is not surprising that the seams burst from time to time. Trials and prisons can do nothing to change this situation.

Appendix V

A Reader's Guide to The Asbestos Strike

by James Boake

Government Agencies
Federal:

National War Labour Board. Created to administer the wartime labour regulations established by Orders in Council during the Second World War, in virtue of the War Measures Act. It intervened in labour-management disputes in the Quebec asbestos industry on more than one occasion.

Industrial Relations Branch. A part of the Department of Labour.

National Selective Service. An agency created during the Second World War to assure that the manpower requirements of the armed forces and essential industries would be met. Regional Selective Service Advisory Boards were established throughout the country.

Provincial:

Legislative Council. An upper chamber of the Quebec Parliament, of which members are appointed for life.

Legislative Assembly. The lower chamber of the Quebec Parliament, of which members are elected.

Department of Labour. The Minister of this department in 1949 was the Hon. Antonio Barrette. Two divisions of this department which figure importantly in the story of the asbestos strike are the provincial Labour Relations Board and the Conciliation and Arbitration Service.

Asbestos companies
Canadian Johns-Manville Co. Ltd. Asbestos, Que. By far the largest asbestos producer in the Eastern Townships; an employer of 2,000 of the 5,000 or so asbestos workers who went on strike; the princi-

pal focus of the dispute. A subsidiary of the Johns-Manville Co., an American firm.

Asbestos Corporation Ltd. Thetford Mines. Negotiations with this company in late 1949 and early 1950 led to the signing of a collective agreement by the miners of Thetford Mines and the three asbestos companies located there: the Asbestos Corporation Ltd., Flintkote Mines Ltd., and Johnson's Co. Ltd.

Nicolet Asbestos Mines Ltd. St. Rémi de Tingwick, Que. A small company which was the first to conclude an agreement with the striking asbestos workers: its 125 employees signed an agreement with it on June 6, 1949; this agreement led to the strike settlement reached with the three bigger companies of Thetford Mines on June 24, 1949.

Other asbestos companies:

Bell Asbestos Mines Ltd. Thetford Township.
Quebec Asbestos Corp. Ltd. East Broughton.
United Asbestos Corp. Ltd. Black Lake.
Chrysotile Asbestos Corp. of Canada Ltd.

Labour organizations
National:

Canadian Trades and Labour Congress (T.L.C.). Grouped many international unions of which the American counterparts often belonged to the American Federation of Labor (A.F.L.). Many of the unions in this group were craft unions, organizing all the workers in a given (and usually skilled or semi-skilled) trade.

Canadian Congress of Labour (C.C.L.). Grouped mainly international unions of which the American counterparts usually belonged to the Congress of Industrial Organizations (C.I.O.). Many of the unions in this grouping were industrial unions. More recent in origin than the craft unions, the industrial unions organized all the workers in a given industry, regardless of their professional skills, or lack of them.

In 1955, the A.F.L. and the C.I.O. amalgamated. The Canadian labour bodies corresponding to them, the T.L.C. and the C.C.L., followed suit the next year: in 1956, they merged to form a new Canada-wide labour body, the Canadian Labour Congress (C.L.C.).

Canadian and Catholic Confederation of Labour (C.C.C.L.) —Confédération des travailleurs canadiens et catholiques (C.T.C.C.). A grouping of Catholic trade unions, known as "national" trade unions in contrast to the "international" unions with American affiliation. Formed at a convention at Hull in 1921, the C.C.C.L. had most of its strength in Quebec, where the majority of Catholic trade unions were located.

In 1960, the C.C.C.L. reorganized and changed its name to Confederation of National Trade Unions (C.N.T.U.)—Confédération des syndicats nationaux (C.S.N.).

Provincial:

Quebec Provincial Federation of Labour (P.F.L.)—Fédération provinciale du travail (F.A.T.). A provincial labour body grouping the T.L.C. membership in Quebec for the most part.

Quebec Industrial Unions Federation (Q.I.U.F.)—Fédération des unions industrielles du Québec (F.U.I.Q.). Founded in 1952. A provincial labour body which mostly groups the C.C.L. membership in Quebec.

Plenary Council of the C.C.C.L.—Conseil plenier de la C.T.C.C. First convened at Montreal on April 9, 1949, for the purpose of aiding the striking asbestos workers.

Joint Conference of Organized Labour of the Province of Quebec —Conférence conjointe du travail syndiqué de la province de Québec. A labour coalition on the provincial level among the C.C.C.L. unions and the "internationals" affiliated with the C.C.L. or the T.L.C. The three Quebec labour bodies joined forces in this coalition shortly before the outbreak of the asbestos strike, to combat the reactionary provincial labour code (Bill 5) which the Duplessis government had tried to enact. Bill 5 was defeated; the joint conference was still in existence when the asbestos strike broke out.

Regional:

Montreal Central Labour Council (C.C.C.L.)
Sherbrooke Central Labour Council (C.C.C.L.)
Quebec City Central Labour Council (C.C.C.L.)
Montreal Labour Council (C.C.L.)
Montreal Labour Council (T.L.C.)

National Federation of Mining Industry Employees, Inc.—Fédération nationale des employés de l'industrie minière incorporée. The Federation is the industry-wide grouping of the local Catholic unions in the asbestos industry, which on the national level are affiliates of the C.C.C.L. Founded in 1936 to group the local Catholic unions of the asbestos industry then in existence, the Federation first took the name National Catholic Federation of Asbestos Employees of the Province of Quebec, Inc; a few years before the strike of 1949, it assumed the new name from which the term "Catholic" was omitted. Most of the negotiations with the Canadian Johns-Manville Co. took place through this Federation.

Local:

Montreal Catholic Teachers' Association—Alliance des professeurs catholiques de Montréal. A teachers' association which contributed substantial aid to the striking asbestos workers.

National Catholic Union of Asbestos Employees of Asbestos, Inc.—Syndicat national catholique de l'amiante d'Asbestos, incorporée. The local Catholic union of employees at the Canadian Johns-Manville Co. mine and works at Asbestos, Que. A few years before the strike, it dropped the word "Catholic" from its name.

National Catholic Union of Asbestos Employees of the Asbestos Corporation, Inc.—Syndicat national catholique de l'amiante d'Asbestos Corporation incorporée. One of the corresponding local Catholic unions at Thetford Mines. The employees of each asbestos company appear to have had their own union; all of these were affiliated with the National Federation of Mining Industry Employees.

Canadian Labour Association—Association ouvrière canadienne. A breakaway labour group founded by Paul Emile Marquette in 1945. He vainly tried to attract workers whose unions were affiliated with the C.C.C.L. His membership was virtually restricted to the employees of the Bell Asbestos Mines Ltd., who did not go out on strike in 1949.

People

Labour leaders:

Jean Marchand, General Secretary of the C.C.C.L.

Rodolphe Hamel, President of the National Federation of Mining Industry Employees.

Daniel Lessard, Secretary of the National Federation of Mining Industry Employees.

Paul Emile Marquette, President of the breakaway Canadian Labour Association.

René Rocque, Assistant Director of Organization for the C.C.C.L. Arrested for conspiracy to commit acts of violence.

Government people:

Maurice Duplessis, leader of the National Union Party then in power in Quebec. Strongly opposed to trade unionism.

Antonio Barrette, Minister of Labour in the Duplessis government.

Journalists:

Gérard Pelletier, special correspondent for *Le Devoir*. Was ordered out of Asbestos by the Provincial Police.

P.E. Trudeau, editor of *Cité libre;* also detained by the Provincial Police.

Management:

Lewis H. Brown, President and Chairman of the Board, Canadian Johns-Manville Co. Ltd.

Church:

Joseph Charbonneau, Archbishop of Montreal. His outspoken advocacy of the workers' cause had an important effect on public opinion; he ordered collections to be taken up at all parish churches in the Province of Quebec in favour of the strikers.

Mgr. Desranleau, Bishop of Sherbrooke. Though absent in Rome at the time of the outbreak of the strike, he expressed his support of the strikers by letter.

Mgr. Roy, Archbishop of Quebec City. His personal intervention led to the final strike settlement.

Abbé Camirand, the parish priest of St. Aimé parish in Asbestos. An outspoken supporter of the strikers, whose remarks were widely quoted in the press.

Mgr. Ferdinand Landry, Rector of Laval University. He forbade Laval students to travel to Asbestos to demonstrate their solidarity with the strikers, on pain of expulsion from the university.

Henri Bourassa, Canon Groulx. Influential thinkers who largely shaped the right-wing interpretation of the social doctrine of the Church which prevailed in Quebec in the late nineteenth and early twentieth centuries.

Laws
Federal:

War Measures Act. An act empowering the federal government to take any measures necessary to ensure national security in wartime (enacted in 1914). During the Second World War, Orders in Council were issued under the Act to set up a whole range of organizations which regulated the relations of labour and management during the war: the National War Labour Board, the Wartime Labour

Relations Board, the Wartime Prices and Trade Board, the National Selective Service, etc.

Riot Act. Part of the federal criminal code. Once read, it makes assembly of more than three persons a crime punishable by life imprisonment. Read at Asbestos, and subsequently used to arrest hundreds of strikers.

Quebec:

Labour Relations Act. First established in 1944.

Bill 5. A proposed provincial labour code (1948), very reactionary in spirit. Defeated partly through the joint efforts of the labour movements in the province.

Juridical Extension of Collective Agreements Act. Enacted 1934; permitted the government to impose uniform wages and hours of work throughout a given industry, on the basis of a collective agreement signed by some companies and labour organizations in the industry.

Quebec Trade Disputes Act. The provincial act regulating the settlement of labour disputes.

Padlock Law. A law prohibiting communist organizations in the Province of Quebec. Liberally employed by the Duplessis government.

Department of Labour Act. The act establishing a Quebec Department of Labour and defining the duties of the Minister of Labour.

Corporatism

Corporatism is a social philosophy which attempts to adapt the guild system of medieval Europe to modern industrial civilization. It advocates that society be organized into professional corporations grouped by industry, with workers and managers belonging to the same corporation and cooperating within it. The theory holds that the corporations should have considerable autonomy; in some versions of corporatism, the professional associations also play a political role. Regarded as a remedy for the class struggles of industrial society, corporatism was recommended by a number of popes, notably Leo XIII in the encyclical *Rerum Novarum* (On the Condition of the Working Classes), 1891; and Pius XI in the encyclical *Quadragesimo Anno* (On Social Reconstruction), 1931. The encyclicals on the social question, especially *Rerum Novarum,* were the inspiration for the Catholic trade union movement.